essentials
Tort Law

CB : 1435-39
     439-42
     445-47 n.5
     457-61
     452-56 n5
     461/64
~~TB : 319-21~~

245-250
366-376, 383-391
391-413

ASPEN PUBLISHERS

essentials
Tort Law

Mark A. Geistfeld
Crystal Eastman Professor of Law
New York University School of Law

Wolters Kluwer
Law & Business

AUSTIN   BOSTON   CHICAGO   NEW YORK   THE NETHERLANDS

Aspen Publishers
Attn: Permissions Department
76 Ninth Avenue, 7th Floor
New York, NY 10011-5201

To contact Customer Care, e-mail customer.care@aspenpublishers.com, call 1-800-234-1660, fax 1-800-901-9075, or mail correspondence to:

Aspen Publishers
Attn: Order Department
PO Box 990
Frederick, MD 21705

Printed in the United States of America.

1 2 3 4 5 6 7 8 9 0

ISBN 978-0-7355-6828-0

Library of Congress Cataloging-in-Publication Data

Geistfeld, Mark.
    Tort law: the essentials / Mark A. Geistfeld. — 1st ed.
        p. cm.
    Includes index.
    ISBN 978-0-7355-6828-0
    1. Torts — United States. 2. Liability (Law) — United States. 3. Damages — United States. I. Title.

KF1250.G45 2008
346.7303dc22

2008025877

About Wolters Kluwer Law & Business

Wolters Kluwer Law & Business is a leading provider of research information and workflow solutions in key specialty areas. The strengths of the individual brands of Aspen Publishers, CCH, Kluwer Law International and Loislaw are aligned within Wolters Kluwer Law & Business to provide comprehensive, in-depth solutions and expert-authored content for the legal, professional and education markets.

CCH was founded in 1913 and has served more than four generations of business professionals and their clients. The CCH products in the Wolters Kluwer Law & Business group are highly regarded electronic and print resources for legal, securities, antitrust and trade regulation, government contracting, banking, pension, payroll, employment and labor, and healthcare reimbursement and compliance professionals.

Aspen Publishers is a leading information provider for attorneys, business professionals and law students. Written by preeminent authorities, Aspen products offer analytical and practical information in a range of specialty practice areas from securities law and intellectual property to mergers and acquisitions and pension/benefits. Aspen's trusted legal education resources provide professors and students with high-quality, up-to-date and effective resources for successful instruction and study in all areas of the law.

Kluwer Law International supplies the global business community with comprehensive English-language international legal information. Legal practitioners, corporate counsel and business executives around the world rely on the Kluwer Law International journals, loose-leafs, books and electronic products for authoritative information in many areas of international legal practice.

Loislaw is a premier provider of digitized legal content to small law firm practitioners of various specializations. Loislaw provides attorneys with the ability to quickly and efficiently find the necessary legal information they need, when and where they need it, by facilitating access to primary law as well as state-specific law, records, forms and treatises.

Wolters Kluwer Law & Business, a unit of Wolters Kluwer, is headquartered in New York and Riverwoods, Illinois. Wolters Kluwer is a leading multinational publisher and information services company.

For my parents

Table of Contents

PART ONE

Conceptual Overview

CHAPTER 1

The Historical Development
of Tort Law   3

CHAPTER 6

The Social Construction of Tort Law   101

PART TWO

Doctrinal Analysis

CHAPTER 7

The Intentional Torts   113

CHAPTER 8

Negligence Liability   151

CHAPTER 9

Causation   239

CHAPTER 10

Multiple Tortfeasors   275

Preface

The story of this book, of course, begins with my first year of law school. It would be natural to assume that I was immediately drawn to tort law, but that was not the case. I found the subject to be a rather dry exercise involving lots of rules that did not cohere in any compelling way. I was not captured by the subject until later, after I had extensively studied products liability. My torts class puzzled me in another way. Outside of the casebook or treatises, there wasn't any other scholarly material to consult. I knew there was a large literature in the law reviews, but it was too extensive and sprawling to be of any use for a harried first-year student. I bought the commercial outlines, unable to understand why there weren't more scholarly expositions like the textbooks I regularly used as a graduate student in economics. The life of a first-year law student continues to be harried, and so it is with some trepidation that I offer something more to study. My hope is to provide students with the kind of resource that I sorely missed when I was in law school.

In the course of learning tort law, I've accumulated way too many debts of gratitude to acknowledge properly here. My previously published work has enormously benefited from the input of many colleagues, and most of that work has been incorporated into this book. The development of the book was then greatly aided by six anonymous tort colleagues who critiqued the manuscript, with a couple helping out more than once. At this point, Tony Sebok dropped the veil of anonymity and helped with the book's organization. Mike Green then read the manuscript, as he has done so often for me in the past, and once again supplied an array of invaluable suggestions. My students over the years have also been of invaluable help in refining virtually all of the arguments I present here. One of them, Jeremy Fischbach, provided superb research assistance.

This project also owes a great deal to the foresight of Carol McGeehan and Steve Errick, who recognized the need for law students to have access to a different type of book. As always, Dean Ricky Revesz of NYU Law School was incredibly supportive. My research and writing was funded by the Filomen D'Agostino Research and Max E. Greenberg Fund of the New York University School of Law.

Those who know me will not be surprised by the repeated reference to traffic accidents in the book. My wife, Janette Sadik-Khan, has long been trying to make the streets of New York City safer and greener. Accidental injury is not a hypothetical problem in her world, and her perspective on the matter has always helped me to counterbalance the abstractions one inevitably gains from reading appellate opinions. For this and countless other reasons, I cannot imagine a better partner.

Our son, Max, makes safety an even more salient issue for me. Unlike any other experience I've had, being a parent has taught me the difficulty of making decisions involving the safety of another — the fundamental issue of tort law. Like other parents, I worry about my son being harmed in any way, and yet I know he must engage in the world to grow up. The art of being a parent shares important similarities with the art of tort law. In a very basic way, my approach to the subject has been shaped by my parents.

MARK A. GEISTFELD

New York City
July 2008

A Note on Using This Book

There is no consensus on how to organize the study of tort law. This book starts with the historical development of tort law, which places the subject in social context while identifying important concepts in need of further development. The book then develops these concepts by reference to the foundational doctrinal issues and the manner in which they are addressed by the varied rationales for tort liability. This conceptual overview constitutes the first part of the book, framing the subject as a whole while supplying the analytical tools employed in the second part. Each chapter in the second part addresses an important doctrine by providing the black-letter rules and extended analysis of the associated issues. This organization departs from the manner in which others have organized the study of tort law, and so the book has been written with this consideration in mind.

Rather than reading the book straight through, you can also use the book as a supplement to a torts casebook, reading particular chapters in conjunction with the associated material in the casebook. The following suggestions are for those who plan to use the book in this way.

Students routinely study tort law in their first year of law school, usually in the first semester. Based on my experience, it is not easy for first-year students to figure out what they are supposed to look for while reading cases. The difficulty is completely understandable. How can you know what to look for if you don't know what tort law is supposed to do? What is the point of the legal inquiry? What are the recurring issues? Having some knowledge of these matters makes it much easier to determine what to look for in a particular case. My advice, then, is to read the book straight through the first two chapters. The sooner, the better. Don't worry about picking up all the nuance or detail. Look for the big picture. Later in the semester, you can take another look at these chapters. Many issues that seemed tangential or confusing will take on new meaning.

How you should proceed after this depends on your preferred style of learning. Many students are attracted to more abstract or conceptual arguments. These students should read the first part of the book in its entirety, although they should recognize that they will not be able to understand the argument fully until they have studied the doctrinal issues more closely. Others find conceptual analysis to be overly abstract unless tied to specific problems, with some strongly doubting that legal analysis requires resort to any type of theory. These students should proceed directly to the second part of the book (having read the first two chapters). A close study of doctrinal issues will reveal the importance of conceptual analysis, creating both the motivation and focus for returning to the earlier chapters in the book that cover the concepts in question.

If you decide to jump ahead to the second part of the book, you will presumably do so to learn about doctrines being covered in your casebook. The casebooks on tort law typically take one of two approaches. The historically faithful approach begins with the intentional torts and then moves on to the problem of accidental harms, with the associated problem of choosing between fault and no-fault forms of liability. The other approach is more functional, recognizing that tort law is dominated by fault-based or negligence liability. This approach starts with negligence liability, leaving the intentional torts and rules of no-fault or strict liability for later coverage. To accommodate these two distinctive approaches, the chapters on the intentional torts and negligence are independent of one another. You can read one without having read the other. Make sure, though, that you first read the introduction to the second part of the book. Whether you begin studying the intentional torts or negligence, you'll soon find yourself poring over the material in Chapter 3 addressing the choice between fault and no-fault liability. Doing so will help clear up a number of puzzling issues and motivate the remaining material in the first part of the book.

Likewise, there is no uniform approach to the study of negligence liability. Some casebooks begin with the element of duty, while others leave that issue for later study. The first three sections in the chapter on negligence liability show why extended analysis of duty can be deferred, but those taking this approach should read these sections before studying the other elements of negligence liability.

You can also read any chapter in the second part of the book without having read the conceptual overview in the first part of the book. Insofar as a doctrinal issue depends on history or a particular concept, the discussion often briefly describes the historical or conceptual matter and always supplies the necessary cross-references to earlier material that develops the point more fully.

Finally, a glossary at the end of the book covers the most important terms, including some of civil procedure that might not be known by those new to the study of law.

Regardless of approach, do not worry if everything is not immediately clear. Themes will recur and concepts will be reapplied in different settings. To understand the complexity of tort law, repeated study is required. Judges, practitioners, and scholars have wrestled with the issues for centuries, underscoring both the difficulty and fundamental importance of tort law.

A Note on Citations

Unlike the traditional law review article or treatise, I have not provided citations for every legal proposition. Aside from the citations for direct quotations, I have tried to supply citations that provide a good entry into the extensive literature on tort law and related issues. Many citations are repeated throughout the book, and for those I have used the following abbreviations:

Dobbs on Torts
> Dan B. Dobbs, *The Law of Torts* (West Group 2000).

Harper, James, and Gray on Torts
> Fowler V. Harper, Fleming James, Jr., and Oscar S. Gray, *Harper, James, and Gray on Torts* (Aspen Pub. 3d ed. 2006).

Prosser and Keeton on Torts
> W. Page Keeton, Dan B. Dobbs, Robert E. Keeton, and David G. Owen, *Prosser and Keeton on the Law of Torts* (West Pub. 5th ed. 1984).

Restatement (Second)
> *Restatement (Second) of Torts* § § 1–503 (1965).
> *Restatement (Second) of Torts* § § 504A–707A (1977).
> *Restatement (Second) of Torts* § § 708–end (1979).

Restatement (Third): Apportionment

Restatement (Third) of Torts: Apportionment of Liability (2000).

Restatement (Third): Liability for Physical Harm

Restatement (Third) of Torts: Liability for Physical Harm (Prop. Final Draft No. 1, April 2005).

Restatement (Third): Products Liability

Restatement (Third) of Torts: Products Liability (1998)

Introduction

We hold these truths to be self-evident, that all men are created equal, that they are endowed by their Creator with certain unalienable Rights, that among these are Life, Liberty and the pursuit of Happiness.

With these stirring words, the Declaration of Independence implicitly defines one of the most difficult problems faced by any government founded on the protection of individual rights: What happens when one individual's right to liberty, essential for the pursuit of happiness, conflicts with another's right to life, also essential for the pursuit of happiness? Contemporary instances of this conflict abound. Each year, hundreds of thousands of people are injured, often fatally, by car crashes, gunshot wounds, or cancer and other diseases caused by toxic chemicals and other substances the marketplace has introduced into the environment. As these injuries illustrate, individuals often exercise their liberty in a manner that causes harm to another. These risk-creating actors cannot have an absolute right to liberty — to do what one pleases without legal consequence — for such a right is incompatible with another's right to life or physical security more generally. So too, an absolute right to life — to be completely secure from the threat of bodily injury caused by the conduct of others — is incompatible with a right to liberty. No one could drive or engage in the myriad activities that create any risk, however slight, of injuring someone else. The pursuit of happiness would be unduly curtailed. To protect each one of these individual rights, the government must somehow balance one individual's interest in liberty with another's interest in being physically secure from harm. That balance must treat all individuals equally as the Declaration forcefully makes clear, but what does equality require in this respect? Life, liberty, and equality as evoked by the Declaration of Independence describe one of the central problems of governance faced by any nation dedicated to the protection of individual rights.

This governance issue is most obviously addressed by the criminal law, which protects individuals from physical assault, theft, and other forms of wrongdoing. The criminal action, however, only lies between the alleged criminal and the state; criminal law does not provide any direct redress for the victims of crime. To compensate the victim of a crime with a damages remedy levied against the criminal wrongdoer, the legal system centuries ago adopted rules that are now part of tort law. In the ensuing centuries, it was unclear whether there was anything more to the law of torts. Insofar as the regulation of conduct is solely a matter of criminal law, tort law is not a proper substantive field of primary legal obligations and instead is remedial only — or so concluded Oliver Wendell Holmes, the intellectual architect of modern tort law.*

A few years later, Holmes famously reached the opposite conclusion after realizing that tort law is a distinctive substantive field addressing the problem of accidental injury.† The problem was of pressing concern in the latter half of the nineteenth century, the time when Holmes first formulated his

---

* Oliver Wendell Holmes, *Book Review*, 5 Am. L. Rev. 340, 341 (1871), reprinted in 1 *The Collected Works of Justice Holmes* 237, 237 (Sheldon M. Novick ed., 1995) (reviewing C. G. Addison, *The Law of Torts* (1870)).

† Holmes began formulating his theory of torts in the 1870s, culminating in his masterful work, *The Common Law* (Little, Brown and Co. 1881).

conception of tort law. In the wake of the Industrial Revolution, unprecedented numbers of workers, consumers, and others in society suffered accidental harms. Holmes understood that most of these injuries were not caused by criminal wrongdoing. These injuries were governed exclusively by tort law, making it not only a worthy substantive field, but also one of fundamental significance. For Holmes, "The 'law of bodily security' and its correlative 'law of personal liberty' is made up of the rules of tort and criminal law, and because tort is the less drastic mode of the two modes of coercion, it draws the law's most basic line between freedom and protection."* The subject matter of tort law, as Holmes discovered, involves the struggle between the rights of liberty and security as described by the Declaration of Independence.

Having identified the substantive domain of tort law, Holmes then looked for its underlying principle. From the great mass of scattered cases and rulings of the earlier era, he discerned a concept explaining how tort law strikes a balance between freedom and protection. The balance is based on an "argument from policy." "[T]he public generally profits by individual activity. As action cannot be avoided, and tends to the public good, there is obviously no policy in throwing the hazard of what is at once desirable and inevitable upon the actor."† To accommodate "desirable" forms of risky behavior, tort law ordinarily limits liability to unreasonable conduct that causes injury to another. As long as individuals act reasonably, they are free to pursue their own ends, which are often socially advantageous as well. Any ensuing injuries are an "inevitable" fact of social life that do not violate the victim's right to physical security, which instead protects the

---

* Thomas C. Grey, *Accidental Torts*, 54 Vand. L. Rev. 1225, 1274–1275 (2001).

† Holmes, *The Common Law, supra* note 2, at 95.

individual from being harmed by the unreasonable behavior of another. The principle of reasonableness, according to Holmes, embodies the policy decision of how to balance liberty and security.

By making the principle of tort liability dependent on policy considerations, Holmes helped to create a dynamic in which tort liability could expand or contract as a matter of policy. For much of the twentieth century, judges and tort scholars maintained that the expansion of tort liability was good public policy. Tort liability promoted safety, provided accident victims with compensation, and did not appear to have any negative impact on the growing economy or the ability of individuals to engage in socially valuable forms of risky behavior. A more expansive tort system could treat accidental harms as a manageable problem of policy rather than an "inevitable" fact of social life.

The growth of tort liability ultimately created a backlash that continues to this day. According to critics, the tort system is now out of control, fueling an overly litigious society and crippling the ability of domestic industry to compete in the global economy. In numerous instances, individuals or organizations have ceased to engage in socially valuable forms of risky behavior out of a concern for "being sued." During the 1980s and 1990s, the vast majority of state legislatures enacted tort-reform measures significantly limiting liability. Tort reform has also become a federal issue, with liability-limiting legislation frequently being introduced in Congress. When you hear politicians railing against the "litigation system" or "trial lawyers," the subject of attack usually is the tort system. Tort law is now highly politicized and controversial.

If the principle of tort law is one of public policy as Holmes concluded, the current debate about tort law is easy to understand. Isn't it good public policy to limit tort liability to promote national wealth and welfare as maintained by the critics of the current system? The strongest counterargument to this position is supplied by the concept of an individual right. Is it fair or just to let individuals suffer accidental injury and premature death merely for the sake of promoting the wealth and welfare of others? The conclusion that tort law is a matter of public policy leaves ample room for disagreement about the appropriate content of that policy.

These issues make tort law one of the most interesting subjects of the common law. They are interesting not only for reasons of political theory and public policy. Understanding the deep issues of tort law is quite important for anyone engaged in the practice of tort law.

As every lawyer quickly learns, the so-called "black letter" rules of law often are ambiguous as applied to the factual circumstances of the case at hand. What does the rule require in these circumstances? Merely invoking "public policy" is unhelpful, particularly when used by an advocate to support a client's position. One instead would like to show that the relevant policy issue has already been resolved by tort law in other cases. In making arguments of this type, a lawyer who draws deep connections between superficially unrelated rules or doctrines can invoke a greater range of legal materials to defend a particular position. Mastering the fundamental concepts is critical for effective lawyering.

For these reasons, the first part of the book provides a conceptual overview of tort law. After describing the historical development of tort law, the book identifies the relevant substantive considerations for evaluating the different forms of tort liability. The second part of the book then applies these concepts to the most important liability rules, often by reference to the leading cases. The doctrinal analysis largely addresses the tort rules governing injury to the person and tangible property — the individual interest in physical security that defines the core of tort law. The analysis shows how these doctrines and their associated controversies can be understood in terms of the basic principles embodied in the "unalienable Rights" of "Life, Liberty and the pursuit of Happiness" that are essential to our system of governance.

essentials

Tort Law

Part One

Conceptual Overview

In deciding how to protect the individual rights to life, liberty, and the pursuit of happiness, the newly united states initially relied on the laws of England. The individual rights in the Declaration of Independence were "endowed" by the "Creator," the ultimate source of law according to the jurisprudence of the time. This divine or natural law included the common law of England, making it perfectly appropriate for America once adjusted to account for differences in circumstances. For these reasons, state after state incorporated the English common law into their own common law.

The common law first developed within the *writ system*, which emphasized the forms of action known as writs rather than the substantive bases of liability. By the mid-nineteenth century, the writ system had fallen into disfavor and was abandoned. Courts were to rely on substantive principles to decide cases, a development that produced a recategorization of the common law into the substantive fields known by lawyers today.

Throughout its history, the evolution of tort law has been driven by the need to identify more precisely the substantive bases of tort liability. The practice of tort law—the meaning of its varied rules and the appropriate scope of their application — ultimately depends on the underlying rationale for liability. Legal rules now called tort law have existed for centuries, yet the rationale for tort liability continues to be unresolved and contentious. To understand tort law adequately, we need to understand the underlying concepts, both historically and analytically.

~ 1 ~

The Historical Development of Tort Law

I. A PREHISTORY OF TORT LAW

The origins of the state or centralized governance can be traced to the problem of injury and its consequences. Lacking any centralized system of governance, individuals tended to congregate in small groups or clans, partly to protect themselves from violence and other threats of injury posed by others. Protection from injury involved self-help, ultimately evolving into ritualized systems of revenge, such as blood feuds between clans or families. These primitive practices importantly influenced the development of law and the state.

According to the conventional view:

[There are] four fundamental stages in the early development of law and the state. Stage one is the state of nature. This is a stage of ordered vengeance and vendetta. In this first stage, clans and/or individuals exact vengeance, in a systematic and rule-governed way, when injured by other clans and/or individuals; in particular, they exact *talionic* vengeance, seeking, in the famous biblical phrase, "an eye for an eye, a tooth for a tooth." In stage two, the early state emerges. The early state does not, however, attempt to prevent violence. Rather, it sets out to supervise the existing system of vengeance. Thus, the early state assumes a kind of licensing power over acts of talionic vengeance, requiring that injured parties seek formal state sanction before avenging themselves. In stage three, the early state itself begins to function as enforcer, taking vengeance on behalf of injured clans. . . . Only in stage four does the early state at last move to eliminate private violence. In this fourth stage, the early state institutes a system of "compositions," substituting money damages for talionic vengeance.[1]

In archaic society, revenge and retaliation were provoked by intentional wrongdoing, like murder. Reprisal was not limited to these wrongs, however. The motive for revenge could stem from simply being injured by another, regardless of fault:

The spirit [*Geist*] of archaic law is the spirit of vengeance, of getting satisfaction for every wrong that befalls one. Not only for intentional wrongs or wrongs where guilt lies, but also for unintentional wrongs and wrongs in which there is no question of guilt.[2]

"Wrong" in this sense means nothing more than "injury caused by another." A wrongdoer of this type could face a response involving revenge, punishment, and the payment of monetary compensation for the harm. Those who were unable to pay the monetary debt faced severe sanctions, "including debt slavery, chattel slavery, killing, beating, mutilation, public disgrace, outlawry, and the blood feud."[3] These responses to injury-causing behavior or wrongdoing combine the retributive features of modern criminal law with the compensatory features of modern tort law, a combination that characterized the early English law governing physical harms.

To help centralize authority, during medieval times the English government instituted permanent royal courts in

London whose decisions were to constitute the *common law* of the entire country.* Under the early common law:

> The distinction between crime and tort was not a difference between two kinds of wrongful acts. In most instances, the same wrong could be prosecuted either as a crime or as a tort. Nor was the distinction a difference between the kinds of persons who could initiate the actions. Victims could initiate actions of both kinds. According to the lawyers, victims who preferred vengeance over compensation prosecuted their wrongdoers for crime. Victims who preferred compensation over vengeance sued their wrongdoers for tort. Royal officers prosecuted wrongdoers for crime on the king's behalf when victims feared or chose not to do so.[4]

These objectives of punishment and compensation correspond to the modern retributive rationale for criminal law and the compensatory rationale for tort law. The nature of the wrongdoing, however, did not depend on any distinction between crimes and torts. Rather, the early common-law courts "approach[ed] the field of tort through the field of crime."[5] Tort actions continued to be quasi-criminal until the late seventeenth century.[6]

For understandable reasons, the common law initially focused on wrongdoing that today would involve criminal liability. "Late medieval England was known throughout Europe for its high rate of crime. . . ." During this period, "the preservation of public order was very often the biggest problem the king had to face."[7] The royal government had limited resources to deal with the problem, forcing it to rely on the community and its members to enforce the law by privately initiated actions.

To initiate proceedings against an alleged wrongdoer, an individual usually had to purchase a *writ* from the royal

---

* The permanent royal courts consisted of Common Pleas, King's Bench, and Exchequer.

government. The writ would specify the nature of the alleged wrongdoing and direct the local sheriff to order the defendant to appear in court. Over time, the writ evolved into standardized forms, and courts required the plaintiff to allege facts fitting the requirements of an established writ. Lacking the ability to do so, the plaintiff would have no legal remedy for the alleged wrongdoing.

The writ of trespass *vi et armis* was one such standardized writ. To satisfy the pleading requirements of this writ, the plaintiff had to allege that the defendant injured the plaintiff with "force and arms" (*vi et armis*) "against the king's peace." The latter allegation was essentially jurisdictional in nature and implied nothing noteworthy about public disorder. "Of far greater importance in moulding the royal courts' action of trespass was the idea of force."[8] The requisite force, though, was slight, "connoting very little more than an invasive interference with the plaintiff's land, goods, or person."[9] The defendant's state of mind — whether the harm was caused intentionally or accidentally — was not part of the plea. The writ "clearly covered unjustified physical interference with the person, land, or goods, and it seems likely that the interference did not have to be deliberate."[10] The writ was limited to non-consensual interferences, for allegations of wrongdoing "were thought to be inappropriate where the defendant had acted with the consent of the plaintiff."[11]

The word *trespass* meant "wrong" inflicted by one individual on another, indicating the nature of this primordial form of tort liability. The word *tort* derives from the medieval Latin phrase "to twist," and came to mean "injury" in Middle English. When considered in relation to the writ of trespass, tort describes a wrongdoing or violation (twisting) of another's right to be free from injury.

The "wrong" implicated by the writ of trespass initially had a broad application. The wrong could involve the breaking of promises, making the writ available for cases now governed by contract law. The writ also covered claims that today constitute distinct torts, including assault, trespass to property, conversion, and false imprisonment. The writ of trespass laid the doctrinal foundation for the modern law of torts.

Despite the myriad wrongdoings covered by the writ of trespass, "[i]t is . . . possible to identify from the early records two ideas at work: affronts to honour, and causation of loss."[12] Over time, concern with dishonor waned and "liability for wrongdoing was exclusively focused on the causation of loss. This became the central feature of the action for trespass, and it has remained the central feature of the English law of tort."[13]

Although quite broad in application, the writ of trespass was only available when the defendant's wrongdoing directly caused the victim's injuries. Restricting the writ to direct causation of loss focused limited government resources on the severe problem of violence, the foremost concern of the newly centralized government. As the royal government amassed more plentiful resources, it could expand the reach of the common law to address a broader range of social problems. By the fourteenth century, the common-law courts adopted a new writ, *trespass on the case*, to address some problematic limitations of the writ of trespass. Rather than requiring the plaintiff to allege that the defendant directly caused harm by "force and arms," the new writ enabled the plaintiff to explain the circumstances of the case that entitled him to relief, providing a legal remedy for a much wider category of injuries than those covered by the writ of trespass.

By the early 1700s, courts required the plaintiff to use the writ of trespass for harms "directly" caused by the defendant, and trespass on the case for harms "indirectly" caused by the defendant. The distinction did not depend on the defendant's culpability or state of mind. The appropriate writ depended entirely on causation — whether the force set in motion by the defendant had come to rest or was otherwise redirected or superseded by another cause, in which case the defendant would be an "indirect" cause of the harm. For example, a defendant who punched the plaintiff would be liable under the writ of trespass. The harm was directly caused by the defendant's force (the punch). By contrast, a defendant who strung a rope across the road to trip the plaintiff's horse would be liable under the writ of trespass on the case. The plaintiff's injury was directly caused by the falling horse, making the defendant's force (stringing the rope) an indirect cause. The distinction between direct and indirect causes was not always clear, however. A plaintiff who chose the wrong writ would lose the case. As one can imagine, this causal inquiry created problems for both plaintiffs and judges.[14]

To simplify matters, the English courts had decided by the nineteenth century that the entire category of accidental harms would be governed by trespass on the case, largely limiting the original writ of trespass to intentional harms. The nature of the defendant's wrongdoing, rather than a distinction of causal forces, determined the appropriate cause of action.

These two writs encompassed the range of legal proceedings that now constitute the main core of tort law. These writs and the associated English common law were incorporated by the states into their own common law.

Despite this initial acceptance, the writ system became increasingly disfavored in the nineteenth century. Critics maintained that the system elevated form and process over substance. The writ of trespass, for example, originally covered actions involving the substantive concerns of wrongdoing against the public ("breach of the king's peace") and the associated concern of punishment and retribution; of wrongdoing against the individual and the associated concern of compensation; and of wrongdoing involving the breaking of promises and the associated concern of assuring stable consensual arrangements in a commercialized society. Over time the writ system evolved to address these different substantive concerns, although it was still notoriously unsystematic and complex. The law was defined by the form of writ and not the underlying substantive obligations.

Beginning with New York's adoption of the Field Code in 1848, the states abolished the writ system, replacing it with the unitary *civil action*. This pleading device lets plaintiffs file multiple claims or causes of action asserting the range of potential legal grounds for the relief being sought against the defendant. This procedural reform produced tort law and the other substantive fields around which the common law is organized today.

The procedural reform also made the tort system more widely accessible to plaintiffs. As proposed, the Field Code "called for freedom of contract for attorneys," and states adopting the Code "correspondingly sanctioned contingency fee contracts," reinforcing the trend toward widespread approval of these contracts in other states.[15] This "distinctly pro-plaintiff innovation" allowed an attorney to represent a plaintiff "free of virtually all charges until a settlement or judgment had been obtained, at which time the lawyer was to receive a percentage of the award, ranging from five percent to fifty percent depending on the type of action, the likelihood of recovery, and the anticipated preparation costs and labor."[16] Indigent accident victims were now able to file suit. Personal injury litigation, which previously had been scarce, sharply increased toward the end of the nineteenth century.[17]

II. INDUSTRIALIZATION AND THE EMERGENCE OF TORT LAW

Once the writ system was abolished in the latter half of the nineteenth century, legal actions no longer could be categorized in terms of writs. They had to be categorized in substantive terms. During this period, torts emerged as one of the recognized substantive fields of law. "The first American treatise on Torts appeared in 1859; Torts was first taught as a separate law school subject in 1870; the first Torts casebook was published in 1874."[18]

The new field of tort law was not composed of newly created legal rules. The abolition of the writ system was supposed to be no more than a procedural innovation. Freed from the formalistic pleading requirements, courts were supposed to rely on the substantive bases of liability that had been implicit in the various writs. The very nature of the writ system, though, made it extraordinarily difficult to identify the substantive bases or principles of tort liability:

> The medieval Common law was a law of actions and procedure. The structure of the law was provided by the forms of action. Legal expertise consisted in the knowledge of the way in which claims should be framed and the ways in which the legal process could be manipulated in order to get the better of one's opponent. It was highly technical, sometimes arcane, likened to a complex game of chess. This formalism tends to conceal substantive principles, but there is no reason to doubt that medieval law was undershot by substantive ideas. The problem is to identify what they were.[19]

Despite the procedural obfuscations of the writ system, the substantive fields of contract, property, and criminal law were all fairly easy to identify, as each governs the evidently separate spheres of consensual exchange; the possession, use, and transfer of property; and wrongdoing against the public order, respectively. Once the fields of the common law were divided in this manner, the only remaining established legal actions involved private or civil actions not based on contract. The field of torts is often defined in precisely this manner today.[20]

Defining torts as the leftover legal actions, the remainder after contract, property, and criminal law have been properly defined makes it unclear whether a principle unites the disparate legal actions. Lacking such a principle, one can rightly question whether tort claims comprise a substantive field of law.

The conceptualization of tort law in substantive terms was largely accomplished by the scholarship of Oliver Wendell Holmes. "Holmes' great breakthrough . . . was his decision to organize tort law around the principle of liability for negligence," which "gave torts a conceptual and doctrinal center."*

At the time of Holmes's breakthrough, there was "no comprehensive standard of liability . . . for tort actions."[21] In the actions we now identify as involving tort law, "the crucial inquiry . . . prior to the 1870s was not whether a defendant was 'in fault' or had otherwise violated some comprehensive standard of . . . liability, but whether something about the circumstances of the plaintiff's injury compelled the defendant to pay the plaintiff's damages. Tort liability was no more precise than that."[22] By the 1860s, some cases and legal commentary had identified a distinctive legal action for negligence, but negligence was commonly understood to be an element of various civil actions in other fields of law, such as bailments. To make matters even murkier, neglect or negligence was also an element pertaining to the required mental state for various causes of action involving breach of a legally specified duty of care. These duties were quite detailed due to the way in which the writ of trespass on the case emphasized the individual circumstances of each case, making it even more difficult to identify their common basis. "However closely allied any two or more of these groups might be, however superficial the differences in the situations with which they dealt, there appeared to the legal mind of the era no need but rather something

---

* Thomas C. Grey, *Accidental Torts*, 54 Vand. L. Rev. 1225, 1257 (2001). This insightful article provides the basis for the ensuing discussion regarding Holmes's conceptualization of tort law.

approaching impiety in seeking to find some general principle as their common basis."[23]

Despite the highly particularized forms of action under the writ system, Holmes realized that many of these rules conformed to a more general principle, with each individual rule being a particular instance of the more general principle. He conceptualized a general rule of *negligence liability* as the violation of an objective, public standard of reasonable conduct that causes harm to another. "This expansion of the concept of negligence brought within its ambit a wide array of legislated and judge-made tort rules that did not in so many words require 'due care' or make liability turn on 'negligence.' These rules could nonetheless be interpreted as defining what counted as reasonable conduct for situations they covered."[24] Having conceptualized negligence liability in this manner, Holmes concluded that it governs "the great mass of [tort] cases."[25]

Holmes knew that this conceptualization of negligence did not cover every relevant rule. He also recognized the important exceptions to negligence liability. Many rules involve an *immunity* that absolves an actor from liability, even though his negligent or unreasonable conduct injured another. At the other extreme, the legal rules of *strict liability* make the actor legally responsible for injuries caused by non-negligent or reasonable behavior. As Holmes depicted tort law, unreasonable behavior usually resulted in (negligence) liability, although not always (immunities), and reasonable behavior could sometimes subject the actor to (strict) liability.

On what basis, then, were the rules of negligence, strict liability, and immunity all properly part of a unified field of substantive law? According to Holmes, "The business of the law of torts is to fix the dividing lines between those cases in which a man is liable for harm which he has done, and those in which he is not."[26] When someone intentionally causes harm, as in cases of assault, battery, murder, robbery, and so on, he ordinarily is subject to criminal liability, leaving accidental harms as a distinctive legal problem. Accidental harms were also a major social problem. With the increasing industrialization of America over the course of the nineteenth century, the problem of accidental injury became widespread. One particularly good study found the rate of fatal accidents in the late nineteenth century to be triple the rate of today.[27] Not only was accidental harm an acute social problem, the highly influential nineteenth-century liberal theory of John Stuart Mill maintained that the government's primary task is to regulate conduct doing "harm to others."[28] The criminal law regulated the intentional harms, making accidental harms the "business" of tort law for Holmes.

Having identified the primary substantive concern of tort law, Holmes then sought to determine whether any principle explains how tort law regulates accidental harms with its rules of negligence, strict liability, and immunity from liability. Each of these rules permits individuals to engage in specific types of behavior potentially causing harm to another, making it possible to characterize each rule by the way in which it balances the actor's liberty interest against a potential victim's interest in physical security. Each type of rule apparently strikes the balance differently, but all require a policy decision on how to mediate an actor's interest in liberty with the conflicting security interests of others.

The nature of this policy decision is something that we explore at great length, so for now it is only necessary to see how any tort rule can be characterized by the way in which it mediates the liberty interests of risky actors with the threatened security interests of potential victims. An immunity lets the actor engage in a specified form of risky behavior without incurring liability, regardless of whether the actor was negligent. The associated liberty interests of the actor are not burdened by any behavioral or compensatory obligations to protect the victim's interest in physical security. The immunities, therefore, privilege or prioritize the liberty interests of the risky actor over the security interests of potential victims. At the other extreme, a rule of strict liability permits a specified form of risky behavior while obligating the actor to pay for the ensuing harms, regardless of whether the conduct was reasonable. Here tort law prioritizes the victim's interest in security over the associated liberty interests of the actor, explaining why the risky actor's (subordinate) liberty interests are burdened by the legal obligation to compensate harms caused to the victim's (prioritized) security interest. In between these two extremes lies the rule of negligence, which prohibits some forms of risky behavior and permits others.* The dividing line cannot be simply stated at this stage of the analysis.† For present purposes, the important point is that negligence liability permits reasonable behavior. Negligence liability does not attach to a reasonable liberty interest, whereas it does attach to an unreasonable liberty interest (or negligent conduct), thereby giving no evident priority to either liberty or security.

Characterizing tort rules in this manner may seem to be unnecessarily complicated, but notice how doing so clarifies their relation. When ordered along a spectrum depicting the relative priority of the conflicting liberty and security interests, negligence stands at the conceptual center of tort law, with the immunities at one extreme and the rules of strict liability at the other.

---

* Some forms of negligence are subject to criminal liability, punitive tort damages, or both, clearly establishing that at least these forms of negligent misconduct are prohibited. *See, e.g., State v. Hazelwood,* 946 P.2d 875 (Ala. 1997) (showing "that the overwhelming majority of jurisdictions allow crimes based on ordinary negligence").

† Identifying the forms of prohibited negligent behavior is important for determining the cases in which punitive damages are appropriate, which is the subject of Chapter 14, section IV.

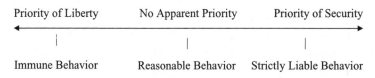

Legally Permissible Harm-Causing Conduct

Priority of Liberty	No Apparent Priority	Priority of Security
Immune Behavior	Reasonable Behavior	Strictly Liable Behavior

To further identify the policy basis of tort law, Holmes conceptualized the forms of harm-causing conduct subject to liability. The writ system had classified causes of action in terms of the type of harm and remedy sought by the plaintiff. Rather than proceeding on this basis, Holmes categorized tort rules in terms of the defendant's state of mind:

- At one extreme are the intentional torts governing cases in which the actor intended the harm, as in the cases of assault, kidnapping, and robbery. The actor is subjectively culpable by virtue of his knowledge that the conduct violated public morals, unless the conduct was motivated by a mistake.
- At the other extreme are the rules of strict liability. The harm-causing conduct subjects the actor to liability even for reasonable conduct; liability does not require subjective culpability or a bad state of mind.
- In contrast to the two extremes of subjective culpability (most intentional torts) and no culpability (strict liability), negligence liability involves *objective* culpability: The actor incurs tort liability for having violated an objectively defined legal standard of reasonable care. Often, the actor was blameworthy for not behaving carefully enough, thereby involving another form of subjective culpability. In some negligence cases, though, the actor merely violated the objective standard without being subjectively culpable. An objective standard formulated in terms of average intelligence, for example, can be violated by someone of below-average intelligence who was acting to the

best of his abilities.[29] Such an actor does not have the bad state of mind required by subjective culpability, illustrating how negligent conduct can function as a rule that does not require personal or subjective fault, just like strict liability.

So conceptualized, tort law consists of three types of liability rules involving differences in culpability. Negligence once again is at the conceptual center, with the intentional torts and rules of strict liability occupying the extremes.

Harm-Causing Conduct Subject to Tort Liability

Subjective Culpability	Objective Culpability	No Culpability
Most Intentional Torts	Negligence	Strict Liability

When conceptualized in this manner, negligence is a compromise between true (subjective) fault and strict liability (not based on any kind of fault). Insofar as most cases of negligence liability involve subjectively culpable misconduct, however, Holmes could conclude "that the law does, in general, determine liability by blameworthiness."[30] The two clear exceptions are the immunities from liability and rules of strict liability, returning us to the previous conceptualization of legally permitted harm-causing conduct, which places negligence at the center, flanked by the immunities and rules of strict liability.

Based on this reasoning, Holmes concluded:

> The theory of torts may be summed up very simply. At the two extremes of the law are rules determined by policy without reference to any kind of morality. Certain harms a man may inflict even wickedly [and avoid liability under an immunity]; for certain others he must answer [under strict liability], although his conduct has been prudent and beneficial to the community.

But in the main the law started from those intentional wrongs which are the simplest and most pronounced cases, as well as the nearest to the feeling of revenge which leads to self-redress. It thus naturally adopted the vocabulary, and in some degree the tests, of morals. But as the law has grown, even when its standards have continued to model themselves upon those of morality, they have necessarily become external [and objective], because they have considered, not the actual condition of the particular defendant [as required by subjective culpability], but whether his conduct would have been wrong [or objectively culpable] in the fair average member of the community, whom he is expected to equal at his peril [or otherwise be subject to the form of negligence liability that functions like strict liability].[31]

This formulation accounts for the way in which tort law originated as a means of preventing revenge and other self-help remedies for wrongdoing. As a matter of practical necessity, the law first dealt with the gravest threat to the king's peace — intentional wrongdoing. This conduct violated the criminal law, making the morality of the criminal law the test of liability within the newly formed civil society. Embryonic tort law merely provided monetary compensation for the victim. Over time, criminal law and tort law diverged over the issue of accidental harms. One who accidentally harms another is not ordinarily subject to criminal liability. Many or perhaps most of these cases involve subjective culpability of carelessness, enabling tort law to retain "the vocabulary" and "tests" of morals. The language of morality, though, can be misleading. "[W]hile the law does still and always, in a certain sense, measure legal liability by moral standards," "[e]very important principle which is developed by litigation is in fact and at bottom the result of more or less definitely understood views of public policy."[32] This policy judgment strikes the appropriate balance between the liberty interest of the actor and the security interest of the accident victim, uniting the overtly moral liability rules and those based expressly on public policy, such as the immunities and rules of strict liability.

By merging morality and public policy in this manner, Holmes was relying on the method of the common law. As the influential judge Lemuel Shaw observed in an 1854 opinion:

> It is one of the great merits and advantages of the common law, that, instead of a series of detailed practical rules . . . the common law consists of a few broad and comprehensive principles, founded on reason, natural justice, and enlightened public policy, modified and adapted to the circumstances of all the particular cases which fall within it.[33]

The judiciary's approach to policymaking stemmed from its governance role of the time. Throughout most of the nineteenth century, the operational characteristics of American government were characterized by the devolution of power to the states — the primary source of American common law — and the lack of regulatory agencies and an extensive civil service to administer them. "The courts had become the American surrogate for a more fully developed administrative apparatus." Consequently, "[i]t fell to the courts . . . to nurture, protect, interpret, and invoke the state's prerogatives over economy and society as expressed in law."[34] Judges adopted a pragmatic, policy-oriented approach to the common law to satisfy the needs of the increasingly industrialized society. "The state and federal courts . . . developed policies in the form of common law rules that tended to spark commercial activity and economic development."[35]

The judicial emphasis on economic development has led some legal historians to conclude that promoting industrialization was the guiding rationale or public policy for tort law in the nineteenth century. According to this view, the early common law involved strict liability. The writ of trespass did not require any fault on the defendant's part; liability was based on the direct causation of loss and not culpability. By the mid-nineteenth century, however, liability for accidental harms required negligence.[36] A shift from strict liability to negligence would reduce costs for industry with its "engines and machines [which] have a marvelous capacity to cripple and maim their servants."[37] The change in liability rules thus amounted to "substantial subsidies for those who undertook schemes of economic development."[38]

Other legal historians have concluded that liability under the early common law typically required fault. The evolution of the writ system to a torts system based on negligence did not produce a substantive change in liability rules, so the newly developing tort law did not "subsidize" industrialization.*

Consistent with this position, an extensive study of all appellate tort decisions in five states during the nineteenth century found that "the nineteenth-century negligence system was applied with impressive sternness to major industries and that tort law exhibited keen concern for victim welfare."[39] Another study of the tort liability incurred by railroads — the

---

* The writ of trespass on the case enabled the defendant to avoid liability if he could prove that the plaintiff's harm was caused by an "inevitable accident." To establish this defense, the defendant could show that he had acted without fault. Liability therefore was limited to faulty conduct under the writ of trespass on the case. The substantive standard of that writ was not different from the substantive standard for the writ of trespass, because the two writs were developed only for jurisdictional reasons and not substantive ones. John H. Baker, *An Introduction to English Legal History* 464 (3d ed. 1990) ("There ought . . . to have been no substantive gaps between the two."); David Ibbetson, A *Historical Introduction to the Law of Obligations* 56 (1999) ("No differences of substance hung on this distinction, and such procedural differences as there were of minimal importance."). Due to the substantive equivalence of the two writs, the writ of trespass must also have been limited to faulty conduct. The writ of trespass could function in this manner due to its requirement of causation, which enabled the jury to conclude that the defendant did not forcibly cause the plaintiff's harm if he were not at fault. The early common law could base liability on causation alone while still requiring fault, so there was no substantive change in liability when negligence emerged in the nineteenth century as the default liability rule for accidental harms.

dominant business enterprise of the late nineteenth century—
concluded that "[b]oth judges and lawmakers attempted to
strike a balance between economic development and railroad
responsibility for personal injuries."[40]

The tort system at this time appeared to be functioning in
the manner described by Holmes. Negligence was the conceptual and doctrinal centerpiece of tort law, and it did not necessarily favor or somehow subsidize business enterprise at the
expense of accident victims. In applying negligence liability,
courts sought to accommodate both the liberty interests of
economic actors and the security interests of those threatened
by the risky activity.

As Holmes had also observed, sometimes tort law privileged
one set of interests over the other. The immunities often protected economic actors from liability. For example, the seller of
a defective product was immunized from liability for harms
suffered by anyone other than the buyer. Judges were
concerned that any expansion of liability beyond the contractual relationship would expose manufacturers and other product sellers to excessive liability, thereby disrupting product
markets to the detriment of society. This immunity (in the
form of a limitation of duty) was expressly justified by public
policy, supporting Holmes's claim that immunity involves a
policy judgment to privilege the activity in question.

So, too, policy reasons could justify rules of strict liability
governing economic actors. For example, a common carrier
such as a railroad was strictly liable for lost or damaged
goods.[41] As one trial judge in New York explained, this rule
of strict liability was "grounded upon great equity and justice."
Liability based on negligence would give common carriers the
incentive "to play the rogue and cheat people, without almost a
possibility of redress, by reason of the difficulty of proving a
default particularly in them." The plaintiff's "witnesses must be
the [defendant] carrier's servants, and they, knowing that they
could not be contradicted, would excuse their masters and

themselves."[42] The plaintiff's inability to prove that the defendant carrier had acted unreasonably — that there was some "default" in its behavior as required by negligence liability — gave judges a reason to impose strict liability on the most important economic actor of the nineteenth century, illustrating Holmes's more general point that strict liability, like immunity from liability, is based on public policy.

The influence of Holmes on tort law is both deep and long lasting. Leading casebooks today often make negligence liability the conceptual and doctrinal center of tort law. Indeed, the evolution of tort law over the twentieth century can be understood in terms of the way in which Holmes had conceptualized the field.

III. TORT LAW IN THE TWENTIETH CENTURY: CONSOLIDATION, EXPANSION, AND BACKLASH

When torts was first formulated as a substantive field of law, the jurisprudence of the time sought to distill general principles from the mass of common-law cases, and from those principles derive an internally consistent body of laws. This approach, known as *Legal Science*, produced the case method of law teaching that is still widely used today. Through the close study of carefully selected judicial opinions, students are supposed to learn to "think like lawyers" by discerning the true rule of decision — the underlying principle — and understanding how it can be extended beyond the particular facts of the case at hand.

The Legal Scientists' reliance on principles helped to consolidate negligence into a rule of general application. The writ system formulated rules in very specific terms, producing a seemingly fragmented body of law. Different relationships in different settings required different liability rules defining the duty of care owed by one to another. By identifying general principles, the Legal Scientists showed how varied rules, typically defined in terms of status, occupation, and so on, could be reconceptualized in general terms of "a universal duty of care owed by persons to their neighbors" growing out of "the civil obligations of those who lived in society."[43] One who violated this duty was legally at fault for the ensuing injuries. As the repository of civil obligation, the fault principle embodied in negligence liability appeared to be the general principle of tort law.

In consolidating negligence liability, the Legal Scientists also tried to rid tort law of doctrines that appeared to be inconsistent with the fault principle, particularly the rules of strict liability. A favored target was the famous nineteenth-century English case *Rylands v. Fletcher*, which decisively affirmed the common-law heritage of strict liability by adopting a liability rule now known as strict liability for abnormally dangerous activities.[44] The first American cases to address *Rylands* emphatically rejected the rule of strict liability on the ground that fault is an essential requirement for tort liability.[45] Legal Scientists relied on these cases to support their claim that the general principle of tort liability is based on legal fault. Some went so far as to claim that any rule of strict liability cannot be squared with the fault principle and should be reclassified into another body of law.[46] Legal Science required logical consistency across liability rules within a substantive field. Strict liability was deemed to be inconsistent with negligence, requiring its removal from tort law.

This aspect of Legal Science was flatly rejected by Holmes. Like the Legal Scientists, Holmes emphasized the need to conceptualize tort law in terms of general principles. The Legal Scientists, though, were also *formalists* who treated law as an autonomous or self-contained body of general principles fully capable of resolving particular legal disputes. This method, deemed by its critics to be "mechanistic jurisprudence," purportedly employed nothing other than formal logic to determine what a general rule required in a particular case. As just discussed, this method led some of the Legal Scientists to conclude that the general principle of fault-based liability was inconsistent with rules of strict liability, requiring the elimination of strict liability from tort law. Unlike the Legal Scientists, Holmes maintained that the "law embodies the story of a nation's development through many centuries, and it cannot be dealt with as if it contained only the axioms and corollaries of a book of mathematics."[47] For Holmes, the general principle of tort law is one of public policy developed by the legal system confronting changed circumstances over the passage of time. As it turned out, the Holmesian conception fairly describes how tort law developed over the twentieth century.

In particular, the public policy reasons for a generalized fault principle enabled courts to considerably expand the scope of tort liability. Under the writ system, the characteristic legal rule was not one of negligence liability but rather one of immunity from liability.* Once the fragmented, individualized rules in the writ system were transformed into a general rule of negligence liability, courts naturally reconsidered the issue of whether a particular form of negligent conduct should be immunized from this general standard of tort liability. The passage of time also made it increasingly difficult for courts to justify the immunities with public policy concerns. Many activities had long been exposed to tort liability without any apparent detrimental effect, making it seem highly dubious that the particular activity protected by an immunity would be unduly restricted by negligence liability. Instead, the salutary features of the fault principle would force the activity to be conducted in a socially reasonable manner, an outcome

---

* Robert L. Rabin, *The Historical Development of the Fault Principle: A Reinterpretation*, 15 Ga. L. Rev. 925 (1981). Many of these rules were expressly ones of immunity, whereas others operated like an immunity by limiting the duty of the risky actor to exclude the negligently caused harms in question or by otherwise privileging the risky conduct.

consistent with the public policy rationale for the fault principle. In hindsight, the considerable expansion of tort liability over the course of the twentieth century is largely attributable to the way in which a consolidated negligence rule of general application combined with public policy to justify eliminating many of the immunities recognized by the early common law.[48]

Negligence liability, however, did not always operate in this manner; it could also conflict with the perceived requirements of public policy. The fault principle was initially formulated when accidents were considered to be the personal fault of someone. This understanding of accidents fundamentally changed during the twentieth century. The last decades of the nineteenth century witnessed the introduction of statistical methods. Like many other statistical phenomena, the rate of accidents over time exhibited a degree of regularity, forcing observers to question whether accidents were largely attributable to systemic forces rather than isolated instances of individual fault. Workplace accidents were particularly troubling at the turn of the century, and those who studied the problem increasingly concluded that for a substantial number of these injuries, "no one is to be blamed."[49] If most accidents were not attributable to fault, then negligence liability typically would provide accident victims without recourse. What justifies a rule making the victims of industrialization bear the cost of their injuries? Why shouldn't industry instead pay for the injuries inevitably caused by their profit-making activities? A limitation of tort liability, according to Holmes, is justified by the public policy of protecting or privileging the risky behavior in question. By the twentieth century, "[c]hanging times and the amazing growth of our industries" showed "that industry not only has no further need of subsidization but also should be made to assume the burden of paying for all damage ensuing from its normal operations."[50] Public policy now apparently favored a rule that would make businesses strictly liable for the inevitable injuries of industrialization, a rule seemingly at odds with the formal purity of a tort system based on the fault principle.

Formalism itself was also under attack in the early twentieth century, and Holmes was one of its most influential critics. Scholars began to evaluate legal rules in terms of their social consequences, producing the jurisprudential school known as *Legal Realism* that dominated American legal thought until at least midcentury. "With the advent of Realism arguments based on public policy revived."[51]

For the Realists, all tort rules inevitably involve some sort of clash between competing social interests. Any justification for negligence liability depends on the way in which it balances these social interests. Negligence could be displaced by a rule of strict liability if doing so would strike a better balance of the competing social interests.

In advocating an increased role for strict liability, Realist tort scholars could rely on the various rules of strict liability that had long been recognized by the common law. These rules had not been eradicated by the Legal Scientists. Most notably, the rule of strict liability in *Rylands v. Fletcher* was ultimately accepted by "a significant majority of the states ... in the late nineteenth and early twentieth centuries," contrary to the claims of leading Legal Scientists.[52] The Realist tort scholars relied on *Rylands* and other common-law rules of strict liability to establish a doctrinal basis for increasing the role of strict liability. On their view, these rules had always depended on public policy concerns that now justified broader application. Circumstances had changed over time, requiring more widespread use of strict liability. The struggle between negligence and strict liability, seemingly resolved in the nineteenth century, gained vigor as the twentieth century progressed.

The doctrinal changes in tort law occurred within broader legal and social contexts, each of which also facilitated the expansion of tort liability for much of the twentieth century. Increased ownership of homes and automobiles substantially increased the number of individuals owning *liability insurance*, a form of insurance protecting the policyholder against certain types of legal liabilities, including tort liability. In a typical tort suit involving an automobile accident, for example, a defendant driver is represented by an insurance company that pays for the legal defense and an adverse tort judgment up to the policy limits. The increased prevalence of liability insurance greatly increased the amount of resources available to tort claimants — it often is worth suing an insured driver who otherwise has no assets to pay for the tort judgment — predictably fueling tort litigation and the associated pressures for expanded liability.[53]

Liability insurance was also increasingly purchased by business enterprises as the twentieth century progressed.[54] Rather than face the uncertain prospect of potentially ruinous tort liability, a business could pay an insurance premium and transfer the risk to a liability insurer. Liability insurance transformed tort liability into a predictable "cost of doing business," reducing the concern that expanded tort liability would curtail business development.

As liability insurance became more widespread and money flowed into the tort system, the plaintiffs' bar became increasingly well organized and financed over the course of the twentieth century. Firms specializing in the representation of tort plaintiffs had the assets to specialize and seek out new, lucrative forms of tort liability. Many firms began to share information in litigating cases of the same type, reducing costs and further adding to the expansionary pressures exerted on tort law.[55]

By midcentury, a number of prominent tort scholars argued that business enterprises should be subject to a rule of strict liability. According to this theory of *enterprise liability*, a business is in a good position to provide compensation for accidental injuries through the purchase of liability insurance.

A social need for compensation and insurance is created by the inevitable fact of accidental injury. Eliminating the fault requirement would enable tort law to increase the scope of tort compensation funded by liability insurance, creating a public policy rationale for strict liability.[56]

Enterprise liability was never fully adopted by tort law, although it helped justify the expansion of negligence liability to cover broader ranges of business activity, thereby allowing more injuries to be compensated by liability insurance.[57] Enterprise liability had its most significant impact on the development of strict products liability, which fully illustrates how tort law consolidated and expanded during the twentieth century, finally creating a backlash triggered by a concern about excessive liability.

A. The Example of Strict Products Liability

Today, manufacturers and other product sellers are strictly liable in tort for physical injuries caused by product defects. The buyer, other users, and bystanders can all recover from the seller of a defective product. Contemporary law starkly contrasts with the law of the nineteenth century, making this area particularly useful for studying the evolution of the common law.

In the 1840s, the English case *Winterbottom v. Wright* concluded that the seller of a defective product could be liable only to the buyer but not third parties.[58] This immunity from third-party injuries was widely adopted in the states. Unlike today, product sellers at that time were immune from both strict liability and negligence liability when their defective products injured parties outside the contractual relationship.

During the 1840s, the common law was still governed by the writ system, and so the resolution of *Winterbottom* depended on whether the plaintiff's claim fit within a recognized writ or cause of action. On the alleged facts, "[t]here simply were no precedents authorizing recovery in tort."[59]

The plaintiff had to argue that the contract itself provided the basis for recovery, and the *Winterbottom* court concluded that one must be a party to the contract or be in *privity* with the defendant to have any contractually based rights.

The privity rule was not absolute, however, because the case law had previously recognized a legal duty involving the delivery of dangerous chattels. Shortly after *Winterbottom* was decided, the New York Court of Appeals affirmed that a defendant could be liable in tort for selling a bottle of mislabeled poison that "put human life in imminent danger," despite the absence of contractual privity between the defendant and poisoned plaintiff.[60] The courts also relied on another exception for cases involving "inherently dangerous" defective products. These cases were consistent with *Winterbottom*, as liability was based on a previously established legal duty and not the contract alone.

This inquiry forced the courts to confront a difficult question. Why were some defective products "imminently or inherently dangerous" and subject to the tort duty, whereas other defective products were governed by the privity-based immunity? The decided cases provided no clear answer, as illustrated by the cases finding defective bottles of water under gas pressure to be inherently more dangerous than defective automobiles.[61] The courts could not identify a defensible distinction between an "imminently or inherently dangerous" defective product and other defective products, even though the distinction was of critical importance for determining whether the privity-based immunity applied to the case at hand.

The distinction was finally demolished by Judge Benjamin Cardozo in the 1916 landmark opinion *MacPherson v. Buick Motor Company*.[62] According to Cardozo, "If the nature of a thing is such that it is reasonably certain to place life and limb in peril when negligently made, it is then a thing of danger [and subject to a tort duty]." By making the tort duty dependent on the foreseeable risk of physical harm posed by the defect, Cardozo turned the "imminently or inherently dangerous" exception to the privity requirement into a general rule of negligence liability. The fact of injury would seem to establish conclusively that the defect made the product a "thing of danger" subject to the tort duty. Any defective product is governed by the tort duty, eliminating any requirement of contractual privity.

In the following years "this decision swept the country" and was "extended by degrees" until it became "in short, a general rule imposing negligence liability upon any supplier, for remuneration, of any chattel."[63]

The *MacPherson* decision shows how the negligence principle became consolidated from more particularized liability rules — those turning on issues of whether there was privity or the product was "imminently" or "inherently dangerous" — into a comprehensive, general standard of tort liability. The more comprehensive liability rule also did not seem to be excessive. Prior to *MacPherson*, the gradual erosion of the privity requirement had shown that tort liability would not lead to "the most absurd and outrageous consequences" as feared by the court in *Winterbottom*.[64] Once the concern of excessive liability was practically eliminated, *MacPherson* could rely on the fault principle to hold product sellers accountable for the physical harms foreseeably caused by their negligence.

The widespread adoption of negligence liability for dangerous products then created a rationale for strict liability. In the landmark case *Escola v. Coca Cola Bottling Company*, Justice Roger Traynor of the California Supreme Court argued in a concurring opinion that the negligence rule, if properly applied, would involve insurmountable problems of proof: "An injured person . . . is not ordinarily in a position to refute [the manufacturer's evidence of reasonable care] or identify the cause of the defect, for he can hardly be familiar with the manufacturing process as the manufacturer himself is."[65] The difficulty of proving fault justified strict liability according to Traynor, as did the public policy rationales of enterprise liability. Strict liability would give product sellers an incentive to distribute nondefective products, and the availability of tort damages for the product-caused injuries was a valuable form of insurance for consumers.

The claim that strict liability could be justified by the difficulties of proving legal fault or negligence was supported by established rules. For example, common carriers had long been strictly liable for lost or damaged goods due to the difficulty plaintiffs would otherwise face in proving negligence.[66] The evidentiary rationale for strict liability was also an important justification for the statutory schemes of workers' compensation that were widely adopted by the states in the early 1900s.

Prior to workers' compensation, an employee ordinarily could recover for workplace injuries only by proving that the injury was caused by the employer's negligence. In light of the staggering toll of workplace injuries that occurred in the late nineteenth and early twentieth centuries, it became increasingly evident that negligence liability did not give employers a sufficient safety incentive. Management engineers and other observers began to understand that workplace injuries were largely attributable to system design, such as the layout and form of production processes, rather than isolated instances of fault. The threat of negligence liability did not give employers an adequate incentive to adopt costly system changes, because a plaintiff ordinarily could not prove that the employer had designed the system in a faulty manner. An injured miner, for example, could rarely prove that the design of the mine was unreasonably dangerous, particularly when the design was customarily employed within the industry. To make the workplace safer while giving workers guaranteed compensation for their financial harms, the states enacted workers' compensation statutes. This legislation removed cases of negligence liability from the tort system in favor of a statutory scheme of strict liability administered within a separate system. In exchange for the uncertain, negligence-based higher tort award covering both monetary and nonmonetary injuries, a worker who is injured on the job now typically receives a guaranteed award for all medical expenses and most lost wages.[67]

The workers' compensation statutes provided particularly strong support for a rule imposing strict liability on the sellers of defective products. After all, if negligence liability did not effectively regulate systems of workplace safety, then presumably negligence liability poorly regulated systems of product safety. Just as strict liability would reduce workplace injuries by giving employers an incentive to adopt safer systems of production, strict liability would reduce product injuries by giving manufacturers an incentive to adopt safer systems of quality control. Faced with the prospect of paying for all injuries caused by defective products, manufacturers would seek to reduce their liability costs by reducing defects (and accidents) through the adoption of safer technologies.

The doctrinal and policy arguments for strict liability were compelling. In 1963, the California Supreme Court accepted Traynor's argument for strict products liability.[68] By 1971, 28 states had adopted the rule of strict liability for product defects; by 1976, 41 states had adopted it. Tort scholars also jumped on the bandwagon, arguing that sellers should be strictly liable for product defects as a matter of sound social policy. The evidentiary rationale for strict products liability is still widely recognized.*

The vast majority of jurisdictions adopted the rule of strict products liability in section 402A of the *Restatement (Second) of Torts*, which was approved by the American Law Institute in 1964. Organized in the 1920s by prominent lawyers, judges, and law professors, the American Law Institute sought to

---

* One justification for imposing strict liability on product sellers for manufacturing defects is that doing so "encourages greater investment in product safety than does a regime of fault-based liability under which, as a practical matter, sellers may escape their appropriate share of responsibility." *Restatement (Third): Products Liability* § 2, cmt. a.

restore "clarity and predictability to American law through the production of a series of massive, annotated 'Restatements' of specific legal subjects" that provide black-letter formulations of the liability rules adopted by the majority of states.[69] Various state courts then often adopt specific Restatement provisions as their own law. Section 402A has been the most influential provision in a Restatement; it is the textual source of modern products liability law.

The growth of products liability has been astounding, with much of it attributable to issues that had not been extensively considered when the rule of strict products liability was promulgated by the American Law Institute in the 1960s. Products liability initially involved cases in which a defect caused the product to malfunction and injure the user, such as an exploding bottle of soda. By the 1970s, the allegations of defect moved beyond malfunctioning products. Even if the product functioned according to design, plaintiffs began claiming that the design itself was defective for not containing a particular safety feature, like a protective guard on a power tool. Plaintiffs also claimed that properly designed and manufactured products were defective for not adequately warning consumers about product risks. The claims of design and warning defects now constitute the bulk of products liability suits. Allegations of warning defects, for example, are involved in the massive number of suits involving asbestos liability. "From an inauspicious beginning in the late 1960s, asbestos litigation has generated over 730,000 claims, at an overall cost of at least $70 billion."[70] The asbestos cases are an extreme example, but they illustrate how the scope of tort liability far exceeds that which was contemplated when state courts first adopted the rule of strict products liability.[71]

Despite the label of strict products liability, this expansion of tort liability has been largely predicated on the fault principle. The rule of strict products liability makes a product seller strictly liable for injuries caused by a defect in the product. When the product performed as intended, the defect cannot be defined by reference to a product malfunction, as in the case of an exploding soda bottle. Absent any malfunction, what makes a design or warning defective? In addressing this issue, most courts have concluded that a design or warning is defective if it creates an unreasonably high risk of physical harm. Under this formulation, the seller continues to be strictly liable for injuries caused by the defect, defined as the absence of a safety feature (like a protective guard or safety instruction) that created an unreasonable risk of harm. The same outcome, though, is obtained under a rule of negligence, which also makes the seller liable for injuries caused by an unreasonable product risk (the defect in design or warning).[72] Like other areas of tort law, the generality of the fault principle enabled courts to expand the scope of tort liability to address issues not covered by more narrowly defined liability rules.

The development of products liability over the course of the twentieth century fully illustrates the development of tort law more generally. The consolidation and ensuing expansion of negligence liability first undermined the common-law immunity conferred on product sellers; negligence was then displaced by a rule of strict liability, which in turn was augmented by negligence liability. The expansion of tort liability could not last indefinitely, however. The development of products liability tested the limits of tort liability. In the last decades of the twentieth century, a burgeoning group of critics claimed that tort liability was excessively burdensome for the economy. The consolidation and expansion of tort liability had created a backlash, with products liability a primary target of reform.

B. The Tort Reform Movement

In 1986, the U.S. Department of Justice issued a report claiming that flaws in the tort system had created a crisis in the market for general liability insurance.[73] From 1984 to 1986, premiums for general liability insurance nearly tripled. Such insurance became unaffordable or unavailable for some, leading to the so-called liability crisis that appeared in myriad forms such as the closing of day care centers and municipal swimming pools due to operator concerns about uninsured exposure to tort liability. The sudden increase in premiums for liability insurance indicated that something might be awry with the tort system.

> There grew a consensus that the source of the insurance crisis was the growth of modern tort law. Changes in liability insurance premiums can be described as reflecting the best estimates of insurers as to what the dimensions of future liability claims will be. . . . The magnitude of current tort claims had generated concern; the estimates that future tort claims would be many multiples greater generated active calls for tort reform.[74]

Products liability was a particular concern. "Major American corporations — such as the Big Three automakers — which had appeared so dominant in the 1960s were now being perceived as fragile, buffeted by consumer resistance and foreign competition."[75] President Bush expressed support in his January 31, 1990 State of the Union address for legislation that would limit a manufacturer's tort liability, and Vice President Quayle stated that such legislation was a "top priority" for the administration.[76]

In response to the dramatically increased cost of liability insurance, the vast majority of states enacted tort reform statutes. From 1985 to 1988 alone, 48 states adopted some form of tort reform legislation.[77] All reforms shared the common attribute of limiting tort liability to reduce insurance rates and restore stability in the market for liability insurance. Undoubtedly affected by this political climate, the courts in most states have largely halted the growth of products liability and tort liability more generally.[78]

Despite the legislative and judicial curbs on liability, problems persisted into this century. Today the crisis is one of medical malpractice, a recurring periodic problem that first appeared in the 1970s. Nearly all physicians purchase insurance to cover them against claims for medical malpractice. The premiums for most malpractice policies have risen sharply in the past few years, allegedly causing many doctors to stop practicing specialties involving a high risk of tort liability (and high malpractice premiums), such as obstetrics and emergency care. In response to the increase in premiums, the American Medical Association and others continue to lobby for limitations of liability in malpractice claims.

Efforts to limit liability, whether for particular areas like medical malpractice or for tort law more generally, are now an established feature of the political landscape. "Few other business issues have generated more controversy, polemics, and campaign spending than the effort to scale back the types of lawsuits people can file and how much they can recover."[79]

A tort reform measure that limits a plaintiff's recovery effectively limits certain types of lawsuits due to its impact on contingency fees. Recall that under this arrangement, a plaintiff's lawyer receives payment for services only if the plaintiff recovers damages from the defendant, a portion of which then goes to the lawyer as remuneration for his or her services.[80] When the plaintiff's damages are limited by tort reform, the attorney's contingency fee is limited as well, with predictable consequences for the types of cases that attorneys are willing to take on this basis.

One study surveyed a number of plaintiffs' lawyers in Texas both before and after Texas adopted a tort reform measure that caps noneconomic damages at $250,000 in cases involving health care, like medical malpractice.[81] The survey questions involve three different types of plaintiffs who suffered the same physical injury, resulting in permanent facial disfigurement, caused by identical forms of physician malpractice: "a

70-year-old retired male for whom economic damages would be minimal (no lost wages, dependents, etc.); a 45-year-old employed married male for whom economic damages would be an issue (lost wages, dependents, etc.); and a 45-year-old married housewife (no lost wages, but dependents)." Without a substantial claim for economic loss, the plaintiff's tort claim is largely limited to the noneconomic damages of pain and suffering. For these types of plaintiffs, the damages cap effectively determines the largest available recovery and the maximum contingency fee for the attorney. Due to the considerable expense the attorney can expect to incur by litigating a case of medical malpractice, the damages cap can reduce the contingency fee to a level that no longer makes the case financially worthwhile for the attorney, regardless of its merits. The damages cap can have differing impacts on the ability of injured individuals to access the tort system, a possibility confirmed by the responses of the surveyed attorneys (the number of whom is denoted by N), as shown in Table 1-1.

Table 1-1

	Before Cap	After Cap
70-year-old retired male	$N = 55$	$N = 59$
Take case	61.8%	13.6%
Take and refer case	25.5%	11.9%
Not take case	12.7%	74.4%
45-year-old employed male	$N = 55$	$N = 59$
Take case	67.3%	37.3%
Take and refer case	25.5%	32.2%
Not take case	7.3%	30.5%
45-year-old housewife	$N = 54$	$N = 57$
Take case	66.7%	24.6%
Take and refer case	25.9%	22.8%
Not take case	7.4%	52.6%

Are results like this justifiable? Tort liability undoubtedly has become increasingly burdensome for business over the course of the twentieth century. Not only did the scope of tort liability expand, so did its consequences. The average compensatory damages award has significantly increased over the twentieth century.[82] Punitive damages awards can be staggering. In one case, a California jury levied a $4.9 billion punitive damages award against General Motors.[83]

The increased burden of tort liability, however, does not imply that there is too much liability. One notable feature of the practice of tort law involves the extent to which valid tort claims are not pursued by accident victims, a problem only exacerbated by reforms that limit liability for the reasons just given.[84] For example, the general level of premiums for medical malpractice insurance is substantially lower than it would be if the tort system functioned perfectly and physicians were liable for all malpractice injuries and absolved of liability in all other cases.[85] Moreover, empirical studies have found that tort damages are often too low. In general, the tort system "tends to undercompensate large losses and overcompensate small losses."[86] The available empirical data, according to a nonpartisan body of the U.S. Congress, are insufficient to support the claim that there is an excessive amount of tort liability.[87]

Problems in the market for liability insurance are also not plausibly attributable to excessive tort liability. The insurance crisis of the 1980s, for example, can largely be explained by a dramatic increase in federal environmental liability that reinforced a cyclical downturn otherwise characteristic of insurance markets.*

---

* The enactment in 1980 of the federal statute known as CERCLA, or Superfund, imposed retroactive strict liability on any entity contributing hazardous waste to a pollution site. That form of liability has involved billions of dollars of unanticipated legal liabilities for insurers. *See* Kenneth S. Abraham, *Environmental Liability and the Limits of Insurance*, 88 Colum. L. Rev. 942 (1988). This unanticipated liability then exacerbated a downturn in the insurance cycle the insurance industry was going through due to extraordinary changes in interest

By the same token, none of the foregoing implies that tort law does not suffer from excesses requiring reform. The cyclical problems of the insurance industry are exacerbated by uncertain tort rules. Substantial and increasing evidence, both theoretical and empirical, reveals that insurance companies raise premiums or withdraw coverage due to increased difficulties in predicting the probability of a given loss or the amount of loss for a given event.[88] When the insurance market is robust and profitable, the problem of uncertainty fades into the background; when the insurance market experiences hard times, uncertainty looms much larger in the profit calculus of insurers, inducing them to raise premiums and withdraw coverage for the most uncertain lines of business. Insofar as tort liability is excessively uncertain, it has contributed to the disruption of insurance markets and merits reform on that basis.

The problem of overly vague tort rules has now become a matter of federal constitutional law. In a line of relatively recent cases, the U.S. Supreme Court has held that a tort award of punitive damages must satisfy the procedural and substantive requirements of the Due Process Clause of the U.S. Constitution.[89] So far, constitutional tort reform has been limited to punitive damages, but such reform is not necessarily limited to this area of tort law. Other important tort practices raise the same sort of due process concerns that the Court has invoked to justify the constitutional tort reform of punitive damages practice.[90] Even if these other tort practices are constitutional, the Court's punitive damages jurisprudence may provide further impetus for reforming

---

rates during the early 1980s. *Cf.* Tom Baker, *Medical Malpractice and the Insurance Underwriting Cycle*, 54 DePaul L. Rev. 393 (2005), describing factors, including interest rate changes, causing the insurance industry to go through cycles. Asbestos liability is the only form of tort liability that plausibly contributed to the crisis, but tort reforms adopted by the states in the 1980s and 1990s typically did not directly target those cases, unlike recent tort reforms.

vague tort rules that compromise the due process values of notice, predictability, and reasoned decision making.

As Holmes observed in his classic formulation of the common law, "the tendency of the law must always be to narrow the field of uncertainty."[91] To understand the current state of tort law and its possible future, we need to identify more clearly what tort liability accomplishes and why these functions are justifiable.

~ 2 ~

Function and Principle

In the first part of the twentieth century, judges and tort scholars rejected the idea that the formal or logical properties of liability rules provide a sufficient or desirable basis for legal analysis. Instead, they began to analyze tort issues in terms of the outcomes produced by tort liability, its functions. Insofar as a liability rule achieves desirable social outcomes, it could be justified in these functional terms, regardless of the rule's formal or logical properties.

Functional analysis fueled the considerable growth of tort liability through the twentieth century, but cannot satisfactorily explain the important limitations of tort liability. Moreover, the primary functions of liability do not always work together in a unified manner, requiring a choice of one function over another. Unless there is some principle to guide these choices, functional analysis can turn the imposition of tort liability into an arbitrary exercise of governmental coercion. A closer look at functional analysis clearly reveals the need for a principled explanation of why liability rules function in a particular manner.

I. WHAT TORT LIABILITY ACHIEVES

Over the years, courts and scholars have ascribed a variety of functions to tort liability. The most important involve injury compensation, the deterrence or prevention of injuries, and the redress of rights violations caused by wrongful conduct.

A. Compensation of Injuries

Tort liability requires the defendant to compensate the plaintiff's injuries and is obviously compensatory from the plaintiff's perspective. In this sense, tort liability necessarily functions as a form of compensation.

When courts and scholars discuss the function of compensation, though, they often mean something else. From a social perspective, tort liability shifts the injury costs from the plaintiff to the defendant. One party is fully compensated and the other bears the entire loss, creating another compensatory problem of the same magnitude. To solve this compensatory problem, tort liability must involve *loss sharing* (also called *loss spreading*). If, for example, the plaintiff is an injured individual and the defendant a business enterprise, then tort liability shifts the injury costs from the individual to the business enterprise, which in turn spreads this particular cost among its customers (via a price increase) and the business owners (via reduced profits), a group often consisting of a large number of shareholders. These groups compensate the plaintiff, and yet no individual suffers a comparable or even significant loss due to the way in which the compensatory payment has been spread among the group members. Loss spreading is characteristic of insurance arrangements. Each policyholder pays a premium for the insurance in exchange for a right to compensation (known as *indemnification*) for any losses covered by the insurance policy. The indemnification is funded by the pool of premiums paid by the group of policyholders, so the insurance arrangement effectively spreads the individual loss among the group of policy-holders. Insofar as insurance functions as a form of compensation, tort liability can do the same.

In most cases, tort liability functions in this manner. When tort law first emerged from the writ system in the latter half of the nineteenth century, courts were confronted by the wide-spread injuries caused by industrialization. Tort liability ordinarily involved injured individuals recovering from business enterprises, thereby functioning as a form of loss sharing. With the development of liability insurance in the twentieth century, tort liability began to function in this manner with increased regularity. Plaintiffs now settle tort suits against individual defendants based on the limits of the defendant's insurance policy, typically seeking recourse against the defendant's personal assets only when they want to extract such "blood money" to hurt the defendant for having behaved in an egregious manner.[1] The practice of tort law largely revolves around the indemnification afforded by liability insurance, enabling tort liability to function as a form of insurance or loss sharing.

B. Deterrence or Prevention of Injuries

In addressing the social problem of accidental harms, tort law is understandably concerned about the deterrence capabilities of a liability rule. By deterring risky behavior, a liability rule protects individuals from injury and reduces the incidence of accidental harms within society more generally.

Despite the evident appeal of deterrence, it may not be apparent how tort liability can function in this manner. A defendant incurs liability for behavior that has already occurred, so how can the liability affect behavior? The answer involves two different ways in which tort law can motivate behavior.

Most tort rules specify the kinds of behavior required of risky actors subject to the tort duty in question. For example, negligence liability requires duty holders to exercise reasonable care. The required behavior is always directed at reducing or eliminating certain kinds of harms that could be suffered by a specified group or class of other individuals — those holding a tort right that is protected by the associated duty. At times, the tort rule states the required behavior in general terms (like "reasonable care"), so the imposition of liability in particular cases can help to clarify the behavior required by tort law. In this respect, tort law can guide the behavior of individuals who want to act lawfully, making the function of deterrence or injury prevention a characteristic aspect of tort liability.

Of course, not all duty holders are interested in acting lawfully merely because it is the right thing to do. Tort law must also recognize that many actors are self-interested and follow the law only when doing so works to their advantage. In these circumstances, the *threat* of tort liability creates a financial incentive for self-interested actors to act lawfully. The self-interested actor compares the personal benefit of the unlawful conduct with the associated liability costs. As long as threatened liability costs are sufficiently high, the self-interested actor will find it advantageous to behave in the legally required manner. For the threat of liability to be credible, those who violate the law must incur liability for having done so. By influencing the personal cost-benefit calculations of self-interested actors, the imposition of liability in an individual case can function in a manner that motivates safe behavior in future cases.

C. Redress of Rights Violations Caused by Wrongful Conduct

A tort suit always involves a defendant who allegedly violated the plaintiff's tort right. By definition, one who violates a right has committed a wrong. An innate function of tort liability, therefore, involves the redress of rights violations caused by wrongful conduct.

The appropriate form of redress ordinarily involves the payment of compensatory damages, but is not necessarily limited to that remedy. In some cases, the appropriate form of redress involves punishment or retribution for the wrongful conduct.

Tort law punishes a defendant through the imposition of punitive damages, a monetary penalty the defendant incurs in addition to liability for compensatory damages. The defendant can only be punished for having behaved in a manner prohibited by tort law. Defendants rarely incur punitive damages, but the liability in these cases enforces the tort prohibition against certain forms of injury-causing behavior, thereby complementing the way in which tort liability otherwise functions to prevent injury.

II. FUNCTIONAL DISUNITY AND THE IMPORTANCE OF PRINCIPLE

The functions of tort liability do not always work in a unified manner. The need for compensation depends only on the occurrence of injury, regardless of its source: "[N]othing about compensation as such justifies its limitation to those who are the victims of deterrable harms." Similarly, the need for deterrence exists whenever someone has engaged in undesirable behavior: "[N]othing about deterrence as such justifies its limitation to acts that produce compensable injury."[2] *Any* injury is an appropriate candidate for compensation, and *any* form of undesirable risky behavior is an appropriate candidate for deterrence. The functions of compensation and deterrence are not mutually dependent and can be decoupled.

Due to this disunity, functional analysis provides a problematic method for justifying tort liability. The function of injury compensation would seem to justify a rule of strict liability, and yet tort law has adopted negligence liability as the default rule for accidental harms. How is this limitation of liability justified by functional analysis? Furthering the compensation function readily explains why both negligence and strict tort liability expanded over the twentieth century, but functional analysis cannot explain the limitations of liability.[3]

To be sure, liability can be limited by the function of compensation as loss sharing. The tort reform movement largely developed in response to the perceived detrimental impact that tort liability was having on the market for liability insurance in the 1980s. If tort liability is supposed to function as a form of loss sharing, then its disruptive effect on insurance markets supplies a compelling reason for cutting back on liability.

By itself, this rationale could justify the elimination of tort liability. Unlike the time when tort law first developed, individuals can now receive injury compensation from private insurance arrangements in addition to governmental insurance programs such as Medicare, Medicaid, and Social Security. These forms of insurance are much more comprehensive and substantially less costly than the compensation provided by the tort system, which requires the injured party to retain the services of an attorney to be compensated for the injuries. If tort liability only serves the function of compensation as loss sharing, then the tort system should largely be scrapped in favor of superior alternative insurance arrangements, the kind of approach taken by New Zealand.[4]

Of course, eliminating tort liability could create problems of inadequate deterrence. Without the threat of tort liability, risky actors may no longer have sufficient financial incentives for preventing harms to others. Again, this problem could be addressed by alternative institutional arrangements, like administrative regulation of health and safety issues coupled with monetary fines for noncompliance.

The functions of compensation and deterrence are connected in this respect, explaining why tort law is regularly analyzed in these functional terms. Tort liability both compensates the plaintiff and deters risky behavior by the defendant and others. The two functions do not always work in a unified manner, however, making functional analysis an inadequate method for justifying tort liability.

When a liability rule can be justified with disparate, non-unified functions, and there is no overarching principle for choosing the appropriate function in a particular case, then judges can arbitrarily decide the outcome of any given case by choosing whatever function would produce the desired result. The function of compensation could justify the award of tort damages for any plaintiff who was injured by the defendant. The deterrence function could instead justify a finding of no liability on the ground that the defendant acted with the desired degree of care. What is the basis for choosing one function over another? Justifying tort liability solely in functional terms could turn tort law into an incoherent mess, an accurate portrayal according to some prominent tort scholars.[5]

The practice of tort law does not suffer from such extreme arbitrariness, indicating that functional analysis does not fully explain how courts decide tort cases. Courts justify their tort decisions with precedent established by prior case law. In the vast majority of cases, prior case law has established the liability rules, and the court only needs to apply an existing rule to justify its resolution of the case at hand. Perhaps the very nature of common-law adjudication eliminates the arbitrariness of functional analysis and obviates the need for judges to rely on an overarching principle for selecting among the varied functions of tort liability.

The nature of common-law reasoning undoubtedly constrains courts, but not in a manner that eliminates the need to identify the principles of tort liability. Like other forms of the common law, the legal inquiry in tort law relies on *analogical reasoning*, "arguing from one case to the next on the basis of perceived likenesses and differences and the location of the instant case in the landscape of common experience painted by the judge or lawyer in command of the full resources of the common law."[6] Because analogical reasoning "is reasoning by or from example . . . from like to like," it "presupposes some degree of (threshold) relevant similarity."[7] To illustrate, consider a case in which the plaintiff solely relies on prior cases that furthered the function of compensation and not deterrence. Suppose the defendant responds by relying on prior cases that denied the plaintiff compensation because liability would not further the function of deterrence. To decide whether the case law supports the plaintiff's recovery, the court must determine which line of cases is sufficiently similar to the present dispute. The court could distinguish each of the prior cases in terms other than compensation and deterrence, but what are the relevant distinctions? Answering that question requires resort to principle. "The major challenge facing analogical reasoners is to decide when differences are relevant. To make this decision, they must investigate cases with care in order to develop governing principles. The judgment that a distinction is not genuinely principled requires a substantive argument of some kind."[8] Consequently, "no clear line of distinction can be drawn between argument from legal principles and argument from analogy. Analogies only make sense if there are reasons of principle underlying them."[9] Rather than obviate the need for courts to rely on principle, the nature of common-law reasoning critically depends on principle or the substantive reasons that explain why liability rules function in a particular manner.

The practice of tort law involves principled decision making by relying on precedent and analogical reasoning, requiring us to look at tort doctrine as the first step in identifying the principles of tort liability.

∼ 3 ∼

The Fundamental Choice: Negligence or Strict Liability?

Tort law is largely negligence law, leading many or perhaps most scholars to deemphasize rules of strict liability on the ground that they are practically irrelevant or otherwise anomalous. So, too, the intentional torts are commonly deemphasized on the ground that they typically involve personally blameworthy misconduct, differing from most negligence cases only in that the misconduct is more egregious. By examining negligence law more closely, one would seem to have the best perspective for identifying the principles of tort liability.

This approach can be criticized for being incomplete, but the problem is more fundamental. Analyzing tort law solely in terms of personal fault makes it easy to justify liability. Any number of reasons can explain why a culpable actor should incur liability for injuries caused by the blameworthy conduct. However, if tort liability is concerned only about the redress of injuries caused by the defendant's culpable misconduct, then the distinctive subject matter of tort law may disappear altogether. An exclusive concern about culpability, personal blameworthiness, or guilt is characteristic of the criminal law. That concern could limit tort liability to behavior that violates criminal principles, making tort law nothing more than a set of remedial rules requiring a criminal wrongdoer to compensate the victim of the criminal misconduct. The substantive behavioral obligations that tort law imposes on individuals would be determined entirely by principles of criminal law. Even if some types of tortious misconduct did not violate an existing criminal statute, tort law would still only be enforcing behavioral obligations derived from the principles of criminal law grounded in notions of culpability and guilt. This conception accurately describes the initial role of tort law in the writ system, but it was decisively rejected by Holmes when he concluded that torts is a field of substantive law precisely because liability attaches to noncriminal behavior.*

Consistent with the Holmesian conceptualization of the field, tort law is conventionally divided into rules of intentional torts, negligence, and strict liability, with judges and scholars commonly contrasting the purely fault-based rules with those that do not require any personal fault to hold the defendant liable. As we have found, these instances of no-fault liability also occur under the objectively defined negligence standard of reasonable care.† The imposition of no-fault or strict liability, in turn, clearly distinguishes tort law from criminal law: "[N]o one seriously argues" that strict liability "provides a potential rationale for routine cases of criminal punishment."[1] The distinctive aspect of tort liability involves the rules of strict liability, whatever their guise, making the choice between negligence and strict liability the fundamental question for tort law.[2]

---

* This aspect of Holmes's approach is discussed in the Introduction to this book, and the writ system is discussed in Chapter 1, section I.

† *See* Chapter 1, section II.

I. NEGLIGENCE V. STRICT LIABILITY

In a case of negligence liability, the defendant breached a duty to exercise reasonable care in a manner that caused the plaintiff to suffer compensable harm. Negligence liability, for example, divides automobile accidents into two subsets, those caused by the defendant driver's *legal fault* or breach of the duty to exercise reasonable care, and those caused by no fault of the defendant driver:

F region:
Set of compensable injuries caused by "fault" of defendant duty holder, where "fault" is a breach of the legal duty to exercise reasonable care.

NF region:
Set of compensable injuries caused by defendant duty holder who was not at "fault."

A negligence rule subjects a driver to liability if he or she was legally at fault for an accident that injured another person, the *F* region. The driver does not incur these injury costs when he or she was legally not at fault, the *NF* region; instead, these costs are borne by the accident victim (who may or may not have insurance covering the losses).

Strict liability eliminates the requirement of legal fault or breach of a duty to exercise reasonable care, thereby requiring the plaintiff accident victim to prove only that the defendant driver caused the compensable harm in question. This causal requirement is satisfied by accidents in both the *F* and *NF* regions, subjecting the driver to liability for this entire class of automobile accidents.

Each rule subjects the defendant to liability when his or her legal fault caused the injury (the *F* region). The choice between negligence and strict liability reduces to the decision of who

[handwritten margin note: only guest. is compens harm]

should incur the cost of injuries not caused by the legal fault of the defendant (the *NF* region). Because the rule of strict liability subjects the defendant to liability for these injuries, it often is called *no-fault liability.*

In considering this choice, we need to look more closely at how tort law defines legal fault in terms of the defendant's breach of the duty to exercise reasonable care. The standard of reasonable care determines both the relative proportions of the *F* and *NF* regions, in addition to the overall number of injuries caused by the risky activity in question (the size of the total diagram). To use an extreme example, suppose the standard of reasonable care requires the total elimination of risk. *Any* injury caused by a driver would involve this form of legal fault, eliminating the *NF* region altogether:

> **F region:**
> Set of compensable injuries caused by defendant duty holder's "fault," where "fault" is defined as the failure to eliminate all risk.

This extreme rule of negligence seems indefensible simply because it manipulates the definition of legal fault to cover the entire class of automobile accidents. Drivers are not always blameworthy or subjectively culpable for causing accidents, so it seems problematic to deem a driver to be at fault merely for having caused an accident. For purposes of negligence liability, however, fault is defined in legal or objective terms, not in the subjective terms of personal blameworthiness. What makes one specification of legal fault more defensible than another?

Unless the question is answered, we have no basis for choosing between the two liability regimes depicted by the two diagrams. The choice between negligence and strict liability (the first diagram) only exists if we first have some reason for rejecting the extreme definition of legal fault (the second diagram). Without a definition of legal fault, we cannot even construct the first diagram (the line cannot be drawn between the *F* and *NF* regions). The reasoning that determines the definition of legal fault, therefore, also affects the choice between negligence and strict liability.

This result confirms our earlier conclusion regarding the foundational importance of strict liability. In addition to providing the clearest distinction between tort and criminal liability, the rules of strict liability are integrally related to the specification of legal fault that is central to negligence liability.

Negligence and strict liability serve the functions of deterrence and compensation in different ways, and courts have chosen the liability rule by relying on these functional considerations. Courts rely on other considerations as well, illustrating how functional analysis must be supplemented by principled reasons or rationales for liability.

II. DETERRENCE AND THE CHOICE OF LIABILITY RULES

Negligence liability directly controls risky behavior by specifying the precautions a duty holder is required to exercise as a matter of reasonable care. To satisfy the requirements of reasonable care, for example, individuals may have to forgo using cell phones while driving automobiles. Someone who violates this behavioral duty would then be subject to liability for injuries caused by this form of unreasonable behavior.

According to the *Restatement (Second)*, whether a risky actor exercised reasonable care requires a determination of "whether the magnitude of the risk outweighs the value which the law attaches to the conduct which involves it."[3] As Judge Learned Hand famously characterized the inquiry,

"If the probability [of injury] be called P; the injury, L; and the burden [of a precaution that would eliminate this risk] B; liability depends upon whether B is less than L multiplied by P: i.e., whether $B < PL$."[4] One who failed to take some precaution for which $B < PL$ acted unreasonably and could be subject to liability in the event that the unreasonable risk caused injury to a right holder.

To illustrate the inquiry entailed by the Hand formula, consider the safety precaution of not using a cell phone while driving an automobile. The precaution inconveniences drivers by preventing them from engaging in these kinds of conversations while driving. In this particular respect, the precaution restricts the freedom of an automobile driver or burdens the liberty interest by some amount (the term B). The precaution also reduces the incidence of automobile accidents insofar as drivers who do not use cell phones are more attentive and perhaps more physically capable of quickly responding to changing conditions on the road. By reducing the probability of such accidents (the term P) that cause a right holder to suffer some amount of harm or loss (the term L), the precaution protects the right holder's interest in physical security. To measure the amount of protection afforded to the security interest, the amount of loss must be discounted by the probability of its occurrence (yielding the term PL), a measure known as the *expected cost* of the risk.* Having determined how a

---

* To identify the rationale for this concept, consider how a duty holder would rationally evaluate a 1 in 100 monthly chance of a crash causing $100 in injury costs for which he or she would be liable. The duty holder does not know whether the crash will occur, so he or she will predictably make mistakes in estimating the outcome. At best, the duty holder can only minimize the cost of these errors. The duty holder might optimistically decide he or she will never crash and estimate the injury cost at zero. If the duty holder drives the car for 100 months, then this estimate probably will be correct 99 times. The error costs for these months are zero. However, the odds are that 100 months of driving will result in one crash. In that month, the duty holder estimates no injury costs but incurs $100 of costs. Over the course of 100 months, then, the duty holder's error costs are $100. At the other extreme, the duty holder might pessimistically

particular precaution like the ban on cell phone use affects the relevant liberty and security interests, the Hand formula then specifies how these conflicting interests should be balanced or mediated. Whenever a precaution imposes a burden on the liberty interest (B) that is less than the associated threat to the security interest (PL), the standard of reasonable care requires the risky actor to exercise the precaution, a legal conclusion compactly expressed by the Hand formulation of reasonable care as requiring precautions for which $B < PL$.

The specification of reasonable care, however, does not necessarily induce the required forms of safe behavior. To recover, the plaintiff usually must prove that the defendant failed to take some precaution required by the standard of reasonable care, and that the precaution, if taken, would have prevented injury. Unless there is such proof, a defendant duty holder can avoid taking such a precaution and avoid negligence liability. Why incur the cost of acting safely if the risky misconduct will not lead to liability? This behavior, although obviously selfish, reduces the actor's costs and is likely to be engaged in by profit-making enterprises. The practical difficulty a plaintiff faces in proving breach or legal fault can substantially diminish the risk-reducing capabilities of negligence liability.

---

assume he or she will crash each month. Over the course of 100 months, he or she is likely to be correct once (zero error costs) but wrong for those 99 months without a crash (error costs of $9,900). Now consider a decision rule based on the *expected value* of injury. A 1 percent chance of incurring a $100 injury in any month yields an expected injury cost of $1 per month. Under this decision rule, the duty holder's estimate is wrong in each month. He or she never suffers a $1 loss in any given month. For the 99 months without a crash, he or she overestimates the injury costs by $99. For the one month with a crash, the duty holder underestimates his or her injury costs by $99. The total estimate over the course of 100 months is correct, however. The duty holder estimated $100 in total injury costs (100 months at $1 per month) and experienced $100 in injury costs. A decision rule based on the expected value of loss therefore minimizes the duty holder's error costs, making it the rational method for quantifying the consequences of probabilistic outcomes.

In these circumstances, the desired safety incentive can be at least partially restored by strict liability. Under a rule of strict liability, the actor only incurs a duty to compensate harms caused by the strictly liable conduct. A strictly liable driver, for example, must pay for the injuries he or she causes to others while driving. This duty does not dictate how the driver should otherwise behave and leaves that decision to him or her. Nevertheless, strict liability affects risky behavior in a predictable manner.

A strictly liable duty holder understands that by engaging in the risky activity, he or she will be liable for the compensable injuries suffered by others. Suppose the actor's full extent of liability for an injury equals the social value of the loss (the term L in the Hand formula). Under these conditions, the actor's liability costs depend on the probability that an injury will occur (the term P) and the total amount of damages for which the actor would be liable in the event of an accident (assumed to be L). Multiplying these two factors together yields the actor's expected liability costs for engaging in the risky activity (PL). The actor can affect the amount of expected liability costs by adopting safety precautions. To exercise a precaution, the actor ordinarily must incur a cost or burden (B), such as the lost usage of a cell phone while driving. A strictly liable driver, therefore, will compare the burden (B) of any given precaution with the expected liability costs that he or she would otherwise incur by not taking the precaution and eliminating this particular liability risk (PL). To minimize total costs, the driver will take any precaution costing less than the expected liability costs he or she would otherwise incur, yielding the behavioral decision rule embodied in the Hand formula ($B < PL$). So, too, the driver will forgo any precautions that are not cost-effective ($B > PL$), as it would be cheaper to save the precautionary costs, create the risk, and incur liability for any ensuing injuries. Under a rule of strict liability, duty holders would rationally adopt the same safety precautions that are required as a matter of reasonable care by the Hand formula.

Insofar as the duty holder would have forgone any of these costly precautions in a negligence regime due to the plaintiff's inability to prove legal fault, then the shift to strict liability will increase precautions and reduce risk.[5] Strict liability can serve the purpose of fostering safe behavior and reducing risk when plaintiffs have a hard time proving that certain forms of risky behavior violate the standard of reasonable care.

This *evidentiary rationale for strict liability* was recognized by Holmes when he observed that "as there is a limit to the nicety of inquiry which is possible in a trial, it may be considered that the safest way to secure care is to throw the risk upon the person who decides what precautions shall be taken."[6] The practical problems a plaintiff faces in proving legal fault "limit the nicety of inquiry which is possible in trial," potentially enabling the defendant and similarly situated duty holders to avoid negligence liability for important forms of risky behavior. In that event, "the safest way to secure care" is to impose strict liability on these actors. Strict liability "throws the risk" of injury on the defendant duty holder and relieves the court of having to make the safety decision based on the plaintiff's proof of legal fault. To minimize costs, the strictly liable actor may take safety precautions he or she would otherwise forgo under the imperfectly enforced negligence standard of reasonable care, thereby reducing these risks below the level attainable by negligence liability.

The evidentiary rationale for strict liability was not invented by Holmes. Other scholars of the time had also justified strict liability in this manner.* As previously discussed, courts

---

* In one of the first tort treatises, Frederick Pollock observed that "the ground on which a rule of strict obligation has been maintained and consolidated by modern authorities is the magnitude of danger, coupled with the difficulty of proving negligence as the specific cause, in the particular event of the danger having ripened into actual harm." Frederick Pollock, *The Law of Torts: A Treatise*

expressly relied on the evidentiary rationale to justify the nineteenth-century rule of strict liability governing common carriers and the contemporary rule of strict products liability.*

These considerations of deterrence or risk reduction would seem to give strict liability a decisive advantage over negligence liability. Because strict liability predictably induces safety behavior characterized by the Hand formula for negligence $B < PL$, whereas negligence liability can fall short in that respect, why not apply a general rule of strict liability and forgo negligence liability altogether?

Such a rationale for strict liability assumes that the Hand formula fully specifies the requirements of reasonable care. Rather than rely on the Hand formula, virtually all jurisdictions instead require duty holders to take any precaution required as a matter of "reasonable care." When interpreting this duty, judges and jurors often rely on the moral intuition that safety (the reduced risk represented by the term PL) is more important than the monetary expenditures or comparable burdens created by the precaution (B).† Under this approach, the risk term (PL) is given some added moral weight that justifies imposing a burden on the duty holder that would otherwise fail the Hand formula (although $B > PL$, the added weight given to the risk term justifies the precaution). If sufficiently enforced, such a demanding standard of reasonable care gives negligence liability a greater capability for reducing risk as compared to strict liability (which only induces precautions for which $B < PL$). The function of deterrence or risk reduction can favor negligence liability, further illustrating how the

---

on the Principles of Obligations Arising from Civil Wrongs in the Common Law 393 (Stevens and Sons 1st ed. 1887).

* See Chapter 1, section II (discussing evidentiary rationale for rule of common carrier strict liability) and Chapter 1, section III.A (discussing evidentiary rationale for strict products liability).

† See Chapter 8, section II.B.

specification of reasonable care or legal fault affects the choice between negligence and strict liability.

To be sure, any time the standard of reasonable care requires precautions beyond the amount required by the Hand formula ($B > PL$), the duty holder has a financial incentive to forgo the more costly precaution (thereby saving the amount B) and face the lower expected liability cost for behaving in such a negligent manner (PL). This type of conduct, though, is subject to punitive damages. Duty holders do not have the option of converting a rule of negligence liability into one of strict liability merely because they are willing to pay compensatory damages in exchange for acting unreasonably. Negligence liability is prohibitory in this respect.[*]

The prohibitory component of negligence liability gives it the potential for exerting more control over risky behavior than a rule of strict liability, providing a deterrence rationale for choosing negligence over strict liability. To make the prohibition effective, tort law supplements negligence liability with punitive measures in the appropriate circumstances, illustrating the complementary relation between the functions of deterrence and punishment.

Analyzing the choice between negligence and strict liability in these functional terms, however, does not explain why tort law has made this fundamental choice. The adoption of negligence liability means that injured plaintiffs will not recover compensatory damages from defendants who exercised the required degree of care. For this class of cases, the function of deterrence requires tort law to forgo the compensation of injuries. Nothing in the prior analysis explains why tort law has chosen one function over the other.

---

[*] *See* Chapter 2, section I.C (discussing the way in which punitive damages identify prohibited forms of conduct) and Chapter 14, section IV (discussing the retributive rationale for punitive damages).

Nevertheless, we can now more fully understand why the activity of automobile driving is subject to negligence liability. Under this liability rule, courts rarely evaluate whether a defendant made a reasonable decision to engage in the activity of driving. This limited role for negligence liability is understandable in light of the evidentiary difficulties a court would face in trying to evaluate a defendant's reasons for driving on a particular occasion, whether the total amount of miles driven by the defendant was reasonable, and so on. Simply put, a plaintiff would have a hard time proving that the defendant acted unreasonably in any of these respects. Rather than address these complex issues, the court instead evaluates how safely the defendant behaved while engaged in the activity of driving. How fast was the defendant driving? Was he or she sufficiently attentive or unreasonably distracted by using a cell phone? These types of issues are amenable to proof by the plaintiff. As compared to this limited negligence inquiry, strict liability does not impose any particular safety requirements on drivers. Consequently, drivers who are subject only to strict liability might take fewer precautions, depending on how the displaced negligence rule defined the requirements of reasonable care. For example, negligence liability could prohibit drivers from using cell phones, whereas some drivers subject only to strict liability might decide to use their cell phones. These strictly liable actors would also consider whether to drive less frequently to reduce their liability costs, although it seems unlikely that strict liability would reduce the total amount of driving. Because strict liability would not significantly reduce the activity of driving and might even increase risk by not establishing required standards of safe conduct, deterrence considerations favor a rule of negligence liability for automobile accidents.

Based on this analysis, we can now define more rigorously how deterrence considerations affect the choice of liability rule. Negligence and strict liability can have different effects on risky behavior, providing a basis for choosing between them. Unlike strict liability, negligence liability employs a standard of reasonable care that specifies the safety precautions required of duty holders while engaged in risky behavior. Negligence liability can require duty holders to exercise greater care than they would otherwise choose under a rule of strict liability. A duty holder's incentive to exercise reasonable care, however, depends on a plaintiff's ability to prove that such a defendant duty holder acted unreasonably. Consequently, strict liability can reduce or discourage a risky activity as compared to negligence liability, where "activity" refers to any component of a duty holder's risky behavior that is not effectively governed by negligence liability due to the difficulty a plaintiff would face in trying to prove legal fault. The relative capabilities of negligence and strict liability to reduce risk accordingly depend on the importance of controlling the duty holder's behavior while engaging in a risky activity (negligence) as compared to the importance of controlling the risky activity itself (strict liability).

The choice between negligence and strict liability is not limited to considerations of deterrence or risk reduction. Sometimes liability functions only as injury compensation, creating a further divergence of function among liability rules.

III. COMPENSATION AND THE CHOICE OF LIABILITY RULES

Having addressed the function of deterrence, we can now consider cases in which the choice of liability rule has no impact on risk reduction. In these cases, which liability rule can be justified by the need to compensate the victim of the accident?

The function of compensation would seem to give strict liability a decisive advantage in these cases. Under negligence liability, the accident victim has no right to a damages remedy when injured by an actor who exercised reasonable care. Yet the compensation of accidental injury is clearly of social concern, and the adoption of strict liability would give the accident victim a right to recover even when injured by someone who was not at fault. This compensatory rationale for strict liability, however, assumes that compensation exclusively depends on the damages remedy.

In evaluating the compensatory nature of tort liability, courts do not limit the inquiry to the damages remedy. Based on a more expansive conception of compensation, courts have concluded that negligence liability is sufficiently compensatory when the participants in an activity impose similar risks on each other. An automobile driver, for example, can injure other drivers, or can be injured by them. The activity of automobile driving has a bilateral structure that affects the compensatory nature of tort liability. Consider a case in which one driver, despite the exercise of reasonable care, causes another to crash and suffer bodily injury. Under the rule of negligence liability, the injured victim does not receive tort damages from the driver who caused the accident without fault. Instead, as the New York Court of Appeals recognized long ago, the victim "receives his compensation for such damages by the general good, in which he shares, and the right which he has to [engage in the risky activity]."[7]

Negligence liability benefits every automobile driver by giving each one the right to drive. Someone who drives with reasonable care does not have to pay for any injuries he or she causes others to suffer—a further benefit for that driver. When an activity involves *reciprocal risks*, the individual benefits from the limitation of liability by an amount that adequately offsets the increased burden the individual faces in the event that he or she is harmed by someone else who has exercised reasonable care. In these circumstances, negligence liability is adequately compensatory, despite the way in which it limits the availability of compensatory damages.

The concept of reciprocity supplies further justification for applying negligence liability to the activity of automobile driving. As the *Restatement (Third)* explains:

> [A]utomobiles are in such general use that their operation is a matter of common usage. Accordingly, at least for this reason, the operation of automobiles is not [subject to strict liability]. . . . Whenever an activity is engaged in by a large fraction of the community, the absence of strict liability can be explained by considerations of reciprocity. Even though various actors may without negligence be creating appreciable risks, the risks in question are imposed by the many on each other.[8]

By this same reasoning, someone who creates an unreasonable risk is subject to liability for the ensuing injuries. The unreasonable risk exposes others to a risk of injury exceeding the amount of risk to which the actor is exposed. The unreasonable risk is not reciprocal. To offset this inequality, the actor is legally obligated to compensate injuries caused by the nonreciprocal (unreasonable) risk, the result attained by negligence liability.

This reasoning creates a compensatory role for strict liability. Because liability applies to nonreciprocal risks, someone who acts reasonably and still injures another with a nonreciprocal risk is subject to liability. This outcome occurs whenever the actor engages in an uncommon activity posing substantial risks. The use of dynamite for reasonable blasting purposes is a paradigmatic example. For risky activities of this type, the negligence rule does not provide an adequate reciprocal benefit for individuals who are exposed to the abnormal risk of injury. Most individuals in the community do not engage in the activity and do not benefit from the right to create the risk with a limitation of liability. Absent such a reciprocal benefit, these individuals must be compensated for their injuries, the result attained by the rule of strict liability for abnormally dangerous activities first recognized in the nineteenth-century English case *Rylands v. Fletcher* involving a burst reservoir.[9]

Based on this case law, we can now define more rigorously how compensation affects the choice between negligence and strict liability. When the choice between negligence and strict liability does not depend on deterrence considerations, the concept of reciprocity provides a basis for choosing between them. Negligence is appropriate for risky activities that are common within the community, whereas strict liability can be appropriate when the defendant, despite the exercise of reasonable care in all respects, injured the plaintiff by engaging in uncommon behavior posing an uncommonly high degree of risk. When formulated in this manner, negligence and strict liability both require the defendant to compensate the plaintiff for injuries caused by nonreciprocal risks.

For these rules, the concept of reciprocity supplements the functional analysis of tort liability. As discussed earlier, negligence liability serves the function of deterrence, which requires the complementary function of punishment in the appropriate cases. Negligence liability, however, limits the availability of compensatory damages to injured accident victims, creating the problem of functional disunity. What justifies furthering the function of deterrence at the expense of limiting the function of injury compensation? An answer is supplied by the concept of reciprocity. The damages remedy is not the only way in which tort liability benefits a plaintiff or the class of similarly situated right holders more generally. Insofar as negligence liability permits these individuals to avoid liability when they injure others, that liability rule may be sufficiently beneficial for them, despite the limitation of compensatory damages for cases in which they are injured by others. The concept of reciprocity explains why negligence liability can limit the damages remedy without being unfair to the plaintiff. Reciprocity then also explains why tort liability can further the function of injury compensation, even when doing so does not serve the deterrence function. In cases involving abnormally dangerous activities, the defendant acted reasonably and did not engage in behavior that tort law wants to deter or prohibit. Nevertheless, the defendant created a non-reciprocal risk, and so (strict) liability appropriately serves the compensatory function. Once again, the concept of reciprocity helps to determine which function tort law can appropriately further when the functions of injury compensation and deterrence are decoupled.

Like functional analysis, the concept of reciprocity does not supply a comprehensive rationale for tort liability. The prior discussion assumed that the choice of liability rules does not involve deterrence considerations. How does reciprocity relate to the deterrence function of liability? More fundamentally, why does reciprocity supply a justification for tort liability? Is reciprocity merely a matter of balancing the costs and benefits of liability for individual actors, thereby finding justification in an economic rationale for tort liability? Or is reciprocity justified by a principle of equality or fairness? If so, why is automobile driving a reciprocal risky activity for a pedestrian who has never driven? What is equal about the risky interaction in those cases? None of these questions can be resolved by the concept of reciprocity.

To address these issues, we need to consider more closely the substantive rationales for tort liability. We know what tort law accomplishes. What are the reasons for doing so?

~ 4 ~

Negligence, Strict Liability, and the Prominent Rationales for Tort Liability

"Innumerable scholars ... have striven to identify the principles and policies underlying judicial decisions concerning whether and to what extent victims of injury should receive compensation."[1] The most influential efforts have tried to identify a unitary rationale for tort liability that explains how and why tort law functions in one manner or another. According to one such rationale, tort liability is a regulatory instrument for minimizing the social cost of accidents, thereby promoting the public policy of economic efficiency. According to another influential justification, tort liability is a form of justice that corrects or redresses the violation of individual rights. These two justifications are now the most prominent rationales for tort liability.

The efficiency and rights-based rationales are incompatible, and neither has gained consensus. Each has its own strengths and limitations. As currently formulated, neither

justification can fully explain the roles of negligence and strict
liability.

I. EFFICIENCY

In the early 1970s, leading scholars published important books
and articles that systematically applied economic analysis to
tort law, and the approach became increasingly popular over
the next few decades.[2] The analysis makes the function of
injury compensation subordinate to the function of deterrence,
yielding a unitary rationale for tort liability.

Efficiency analysis assumes that the objective of tort liability is to minimize the social cost of accidents. Cost minimization increases social wealth and the welfare or well-being of
individuals in society, thereby allocating scarce resources in an
efficient manner. For this purpose of *allocative efficiency*, the
social cost of accidents is made up of three components:

1. The cost of injuries discounted by the probability of their
   occurrence (yielding the expected cost of injuries).*
2. The cost of safety precautions.
3. The cost of administering the tort system and related
   insurance mechanisms.

All three categories of cost cannot be simultaneously reduced,
as the reduction of one causes an increase in one or more of
the others. For example, safety precautions reduce the probability of accident and the expected cost of injuries, but these
safety measures have their own costs, such as increased time,
effort, or financial expenditures on safety technologies. Risky
behavior necessarily creates costs, just as precautionary behavior necessarily creates costs. These social costs cannot be

---

* For discussion of this concept, see the first footnote in Chapter 3,
section II.

eliminated by the tort system, leading many scholars to conclude that tort law should strive to minimize the social cost of accidents.

Efficiency analysis is not indifferent to issues of fairness, but instead recognizes that tort liability creates a gain of wealth by one party (the plaintiff) that is fully offset by another party's loss of wealth (the defendant). The defendant's payment of damages does not affect total social wealth, nor does the payment necessarily transfer money from the wealthy to the poor. A poor defendant can be obligated to compensate a wealthy plaintiff, making tort liability an unsatisfactory mechanism for redistributing wealth. Insofar as fairness involves the equitable distribution of wealth across society, the most efficient way to promote fairness typically is via income-tax transfers.[3] Rich people, for example, can pay higher income taxes, and poor people can receive income transfers from the government. Because the fair distribution of wealth is best pursued outside of the tort system, the economic analysis of tort law focuses exclusively on minimizing the social cost of accidents to attain the efficient allocation of scarce resources.

The compensatory function of tort damages can improve allocative efficiency only by serving as a cost-effective form of insurance for accident victims. Once again, tort damages fare poorly in comparison to other institutional arrangements. Tort damages provide a noncomprehensive, costly form of accident insurance as compared to alternative forms of insurance. For those injuries compensable by tort law, the plaintiff needs to hire a lawyer to receive indemnification for the injury. Accident victims can more cheaply and expeditiously receive indemnification for these losses from an insurance company by filing a valid claim for reimbursement, which ordinarily is easy to prove (e.g., submitting medical bills) and does not require legal representation. As compared to the insurance supplied by the private market or governmental programs, tort damages are a significantly more costly form of injury indemnification, making their sole economic function one of deterrence.

Consider the rule of strict liability from this perspective. Under strict liability, the risky actor incurs either the burden of a safety precaution (B) or the expected cost of injuries that would be prevented by the precaution (PL). To minimize his or her total costs, the actor will take any precaution costing less than the expected liability costs he or she would otherwise incur, yielding the behavioral decision rule embodied in the Hand formula ($B < PL$). This amount of care minimizes the social cost of accidents and is allocatively efficient. When the cost of a precaution exceeds the expected cost of injuries that would be avoided by the precaution ($B > PL$), the strictly liable actor will forgo the precaution and create the risk. Once again, the decision minimizes the social cost of accidents. In effect, strict liability forces the risky actor to internalize the social cost of accidents through the payment of compensatory damages, thereby creating a financial incentive for actors to exercise the efficient amount of care. Injury compensation serves the deterrence function.

To induce this same behavior, tort law can instead adopt a rule of negligence liability based on the Hand formula for reasonable care. Under this rule, the risky actor can avoid liability by taking any precaution for which $B < PL$. Such conduct is reasonable, absolving the actor of negligence liability for any ensuing injuries. If the rule is sufficiently enforced, the actor will find it cheaper to incur the cost of a precaution (B) rather than the associated liability costs that would be created by the negligent conduct (PL). In effect, negligence liability uses compensatory damages to create a threat of liability that gives risky actors a financial incentive to exercise the efficient amount of care. As in the case of strict liability, the function of injury compensation only serves the function of deterring risky behavior in an efficient manner.

Although the two liability rules are equivalent in this respect, efficiency analysis favors negligence liability as the default rule for accidental harms. Strict liability gives actors the legal obligation to pay for all injuries caused by their risky behavior, thereby increasing the total number of tort cases and the total amount of tort damages paid to accident victims relative to a rule of negligence liability. The associated increases in administrative cost and insurance cost (as compared to other insurance arrangements) that would occur under a general rule of strict liability make negligence the less costly liability rule.[4]

In addition to explaining why the tort system has adopted negligence liability as the default rule for accidental harms, efficiency analysis explains why tort law has adopted limited rules of strict liability. Negligence liability does not work well for complex forms of safety precautions like those involving systems of product quality or workplace safety. To prove that such precautions are required as a matter of reasonable care, the plaintiff would need evidence that is not feasibly attainable, effectively immunizing these types of safety investments from negligence liability. Without the threat of such liability, the defendant and similarly situated risky actors do not have an adequate financial incentive for incurring the costs of these safety measures. The deterrence incentive is restored by strict liability, explaining why courts have adopted the evidentiary rationale for strict liability.*

Although it provides a good description of tort law in these respects, efficiency analysis is often criticized for assuming that risky actors make safety decisions only by reference to a personal cost-benefit calculus. This kind of decision making involves a specific type of rationality based on knowledge of the law and its financial consequences. Presumably, this kind of decision making is engaged in by business enterprises, but it

---

* *See* Chapter 3, section II.

seems to be much less descriptive of how ordinary individuals behave.

This problem is not fatal to the economic analysis of tort law. As a practical matter, the most important forms of tort liability, such as products liability, involve the safety decisions made by business organizations, like product manufacturers. Even if ordinary individuals do not usually make safety decisions in a similar manner, the relevant question then becomes one of deciding how a legal rule should account for such behavior. Should the law assume that individuals will always comply with their legal obligations because it is the right thing to do? Or should the law instead recognize that individuals often act in a self-interested manner and disregard their legal obligations when it is in their personal interest to do so? Both types of actors undoubtedly exist, and the same person can act in each manner at different times. By formulating liability rules in terms of self-interested actors, though, tort law can still attain the efficient result. Some will act efficiently because the law requires them to do so; others will act efficiently because it is in their self-interest to do so. Of course, many or perhaps most individuals may not even know what the law requires of them in particular respects, but this would seem to pose a problem for any liability rule and does not provide a distinctive reason for rejecting efficient liability rules.

Efficiency analysis is vulnerable to critiques that are more fundamental. Costs can only be minimized if they can be measured. Efficiency analysis depends on prices, which in turn depend on the initial allocation of property rights or legal entitlements.[5] Who owns the entitlement? What does it consist of? Can the entitlement be transferred only by consent? By forced transfer at a price determined by the court via the damages remedy? Each question is determined by the initial entitlement, the complete specification of which determines the liability rule that protects the entitlement.[6] Because the entitlement cannot be determined by efficiency analysis, the economic approach assumes the existence of a liability rule and then determines whether an alternative rule would reduce costs. The liability rule does not originate with efficiency analysis, and so allocative efficiency cannot explain why tort law first adopted the rule in question. The animating principle of liability must be supplied by some norm other than efficiency.[7]

In addition, efficiency analysis does not adequately explain a number of important tort doctrines. It assumes that negligence liability defines the standard of reasonable care in the cost-benefit terms of the Hand formula, but jury instructions are not formulated in this manner.[*] Efficiency analysis also requires a deterrence rationale for tort liability, yet some tort rules are purely compensatory and not dependent on risk reduction, such as the rule of strict liability for nonreciprocal risks.[†] Indeed, any approach that relies exclusively on the deterrence function cannot explain many fundamental requirements of tort liability. If tort damages only serve the purpose of deterrence, the role of the plaintiff is not limited to someone who was harmed by the accident. The efficient incentives for risky behavior merely require a credible threat of tort liability, regardless of the plaintiff's identity. Efficient behavior could be induced if unreasonably risky actors were sued by anyone, leaving efficiency analysis unable to explain persuasively why tort liability requires plaintiffs who have suffered particular types of harm. The way in which tort liability provides compensation to injured accident victims is an essential feature of tort law that is not adequately recognized by efficiency analysis.

Nevertheless, efficiency analysis has been highly influential for good reasons. It has greatly enhanced our understanding of how tort law can deter risky behavior, one of the primary

---

* *See* Chapter 8, section II.B.
† *See* Chapter 3, section III.

functions of tort liability. Efficiency analysis has also precisely specified otherwise ambiguous concepts like reasonable care, showing that the important doctrines of tort law do not have to be vague. By providing much-needed structure to the legal inquiry, efficiency analysis has furthered the development of tort law, even though allocative efficiency does not appear to be the underlying rationale for tort liability.

II. CORRECTIVE JUSTICE AND THE REDRESS OF RIGHTS VIOLATIONS

Around the same time that economically oriented scholars were developing a unified conception of tort law based on allocative efficiency, philosophically oriented scholars started offering alternative justifications for tort liability based on the correction or redress of individual rights violations.[8] The two approaches have produced an ongoing, contentious debate about their respective merits.

The tenor of the debate is not surprising. The claim that tort law should only minimize accident costs and pay no concern to other matters of fairness has predictably provoked an equally extreme response. The most forceful critique has come from those who maintain that tort liability is a form of *corrective justice*, which gives "individuals who are responsible for the wrongful losses of others . . . a duty to repair [or correct] those losses."[9] A wrong involves the violation of a right, and so corrective justice imposes a duty of repair or compensation on a defendant who wrongfully violated the plaintiff's tort right. Such a rights-based rationale for tort liability "rules out the economic analysis of [tort] law."[10] As one would expect, proponents of efficiency analysis dismiss these rights-based interpretations of tort law.

A rights-based interpretation of tort law fundamentally differs from the efficiency interpretation. Efficiency analysis assumes that fairness is solely a matter of *distributive justice*, a form of justice involving the equitable distribution of resources among all members of society. A distributive principle of justice, for example, could justify transfers of income from the wealthy to the poor through the tax system to remedy unfair wealth inequalities. By recognizing only these forms of injustice, efficiency analysis ignores the inequalities redressed by corrective justice. In addition to dictating the fair distribution of resources within society, a principle of equality can also govern the way in which individuals interact with one another, requiring equal treatment of the interacting parties, regardless of their wealth or relative status in the overall distributive scheme. Each individual has the same right in this respect vis-à-vis other individuals, making the right of one individual correlative to the duty of another. If a duty holder violates another's right, the wrong creates an inequality that must be corrected as a matter of justice or fairness between the two parties. By redressing such a rights violation, tort liability involves a form of transactional justice limited to the interacting parties, a form of (corrective) justice distinctive from the type of (distributive) justice that could be achieved by an efficient tort system that increases the total resources available for tax redistributions.

Like an efficient tort system, a rights-based tort system relies on other governmental institutions, particularly the tax system, to implement the redistributions required by distributive justice. An efficient tort system, however, is only a mechanism for pursuing this collective good — it reduces accident costs and increases the amount of social wealth or welfare that other governmental institutions can then redistribute within society. A rights-based tort system, by contrast, limits or constrains the ability of the government to pursue this collective aim at the expense of the individual right holder.

The rationale is a familiar one within modern liberal democracies. An individual right protects individuals or minority groups from being used by the government as an instrument for furthering majoritarian interests.[11] Consequently, the individual tort right protects morally fundamental interests, such as one's interest in physical security, from burdens justified solely on grounds of social expediency, including the pursuit of social welfare via the minimization of accident costs. Social welfare still matters, but a rights-based tort system protects individuals from being subjected to accidental injury and premature death merely because the risky activity promotes the wealth and welfare of others.*

Efficient and rights-based tort rules also employ the functions of tort liability in fundamentally different manners. Tort liability can minimize accident costs only by deterring accidents in the future, making efficiency analysis a forward-looking inquiry that uses the compensation function only to create the financial incentives required by the deterrence function. By contrast, rights-based liability rules ask the backward-looking question of whether compensation in this case is warranted because the defendant duty holder is responsible for having violated the plaintiff's right. The redress of such a rights violation will create financial incentives for future actors to avoid behaving in a manner that would result in their incurring such liability costs, but deterrence is entirely incidental to the plaintiff's injury compensation. Rights-based liability rules make the function of deterrence subordinate to the function of injury compensation, exactly opposite to the way in which the functions are employed by efficient rules.[12]

For these reasons, rights-based theories can readily account for those tort doctrines that are hard to square with efficiency analysis. The individual tort right creates a corresponding duty of care for a risky actor, so a tort suit necessarily involves one

---

* It is a separate question whether an individual right to physical security requires tort liability as compared to alternative institutional schemes for protecting the individual interest in physical security. That issue is discussed in Chapter 15.

party whose injury (rights violation) was allegedly caused by the other party's breach of the corresponding duty. The structure of tort litigation is entailed by the logic of rights-based liability rules that obligate the defendant to provide compensation for having violated the plaintiff's tort right. Efficiency analysis, by contrast, only requires deterrence and not injury compensation, leaving it unable to persuasively explain why the tort suit requires a plaintiff who suffered compensable injury caused by the defendant. The required structure of a tort suit can block the pursuit of deterrence, contrary to the requirements of economic efficiency.* Tort liability must involve the redress of individual rights violations, regardless of the ensuing consequences for allocative efficiency.

So, too, doctrines that are easily explained by efficiency analysis have been problematic for rights-based interpretations. An efficient liability rule utilizes injury compensation to deter risky behavior, the type of functional relationship embodied in the evidentiary rationale for strict liability.† A rights-based liability rule, by contrast, uses the compensation function to redress a rights violation. The deterrence function is only an incidental effect of liability that is not of intrinsic importance for the liability rule. What explains why courts have adopted rules of strict liability to solve the deterrence problems created by the practical inability of plaintiffs to prove legal fault? Lacking a good answer, a rights-based interpretation of tort law can be criticized for not giving adequate importance to the function of deterrence, just like the economic interpretation can be criticized for doing the same with respect to the function of injury compensation.

Rights-based theories have also had a hard time explaining rules of strict liability that only function as a form of

---

* For a good example, *see* Chapter 10, section III, discussing the problem of market-share liability.
  † *See* Chapter 3, section II.

compensation. Some rights-based theories maintain that the "wrong" to be redressed by liability requires faulty or unreasonable behavior on the defendant's part, leaving them unable to explain *any* rule of strict liability.* Other rights-based theories use the concept of reciprocity to explain why the tort system has adopted both negligence and strict liability.[13] According to these theories, all tort liability involves a defendant who is responsible for a nonreciprocal risk that caused injury to the plaintiff. By causing injury, the nonreciprocal risk created an inequality between the parties that is corrected by the damages remedy. Unreasonable behavior creates the nonreciprocal risks subject to negligence liability, and abnormally dangerous activities create the nonreciprocal risks subject to strict liability. These theories, though, do not fully specify the requirements of reciprocity. What makes an automobile accident between a driver and pedestrian reciprocal? In situations of equality or reciprocal risky interactions, these theories also have no evident implications for the liability rule. What is unfair about a rule of strict liability that applies to reciprocal and nonreciprocal risks? The rule equally applies to everyone, so how does it violate the requirement of equality? Like the other rights-based theories, reciprocity theory does not adequately explain how tort law has made the choice between negligence and strict liability.

Despite these problems, it seems incontrovertible that the redress of rights violations is an essential aspect of tort law. Within the writ system, the rules that are now part of tort law

---

* These theories interpret the rules of strict liability as presumptively involving unreasonable behavior, turning strict liability into a form of negligence liability. *E.g.*, Arthur Ripstein, *Equality, Responsibility, and the Law* 70 (Cambridge U. Press 1999); Ernest Weinrib, *The Idea of Private Law* 171–203 (Harvard U. Press 1995). This interpretation ignores judicial claims to the contrary. *See* Chapter 12, describing rule of strict liability for abnormally dangerous activities. The interpretation is also inconsistent with the rule of strict products liability. Retailers routinely incur strict liability even when they had no reasonable opportunity to inspect the goods in question and did not act in any other way that could be described as being unreasonable. *See* Chapter 13, describing the rule of strict products liability.

provided injury compensation to the victims of criminal wrong-doing.* Tort law did not have to specify how duty holders should behave as long as liability involved criminal misconduct. The criminal law proscribed certain types of behavior, and the threat of criminal sanctions provided the necessary incentives for deterring individuals from engaging in the prohibited behavior. As it first developed within the writ system, tort law only served the function of providing injury compensation to those individuals whose rights had been violated by the defendant. The tort suit is still structured to redress rights violations caused by wrongful conduct, providing decisive support for a rights-based interpretation of tort law.[14]

---

* *See* Chapter 1, section I.

~ 5 ~

Compensation as a Unified Rationale for Tort Liability

I
n making the choice between negligence and strict liability, tort law relies on the function of deterrence in some cases, and in others, it relies on the function of injury compensation. Because the functions can be decoupled, there must be some underlying principle of liability that justifies how tort law selects between them. Without an underlying principle or rationale for tort liability, a judge could freely choose one function over the other, turning the imposition of tort liability into an arbitrary exercise of governmental coercion.

The most prominent rationales for liability give an independent role to only one of these functions. The efficiency rationale relies on the function of deterrence and does not require injury compensation, whereas the prominent fairness rationales require injury compensation and make deterrence an incidental function. Neither rationale is able to explain how tort law has made the fundamental choice between negligence and strict liability.

Tort liability is structured to redress rights violations, so the most plausible rationale for liability involves the protection of individual rights. To be fully persuasive, however, such a rationale must account for the function of deterrence in a manner that explains its importance within tort law, an omission that has prevented a rights-based rationale from gaining widespread acceptance.

Under a rights-based rationale for tort liability, the compensation of injury provides redress for the associated rights violation, making it easy to understand why the function of compensation is so important. Insofar as compensation consists entirely of the compensatory damages remedy — the assumption conventionally made by tort scholars — it is hard to understand why the function of deterrence is also important. The concept of compensation, though, is not necessarily limited to the compensatory damages remedy. A broader conception of compensation can readily account for the importance of deterrence within tort law.

Recall that in explaining why the limitation of the damages remedy under negligence liability is fair for plaintiffs, the New York Court of Appeals observed that each plaintiff "receives his compensation for such damages by the general good, in which he shares, and the right which he has to [engage in the risky activity]."[1] By relying on a broad conception of compensation that is not limited to the damages remedy, the court was able to justify negligence liability with the concept of reciprocity.* Such a broad conception of compensation can also explain why tort law values deterrence or risk reduction. Just as a plaintiff or any other right holder can be compensated by negligence liability insofar as he or she shares in the "general good" and has a similar right to engage in the risky activity, these individuals can also be compensated by negligence liability insofar as that rule is more capable of reducing risky behavior and protecting them from injury. A broad conception of compensation values the risk-reducing capabilities of a liability rule, enabling a compensatory tort right to unify the function of deterrence with the function of injury compensation via the damages remedy.

---

* *See* Chapter 3, section III.

Such a compensatory tort right has evident appeal. Recall that Holmes first conceptualized "torts as a body of substantive law formed by the active accommodation of conflicting considerations of policy, in particular the prevention of harm, and the freedom to engage in valued activity."[2] When the exercise of one party's liberty threatens another with harm, the conflict of interests creates the policy question identified by Holmes. Tort law can mediate these conflicting interests by requiring the actor to adequately compensate the potential victim. Such a compensatory obligation incurred by the actor as duty holder must be correlative to the compensatory right of the potential victim, the type of relationship required by the structure of tort liability. The duty gives the actor the opportunity to engage in the risky behavior and relies on a norm of compensation to ensure that the interaction does not unfairly disadvantage the right holder. As compared to other bodies of the common law, the characteristic aspect of tort law involves injury compensation, so it would not be surprising if tort law resolves its distinctive policy problem with a compensatory tort right.

I. THE NATURE OF A COMPENSATORY TORT RIGHT

To be protected by a right, an individual must have some interest that the law prevents others from interfering with merely because doing so would further their own interests or those of society more generally.* This formulation of the tort right occurs at the outset of the multivolume *Restatement (Second)*:

> If society recognizes a desire as so far legitimate as to make one who interferes with its realization civilly liable, the

---

* *See* Chapter 4, section II.

interest is given legal protection generally against all the world, so that everyone is under a duty not to invade the interest by interfering with the realization of the desire by certain forms of conduct. Thus the interest in bodily security is protected against not only intentional invasion but against negligent invasion or invasion by the mischances inseparable from an abnormally dangerous activity.[3]

An individual interest that "is protected against any form of invasion . . . becomes the subject matter of a 'right.'"[4] A rule that protects the individual interest in physical security, for example, gives the security interest of the right holder some sort of legal priority over the conflicting or "invading" liberty interest of the duty holder. To do so, the liability rule must first distinguish these interests in a manner that justifies a priority for the security interest. The nature of the priority then defines the content of the tort right and correlative duty, making it possible to characterize rights-based liability rules in terms of an underlying priority that gives one set of interests legal protection over another set of conflicting or invading interests.

Consider a tort rule governing risky interactions between an automobile driver and a pedestrian. The transportation enables the driver to pursue various liberty interests, including economic interests. As an unwanted by-product of that activity, the driver exposes pedestrians to a risk of bodily injury. A pedestrian is also acting in furtherance of his or her liberty interests, including economic interests. In the event of a crash that physically harms the pedestrian, by definition, his or her interest in physical security has been injured. The pedestrian also suffers emotional harm (pain and suffering) and economic harm (like medical expenses). If the driver were obligated to pay compensatory damages for any of these harms, the monetary payment would be detrimental to his or her economic interests. Any precautionary obligations that tort law imposes on the driver, such as a duty to drive slowly, are detrimental to the associated liberty interests. Similarly, any precautionary obligations that tort law imposes on the pedestrian (no jaywalking) restrict those liberty interests. The way in which tort law regulates the risky interaction will burden or threaten at least one party's interests: either the pedestrian's interests in liberty and physical security; the driver's liberty interests, including the economic interest; or the interests of both parties. How these conflicting interests should be mediated is the basic question of policy or fairness that must be addressed by tort law, and different resolutions of the problem are provided by different specifications of the tort right.

An absolute right to physical security, for example, would prohibit the driver from threatening the pedestrian's security in any way. The pedestrian's interest in physical security would have absolute priority over the driver's conflicting liberty interest, justifying the negation of the conflicting (absolutely subordinate) liberty interest by a liability rule that prohibits driving whenever the activity would threaten injury to a pedestrian, even if the risk of injury were miniscule.

As this particular rule illustrates, a rights-based liability rule can be characterized by the way in which it prioritizes the conflicting interpersonal interests of the right holder and duty holder (an approach we will call *interest analysis*). "This process of weighing the interests is by no means peculiar to the law of torts, but it has been carried to its greatest lengths and has received its most general conscious recognition in this field."[5]

For reasons suggested by the extreme liability rule that would virtually prohibit driving, tort law does not give the right holder's security interest an absolute priority over the conflicting liberty interests of another. As Holmes observed, the early common law did not give the individual "an absolute

right" "to his person, and so forth, [to be] free from detriment at
the hands of his neighbors."[6] An absolute right would require
the wholesale elimination of risk, preventing individuals from
exercising their liberty in social settings any time the conduct
might pose any risk, however slight, of causing physical harm to
another. An absolute right to physical security would largely
block social interactions, thereby violating the reason for prioritizing the security interest in the first instance.

The rights-based protection of the security interest typically is justified by autonomy or self-determination, an ideal
that individuals should be able to live the life of their own
choosing. To be autonomous agents, individuals must have
liberty, a requirement vividly expressed by the New Hamp-
shire state motto, "Live free or die." Without liberty, physical
security may not be worth having. Liberty, however,
depends on security. Unless our bodies and personal possessions are adequately secure, the threat of physical harm
severely compromises our ability to make plans and live the
life of our choosing. The aftermath of September 11, 2001
provides a sobering illustration. Autonomy requires both
security and liberty, and within this common moral metric,
security is prior to or more fundamental than liberty. Consequently, leading justice theorists maintain that rights-
based tort rules prioritize the individual interest in physical
security over the conflicting liberty and economic interests
of others.[7]

This reason for prioritizing the security interest over a
conflicting liberty interest does not justify an absolute priority.
The security interest is prioritized only because individuals
must be adequately protected from the threat of physical
harm before they can meaningfully exercise their liberty. An
absolute priority would eliminate most social interactions and
unduly curtail the ability of individuals to exercise their liberty
in a meaningful way, contrary to the rationale for prioritizing
the security interest.

Because the priority cannot be absolute, it must be relative. The priority is justified by a principle of equality that values individual autonomy or self-determination, making the priority relative to that overarching, general principle. This general principle holds that each person has an equal right to freedom (or autonomy or self-determination), and it then gives different values to the individual interests in physical security and liberty, depending on their relative importance for the exercise of the general right. In this respect, a tort right of security must be relative to the right of liberty. Consistent with this reasoning, courts have long recognized that "Most of the rights of property, as well as of person, are not absolute but relative."[8]

When the security interest of a right holder has a relative priority over the conflicting liberty interests of a duty holder, tort liability can be formulated so that its primary purpose is to "give compensation for harms" — the primary rationale for liability according to the *Restatement (Second)*.[9] If a duty holder's exercise of liberty causes physical harm to a right holder, a compensatory liability rule burdens the duty holder's subordinate liberty interest by the obligation to compensate the harms inflicted on the prioritized security interest of the right holder. This duty permits the duty holder to engage in risky behavior by relying on compensation to protect the security interest of the right holder, the type of outcome required by a right of physical security that is relative to a right of liberty.

Tort law was conceptualized in compensatory terms from its very beginning when the writ system gave individuals the opportunity to obtain compensation for their harms caused by the criminal misconduct of another. After the legal system separated tort law from criminal law, tort law could provide compensation for harms not caused by criminal wrongdoing. The distinctive attribute of tort liability has always involved the compensation of injury.

The early common law often justified liability in these cases with the maxim *sic utere tuo ut alienum non laedas* — use your own so as not to injure another.* The maxim locates the compensatory duty in the fact of injury-causing conduct rather than the unreasonableness of the injurer's behavior, and so it has frequently been invoked by courts and commentators to justify rules of strict liability.[10]

A compensatory tort system, however, will not ordinarily rely on rules of strict liability. Due to the inherent limitations of the damages remedy, a compensatory tort system utilizes negligence liability as the default rule for accidental harms, providing two limited roles for strict liability — one based on the function of deterrence, and the other based on the function of injury compensation by the damages remedy.

II. NEGLIGENCE LIABILITY AND THE INHERENT LIMITATIONS OF THE DAMAGES REMEDY

A tort right cannot be adequately protected by the compensatory damages remedy for reasons starkly illustrated by a case of wrongful death. In the event of a fatal accident, the defendant duty holder does not have to pay damages for the decedent right holder's loss of life's pleasures.† A rights-based liability rule uses the damages remedy to provide redress to the plaintiff for the violation of his or her right, and an award of

---

* The maxim literally means "use your own property in such a manner as not to injure that of another." *Black's Law Dictionary* 1238 (5th ed. 1979). As applied to risky behavior not involving the use of property, the maxim yields a common-law principle that "under the common law a man acts at his peril." Oliver Wendell Holmes, *The Common Law* 82 (Little, Brown, and Co. 1881) (stating that some of the "greatest common law authorities held this view").

† Under the common law, death was not a compensable harm. This rule was legislatively altered by *wrongful-death statutes* that enable statutorily specified plaintiffs to recover from the defendant for their own injuries caused by the violation of the decedent's tort right. The decedent's loss of life's pleasures, however, is not compensable by the damages remedy in the vast majority of states. *See* Chapter 14, section II.

damages could not compensate a dead right holder for the premature loss of life. It would be "cheaper for the defendant to kill the plaintiff than to injure him."* This inherent limitation of the compensatory damages remedy has important implications for the choice between negligence and strict liability.

Recall that a strictly liable actor can choose how to behave, incurring only a duty to pay compensatory damages to an injured right holder. A duty framed exclusively in terms of the compensatory damages remedy, not surprisingly, is unappealing when applied to injuries for which the remedy is clearly inadequate. In the event of a fatal accident, the strictly liable actor incurs no obligation to pay damages for the decedent's loss of life's pleasures and therefore owes no duty with respect to that harm. The compensatory duty under strict liability cannot encompass the premature loss of life, and yet that harm is the most serious setback to the right holder's interest in physical security. This problem with strict liability is most pronounced in the case of premature death, although a significant compensatory problem also exists for any nonconsensual risk causing severe bodily harm.†

Whereas strict liability exclusively relies on compensatory damages to protect the right holder's interest in physical security, negligence liability directly protects the security interest by giving the duty holder an obligation to reduce the risk of fatal accidents as a matter of reasonable care.[11] The duty of reasonable care specifies required forms of precautionary behavior that would prevent the right holder from suffering injury in

---

* Prosser and Keeton on Torts § 127, at 945. For empirical support of this claim, *see* Chapter 14, section II.

† For severe bodily injuries, compensatory damages do not make the victim "whole." A damages award for the loss of life's pleasures — a form of damages for pain and suffering — is not supposed to "restore the injured person to his previous position" but should instead only "give to the injured person some pecuniary return for what he has suffered or is likely to suffer." *Restatement (Second)* § 903 cmt. a.

the first instance. Under negligence liability, the duty holder satisfies the compensatory obligation by incurring the expenses of the required forms of reasonable care, a more valuable expenditure of compensatory resources for the right holder as compared to the equivalent expenditure on the inherently inadequate damages remedy.* Within a compensatory tort system, the default rule of negligence liability is justified by the deterrence function.

This deterrence rationale explains why only a certain type of unreasonable conduct is blameworthy and subject to punishment. To protect adequately the right holder's interest in physical security, tort law has adopted a rule of negligence liability that gives risky actors a duty to exercise reasonable care. One can violate this duty without rejecting the tort right. Unreasonably risky behavior is often the result of inadvertence, mistake, or even adherence to conventional practices (like exceeding the speed limit on a highway). These common forms of unreasonable conduct do not exhibit any fundamental disrespect for the plaintiff's right to physical security and do not merit retribution. Punitive damages are the exception, not the norm.

A defendant who rejects the duty to exercise reasonable care in exchange for paying the inherently inadequate "price" of compensatory damages, though, is subject to moral condemnation. In the event of an accident, such a decision would not be excused or justified. The payment of damages cannot compensate a decedent right holder for the premature loss of life, nor can monetary damages fully restore a plaintiff's loss of health or physical capabilities. By rejecting another's right to be protected by reasonable care, a defendant has the "bad state

---

* As discussed in Chapter 8, section II.B, the rule of negligence liability can be formulated so that the precautionary burden incurred by a duty holder equals the total burden the duty holder would incur under ideal conditions in which the right holder is always fully compensated by the duty holder. *See also* Mark Geistfeld, *Negligence, Compensation, and the Coherence of Tort Law*, 91 Geo. L.J. 585, 602–608 (2003).

of mind" that subjects him or her to punitive damages.* In a compensatory tort system, the functions of deterrence and punishment coherently work together to offset the inherent limitations of the compensatory damages remedy.

During the nineteenth century when tort law emerged from the writ system and adopted negligence as the default rule for accidental harms, most observers thought that negligence liability served the purpose of punishing or deterring civilly blameworthy or "negligent" behavior.[12] The justification for negligence liability involved its ability to reduce injuries by controlling risky behavior, a rationale frequently invoked by courts of that era.[13] Both the history and logic of negligence liability are rooted in the function of deterrence, an attribute of the liability rule that can be justified by a compensatory tort right.

III. STRICT LIABILITY AND IMMUNITY FROM LIABILITY

Unlike strict liability, negligence liability can directly control risky behavior by specifying the requirements of reasonable care, which ordinarily gives it a decisive advantage for protecting a compensatory tort right. If negligence liability loses this deterrence advantage, then the compensatory tort right is best protected by a rule of strict liability.

As compared to negligence liability, strict liability can more effectively reduce risk whenever problems of proof make it difficult for the plaintiff to show that the defendant breached the duty to exercise reasonable care. Without a credible threat of being subjected to negligence liability, the defendant and similarly situated duty holders do not have an adequate financial incentive to take the costly precautions required by the

---

* *See* Chapter 14, section IV (discussing punitive damages).

duty of reasonable care. In these circumstances, the adoption of strict liability could induce duty holders to take these costly safety precautions to reduce the incidence of the more costly injuries for which they are (strictly) liable.*

This evidentiary rationale for strict liability, long recognized by courts, is a direct implication of a compensatory tort right. When problems of proof prevent right holders from enforcing the duty of reasonable care, strict liability provides the better method for regulating risk while allowing the plaintiff to recover compensatory damages in more cases than negligence liability. The two primary instruments for protecting a right holder's interest in physical security — injury prevention and the compensation of injuries with the damages remedy — both favor strict liability under these conditions.

The compensatory tort right creates another role for strict liability, one having nothing to do with the function of deterrence or injury prevention. Consider a defendant who exercised reasonable care. The defendant acted in the manner required by the compensatory tort right, eliminating deterrence as a rationale for strict liability. The only remaining rationale involves the compensation of injuries with the damages remedy. A rule of strict liability in these circumstances could provide a compensatory supplement to negligence liability, which would continue to operate as a default rule requiring risky actors to exercise reasonable care.

As we have found, if both the defendant and plaintiff were engaged in a reciprocally risky activity like automobile driving, then negligence liability is sufficiently compensatory. The plaintiff is unable to recover damages for any injuries caused by the defendant's reasonably safe driving, but he or she nevertheless is sufficiently compensated by the way in which negligence liability otherwise works to his or her advantage when

---

* *See* Chapter 3, section II (developing the evidentiary rationale for strict liability).

imposing an equal amount of reasonable risk on others while engaged in the activity of driving.*

Because negligence liability is sufficiently compensatory for reasonable, *reciprocal* risks, the only potential compensatory role for strict liability involves cases in which the defendant is responsible for a reasonable, *nonreciprocal* risk that injured the plaintiff. Strict liability allows the plaintiff to recover compensatory damages for these injuries, creating the necessary compensatory rationale for using this form of liability to supplement the default rule of negligence liability. In a compensatory tort system, strict liability should govern injuries caused by reasonable, nonreciprocal risks, the result attained by the rule of strict liability for abnormally dangerous activities that has been widely adopted by courts.†

As discussed earlier, an activity is not abnormally dangerous if it is common within the community, explaining why the activity of automobile driving is governed by negligence liability.‡ Many people, though, do not own cars, and yet tort law assumes that the activity of automobile driving is a reciprocal risky interaction for them as well. Tort law does not distinguish between those plaintiffs who drive and those who do not. The reason for doing so makes it possible for us to uncover the full relation among negligence, strict liability, and immunity from liability.

To determine why a plaintiff's decision to not drive is irrelevant to the liability rule, we need to identify the conditions under which either the plaintiff right holder or defendant duty holder can unilaterally alter the liability rule. Presumably, one or both of the parties can alter the liability rule in some

---

* See Chapter 3, section III. For a more rigorous demonstration of this point, *see* Chapter 8, section II.B.

† *See* Chapter 3, section III (explaining how courts have relied on the concept of reciprocity as the reason for applying strict liability to abnormally dangerous activities).

‡ *Id.*

circumstances. What prevents a pedestrian from unilaterally triggering the rule of strict liability by choosing not to drive?

A compensatory tort right finds justification in the value of autonomy or self-determination, requiring liability rules that equally respect the autonomy of both the right holder and duty holder. The requirement of equality would permit the pedestrian to unilaterally relieve a driver of legal responsibility for the conduct in question. The pedestrian's exercise of autonomy would not limit the autonomy of the driver as duty holder, so by allowing the pedestrian right holder to alter the liability rule in these circumstances, tort law would not unfairly advantage the autonomy of one party over the other. The equal respect for autonomy, therefore, justifies liability rules that can be unilaterally altered by either the right holder or duty holder if doing so would not limit the autonomy of the other party.

For these same reasons, tort law cannot allow one party to unilaterally determine the content of a liability rule in a manner that would restrict or limit the autonomy of the other party. A pedestrian's unilateral choice not to drive cars, for example, cannot subject an automobile driver to a more demanding standard of tort liability, the outcome that would occur if the rule of strict liability for abnormally dangerous activities were triggered by the particular choices made by the plaintiff. Such a liability rule would favor the plaintiff's autonomous choices to the detriment of the defendant's autonomy, violating the requirement of equal treatment.

When an attribute of a rights-based liability rule cannot be formulated by reference to the individual choices of the plaintiff or defendant, it must instead depend on some impartial or objective measure. Whether an activity such as automobile driving is abnormally dangerous and subject to strict liability, for example, depends on whether the activity is common within the community. By defining the liability rule in objective terms, tort law can equally respect the autonomy of the plaintiff right holder and defendant duty holder, satisfying the requirement that "the law can have no favorites."[14]

Due to the objective nature of tort liability, tort law often requires legal conclusions that do not accurately describe the particular facts or subjective traits of the parties in any given case. The objectively defined liability rule, for example, deems automobile driving to be a reciprocal activity even for those individuals who have never driven. Once the objective nature of a liability rule is compared to the actual, subjective traits of the parties in a lawsuit, it becomes apparent that negligence liability has components of personal fault, strict liability, and immunity from liability.

First, consider how an objective standard can create an immunity from liability. Automobile driving involves an objective reciprocal risk whenever the activity is common within the community, yielding a rule of negligence liability. As a factual matter, however, a driver who exercises reasonable care does not impose an equal or reciprocal risk on a pedestrian who rarely or never drives. If defined by reference to this subjective nonreciprocal risk, the liability rule would be one of strict liability. By comparing this subjectively defined rule of strict liability to the objectively defined rule, it becomes apparent that the objective liability rule immunizes automobile drivers from the rule of strict liability they would otherwise face when imposing risks on pedestrians who rarely or never drive.

In adopting an immunity, tort law overrides the priority of the right holder's interest in physical security and instead gives that interest the same normative weight as the duty holder's conflicting liberty interest. Without any normative distinction between these interests, tort law has no basis for shifting the injury costs from one set of interests (those of the plaintiff) to the other (those of the defendant). The loss must lie where it fell, on the plaintiff as accident victim, thereby immunizing the defendant from liability.

What justifies an immunity? Tort law prioritizes the security interest for reasons of autonomy or self-determination, and so tort law can override the priority with an immunity only when doing so is required as a matter of autonomy. As just discussed, an equal concern for autonomy can require objectively defined liability rules. The objective nature of liability, in turn, creates pockets of immunity within negligence liability that protect an individual duty holder (the frequent driver) from being subject to strict liability when interacting with an individual right holder who does not, in fact, equally participate in the risky activity (the pedestrian who never drives). Like this particular form of immunity, tort law can adopt other immunities when doing so is required as a matter of autonomy.

Due to the objective nature of negligence liability, it also contains pockets of strict liability. An individual duty holder's reasons for creating risk, whether well considered or otherwise, cannot reduce the amount of protection that tort law would otherwise provide to a right holder. A rights-based tort system cannot allow one party to unilaterally determine the content of a liability rule in a manner that would be detrimental to the other party's autonomy. Like the issue of reciprocity, the standard of reasonable care must be objectively defined. The objective component of the liability rule means that some duty holders will be deemed negligent, even though they cannot be "blamed" for their conduct in light of their own subjective traits. In the absence of any personal fault or blameworthiness, the imposition of negligence liability functions as a form of no-fault or strict liability.

As Holmes explained:

> If, for instance, a man is born hasty and awkward, is always having accidents and hurting himself or neighbors, no doubt his congenital defects will be allowed for in the courts of Heaven, but his slips are no less troublesome to his neighbors than if they sprang from guilty neglect. His neighbors

accordingly require him, at his proper peril, to come up to their standard, and the courts which they establish decline to take his personal equation into account.[15]

In these cases, the liability rule is framed exclusively in terms of negligence — the defendant's failure to comply with an objectively defined standard of reasonable care subjects the defendant to negligence liability for the ensuing injuries — but any rationale for liability must consider how the objective rule applies to individuals who are simply unable to comply with that standard. These defendants are not blameworthy for their "congenital defects," but there is nothing unfair about subjecting them to negligence liability. One who fails to comply with the objective standard of reasonable care creates an objectively defined nonreciprocal risk and is fairly subject to (strict) liability for the resultant injuries.

For reasons suggested by this analysis, a complete understanding of negligence liability depends on the concepts of strict liability and immunity from liability. The reasons negligence liability does not require personal fault, for example, also explain why tort law does not punish or prohibit every form of negligent behavior. Without any personal fault or "guilty neglect," as Holmes put it, tort law has no basis for punishing the defendant. Due to these pockets of strict liability, tort law prohibits only some forms of negligent behavior (involving "guilty neglect") and subjects the actor to punitive damages, whereas other forms of negligent behavior (lacking personal fault) only subject the actor to liability for compensatory damages (as per a rule of strict liability). As we found when first considering the issue, the specification of legal or objective fault for purposes of negligence liability also determines the roles of fault and no-fault liability.*

---

* *See* Chapter 2, section I.

IV. A UNIFIED RATIONALE?

By specifying the intrinsic relationship among negligence liability, strict liability, and immunity from liability, a compensatory tort right can explain the important substantive doctrines of tort law. Within a compensatory tort system, these doctrines work together in a manner that unifies the important functions of liability. As a study of the case law quickly reveals, courts analyze tort issues in terms of fairness, responsibility, compensation, deterrence, and even retribution at times. Each matters for a compensatory tort right, unlike other conceptions of the individual right to physical security that deny the fundamental importance of deterrence.*

Throughout the twentieth century, most participants in the tort system believed that tort liability can be justified by the functions of deterrence and the compensation of injuries with the damages remedy.[16] These functions can be decoupled, however, creating the problem of functional disunity that requires resort to some principled rationale for tort liability. A tort norm of compensation makes each function fundamentally important for protecting the individual right to physical security, unlike the prominent rationales for liability. Unless one believes that most participants in the tort system have had an incoherent or unprincipled understanding of tort liability, a rights-based norm of compensation plausibly describes their interpretation of tort law.

So, too, the norm of compensation incorporates economic analysis into the rights-based legal inquiry. A compensatory tort right finds justification in the value of individual autonomy, and self-determination or individual choice is the point of departure for economic analysis. The ability of a tort rule to reduce risk, for example, is critical for protecting the

---

* *See* Chapter 4, section II.

compensatory tort right, and economic analysis is formulated to address that question. Indeed, for important classes of cases, the fair protection of a compensatory tort right involves safety decisions governed by cost-benefit analysis.* A compensatory tort right will not always yield liability rules that minimize costs, but the rules nevertheless satisfy the relevant requirements of welfare economics.†

Departures from allocative efficiency are not ruled out by the economic analysis of tort law. While maintaining that allocative efficiency is an important consideration for legal decision makers, many, if not most, law and economic scholars also recognize that "fairness is the final test which any system of accident law must pass."[17] A compensatory tort system employs economic analysis to formulate fair liability rules, thereby unifying the economic analysis of tort law with a rights-based rationale for tort liability.

To be sure, the interpretation of tort law is highly contested. Any effort to analyze tort law must be understood within this context. By analyzing tort law in compensatory terms, though, we must consider issues of fairness and efficiency, of deterrence and compensation, and of fault and no-fault liability, thereby canvassing the range of considerations that factor

---

* *See* Chapter 8, section II.B (showing why cost-benefit analysis appropriately governs safety decisions for cases involving reciprocal risks or parties in a contractual relationship).

† When tort liability determines the fair distribution of accident costs, the efficiency properties of a rule depend on whether it is the most cost-effective means for attaining the required distribution, and not on whether the rule is allocatively efficient. Analyzed as a distributive mechanism, compensatory liability rules satisfy the efficiency conditions conventionally employed by welfare economics, and they are more faithful to the efficiency criterion of Pareto optimality than are cost-minimizing tort rules. The ideal outcome in a compensatory system requires risky interactions that make no one worse off as per the Pareto criterion, whereas the ideal outcome in a cost-minimizing tort system gives no independent weight to this consideration. *See* Mark A. Geistfeld, *Efficiency, Fairness, and the Economic Analysis of Tort Law,* in *Theoretical Foundations of Law and Economics* (Mark D. White ed., Cambridge U. Press 2009).

into the varied interpretations of tort liability. Analyzing tort law in compensatory terms provides a unified way to consider the issues relevant to any plausible rationale for tort liability, an attribute that makes the analytical approach particularly useful for the study of tort law.

ᗒ 6 ᗕ

The Social Construction of Tort Law

L
ike any other cooperative human enterprise, tort law is socially constructed. The participants are engaged in purposive activity, not merely random interactions. The practice of tort law provides further evidence about the point of tort law.

In an allocatively efficient tort system, for example, the practice of tort law is largely empirical or factual in nature. The correct result in each case typically depends only on an accurate measuring of the relevant costs and benefits of tort liability. If the tort system were guided by such a norm, tort disputes would involve problems of measurement, and not the disagreements about cultural or social values that characterize so many tort disputes.*

---

* *See* Marshall S. Shapo, *Tort Law and Culture* (2003) (showing how tort law reflects national or local culture and illustrating this thesis by showing how doctrinal controversies can be understood as "mirrors of cultural conflict"). Recognizing this problem, some law and economic scholars have maintained that the structure of tort litigation nevertheless causes tort law to evolve toward allocatively efficient liability rules, a dynamic akin to the "invisible hand" theory of Adam Smith. *See, e.g.*, Richard A. Posner, *Economic Analysis of Law* 320–328

In a rights-based tort system, by contrast, tort disputes often involve cultural and moral matters. To use the familiar terms of the Declaration of Independence, a rights-based tort system gives everyone an equal right to "the pursuit of Happiness" (autonomy or self-determination), which in turn supplies the value for determining how one individual's "right to Life" must be mediated against another's "right to Liberty." Both are necessary for the purpose of self-determination, but each does not have to be equally important in this respect. Based on the judgment that our bodies and tangible possessions must be adequately secure before we can meaningfully exercise our liberty in the pursuit of happiness, tort law can prioritize the individual interest in physical security over the conflicting liberty interest of another. The priority yields a tort right to physical security that must permit others to create risk in the pursuit of their own happiness, making the individual right to security relative to another's right to liberty. The appropriate relation of these two rights will always be contestable in light of the changing facts of social life, the importance of particular types of risky conduct for purposes of self-determination within different communities, and the consequences of injury for leading the life of one's own choosing.

A good example is provided by workplace injuries. The tort system in the late nineteenth century routinely barred injured workers from recovery for workplace injuries whenever the worker chose to face the risk by not quitting the job in question. The bar to recovery was based on a doctrine that permits a right holder to exercise his or her autonomy by choosing to face a known risk, thereby relieving the duty holder of legal responsibility for that risk.* In limiting liability, the nineteenth-century courts relied on a concept of choice that is indefensible

---

(Little, Brown Pub. 1973). Rigorous analysis shows otherwise. *See* Gillian Hadfield, *Bias in the Evolution of Legal Rules*, 80 Geo. L.J. 583 (1992).

* *See* Chapter 11, section I (discussing doctrine of assumption of risk).

by today's standards.* At the time, however, the idea of free choice in the workplace was inextricably linked to the ideology of free labor within a social milieu deeply influenced by the practice of slavery. The abolition of slavery translated into an extreme emphasis on worker autonomy. No one other than the individual worker could be the complete master of his own choices. The worker always had the right to quit the job, making him responsible for injuries he suffered at the workplace. In light of this particular conception of workers as free men, the limitations of tort liability for workplace injuries during the nineteenth century are understandable. The conception of worker autonomy then changed over time. Slavery became more distant, and the workplace more systematized and technologically complex. Individual workers clearly did not control the workplace, and the associated threat to their physical security ultimately justified a rule of strict liability (under workers' compensation) for this class of injuries. The rules have changed dramatically over time in a manner that reflects changes in the underlying cultural values.†

The social construction of autonomy and liberty also influenced the liability of railroads and streetcars in late-nineteenth-century America. "An overwhelming majority of Americans used railroads or streetcars; all Americans' lives were touched by them."[1] When women utilized the transportation services provided by these common carriers, they often interacted with the machines quite differently than men. For example, a woman's dress could get caught on a moving train

---

* *See* Chapter 11, section I.C (defining the nature of the choice required for a worker to assume the risk).

† For discussion of the ideology of free labor as the justification for limiting employer liability, *see* John Fabian Witt, *The Accidental Republic: Crippled Workingmen, Destitute Widows, and the Remaking of American Law* 29–35 (2004). For discussion of the ensuing change in the conception of worker autonomy and its relation to the development of workers' compensation, *see id.* at 63–70; *see also* Chapter 1, subsection II.A (describing reasons for adoption of workers' compensation).

and cause her to fall while exiting. "Courts might have placed on women the 'cost'—economic and physical—of apparel that presented such an obvious safety hazard, yet they refused to do so."[2] Railroads were responsible for ensuring the safety of female passengers. The late-nineteenth-century ethos of "free men," which held adult males solely accountable for their safety choices on trains and at the workplace, did not apply to women. Liberty, and the associated concept of responsibility for one's autonomous choices, appears to have been a gendered notion.[3]

As more women filed suit, these conceptions changed as well:

> In effect, the daily parade of injured women had contributed to a shift in legal attitudes about those who suffered injury and toward those who increased the danger of daily life in much the same way that highlighting women and children as victims of warfare generates outrage and condemnation. In significant areas of the law, where injury sometimes involved a woman and sometimes a man, courts without consciously deciding that the ideal of "free men" was outmoded, replaced the image of "free men" with one of women. [T]he collective [impact of these] claims and the risk of state court judgments imposing liability for personal injury, in part, led railroad and streetcar companies to adopt operating policies and techno-logical innovations—limited stops, elevated trains, gates on car doors, enclosed cars—that safeguarded life by reducing opportunities to exercise individual judgments of safety and danger. The concomitant of recognition of a right to bodily integrity was a circumscribed individual autonomy.[4]

In this area as in others, changing social conditions affected the way in which tort law mediated one individual's right to secu-rity against another's right to liberty. One right is relative to the other, so the expanded protection of security entailed restrictions on liberty involving required forms of precautionary behavior, like those adopted by railroads and streetcar companies.

Rights-based liability rules are also sensitive to changing economic conditions and the impact that liability would have on economic development. A business organization is the collective undertaking of individual owners, employees, and customers. Their reasons for participating in the market — the need to earn a living or to purchase goods and services — are not fundamentally different from the reasons individuals engage in other types of risky behavior (such as driving) outside of markets. The liberty interests of market participants are also burdened by tort liability, just like the liberty interests of any other duty holder. A business includes its liability costs in the price of the goods or services it sells to others. At least part of the cost of tort liability is passed on to customers in the form of higher prices. The costs that are not passed on to customers are borne by the business itself, due to lower sales stemming from any price increase or to reduced profitability for a given level of sales. This outcome can be costly for the owners, it can cost some employees their jobs, and it may have detrimental effects on other individuals in the community. As in other contexts, any tort rule governing business activity will mediate the individual liberty interests of risk-creating actors (the participants in the business enterprise) with the liberty and security interests of those facing the risks generated by the business. A liability rule that unduly curtails economic development is overly burdensome for the liberty interests of the affected market participants, so the impact that liability would have on economic activity is of fundamental importance in a rights-based tort system.

For example, in the early stages of economic development, a society must expend most of its wealth to satisfy basic needs like hunger and shelter. One individual's interest in physical security is hard to distinguish from another's economic interest directed toward maintenance of the basic conditions required for a healthy existence. In these social circumstances, a rights-based tort system would adopt various immunities justified by the concern that liability would have an overly detrimental impact on economic development, a characteristic aspect of the tort system before the twentieth century. As the twentieth century progressed, social wealth accumulated and individuals were increasingly able to expend their economic resources in a discretionary manner. Due to this change in social circumstances, tort law could more sharply distinguish between one individual's interest in physical security and another's economic interest, making it possible for judges to rely on the rights-based protection of physical security as the reason for eliminating immunities concerned with economic development. The expansion of tort liability through the twentieth century fully illustrates how rights-based liability rules can change in response to altered economic conditions.*

Over the years, tort law has dramatically changed its approach to injuries on railroads, in the workplace, and elsewhere, perhaps confirming that there is no underlying principle or rationale for tort liability.

> [A] different view is possible if an effort is made to fit the theory of [tort] justice into a theory of social justice — to see the purposes of [tort] law in their relation to the purposes of the law as a whole. Man is a social animal, and the function of law is to enable him to realize his potentialities as a human being through the forms and modes of social organization.[5]

By recognizing that the ultimate function of tort law is to give each of us an equal chance for realizing our potentialities as a human being, we can begin to see why the appropriate balance between liberty and security is highly context dependent. The balance not only depends on case-specific features like the reciprocity of risk, it also critically depends on how judges and juries value the importance of the risky

---

* *See* Chapter 2, sections II and III (describing how tort law developed over this period).

activity for purposes of autonomy or self-determination within the community. The meaning of worker autonomy today is quite different than it was in the aftermath of the Civil War. A liability rule that makes sense in one set of social circumstances can be indefensible in another.

Recognizing this dimension of tort law is critical for effective lawyering. Liability rules frequently differ from one another due to a difference in circumstance and the like, and yet each can provide the same answer to an underlying issue of policy. Apparent differences often disappear once doctrines are scrutinized by policy analysis, enhancing one's ability to rely on a wider range of cases as analogical support for one side of a contested issue. As Holmes observed, every tort rule "is in fact and at bottom the result of more or less definitely understood views of public policy."[6] Having learned how to identify the relevant policy considerations, we now have the capability to analyze the important doctrines of tort law.

Part Two

Doctrinal Analysis

E ach tort consists of a set of *elements*, with each element specifying a particular requirement that must be satisfied for the legal system to enforce the liability rule against the defendant. Ordinarily, the plaintiff must prove each element of the *prima facie* case for liability. The plaintiff has the burden of producing admissible evidence that would enable a reasonable juror to conclude that each element, more likely than not, is satisfied. Unless the plaintiff has proven each element of the prima facie case by such a *preponderance of the evidence*, he or she cannot prevail. Adequate proof of the prima facie case, however, does not necessarily mean the plaintiff can recover. The defendant may be able to rely on an *affirmative defense*, which consists of elements the defendant must prove by a preponderance of the evidence to avoid liability. If the evidence is so conflicting that a reasonable juror could find for either the plaintiff or defendant, the judge must instruct the jury about the findings it must make to conclude that the plaintiff is entitled to recovery.

The evidentiary standard allows for the possibility that some innocent defendants will incur liability. It also allows for the possibility that some deserving plaintiffs will not be compensated. Mistakes like this are inevitable in a world of limited information and factual uncertainty. The evidentiary

109

standard accordingly determines who should bear the risk of legal error.

For example, suppose the plaintiff establishes all the required elements but one. If the evidence shows there is a 50.1 percent chance that the remaining element is satisfied, the plaintiff can recover, despite the 49.9 percent chance that the element is not actually satisfied. Conversely, if the evidence shows there is a 50.1 percent chance that the element is not satisfied, the plaintiff cannot recover, despite the 49.9 percent chance that the element actually is satisfied. As this example illustrates, the ordinary evidentiary standard expressly allows for a 49.9 percent chance that the defendant will be erroneously subjected to liability (a "false positive") and a 49.9 percent chance that the plaintiff will be erroneously denied recovery (a "false negative").

By giving equal treatment to false positives and false negatives, tort law has adopted a norm that gives equal weight or concern to (1) the interest of an innocent defendant in avoiding liability judgments based on limited factual information (a false positive), and (2) the interest of a deserving plaintiff who cannot establish his or her right to compensation only because of limited factual information (a false negative). The tort norm, in other words, strives to apportion equally the burden of factual uncertainty or erroneous legal determinations between an innocent defendant and a deserving plaintiff. The apportionment recognizes that the interest of one party cannot be distinguished from the other, making it fair to divide the burden equally between the two.

This conclusion has an important implication. Consider a case in which the evidence is in equipoise, showing that there is only a 50 percent chance that a required element of the prima facie case is satisfied. The plaintiff loses. The proof only establishes an equal likelihood that the plaintiff is deserving and the defendant is innocent. Given the normative equivalence of these two conflicting interests, tort law has no basis for shifting the loss from one party to the other. The loss must lie where it fell, on the plaintiff seeking compensation for his or her injuries. To recover, the plaintiff must show that his or her interest in recovery exceeds the conflicting interest of the defendant in avoiding liability, explaining why the plaintiff bears the *burden of production* or the initial burden of producing proof that each element of the prima facie case, more likely than not, is satisfied.

As revealed by the structure of a tort suit, tort liability requires some basis for distinguishing between the conflicting interests of the plaintiff and defendant. Having developed the components of interest analysis, we can utilize it to study the important doctrines of tort law.

7

The Intentional Torts

The first torts, although not denominated as such within the medieval writ system, involved intentional harms. The newly centralized royal government needed to suppress violent behavior and the ensuing cycle of revenge and retaliation, resulting in a body of legal rules that protected one from being intentionally harmed by another.*

These ancient torts continue to provide redress for the victims of violence, but they now apply to distinctive contemporary problems as well, illustrating the adaptability of common-law rules. Over time, the legal system has also become more capable of redressing a broader range of social ills, enabling courts to recognize new torts involving intentional harms less connected to the problem of physical violence.

---

* *See* Chapter 1, section I.

I. THE PRIMA FACIE CASE

A. Intent

All of the intentional torts share the common element of intent, which typically is defined in two different ways:

A person acts with the intent to produce a consequence if:

1. The person acts with the purpose of producing that consequence; or
2. The person acts knowing that the consequence is substantially certain to result.*

The first definition of intent supplies an obvious rationale for tort liability. One who purposefully punches another wanted to cause that person bodily injury, establishing a prima facie case for liability.

This example is deceptive, however. What if the defendant was acting in self-defense or had some other reason for striking the plaintiff that did not entail any disrespect for his or her physical security? Perhaps the defendant needed to knock out the plaintiff to protect him or her from more serious harm. In these cases, the rationale for liability is no longer obvious.

Regardless of the defendant's motive, the definition of intent is still satisfied in these cases. The defendant swung his or her fist with the purpose of hitting the plaintiff; the reasons for doing so are irrelevant. The legal definition of intent does not distinguish between good and bad motives. As long as the defendant acted with the purpose or desire of producing the consequence in question, the particular motivation for the conduct is irrelevant. The element of intent has been satisfied.

To avoid liability, the defendant must instead prove an affirmative defense. These separate rules specify the types of

---

* *Restatement (Third)* § 1. Outside of a few limited exceptions, the *Restatement (Third)* "does not address the specific intentional torts or their elements. That law has not undergone significant change since the Second Restatement of Torts and remains governed by it." *Id.*, Introduction.

motives or reasons that justify the defendant's conduct, enabling him or her to avoid liability for having intentionally harmed the plaintiff.*

In this respect, the intentional torts illustrate the more general principle that tort law objectively determines the value of any particular form of conduct. An actor's motives or reasons are relevant only insofar as tort law finds them to be relevant. One who acts with *any* desire or purpose to physically harm another is subject to liability for the resultant injuries, unless tort law deems the conduct to be objectively justifiable and governed by one of the affirmative defenses to be discussed later, such as self-defense or necessity.

Under the second definition of intent, if the actor knows that his or her conduct is substantially certain to produce a consequence, then the choice to engage in the conduct establishes the intent to cause that consequence. The substantial-certainty definition eliminates purpose altogether, substituting a requirement that the actor had knowledge — the only subjective consideration — of the substantial certainty that the consequence would occur.

Tort law can define intent in these terms for a basic reason. One who knows he or she is acting in such a way that is substantially certain to injure another has created a nonreciprocal risk. The unequal nature of the risk is sufficient to justify liability for the ensuing injuries, regardless of the actor's motives, personal fault, or blameworthiness.†

This rule is "limited to situations in which the defendant has knowledge to a substantial certainty that the conduct will bring about harm to a particular victim, or to someone within a small class of potential victims within a localized

---

* *See infra* Part II.
† *See* Chapter 3, section III (explaining why an actor incurs strict liability for injuries caused by nonreciprocal risks); Chapter 5, section III (explaining why an uncommonly dangerous activity creates a nonreciprocal risk).

area."[1] The limitation is required because the black-letter rule is literally satisfied by the conduct of most mass manufacturers and other actors who create recurring, low-level risks. Due to the prevalence of automobile accidents, for example, a large automobile manufacturer knows or is substantially certain that some of its consumers will be hurt in car crashes. By selling automobiles, however, the manufacturer only exposes each individual consumer to the ordinary risk of being injured in a car crash. The manufacturer does not subject any particular consumer to a substantial certainty of injury, explaining why the element of intent is not satisfied unless the manufacturer "has knowledge to a substantial certainty that the conduct will bring about harm to a particular victim, or to someone within a small class of potential victims within a localized area."

As this example illustrates, literal application of a black-letter rule can lead to erroneous outcomes, underscoring the need to understand the underlying rationale for the rule in question. A conceptual understanding also clarifies a number of otherwise puzzling cases involving nonculpable actors who incur liability and reprehensible actors who avoid liability.

Recall that an objective standard creates pockets of strict liability and immunity from liability within a liability rule that appears to require blameworthy or culpable misconduct. The objectively defined rule of negligence liability, for example, requires faulty conduct on the defendant's part, and yet it has pockets of strict liability and immunity from liability. Due to the objective definition of intent, the intentional torts also contain pockets of strict liability and immunity from liability.

As we discover soon, the difficult cases involve a mismatch between personal culpability and tort liability. Some defendants incur liability even though they acted for laudable

---

* *See* Chapter 5, section III.

reasons, and other abominable actors avoid liability altogether. These outcomes stem from the objective definition of intent, which makes the defendant's actual or subjective motive irrelevant. The objective definition can yield outcomes in which the defendant acted with perfectly acceptable motives and still incurred (no-fault or strict) liability for an intentional tort. The objective definition can also yield outcomes in which a defendant acted with bad motives and was not subject to (or immunized from) liability. By ignoring the defendant's actual, subjective motive, the objective definition of intent creates these pockets of strict liability and immunity from liability, thereby severing any necessary link between personal culpability and the incidence of liability.*

To be liable, the defendant must have intended to produce a consequence that is prohibited by tort law. The different types of prohibited consequences are defined by the different intentional torts.

B. Battery

A defendant commits a *battery* if he or she intends "to cause a harmful or offensive contact" with the "person" of the plaintiff or another, and such contact with the plaintiff "directly or indirectly results."† This ancient tort obviously protects the individual interest in physical security, and its origins can be traced to the problem of physical violence. Scuffles or affronts to honor and dignity predictably produce violent responses,

---

* *See* Thomas Cooley, *Torts* 497 (1st ed. 1888) ("Malicious motives make a bad case worse, but they cannot make that wrong which is in its essence lawful."). *Compare* Chapter 14, section IV (explaining how bad motive can subject the defendant to punitive damages).

† *Restatement (Second)* § 13 (harmful contact), § 18 (offensive contact). As this definition implies, the defendant's intent to harm one person can be transferred to another under the doctrine of *transferred intent*. The doctrine is a vestige of the writ system and is limited to the directly caused harms compensable under the writ of trespass. *See* Dobbs on Torts § 40, at 76–77.

and so "keeping the peace" requires a legal prohibition of such conduct, the result attained by the tort of battery.

The imposition of liability is easy to understand when one maliciously hurts another directly by a punch or indirectly by a thrown object or gunshot. The conduct is the exact kind of behavior the government wants to prohibit and can be readily condemned for numerous reasons.

The hard cases involve defendants who acted without blameworthy intent. The element of intent is satisfied whenever the defendant had any desire or purpose to cause a harmful or offensive contact with the plaintiff. An insane person who had a deluded reason for striking the plaintiff, for example, would have the requisite intent for committing battery. He or she had a desire or purpose to hit the plaintiff. Such defendants cannot be faulted for their mental condition, and yet they are liable.

These cases illustrate the disjunction between tort law and criminal law. Insanity is a defense in criminal law. Unlike criminal liability, tort liability can attach to behavior that does not merit punishment. Tort liability is compensatory, an attribute that depends on injury and not blameworthy conduct. When an insane person commits a battery on another, the imposition of liability is a form of no-fault or strict liability that only obligates the insane defendant to pay compensatory damages to the injured plaintiff. Tort law, after all, cannot prohibit an insane person from acting in an insane way or punish that person for having done so. Nevertheless, tort law can still require these individuals to compensate others whom they have injured. Regardless of motive (deluded or otherwise), one who has the purpose or desire of causing another to suffer harmful or offensive contact has engaged in a nonreciprocal risky activity. The common member of the community does not cause others to suffer unwanted, intentional contacts on their bodies, nor does such conduct give equal respect to the other's interest in physical security. Having injured the plaintiff with such nonreciprocal behavior, an insane defendant incurs a tort obligation to compensate the plaintiff for his or her injuries, a compensatory rationale for liability that fundamentally differs from the punitive or retributive rationale for criminal liability.*

The requisite intent also exists if the defendant knew his or her conduct was substantially certain to cause a harmful or offensive contact on the plaintiff. In *Garratt v. Dailey*, for example, a five-year-old boy pulled a lawn chair out from under the plaintiff as she was about to sit on it, causing her to fall and suffer a fractured hip and other injuries.[2] The trial court found that the defendant "did not have any intent to injure the plaintiff, or any intent to bring about any unauthorized or offensive contact with her person." On appeal, the Washington Supreme Court concluded that these facts were sufficient to establish a battery "if, in addition to plaintiff's fall, it was proved that, when [defendant] moved the chair, he knew with substantial certainty that the plaintiff would attempt to sit down where the chair had been." This proof would not show that the defendant was a bad little boy, as the trial court had concluded that he did not want to injure the plaintiff. The proof could only show that the child knew he had imposed the substantial certainty of injury — a nonreciprocal risk — on the plaintiff, subjecting him to (strict) liability for the injuries.

Another instance of strict liability occurs in the well-known case *Vosburg v. Putney*.[3] The defendant and plaintiff were classmates, sitting across the aisle from one another. "The defendant reached across the aisle with his foot, and hit with his toe the shin of the right leg of the plaintiff. The touch was slight."[4] Unknown to the defendant, the plaintiff had an underlying diseased condition of the leg that was

---

* *See* Chapter 3, section III (explaining why a compensatory norm entails strict liability for injuries caused by nonreciprocal risky behavior); Chapter 5, section III (identifying conditions under which reciprocity is objectively determined and not dependent on the subjective traits of the defendant or plaintiff).

aggravated by the kick, leading to permanent injury. In concluding that the defendant was liable for battery, the jury found that the defendant did not intend to harm the plaintiff. The defendant appealed, and the Wisconsin Supreme Court upheld the verdict on the ground that although "the defendant being free from malice, wantonness, or negligence, and intending no harm to the plaintiff in what he did," the defendant acted with an "unlawful" intent and was liable for the injurious consequences. Lacking any indicia of personal blameworthiness, the liability is a form of no-fault or strict liability.

This case poses difficult questions about the requirement of intent in a case of battery, as generations of law students will attest. The defendant did not know that his intentional "slight touch" of the plaintiff's leg would cause injury, suggesting that a battery only requires the single intent to cause a contact that turns out to be harmful or offensive. In that event, the defendant intended a "harmful or offensive contact" as literally required by the black-letter rule. The rule, though, is also literally satisfied by the requirement that the defendant must have two intentions: the first to make contact, and the second to cause harm or offense. The rule is ambiguous in this important respect. By apparently adopting the requirement of a single intent to cause contact that unexpectedly turns out to be harmful, *Vosburg* clarifies this aspect of the liability rule without explaining why that interpretation is better than the other one requiring the dual intent of both contact and harm or offense.

The single-intent definition, however, is problematic. Suppose a manufacturer sold a drug to the plaintiff, who was then severely injured by an adverse drug reaction that could not have been foreseen at the time of sale. No one knew or reasonably could have known that the drug would have this effect on some users. The manufacturer had the purpose or desire of bringing the drug into contact with users, including the plaintiff, and that contact ultimately injured the plaintiff. This type of conduct involved an intended "harmful contact," but it does not subject a manufacturer to liability for battery. The manufacturer did not have the desire or purpose of injuring its consumers and only exposed each one to the ordinary (reasonable) risk of suffering injury by an unknown side effect of the drug.* Battery apparently requires more than just the single intent to cause a contact that turns out to be harmful.[5]

The problem is not easily resolved by formulating the liability rule to require the dual intent of causing contact and causing harm or offense. In *Vosburg*, the trial court specifically found that the defendant did not have any intent of injuring the plaintiff, suggesting that battery only requires the single intent of causing a physical contact with the plaintiff that unintentionally causes harm or offense. The single-intent requirement also explains the battery cases involving insane defendants, creating further difficulties for the dual-intent interpretation.

Not surprisingly, courts continue to disagree about the definition of battery. The single-intent and dual-intent interpretations each satisfy the black-letter rule for battery liability, and each has been adopted by a substantial number of courts.[6]

Without directly addressing this issue, the *Restatement (Second)* maintains that the defendant in a case like *Vosburg* committed an offensive battery.[7] This conclusion is puzzling. Damages in the case involved compensation for physical harm to the plaintiff's leg, so how can liability be predicated on an offensive contact? Moreover, the defendant did not intend to cause *any* harm, so how could he have intended an offensive contact? These questions are not addressed by the *Restatement (Second)*, so its solution has not gained widespread acceptance. On closer inspection, however, it becomes apparent that

---

* *See Restatement (Third)* § 1 cmt. e (explaining why the requirement of intent is not satisfied in these circumstances).

Vosburg can be interpreted as a case of offensive battery, and that doing so can resolve the perplexing issues posed by the case.

As illustrated by contemporary cases involving sexually transmitted diseases, courts award substantial damages for physical harms caused by an offensive battery. Someone with HIV or a venereal disease who knows of the condition "and does not disclose this to his or her sexual partner can be liable for battery."[8] In these cases, the defendant sexual partner did not want to physically harm the plaintiff, and the contact was not substantially certain to transmit the disease. The physical contact was tortious only because the plaintiff's consent to the sexual relations was ineffective due to the defendant's failure to disclose that he or she was infected. Sexual contact to which one has not consented is highly offensive. By committing an offensive battery, the defendant becomes liable for the injuries caused by the tortious contact, including the sexually transmitted disease. The damages compensate the plaintiff for physical harm (disease), but the defendant's liability is based on the offensive nature of the physical contact, just like the damages in *Vosburg* compensated the plaintiff for a physical harm (the disabled leg) caused by the offensive nature of the intended physical contact (a slight kick of the leg).

Why would the defendant's slight kick of the plaintiff's leg in *Vosburg* be an offensive contact? The tort of battery originated in the writ of trespass, for which "[i]t is . . . possible to identify from the early records two ideas at work: affronts to honour, and causation of loss."[9] At that time, the legal system was primarily concerned about suppressing violence and maintaining public order, a concern that required legal redress for affronts to honor within a status-based culture. A man who spat on another caused him no physical harm, yet the dignitary harm could predictably trigger a violent response to defend one's gentlemanly honor. Over time, the concern with dishonor waned, and "liability for wrongdoing was exclusively focused on the causation of loss."[10] The ancient tort of battery continued to provide redress for an offensive contact on the plaintiff's "person," including his or her body and any physical extensions defining his or her personal space, but the loss in question evolved into one of autonomy and not merely honor. By the mid-twentieth century, the *Restatement (Second)* could describe the rule in these terms: "the essence of the plaintiff's grievance consists in the offense to the dignity involved in the unpermitted and intentional invasion of the inviolability of his person and not in any physical harm done to his body."[11] The offense depends on the nonconsensual nature of the contact and not the defendant's motive, the same conditions that existed in *Vosburg*.

For example, a doctor who performs unwanted surgery on a patient is liable for medical battery. These defendants typically only want to help the plaintiff by preventing future harm, and yet they will incur liability for touching the plaintiff in a manner to which he or she did not consent. As Judge Cardozo famously explained, "Every human being of adult years and sound mind has a right to determine what shall be done with his body; and a surgeon who performs an operation without his patient's consent, commits an assault [a synonym for battery in this context], for which he is liable in damages."[12]

Due to the importance of protecting individual autonomy, a defendant can incur liability for physical harms without having intended any physical harm. As in *Vosburg*, the defendant must only have intended to make physical contact with the plaintiff, knowing that the plaintiff had not consented. The defendant, for example, might have been playing a prank or practical joke on the plaintiff that went awry and physically harmed the plaintiff.[13] Liability in these cases is justified by the *Restatement (Second)* on the ground that the individual's "interest in freedom from either [a harmful or offensive] contact . . . is so far a part of [the] interest in his bodily security that the intention to inflict an offensive contact . . . is sufficient to make the actor liable for a harmful contact resulting therefrom, even though such harmful contact was not intended."[14]

To be sure, the defendant may not have intended any offense whatsoever, as in *Vosburg*. Due to the requirement of equality, however, the defendant cannot unilaterally determine whether any given contact is offensive.* Otherwise, a physician could subject a patient to any course of unwanted treatment that the doctor honestly believes is in the patient's best interests. An offensive contact must instead be objectively determined, and so an offensive contact is a "bodily contact" that "offends a reasonable sense of personal dignity."[15] By intending to make such a contact, the defendant in *Vosburg* committed an offensive battery. The objective nature of the liability rule renders the defendant's actual motive or beliefs irrelevant.

We can now see why courts have adopted different definitions of the liability rule. Suppose battery only requires the single intent of causing a physical contact on the plaintiff's person. To limit this rule so that it does not subject drug manufacturers to battery liability for unforeseeable adverse drug reactions, the physical contact must be "unlawful" or tortious. One who intends such a contact would then have the "unlawful" intent required by *Vosburg*. The contact would be unlawful or tortious if the defendant knew or desired that it would injure the plaintiff. The contact would also be tortious, though, if it "offends a reasonable sense of personal dignity," an objective standard that has nothing to do with the defendant's knowledge or desires. The requirement of a single "unlawful" intent in *Vosburg*, therefore, involves two requirements: (1) the defendant intended to cause contact on the plaintiff's person, and (2) that contact was unlawful either because the defendant intended harm or offense, or tort law otherwise prohibited that contact on the ground that it is objectively harmful or offensive.

---

* *See* Chapter 5, section III.

By contrast, the dual-intent approach requires proof showing that (1) the defendant intended to cause contact on the plaintiff's person, and (2') the defendant intended the contact to be harmful or offensive. Now compare the two approaches. They expressly differ only with respect to the second requirement when the defendant did not have a desire or purpose to cause harm or offense, as in *Vosburg*. In a case like *Vosburg*, though, the defendant's intended contact as per requirement (1) is also "substantially certain" to cause an objectively defined harmful or offensive contact, thereby satisfying the definition of intent that does not depend on desire or purpose.* In other words, the defendant in *Vosburg* (objectively) intended the contact to be offensive, as his intent to kick the plaintiff's leg was substantially certain to cause an offensive contact, satisfying both (2) and (2'). *Vosburg* satisfies both the single-intent and dual-intent approaches, and so does any other case of battery. Both the single-intent and dual-intent definitions turn out to be equivalent, explaining why courts could defensibly adopt one or the other.

Just as the defendant's subjective beliefs cannot unilaterally determine whether he or she can touch the plaintiff without liability, the plaintiff's beliefs cannot unilaterally determine whether any given touching is offensive. "A bodily contact is offensive if it offends a reasonable sense of personal dignity."[16] The standard of reasonableness is objective, so an overly sensitive plaintiff who takes offense at some touching, like a tap on the shoulder to gain attention, cannot recover if that contact was reasonable in the community and the defendant did not know that the plaintiff would be offended in this manner.†

---

* *See supra* Part I.

† A defendant who had such knowledge would then make the contact with the intent to cause offense, thereby completing the tort.

Like any other objective component of a liability rule, the objective standard of reasonableness can function as an immunity for the actor.* A good illustration is provided by cases involving patients who sued their physicians for providing treatment without disclosing that they were infected with HIV or had contracted AIDS.

> Courts have been reluctant to allow a battery claim when the doctor's treatment had no realistic chance of infecting the patient. This position is somewhat surprising, insofar as the patient is arguably mistaken about the essential nature of the invasion, and insofar as it is arguably quite reasonable for the plaintiff to suffer offense once she realizes the nature of the contact. Nevertheless, some courts have expressed an understandable concern about the long-term policy implications of permitting tort recovery when the mode of treatment, despite the medical provider's condition, did not objectively present a significant risk of infection to the patient.[17]

The policy concern involves the way in which a successful battery claim based on a "fear of AIDS" would "contribute to the phobia" and "widespread public misperception" about HIV transmission.[18] To avoid liability, health-care workers would have to disclose their condition to their patients. The disclosure would then make it quite difficult for infected health-care providers to practice their occupations, even though "[t]he risk of HIV transmission from a health care worker to a patient during an invasive medical procedure is very remote."[19] An infected or diseased person has an equal right to engage in the occupation of his or her choice as long as that choice does not impose a significant risk of physical harm on others. To protect this important interest in self-determination, the objective standard immunizes these health-care providers

---

* *See* Chapter 5, section III (illustrating the point with the objective conception of reciprocal risks).

from battery liability by deeming their patients' "fear of AIDS" to be unreasonable.*

The ancient tort of battery ultimately reveals the full complexity of tort law. A battery case ordinarily involves blameworthy conduct that is understandably subject to liability, and yet the tort does not require such conduct in every instance, leading to hard questions. Given that the defendant in *Vosburg* had to pay for injuries that he did not want to cause, why does a physician infected with HIV not have to disclose that condition to a patient who becomes greatly upset on learning about the infection after having received the treatment? In both cases, the defendant is not personally blameworthy and the plaintiff suffered harm, so what distinguishes them? The answer is not supplied by the black-letter rule of battery liability, and instead requires deeper policy analysis. The objective components of the liability rule can create pockets of strict liability and immunity from liability. Consequently, a battery case can involve blameworthy conduct as in the typical case, no-fault liability as in *Vosburg*, or an immunity from liability as in the HIV cases. Each type of battery case promotes individual autonomy equally for right holders and duty holders, illustrating how policy analysis can reconcile cases that otherwise appear to be conflicting.

These varied considerations apply to all of the intentional torts. Rather than repeat the analysis, we instead focus on other issues distinctive of the particular torts.

C. Assault

One commits an *assault* with an act either (1)(a) intending to cause a harmful or offensive contact with the person of

---

* A patient's fear would be reasonable if the procedure directly exposed him or her to HIV. *Brzoska v. Olson*, 668 A.2d 1355, 1363–1364 (Del. 1995). In addition, if a patient first asks the physician about the matter and the physician fails to disclose the infection or disease, then the patient may recover the economic cost of treatment under the tort of fraudulent misrepresentation. *Id.* at 1366–1367.

another, or (1)(b) intending to put another in imminent apprehension of such contact; and (2) "the other is thereby put in such imminent apprehension."[20] In a case of assault, the plaintiff's harm consists of the apprehension that he or she will suffer an imminent battery. If the defendant's conduct completes the battery, any injuries the plaintiff suffered with respect to the immediately prior assault merge into those recoverable for the battery. The link between the two torts is expressed by the commonly used phrase "assault and battery" or the usage of assault as a synonym for battery. The two torts are different, however. One can commit an assault without committing a battery (a punch can miss, for example), and one can commit a battery without committing an assault (the plaintiff might not be aware of the oncoming punch).

Like an offensive battery, assault protects the individual right holder from a particular type of dignitary harm closely connected to the problem of physical violence. As in the case of an actual attack, conduct evincing an imminent attack is quite likely to provoke a violent response to the detriment of public order. An assault, therefore, "is an inchoate violence, amounting considerably higher than bare threats."[21]

The nature of the social problem first addressed by the tort of assault explains its other important limitations. The defendant's conduct must put the plaintiff in *apprehension* of an imminent harmful or offensive contact. The plaintiff does not have to be afraid, perhaps because his or her advanced skills in the martial arts would easily protect him or her from the defendant's attack. The defendant, however, does not have the right to force the plaintiff to defend himself or herself, so the mere threat infringes the plaintiff's autonomy and constitutes a compensable harm. Requiring the plaintiff to fear for his or her safety would also mean that the tort provides no protection to those who are unafraid, forcing them to protect themselves — the very type of violent confrontation that tort law wants to avert.

To constitute an assault, the threatened contact must also be *imminent*. A conditional threat, including one based on the passage of time, is not sufficient ("If the weather today were not so pleasant, I would smack you"), unless the condition would require the plaintiff to forgo one of his or her rights ("Your money or your life"). When not confronting an imminent threat, the plaintiff has time to seek protection from the authorities. By discouraging reliance on self-help remedies and the associated problem of escalating violence, the tort of assault channels disputes into the legal system for peaceful resolution.

D. False Imprisonment

Tort law is concerned about both liberty and security, so it protects the individual interest in freedom of movement. The tort of *false imprisonment* is completed whenever the defendant (1) intentionally confines the plaintiff, (2) against his or her will, when (3) the plaintiff is aware of the confinement. In a substantial number of jurisdictions, false imprisonment does not require the plaintiff to be aware of the confinement.[22] Liability in such cases can be justified by the manner in which the defendant's intentional confinement fundamentally disrespects the plaintiff's legally protected interest in self-determination, thereby constituting tortious harm per se.

Like assault and battery, false imprisonment was initially formulated to address the problem of violence and public disorder. In medieval England, "[c]harges of abduction and rape were very common" with respect to unmarried women of wealthier classes.* An egregious example of false imprisonment involves the modern crime of kidnapping.

---

* John Bellamy, *Crime and Public Order in England in the Later Middle Ages* 58 (U. Toronto Press 1973). These charges were often fabricated to avoid a prearranged marriage and allow a "woman of station [to] marry the man she preferred." "The indictment of the new husband would follow and he would have to purchase a pardon." *Id.* In these cases, the women were not restrained against their will, but

To recover, the plaintiff must prove that he or she was completely confined within boundaries fixed by the defendant. The area of confinement "may be large and need not be stationary." The confinement is complete if the plaintiff, to escape, is "required to run any risk of harm" to himself or herself, his or her chattels, or third parties. Partial obstruction is not sufficient, unless the plaintiff was unaware of the "reasonable means of escape."[23]

The tort of false imprisonment also protects international human rights. Under a federal law known as the Alien Tort Statute, federal district courts have "original jurisdiction over civil actions brought by aliens for torts committed in violation of the law of nations or a treaty of the United States." Based on this statute, six "prominent Haitian citizens, opponents of the ruling military regime," received a damages judgment for "torture and false imprisonment directed by Prosper Avril who was then military ruler" of Haiti and at the time of suit a resident of Florida.[24] Unlawful detention is a serious international human rights problem that is partially redressable by the ancient tort of false imprisonment.

E. Trespass and Conversion

An individual has various interests in tangible property, including the interest in exclusive possession and ownership. These latter interests are protected by three of the ancient intentional torts.

One is liable to another for *trespass on land* if he intentionally:

(a) enters land in the possession of the other, or causes a thing or a third person to do so, or
(b) remains on the land, or
(c) fails to remove from the land a thing which he is under a duty to remove.[25]

---

the law instead assumed as much based on social convention, providing another example of how tort law has been affected by gendered notions of equality.

This tort protects the individual interest in exclusive possession of land by giving the possessor a legal right to exclude others from occupying the land. This possessory interest includes any tangible property permanently on the land, such as residential buildings, and encompasses certain entries above and below the surface. One who rents an apartment, for example, has a possessory interest in the space that is protected by this tort right.

In addition to having an interest in the exclusive possession of land or *real property*, individuals have a similar interest in *chattels* or movable forms of tangible property. One has "possession of a chattel" if he "has physical control of the chattel with the intent to exercise such control on his own behalf, or on behalf of another."[26] This possessory interest is protected by the tort of *trespass to chattels*, which makes one liable for intentionally:

(a) dispossessing another of the chattel, or
(b) using or intermeddling [by bringing about a physical contact] with a chattel in the possession of another.[27]

Because trespass on land and trespass to chattels both protect the individual interest in exclusive possession of tangible property, the two liability rules are virtually identical. They differ in one important respect. To recover for trespass on land, the plaintiff does not need to prove actual harm. The defendant's intended entry on the land violates the plaintiff's right to exclusive possession, and the rights violation establishes the compensable harm (which is nominal for cases in which the trespass causes no other harm). To recover for trespass to chattels, the plaintiff cannot merely prove that his or her right to exclusive possession was violated by the defendant. The plaintiff must also prove that the trespass caused harm consisting of either actual dispossession, damage to the chattel's condition, loss of use for a significant period, or some physical harm to the plaintiff's person or chattels or to some other person in whom the plaintiff has a legal interest.[28] Lacking proof of actual harm, the plaintiff cannot recover for trespass to chattels, even though such proof is not required by trespass on land.

To be defensible, any substantive difference between the two liability rules requires justification by reference to a substantive difference between chattels and land. According to the conventional view, the individual interest in exclusive possession of land is simply more important than the individual interest in exclusive possession of chattels, perhaps because "the resentment on the part of the ordinary person toward another who intermeddles with one's chattels without consent is not the same as that toward an unlicensed intruder on one's land."[29] The more important interest in exclusive possession of land explains why the mere rights violation satisfies the liability rule, whereas the less important interest in the exclusive possession of chattels does not merit such protection and instead requires additional proof of actual harm.

Tort law, however, does recognize that one's possessory interest in chattel is inviolable. "Sufficient legal protection of the possessor's interest in the mere inviolability of his chattel is afforded by his privilege to use reasonable force to protect his possession against even harmless interference."[30] Possessors can ordinarily protect their chattels against interference by others in a very simple way. Possessors can always move the chattel to somewhere else such as their home, where it is protected by the tort of trespass on land. Given the effectiveness of this easy self-help remedy, tort law does not need to protect the individual interest in exclusive possession of chattels, unless the trespass causes actual harm.

Unlike chattels, the possessor cannot move land.[31] If someone trespasses on land without causing actual damage, the possessor's self-help remedies to prevent future trespasses are much more costly and burdensome (like keeping a vigilant watch or fencing the property). Rather than force the possessor to incur these costly measures of self-protection, tort law employs other remedies. An award of compensatory damages is required for a court to grant the additional remedies of punitive damages or injunctive relief.[32] By allowing the land possessor to recover nominal damages without proof of actual harm, tort law can protect the right to exclusive possession with an award of punitive damages or injunctive relief prohibiting future incursions on the land. The nonmovable nature of land explains why tort law does not require proof of actual harm for this type of trespass.*

Because chattels are movable and land is not, tort law recognizes a distinctive tort for chattels that is unavailable for real property. The tort of *conversion* involves "an intentional exercise of dominion or control over a chattel which so seriously interferes with the right of another to control it that the actor may justly be required to pay the other the full value of the chattel."[33] For example, if I mistakenly take your hat when leaving a restaurant and then immediately return it, I have only committed a trespass to chattels and not conversion (further

---

* Consider how this reasoning applies to cases in which the plaintiff claims that the defendant trespassed on a computer system by sending unwanted e-mails or "spam." An e-mail address is a fixed location in cyberspace, making it analogous to the fixed location of land. *See Intel Corp. v. Hamidi*, 731 P.3d 296, 309 (Cal. 2003) (ascribing this view to Professor Richard Epstein). Drawing the analogy between cyberland and real property, however, does not turn the claim into one of trespass on land. A defendant who sends a few unwanted e-mails does not physically interfere with the plaintiff's possessory interest in the computer system, but instead affects the plaintiff's ability to use or enjoy the computer. The interest in the use or enjoyment of real property — and by analogy, of e-mail systems in cyberland — is protected by the tort of *nuisance*, which compares the amount and reasonableness of the defendant's interference with the plaintiff's use of (cyber)land. To resolve this issue, the court would have to consider the plaintiff's interest in excluding unwanted e-mails in relation to the social cost that would be created by such an exclusionary right, including the need for each Internet user to "get permission in advance from anyone with whom they want to communicate and anyone who owns a server through which their messages may travel." *Id.* at 310 (quoting Professor Mark Lemley and then holding that the plaintiff must establish that the unwanted e-mails caused actual harm to prove trespass to chattels).

illustrating the important strain of strict liability in all these torts). If I took the hat intending to steal it, then I have committed conversion, the same liability outcome as would occur in the event that I kept your hat for three months before returning it.[34] In effect, conversion requires the defendant to buy the chattel "at a forced judicial sale" equaling the "full value of the chattel, at the time and place of the tort," whereas trespass to chattels involves compensation to the owner "for the diminished value of his chattel because of any damage to it, or for the damage to his interest in its possession or use."[35] Conversion does not apply to trespass on land. One who trespasses on land can only interfere with possession or use and not ownership, presumably because land is not movable and subject to theft.

F. Evolution in the Common Law: The Intentional Infliction of Emotional Distress

The early common law was primarily concerned with protecting the King's peace, so it adopted liability rules addressing problems of violence and dishonor. As we have found, these torts give the individual some protection against dignitary harms, and their limitations can be understood by reference to the predominant concerns and limited capabilities of the newly centralized royal government. With the maturation of the legal system and increased stabilization of civil society, tort law could address a broader range of emotional harms by recognizing new forms of action.

An excellent example is provided by the tort known as the *intentional infliction of emotional distress*. In a hugely influential article, Calvert Magruder persuasively showed that tort law had long protected the individual interest in emotional tranquility as an incident to other torts.[36] That protection, however, is limited. The tort of assault, for example, requires the threat of an *imminent* harmful or offensive contact, even though one can be greatly upset by verbal threats not involving an immediate attack.[37] To address this problem, the tort system in the twentieth century adopted a new tort making one liable for intentionally causing another "severe emotional distress" by engaging in "extreme and outrageous conduct."[38] Mere "insults, indignities, threats, annoyances, petty oppressions, or other trivialities" intended to cause emotional upset are not enough: "There must still be freedom to express an unflattering opinion, and some safety valve must be left through which irascible tempers may blow off relatively harmless steam." Hence liability is limited to cases "in which the recitation of the facts to an average member of the community would arouse his resentment against the actor, and lead him to exclaim, 'Outrageous!'"[39]

In addition to illustrating how the common law evolves, the tort of intentional infliction of emotional distress further reveals the extent to which tort rules mediate one's interest in being free from (emotional) harm against another's freedom to engage in behavior threatening such harm (by expressing "an unflattering opinion" and so on). Due to the importance of this liberty interest, courts have significantly limited the availability of this tort, enabling the plaintiff to recover only in exceptional circumstances involving "EXTREME AND OUTRAGEOUS" conduct.*

G. Absence of Consent

The plaintiff's consent to an intentional invasion of a legally protected interest ordinarily bars recovery.

> It is not, strictly speaking, a privilege, or even a defense, but goes to negative the existence of any tort in the first instance.

---

* *Compare Jones v. Clinton*, 990 F. Supp. 657, 677 (E.D. Ark. 1998), the infamous case in which Paula Jones accused then-Governor Bill Clinton of conduct the court found to be insufficiently outrageous because it was "a mere sexual proposition or encounter, albeit an odious one, that was relatively brief in duration, did not involve any coercion or threats of reprisal, and was abandoned as soon as plaintiff made clear that the advance was not welcome."

It is a fundamental principle of the common law that *volenti no fit injuria* — to one who is willing, no wrong is done. The attitude of the courts has not, in general, been one of paternalism.[40]

Consent effectively defines the domain of tort law, distinguishing tortious behavior from socially acceptable behavior. "For example, consent turns trespass into a dinner party; a battery into a handshake; a theft into a gift; an invasion of privacy into an intimate moment; a commercial appropriation of name and likeness into a biography."[41]

Because the domain of tort law is limited to nonconsensual interactions, the significance of consent is critically important for understanding tort liability. Informed consent allows individuals to structure their relationships in the manner that best promotes their individual welfare as per the requirements of allocative efficiency.* The "moral magic of consent" is based on individual autonomy:

> By consenting to another's touch, one puts that person at liberty to do what was antecedently obligatory of her not to do. By consenting to another's intrusion onto one's land, one dispels a duty that antecedently obligated that person to keep off private property. . . . To have the ability to create and dispel rights and duties is what it means to be an autonomous moral agent. To respect persons as autonomous is to recognize them as givers and takers of rights and duties. It is to conceive of them as very powerful moral magicians. The capacity for autonomy is the capacity for self-legislation.[42]

Because tort law protects individual autonomy, a prima facie case for liability will always require proof that the

---

* According to the *Coase theorem*, when individuals have full information of all the relevant variables and do not incur any other costs in bargaining with others, voluntary agreements among right holders and duty holders will produce allocatively efficient outcomes. *See* Ronald Coase, *The Problem of Social Cost*, 3 J.L. & Econ. 1 (1960).

defendant interfered with one of the plaintiff's protected autonomy interests like that of physical security — proof necessarily including the plaintiff's lack of consent to the contact in question. Proof of a negative is not feasible, however, and so the plaintiff can allege the absence of consent, giving the defendant the opportunity to deny that allegation. The form of argument creates the appearance that consent is an affirmative defense, even though the plaintiff bears the burden of proving that he or she did not consent and will lose if the conflicting evidence is in equipoise.

To consent, the plaintiff must make an *informed choice*. He or she must adequately understand the relevant factors, making consent ineffective when based on limited information, as in the battery claims involving sexually transmitted diseases.* The plaintiff must also have the capacity for understanding the requisite information, so children and mentally impaired individuals cannot consent to many types of contacts. Consent usually is limited to certain types of contacts. One can commit an intentional tort by exceeding the scope of consent. This type of conduct is involved in many medical battery cases, in which the plaintiff consented to a particular procedure and the physician committed battery by performing an unrelated procedure. Consent is also ineffective when made under duress or coercion, which robs the decision of the requisite element of choice.

Consent can negate liability in another way. The defendant avoids liability if a reasonable person in the defendant's position would have believed that the plaintiff had consented to the contact in question, and the defendant actually believed as much. A rationale for this rule is evident in a case of offensive battery. If the circumstances were such that the defendant actually and reasonably believed that the plaintiff had consented to the bodily contact, then the defendant did

---

* *See* section A above.

not have the intent to cause an offensive contact. The defendant did not have the desire or purpose of causing an offensive contact, nor did he or she know or have reason to know that the contact was substantially certain to be offensive. An actual, reasonable belief in consent accordingly relieves the defendant of liability for offensive battery, even if the plaintiff can prove that he or she did not truly consent to the physical contact.[43]

Like other objectively defined liability rules, consent can function as an immunity in some cases. For example, the "defendant is sometimes at liberty to infer consent as a matter of usage or custom, and to proceed upon the assumption that it is given. Thus the general habit of the community to permit strangers to enter at will upon wild land may justify a trespass. . . ."[44] At first glance, the rule looks puzzling. Trespass on land can involve honest mistakes, so the defendant could incur liability by going on another's land in the mistaken belief that the landowner had consented. Trespass only requires proof that the defendant intended to be on the plaintiff's land; social custom is irrelevant. By allowing the defendant to rely on social custom or objective consent, tort law immunizes the defendant from the (strict) liability he or she would otherwise face for entering the plaintiff's land on the reasonable but mistaken assumption that the plaintiff had consented to the entry.

This immunity must find justification in the concern for autonomy that makes consent fundamentally important for tort law. A contrary rule that subjected the defendant and others to liability for reasonable mistakes of this type would leave them unable to rely on social custom or any other reasonable appearance of consent, substantially limiting their autonomy or ability to act in the world. As the underlying normative value of tort law, the concern for individual autonomy must apply equally to both plaintiffs and defendants. The autonomy of plaintiffs (or right holders in general) is protected by the rule negating liability for cases in which they consent, just like the autonomy of defendants (or duty holders) is protected by the rule negating liability for cases in which they have an actual, reasonable belief that the plaintiff consented. Once again, the varied permutations of the liability rule can all be understood by reference to its substantive rationale.

II. AFFIRMATIVE DEFENSES

Unlike criminal law, tort law does not permit the defendant to defend himself or herself by relying on excuses such as insanity, creating a significant strain of no-fault liability within the intentional torts. The affirmative defenses in tort law instead justify or privilege certain forms of conduct, enabling the defendant to avoid liability by proving that he or she engaged in such conduct.

According to the influential tort scholar Francis Bohlen, "all agree that the existence of a privilege is determined by a comparison of the respective interests involved. . . ."[45] Bohlen also observed that the comparison of interests gives an interpersonal priority to the individual interest in physical security over a conflicting liberty interest: "[I]n new fields the interest of the safety of human life and limb is recognized as superior to no matter what interests of property."[46] By employing this type of interest analysis, we can readily understand the affirmative defenses.

A. Self-Defense and Defense of Property

Due to the inherent inadequacy of the compensatory damages remedy (as clearly revealed by a case of wrongful death), someone who faces an imminent attack is not adequately protected by the right to receive compensatory damages from the wrongdoer.* The privilege of *self-defense* entitles the individual to use reasonable force when he or she reasonably believes that another is about to commit an actionable battery on him or her. The privilege also applies to conduct aimed at defending others who reasonably appear to be threatened by such an imminent attack.

To be reasonable, the force "must not be disproportionate in extent to the harm from which the actor is seeking to protect" himself or herself.[47] A punch is a reasonable way to protect oneself from a threatened punch, but not from a threatened poke in the arm. "Since the means used must be proportionate to the danger threatened, it is obvious that one is not privileged to protect one's self even from a blow which is likely to cause some fairly substantial injury by means which are intended or likely to cause death or serious bodily harm."[48] One who is threatened by a mere punch cannot justifiably shoot the attacker. Self-defense with potentially deadly force is reasonable only when the threat reasonably appears to involve "peril of death or serious bodily harm or ravishment."[49] To justify defense with potentially deadly force, the threatened punch must carry an implied threat of grave bodily harm in light of the circumstances. One can also defend himself or herself against another's negligent conduct that threatens "harmful or offensive contact or bodily harm," but the force will be unreasonable and excessive if "intended or likely to cause death or serious bodily harm."[50]

An individual is not privileged to use force in excess of the amount that is required for self-protection. One who responds with excessive force is liable to the other for battery with respect to the excessive force and not the actual force (some of which is privileged).

---

* *See* Chapter 5, section II (discussing the inadequacy of the compensatory damages remedy and arguing that it explains why tort law has adopted negligence liability as the default rule for accidental harms).

Courts are divided on the issue of whether deadly force is justified when the individual has the option of safely retreating from the attack. In the jurisdictions requiring retreat, courts reason that the attacker's interest in bodily security has priority over the conflicting liberty interest of the one forced to retreat. This rule does not condone the attack—that attacker is subject to liability for assault, battery, or both—but instead recognizes that the confrontation will likely cause bodily injury that is worse than the loss of dignity suffered by the party forced to retreat. By contrast, in "the West and South, where most of these authorities are found [not requiring retreat], it is abhorrent to the courts to require one who is assailed to seek dishonor in flight. The ideal of these courts is found in the ethics of the duelist. . . ."[51] In these jurisdictions, courts have concluded that retreat involves a loss of dignity or self-respect that undermines autonomy to the same extent as the associated threat to the security interest of the attacker. The confrontation may cause bodily injury, but that outcome is not any worse than the loss of dignity caused by the forced retreat. As revealed by the divided case law, the rule regarding retreat depends on the social construction of honor or dignity within a particular community, illustrating the dependence of liability rules on cultural norms.*

The defendant can assert the privilege of self-defense against an innocent plaintiff—either someone who was not actually going to attack the defendant, contrary to reasonable appearances, or even a bystander wounded by the defendant's use of reasonable force in defending himself or herself from an attack by a third party. These cases implicate the security interests of both the physically injured plaintiff and the defendant who only engaged in the conduct for purposes of self-defense. When the defendant employed reasonable force, the conflicting security interests of the two parties are indistinguishable. The defendant

---

* *See* Chapter 6 (discussing the social construction of tort law).

and bystander plaintiff each acted reasonably, and the interaction implicated the security interest of each party to the same extent (to be reasonable, the defendant's use of force must have been proportionate to the threatened harm). Without any normative distinction between the conflicting interpersonal interests in physical security, tort law cannot shift the loss from one party to the other. It must lie where it fell, on the plaintiff.[52]

Individuals are also privileged to protect their property from imminent harm, including unwanted intrusions on land, caused by another. An individual's interest in property, however, does not have priority over the intruder's interest in physical security. Consequently, the individual must first ask the other "to desist from, or terminate his intrusion" when warranted by the circumstances.[53] If the request is ineffective or otherwise impractical, the individual can use reasonable force to prevent the intrusion or other property damage, but the force cannot be "intended or likely to cause death or serious bodily harm."[54] The individual's interest in property has lower priority than the intruder's interest in bodily security, and so tort law does not let individuals protect their property by *any* force likely to cause serious physical injury.[55] Such force is reasonable only when the intrusion also poses an implied threat to the individual, such as when a burglar enters an occupied dwelling.

Property in the form of chattels is movable, creating the opportunity of recapture by the owner. The owner can recapture the chattel by exercising reasonable force only if "he acts promptly after his dispossession or after his timely discovery of it."[56] If one's bike is stolen, for example, he or she cannot use force to recapture the bike after seeing it on the street a couple months later.

> There is a period of time, depending on the circumstances of the particular case, at the expiration of which the actor's discovery of his dispossession ceases to be timely and the

privilege of recaption no longer exists. The public interest in the preservation of the peace requires that one who no matter how innocently and unavoidably has permitted another to remain in long continued and undisturbed possession of his chattel shall be required to assert his possessory rights by bringing an action rather than by self-help.[57]

After the passage of time, the current possessor of the bike may sincerely believe that he or she owns it. Perhaps the possessor purchased it from someone else, not knowing that it was stolen. The owner's effort to recapture the bike at this point is likely to cause the other to defend possession of the bike, with the consequent possibilities of escalating violence. At this point, the bike owner must seek help from the police or otherwise file a tort claim, illustrating once again how tort rules are formulated to prevent self-help remedies not otherwise required by the exigencies of the moment.

B. Necessity

To protect oneself from harm, an individual may have to interfere with the property interests of an innocent third party. One who had been camping in the wilderness, for example, might have to trespass on another's land to escape from a raging forest fire. This conduct is justified under the doctrine of *private necessity*, which gives actors the privilege to interfere with someone else's property right to avoid a greater private harm threatened by natural forces or some independent cause unconnected to the property owner. Conduct that otherwise would constitute trespass on land, trespass to chattel, or conversion is privileged under these conditions, thereby giving the party in need of protection the right to use the other's property for this limited purpose.

In *Ploof v. Putnam*, for example, the plaintiff and his family were out on Lake Champlain when unexpectedly bad weather forced them to tie their sloop on the defendant's dock. A servant of the defendant unmoored the boat, "whereupon it was driven upon the shore by the tempest, without the plaintiff's fault; and . . . the sloop and its contents were thereby destroyed, and the plaintiff and his wife and children cast into the lake and upon the shore, receiving injuries." The court held that these allegations, if proven, would mean that the plaintiff was privileged to use the dock. Once the plaintiff had a right to use the dock, the defendant could not lawfully prevent the plaintiff from using the dock for this purpose. Consequently, the plaintiff could recover either for the trespass the defendant's servant committed by unmooring the boat, or, alternatively, for the defendant's breach of duty "to permit the plaintiff to moor his sloop to the dock, and to permit it to remain so moored during the continuance of the tempest."*

In a case of private necessity, the emergency creates a conflict between the threatened person's interest in physical security and the other's interest in property. Because the threatened individual was not at fault for creating the emergency, the case involves a conflict of one party's security interest with another's property interest. Due to the priority of the security interest, the subordinate property interest must give way — individuals must have the right or privilege to use another's property for the limited purpose of self-protection. By extension, the privilege applies to cases in which the emergency forces one to protect his or her more valuable property by invading the less valuable property right of another.

---

* 71 A. 188 (Vt. 1908). The people in the boat were known in the area as thieving pirates, making the conduct of the defendant's agent more understandable (although still not justifiable). *See* Joan Vogel, *Cases in Context: Lake Champlain Wars, Gentrification, and* Ploof v. Putnam, 45 St. Louis U. L.J. 791 (2001).

A more puzzling issue is raised by *Vincent v. Lake Erie Transportation Co.*, in which the court held that the defendants properly exercised the privilege of private necessity to protect their ship during a storm, but still had to pay for the resultant damage to the dock owned by the plaintiff.[58] The privilege to use another's property for purposes of self-protection entails an obligation to compensate the property owner for any damage thereby caused to the property. The privilege is incomplete in this respect, an aspect of the liability rule that has caused considerable debate.

The issue has garnered so much attention because it involves liability without legal fault: The self-help actor in *Vincent* reasonably used another's property and still incurred liability for the property damage. As we have found, the intentional torts often create implicit forms of no-fault liability due to mismatches between the objective aspect of a liability rule and the subjective traits of the defendant, but *Vincent* involves conduct that was *objectively* reasonable and still subject to liability. By imposing liability on a defendant who exercised reasonable care, *Vincent* expressly raises the issue of how tort law should choose between negligence and strict liability.

According to one prominent rationale for the outcome in *Vincent*, "[a]s between the individuals concerned, it is obviously just that he whose interests are advanced by the act [of self-help] should bear the cost of doing it," as the other "derives no benefit from the act."[59] This rationale can be reframed as a matter of "restitution . . . justified on the general principle that a person who obtains — though not necessarily tortiously — a benefit at the expense of another through appropriation of a property or quasi-property interest held by the other is unjustly enriched and should be liable to the other for any benefit attributable to the appropriation."[60]

As formulated, these rationales are unpersuasive. Individuals often act for their own benefit in a manner that necessarily exposes others to injury without incurring strict liability for those injuries.* What distinguishes these cases from *Vincent*? Reframing the rationale as one of restitution for an unjust enrichment does not fully solve the problem. Tort law privileges the actor to use the other's property for purposes of self-protection, so in what way has the actor "appropriated" the property of another? Invoking the label of *unjust* enrichment merely begs the question of what justice requires. The mere fact that one party benefits at the other's expense is unsatisfactory, for it returns us to the question of why others who act in this way do not incur strict liability. On scrutiny, the varied rationales for *Vincent* are unpersuasive, yielding an important "failure of tort theory."[61]

The difficulty of explaining *Vincent* is understandable. Over the years, courts have developed two different rationales for imposing strict liability on defendants whose conduct was objectively reasonable. Neither rationale, though, persuasively explains *Vincent*.

Under the evidentiary rationale for strict liability, courts apply strict liability to forms of risky behavior that cannot be adequately regulated by negligence liability due to the plaintiffs' practical inability of proving legal fault.† The cases of

---

* The construction of dams or other large projects like mines, for example, requires large amounts of workers to face dangerous conditions, predictably resulting in a number of deaths. Under the common law (that is, prior to the adoption of workers' compensation), the employer only faced negligence liability for these injuries. One might try to distinguish these cases on the ground that a nonnegligent employer exposes each individual worker to a risk of harm, whereas the defendant's conduct in *Vincent* was virtually certain to harm the plaintiff's dock. This difference in the magnitude of the risk, though, is not normatively relevant. In both types of cases, the defendant acted reasonably. Given the normative equivalence of the behavior, the magnitude of the risk is normatively relevant only insofar as it is affected by considerations of reciprocity. For reasons to be discussed in the text, strict liability in *Vincent* cannot be justified on the ground that the defendant imposed a reasonable, nonreciprocal risk on the plaintiff. Consequently, this particular method of justifying *Vincent* does not persuasively distinguish the case from the construction cases.

† *See* Chapter 3, section II.

private necessity, however, involve discrete safety decisions that can be effectively governed by negligence liability. For example, the self-help conduct in *Vincent* could be readily evaluated in a negligence case. The defendant's decisions to secure the ship to the dock, replace the fraying ropes, and so on, do not fundamentally differ from the types of safety decisions routinely scrutinized in negligence cases. Cases of private necessity do not plausibly involve important forms of unreasonable behavior that are beyond proof, requiring some other rationale for strict liability.

The other widely recognized rationale for strict liability involves the fairness of making the defendant pay for injuries caused by nonreciprocal risks.* The cases of private necessity, however, do not involve this type of risk. The concept of reciprocity is relevant for determining how to mediate the conflicting interpersonal interests of the plaintiff and defendant — the defendant must have injured the plaintiff with a nonreciprocal risk to justify liability. Such an interpersonal conflict of interests is not present in cases of private necessity. Having established necessity, the actor is privileged or has a right to use the property for purposes of self-protection, so these safety decisions only implicate the actor's interests. The defendants in *Vincent*, for example, had a protected interest in their ship that conflicted with their protected interest or right to use the dock for purposes of self-protection. This *intrapersonal* conflict of interests in a case of private necessity fundamentally differs from the *interpersonal* conflict involved in the nonreciprocal risky interactions that can justify strict liability.

This attribute of the privilege, however, is sufficient for justifying the duty to compensate. Necessity gives the self-help actor legal control over the property, which then entails

---

* *See* Chapter 3, section III.

legal responsibility for the exercise of that control. As the *Vincent* court explained:

> The situation was one in which the ordinary rules regulating property rights were suspended by forces beyond human control, and if, without the direct intervention of some act by the one sought to be liable, the property of another was injured, such injury must be attributed to the act of God. . . . But here those in charge of the vessel deliberately and by their direct efforts held her in such a position that the damage to the dock resulted, and, having thus preserved the ship at the expense of the dock, it seems to us that her owners are responsible to the dock owners for the extent of the injury inflicted.[62]

The liability was not based on trespass or wrongful use of the property — the emergency "suspended" the "ordinary rules regarding property rights," thereby giving the defendant ship owners the privilege or right to use the dock. The right then placed the defendants' protected interest in the ship in conflict with their protected interest in the dock, and the defendants exercised their right over these conflicting interests by "deliberately" preserving "the ship at the expense of the dock." Their exercise of this right made the defendants legally "responsible" for damage to the dock.

The *Vincent* court could have done a much better job of explaining this reasoning. As implied by the doctrine of consent, a right holder is unilaterally empowered to make decisions with respect to his or her legally protected interests. Consent can turn an offensive battery into a kiss. By exercising one's autonomy or right in this respect, the actor becomes responsible for the foreseeable consequences of that choice. In a case of private necessity, the same concept of responsibility justifies a duty to pay for any property damage once the emergency has passed and the property interest has devolved back to the original property owner. As in the case of consent, the defendants in *Vincent* exercised a right (to use the dock) that made them legally responsible for the consequences of that choice (damage to the dock).

This reasoning explains why the actor incurs no compensatory duty in a case of *public necessity*, which privileges the actor to use or even destroy another's property to avoid "imminent public disaster."[63] "Thus, one who dynamites a house to stop the spread of a conflagration that threatens a town, or shoots a mad dog in the street . . . is not liable to the owner, so long as the emergency is great enough, and he has acted reasonably under the circumstances."[64] By definition, the actor's decision is limited to matters of public interest. The actor is not deciding how to mediate conflicts between two of his or her own protected interests (like the ship and dock). The actor instead mediates conflicting public interests (the sure destruction of one house by dynamiting as opposed to the possible destruction of the entire town). If the actor mediates this conflict in a reasonable manner, any ensuing losses are an inevitable fact of social life for which the actor is not legally responsible.

Of the varied privileges or affirmative defenses, private necessity is the only one requiring the actor to pay compensation for harms caused by reasonable conduct. Of the varied privileges, private necessity is the only one involving an intrapersonal conflict of the actor's legally protected interests. How the actor resolves that conflict is solely a matter of individual autonomy, explaining why the actor is legally responsible for the consequences of that choice.

In addition to explaining *Vincent*, an autonomy-based rationale for liability can justify a compensatory tort right.* Such a right is clearly contemplated by the conventional "unjustment enrichment" rationales for *Vincent*. As these rationales recognize,

---

* *See* Chapter 5, section I.

the normative problem involves individuals who exercise their liberty for their own benefit in a manner that threatens injury to others who do not necessarily benefit from the activity. The conflicting interests in liberty and security are normatively distinguishable, justifying a priority of the security interest — repeatedly recognized by the affirmative defenses — that is protected by a compensatory tort right. The compensatory tort right creates a correlative compensatory duty that can be triggered by the fact of injury and not any faulty or unreasonable behavior by the defendant, as in *Vincent*. A compensatory tort right does not justify a general rule of strict liability, however, because the inherent inadequacies of the damages remedy — also repeatedly recognized by the affirmative defenses — make negligence liability the default rule for accidental harm.*   Within a compensatory tort system, the affirmative defenses rely on principles that can explain *Vincent* in a manner that unites the intentional torts with both strict liability and negligence liability.

---

* *See id.*, section II.

∼ 8 ∼

Negligence Liability

Tort law is often called "accident law" for good reason. In the vast majority of cases, individuals suffer injuries due to accident and not intentional wrongdoing. Accidental harms are governed by negligence liability, with strict liability providing an additional cause of action in certain types of cases.

The prima facie case of negligence involves the four elements of *duty*, *breach*, *causation*, and *damages*. By contrast, strict liability involves a legal duty to compensate physical harms caused by the conduct governed by the duty. Strict liability does not require any proof that the defendant's conduct was unreasonable. The distinctive attribute of negligence liability accordingly involves the issue of whether the defendant's conduct failed to satisfy the standard of reasonable care — the element of breach.

We cannot study reasonable care without first defining the prior element of duty. Their inherent connection is reflected in the common practice of using "duty" to refer to both elements, as in, "One has a duty to exercise reasonable care." Duty, however, is analytically distinct from the standard of reasonable care, making each a separate element of negligence liability.

I. DUTY

A rule of no duty absolves the defendant of legal responsibility for the injuries in question, so the element of duty determines the types of harms or associated risks for which the defendant is responsible as a matter of tort law. Having identified the harms or risks governed by the duty, the tort inquiry can then determine how a duty holder like the defendant should behave in light of those harms or risks. As a functional matter, the standard of reasonable care — the second element of negligence liability — must be defined by reference to the harms or risks for which the duty holder is legally responsible, explaining why the specification of duty is the first element of negligence liability.

To serve this function, duty cannot depend on "factors specific to an individual case" but instead must be "applicable to a general class of cases" involving "categories of actors or patterns of conduct."[1] By defining the element of duty in categorical terms, tort law can then specify the requirements of reasonable care in terms applicable to all similarly situated actors within the category.

The categorical determinations inherent in the element of duty are made by judges as a matter of law. Judges have experience with a broad range of cases, enabling them to identify the general concerns of relevance for the categorical decision, unlike juries, whose comparative advantage resides in factual and evaluative judgments of case-specific matters.

Judges resolve duty questions by relying on various factors, but these "factors are so numerous and so broadly stated that they can lead to almost any conclusion."[2] Consequently, "no universal test for [duty] ever has been formulated. . . . There is little analysis of the problem of duty in the courts."[3]

Despite the absence of extensive analysis in the case law, the element of duty can still be understood in substantive terms. Duty involves issues of law that are determined by judges on the basis of categorical considerations, and so the specification of duty inevitably depends on the most important categorical decision of all — the reasons or rationales for imposing tort liability on any defendant.

A. The Requirement of Feasance or Action

Duty ordinarily is limited to risks created by some affirmative action taken by the duty holder, known as the requirement of *feasance*. An actor who creates a risk incurs a duty to control the risk in a reasonable manner. The requirement can be satisfied even if the direct cause of the injury involved the defendant's failure to act. A driver who did not brake can still be liable for the ensuing accident. Having engaged in some affirmative act that created the general risk of an automobile accident, the driver has a duty to continue acting in a manner that reasonably reduces the risk.

The requirement of feasance has some exceptions, the most important of which is discussed later.* There is no exception involving a duty to rescue. For example:

> A sees B, a blind man, about to step on the street in front of an approaching automobile. A could prevent B from so doing by a word or touch without delaying his own progress. A does not do so, and B is run over and hurt. A is under no duty to prevent B from stepping into the street, and is not liable to B.[4]

Bystander A did not affirmatively create the risk, but merely failed to prevent it from materializing. The requirement of feasance is not satisfied, and the absence of duty absolves the bystander of liability for not protecting or rescuing the blind man from injury.

---

* *See infra* section F (discussing duty created by special relationships).

Without a duty to rescue, the requirements of tort law can diverge from the requirements of morality. As courts have recognized, the bystander might be a "moral monster" for failing to rescue, but that is a matter for his or her conscience and not tort law.[5]

This limitation of tort liability could stem from an unappealing aspect of individual autonomy. The concept is contentious in important respects, but autonomy "is generally understood to refer to the capacity to be one's own person, to live one's life according to reasons and motives that are taken as one's own and not the product of manipulative or distorting external forces."[6] Someone who chooses not to rescue another is living his or her "life according to reasons and motives that are taken" as his or her own; for tort law to impose some other choice on the individual could be "manipulative" or paternalistic. The need to protect individual autonomy might explain this limitation of duty, even though it allows a "moral monster" to escape liability for not undertaking an easy rescue.[7]

This rationale becomes problematic once we consider how tort law regulates risky behavior that is governed by the tort duty. For this behavior, tort law requires the actor to exercise precaution as a matter of reasonable care. Why isn't this requirement a form of paternalism that impermissibly intrudes on the actor's ability to live "life according to reasons and motives that are taken" as his or her own? Any form of tort liability necessarily limits the autonomy of a duty holder in a particular manner, which is why tort law must give equal weight or concern to the autonomy of all individuals, not merely a specific right holder or duty holder. The injury suffered by the blind man who was not rescued severely impairs his autonomy. Why doesn't the equal concern for his autonomy justify a duty for the bystander to incur the slight burden of undertaking an easy rescue? As these questions suggest, the concern that a duty to rescue would unfairly limit individual autonomy does not persuasively explain why tort law rejects the duty.[8]

A stronger rationale involves the practical considerations of administrability and institutional choice. A tort duty requiring an easy rescue would be difficult to limit. What would prevent the duty from being applied to wealthy individuals who could easily save others by paying for medicine and food? Such a duty could eventually require massive redistributions of wealth and effort, an outcome far removed from the case of a blind man crossing the street. The liability rule must somehow distinguish the "easy rescue" of the blind man from these other, more problematic forms of rescue. When this line-drawing problem is evaluated as a matter of institutional choice, the appeal of criminal liability becomes evident. Prosecutorial discretion can limit criminal liability to cases of easy rescue. Prosecutors can indict a bystander who lets a blind man be hit by an oncoming car and ignore individuals who do not redistribute their wealth to reduce hunger. Criminal penalties are also flexible, unlike tort liability fixed at the level of compensatory damages. A small criminal fine, such as $100, can be a sufficient sanction for a bystander's failure to undertake an easy rescue. Consistent with this reasoning, a few states have adopted criminal statutes that levy a small fine on individuals in these cases.[9] The flexibility afforded by the criminal law is a decisive advantage in this context, providing a good example of how duty can be defensibly limited by concerns of "institutional competence and administrative difficulties."[10]

B. Foreseeability

"In order that an act may be negligent it is necessary that the actor should realize that it involves a risk of causing harm to some interest of another, such as the interest in bodily security, which is protected against unintended invasion."[11] If the actor knew or should have known that his or her conduct would create a risk of injury, then the risk is *foreseeable* and governed by the duty to exercise reasonable care.

As Holmes explained, "the only possible purpose of introducing this moral element is to make the power of avoiding the evil complained of a condition of liability. There is no such power where the evil cannot be foreseen."[12] This rationale has been more extensively developed by legal philosophers:

> The normative power of this conception . . . resides in the idea that the exercise of a person's positive agency, under circumstances in which a harmful outcome could have been foreseen and avoided, leads us to regard her as the author of the outcome. Others can appropriately say of her, and she can say of herself, that she did it, and this is true even if other factors (some of which might be the acts of other persons) also causally contributed to the harm. The agent acted and caused harm under circumstances in which she had a sufficient degree of control to avoid its occurrence, and for that reason she has a special responsibility for the outcome that other persons do not have. That we view outcome-responsibility as reason-affecting in this way is part of our deepest self-understanding of what it means to be a moral agent capable of both acting in the world and acknowledging responsibility for what one has done.[13]

This rationale explains why the element of duty is limited to the foreseeable outcomes of the individual's affirmative conduct. Unforeseeable outcomes are not fairly attributable to the individual's exercise of autonomy, preventing tort law from making the actor legally responsible for such harms.

A foreseeable risk refers to a category of accidents that a reasonable person would consider in deciding whether to take a particular safety precaution. While driving an automobile, for example, the reasonable person would consider how a particular form of safe driving would reduce the risk of injury for other drivers, pedestrians, and nearby property owners. The

safety decision does not depend on the identities of other drivers, pedestrians, or landowners, but instead is made by
reference to the general categories of other drivers, pedestrians, and so on. An unforeseeable risk, by contrast, involves
a categorical harm that would not be contemplated by the
reasonable person at the time of the safety decision. Because
an unforeseeable risk does not factor into the safety decision, it
is excluded from the standard of reasonable care by a limitation
of duty, illustrating how duty defines the risks encompassed by
the standard of reasonable care.

Due to the requirement of foreseeability, negligence liability
has a relational structure that was famously recognized in
Palsgraf v. Long Island Railroad Co., which held that a plaintiff
can recover only by showing that the defendant's breach of duty
constitutes " 'a wrong' to herself; i.e., a violation of her own right,
and not merely a wrong to someone else, nor conduct 'wrongful'
because unsocial."[14] According to the *Restatement (Second)*,
this requirement is satisfied only if the defendant "create[d] a
recognizable risk of harm to the [plaintiff] individually, or to a
class of persons — as for example, all persons within a given area
of danger — of which the [plaintiff] is a member."[15] A defendant's duty is limited to those right holders who were foreseeably
threatened by the conduct in question, making negligence
liability relational in this sense.

Is this a rule of duty, however? Whether the plaintiff in
Palsgraf was a foreseeable victim depended entirely on the
particular circumstances of that case — the nature of the conduct in question, the plaintiff's location relative to the tortious
conduct, and so on. These are case-specific issues for the jury
and not categorical issues governed by duty analysis, explaining
why courts and scholars have long disagreed about the meaning of *Palsgraf*.[16]

The confusion stems from two different holdings in *Palsgraf*
that the court needed to make to conclude that the defendant

owed no duty to the plaintiff. The court first adopted a rule limiting duty to the foreseeable victims of the unreasonable conduct. This rule is entirely categorical in nature and has nothing to do with the particular aspects of the case, making it a rule of duty. Having decided this categorical duty issue, *Palsgraf* then addressed the separate case-specific question of whether the plaintiff was in fact within the category of fore-seeable victims. Like any other case-specific issue, the matter should be resolved by the jury. Like any other jury question, judges can make the finding as a matter of law by determining that no reasonable juror could find otherwise. *Palsgraf* made such a determination. The court held that "varying inferences" about foreseeability were not possible, as the parties "by conces-sion" agreed that the risk to the plaintiff was not foreseeable.[17] This holding, in effect, meant that a reasonable juror could only conclude that the plaintiff was an unforeseeable victim.[18] Based on the court's prior holding that duty excludes unforeseeable victims, it followed that the defendant owed no duty to the plaintiff with respect to the injuries in question.

Despite these two distinctive holdings in *Palsgraf*, many courts have mistakenly deemed any duty issue to be purely a matter of law for resolution by judges, without recognizing that the issue of whether the particular plaintiff was a foreseeable victim depends on whether a reasonable juror could make "varying inferences" about this case-specific matter. The reasonable-juror standard constrains the discretion of judges. By ignoring this standard, these courts have enhanced the decision-making power of judges at the expense of the jury.

To avoid this usurpation of the jury's role, the *Restatement (Third)* has moved this particular issue from the element of duty to the element of proximate cause, which requires the jury to find that the plaintiff's injury was caused by a foresee-able risk created by the defendant's negligence.[19] By defini-tion, the injuries of an unforeseeable plaintiff must have been caused by an unforeseeable risk, so the defendant's negligence is never the proximate cause of an injury suffered by an unforeseeable victim. The absence of proximate cause is a sufficient ground for explaining why an unforeseeable victim cannot recover, as in *Palsgraf*. By relocating the case-specific issue of foreseeability to the element of proximate cause, the *Restatement (Third)* approach ensures that courts will treat the issue as a jury question. This approach leaves untouched the other holding in *Palsgraf* that defines duty in the categorical, relational terms of foreseeability.

To be sure, the relational conception of duty is also controversial. As the dissenting opinion in *Palsgraf* powerfully argued, "[d]ue care is a duty imposed on each one of us to protect society from unnecessary danger, not to protect *A, B,* or *C* alone."[20]

A relational conception of duty, though, does not have to be limited in the manner suggested by the *Palsgraf* dissent. Rather than limiting duty "to protect *A, B,* or *C* alone," the requirement of foreseeability turns the duty to exercise reasonable care into a rule generally applicable to different categories of foreseeable victims whose identity changes along with the risky conduct. As you drive up the street, the other drivers and pedestrians to whom you owe a duty are continually changing. When you get out of the car and engage in some other type of risky behavior, the categories of foreseeable victims change again. The tort duty can govern any form of affirmative conduct creating a foreseeable risk of harm "to others even though the nature of that harm and the identity of the harmed person or harmed interest is unknown," and so in this essential respect "everyone has a duty of care to the whole world."[21]

C. The Ordinary Duty of Care

The typical negligence case involves a plaintiff who has suffered *physical harm* consisting of bodily injury or damage to tangible property—the components of the individual interest in physical security.* When the security interest has been harmed, the plaintiff can also recover for consequential harms to the other interests in emotional tranquility and intangible forms of property like money. For example, a negligent driver who hits a pedestrian is liable for damages that compensate the pedestrian's physical harms and other harms such as pain and suffering, lost wages, and medical expenses caused by the physical harm.†

A right holder is protected against this category of harms by the *general* or *ordinary duty of care*, which we can express in more formal terms that will be useful in later discussions. The requirements of reasonable care depend on a balancing of "the overall level of the foreseeable risk created by the actor's conduct" with "the burdens that the precautions, if adopted, would entail" for the actors or others.[22] Thus, if B represents the burden or cost of a precaution that the duty holder must exercise as a matter of reasonable care ® to eliminate a probability P of causing a loss L, then the general or ordinary duty of care can be compactly expressed in these terms. That is, for any accident involving physical harm, a risk-creating actor has a duty to take any precaution for which

$$B \text{ ® } P \bullet (L_{physical} + L_{emotional} + L_{economic})$$

As this formulation makes clear, the element of duty defines the risks for which the actor is legally responsible

---

* Tangible property is an important component of individual identity, so the concern for autonomy or self-determination explains why the security interest includes this form of property. *Compare* Oliver W. Holmes, *The Path of the Law*, 10 Harv. L. Rev. 457, 477 (1897) ("A thing which you have enjoyed and used as your own for a long time, whether property or an opinion, takes root in your being and cannot be torn away without you resenting the act and trying to defend yourself, however you came by it.").

† *See* Chapter 14, section I (describing categories of compensatory damages).

(the $P \bullet L$ terms). Consequently, duty must first be specified before tort law can determine the burdens or safety precautions (represented by the term B) required as a matter of reasonable care (the logical operator ®), explaining why duty is the first element of negligence liability.

The ordinary duty of care is so well established that it is presumed to exist. "[I]n cases involving physical harm, courts ordinarily need not concern themselves with the existence or content of this ordinary duty."[23]

For this reason, one can study negligence law by assuming the existence of the ordinary or general duty, leaving the permutations of this duty for later study. Those taking this approach can skip ahead to the next section covering the standard of reasonable care.

Like any other tort issue, extended analysis of duty enables one to gain insights about the underlying nature of tort liability. Duty typically excludes emotional or economic harms unless they stem from a tortiously caused physical harm. The nature of harm affects duty, requiring some explanation for why duty is formulated in this manner.

D. Emotional Harms

Consider again the car driver who negligently hits a pedestrian, and now consider the bystanders and family members who suffer emotional distress as a result. These third parties are foreseeable victims of the negligence, yet the defendant ordinarily has no duty to compensate their emotional harms. Traditionally, courts denied recovery for stand-alone emotional harms, unless the defendant's conduct was not merely negligent but amounted to some other tort such as libel or slander. The bar to recovery partially eroded over time, and today most jurisdictions allow recovery for the negligent infliction of emotional distress under limited conditions. Typically, such a claim is available only if the plaintiff was within the "zone of danger"

[handwritten: Limitation by zone of danger]

or physically threatened by the defendant's unreasonable conduct, causing him or her to suffer the emotional distress.[24]

This limitation on duty seems arbitrary. Why is a grieving mother who was not in the "zone of danger" denied recovery for emotional distress when she saw the accident that killed her child? Unable to answer this question, some jurisdictions allow parents and close family members to recover in these cases while still limiting duty in other ways that seem equally arbitrary.[25]

[handwritten: why limit duty?] According to courts, the reasons for limiting duty include the difficulty of determining monetary damages for purely emotional harms; the difficulty of assessing the existence and severity of emotional injuries; the difficulty of knowing whether monetary damages meaningfully compensate emotional injuries; and the difficulty of limiting the number of emotional claims that can be brought as the result of a single tortious accident.

These rationales for limiting duty are unsatisfactory. The concerns regarding the computation and compensatory nature of emotional distress damages are hard to defend given that such damages are available in the ordinary negligence case involving physical harm. *[handwritten: Fraud regrads more valid]* The separate concern about fraud is valid, due to the possibility that stand-alone emotional distress claims are more easily faked or exaggerated than other claims. That concern, though, does not require a limitation of duty, as the problem of fraudulent claims could be addressed by more stringent standards of proof. Indeed, these concerns "have been answered many times, and it is threshing old straw to deal with them."[26] The only remaining concern pertains to the "floodgates problem" of too many suits. This concern merely begs the question. Any limitation of duty necessarily limits liability, presumably because liability would otherwise be excessive. What makes liability for stand-alone harms excessive?

According to the conventional rationale:

> It would be an entirely unreasonable burden on all human
> activity if the defendant who has endangered one person were

to be compelled to pay for the lacerated feelings of every other person disturbed by reason of it, including every bystander shocked at an accident, and every distant relative of the person injured, as well as all his friends.[27]

Like the other rationales for limiting duty, this one begs the question of why liability for stand-alone emotional harms would be excessive. Perhaps such liability would be "entirely unreasonable" because a negligent defendant would then incur an amount of total liability disproportionate to the wrongdoing. Proportionality certainly matters for purposes of retribution — the punishment should "fit" the crime — but the tort obligation in question is one of compensation and not retribution. As a matter of compensation, the tort obligation is not disproportionate given that the defendant's negligence foreseeably caused the emotional harms, leaving us with the unanswered question of why liability for stand-alone emotional harms would be excessive.*

The conventional justification for the duty limitation also casts tort law in a bad light. If a negligent actor's interests justify the limitation of duty, then tort law would give the unreasonable liberty interests of the negligent actor legal priority over the emotional interests of a foreseeable victim. Such a priority would devalue emotional interests in a manner that

---

* Moreover, if the total compensatory obligations of a negligent defendant can be limited on grounds of proportionality, then a mitigation defense should be available to those unlucky defendants whose negligence consisted of slight inadvertence that caused severe physical harms to another. Such a defendant could face financially ruinous liability for an act that does not even merit personal reproach. Tort law does not reduce the defendant's liability in these cases, presumably because the damages merely compensate the plaintiff's physical harms. The absence of a mitigation defense indicates that duty is not limited out of some concern that the obligation to pay compensatory damages must always be proportionate to the wrongdoing. For a good discussion of the associated normative issues, *see* Jeremy Waldron, *Moments of Carelessness and Massive Loss*, in *Philosophical Foundations of Tort Law* 387 (David G. Owen ed., Oxford U. Press 1995).

is hard to defend, making tort law vulnerable to withering criticism that some indefensible rationale, like gender bias, explains the rule.[28]

Any limit on recovery for those who suffer stand-alone emotional harms must mean that their emotional interests are subordinate to someone else's prioritized interests. The most obvious interests having such a priority are the security interests of those individuals who were also harmed by the negligent conduct. The autonomy of these individuals is limited by their physical harms and the consequential emotional harms, explaining why each type of harm is compensable and encompassed within the duty of ordinary care. Nevertheless, as a categorical matter (the relevant frame for duty analysis), an individual's ability to act in the world is more restricted by physical harm than emotional distress. Each matters, but physical harms are generally of greater concern than emotional harms. A priority of the security interest, therefore, could explain why the duty of a negligent defendant excludes most stand-alone emotional harms.

To determine whether protection of the security interest justifies such a limitation of duty, consider the duty that would exist if the negligent car driver were liable for all foreseeable emotional injuries. A rule of no-duty decides a case only when the defendant's unreasonable behavior caused injury to the plaintiff. To have acted unreasonably, the defendant must have breached an established duty of reasonable care — the ordinary duty in cases involving physical harm. That breach makes it possible to ask whether the negligent defendant's duty should be expanded to include stand-alone emotional harms. Suppose the risk of an automobile accident threatens a total of n individuals: the pedestrian who faces the risk of bodily injury (individual 1) and other $(n-1)$ individuals such as family, friends, and bystanders who would foreseeably suffer emotional distress in the event that the pedestrian were injured. In this case, the driver's ordinary duty changes to the following expanded duty:

$$B ® P \bullet \{(L_{1:physical} + L_{1:emotional} + L_{1:economic})$$
$$+ L_{2:emotional} + \cdots + L_{n:emotional}\}$$

If a driver negligently causes an accident, all *n* individuals could seek full compensation for their injuries. Such a duty would create a "floodgates problem" of excessive liability as courts have long maintained. Frequently, the sum total of these judgments will exceed the insurance and other assets of the ordinary defendant within the category of negligent actors. Unless the number of claimants for any given negligent act is limited, bankruptcy becomes a concern.

In the event that a defendant goes bankrupt, the law of bankruptcy determines how the limited assets of the defendant's bankrupt estate must be distributed to satisfy a total amount of debt exceeding those assets. The claim of each debtor cannot be fully satisfied. Each of these claimants does not have to be treated equally, however, if there are substantive differences in the nature of their claims against the bankrupt estate. Insofar as the claims can be prioritized, bankruptcy law permits some claimants to recover more than others. Some can even be fully compensated, with others receiving nothing.

Within the priority scheme adopted by bankruptcy law, no special priority attaches to tort plaintiffs who are owed money for compensatory damages from the bankrupt defendant. As a matter of bankruptcy law, each tort claimant gets less than full recovery from the bankrupt estate, including the physically harmed victims. Any form of tort liability that is likely to bankrupt the defendant, therefore, will predictably prevent all tort claimants from receiving full recovery.[29]

In theory, tort law could try to address this problem with a procedural rule like the "worst go first," but common-law courts were not traditionally equipped with the procedural powers of case consolidation and the like that are required by such a procedural rule.* To address the problem of bankruptcy and the associated limitations of recovery for all tort claimants, tort law could only adopt substantive rules that prioritize among claimants as a means of staving off bankruptcy.

Courts have long recognized that a duty encompassing all stand-alone emotional harms would predictably lead to bankruptcy. They could defensibly address this problem by limiting the defendant's duty to exclude stand-alone emotional harms. The limitation of liability significantly reduces the number of potential tort claimants, thereby reducing the likelihood of bankruptcy and increasing the likelihood that the physically harmed victims will receive full compensation. The priority of the security interest can justify the limitation of liability for reasons that are consistent with the concern of excessive liability repeatedly invoked by courts.[30]

For these same reasons, courts can defensibly limit duty for stand-alone emotional harms in seemingly arbitrary ways, such as the "zone of danger" rule. The limitations serve the purpose of limiting duty to a small enough group of claimants capable of being fully compensated by the ordinary defendant in most cases. How the line is drawn will inevitably appear unfair in some cases. A general concern about bankruptcy, for example, is not apparent in a particular case involving a wealthy defendant.[†]

---

* Today courts can consolidate cases or control their dockets in a manner that would allow those tort claimants with the most severe injuries to litigate their claims first. Many courts have done so in the asbestos context. Any tort procedure that is designed to exhaust the defendant's assets in some prioritized manner, however, will predictably induce many defendants to file for bankruptcy. Once the defendant files for bankruptcy, the tort claims are governed by bankruptcy law, which consolidates all the tort proceedings before the bankruptcy court and administers those claims according to the rules of bankruptcy, an outcome that leaves each tort claimant with less than full recovery. A procedural approach does not adequately solve the compensatory problem.

† It also would be difficult to justify a duty that depended on the defendant's wealth. The duty of reasonable care does not include an obligation to earn money in order to protect the security interests of right holders, making the duty holder's wealth irrelevant to the substantive content of the duty.

A categorical concern about the compensation of physical harms is also not apparent in a case involving little or no such harm. Any apparent unfairness in a particular case can be countered, though, if courts adequately explain why liability must be limited for the general category of cases under consideration — the type of inquiry mandated by duty analysis.

This rationale for limiting liability complements the conventional rationale that it would be unreasonably burdensome for a negligent defendant to compensate every foreseeable stand-alone emotional harm. Any negligent actor faces the threat of bankruptcy by causing extensive physical harm, so the mere threat of bankruptcy does not sufficiently justify a limitation of duty (as illustrated by the asbestos cases).* Anyone, though, can slip up and negligently cause an accident. Insofar as an inadvertent mistake becomes increasingly likely to cause financial ruin, the associated duty becomes increasingly burdensome. By itself, that burden does not justify a limitation of duty, but the overall concern for autonomy — protection of both the right holder's security interest and the duty holder's liberty interest — can justify limiting duty to exclude most stand-alone emotional harms.

E. Economic Loss

Consider again the negligent driver who physically harms a pedestrian. Suppose the injured pedestrian is a sole proprietor

---

* So far, asbestos liabilities have driven at least 75 companies into bankruptcy. "The original villains, companies like Johns Manville and Raybestos Manhattan, caused far more harm than they could pay for. The rest of American industry [that used asbestos-containing products] has been made to fill the gap. That is not fair." Patrick M. Hanlon & Anne Smetak, *Asbestos Changes*, 62 N.Y.U. Ann. Surv. Am. L. 525, 535 (2007). The alleged unfairness involves liability that is disproportionate to the wrongdoing of many current asbestos defendants. As previously discussed, however, tort liability does not always have to be disproportionate to the wrongdoing. Having caused extensive physical harm, the current asbestos defendants are fairly subject to compensatory liability, despite the high likelihood that they will be driven into bankruptcy as a result.

who employs five individuals, and those five workers lose their jobs because the injured proprietor can no longer run the business. Although the injured proprietor (as pedestrian) can recover for the lost profits caused by the physical harm, the workers cannot recover their lost wages from the negligent driver pursuant to the *economic loss rule*.[31]

These cases pose many of the problems present in the cases involving stand-alone emotional harms. "The common thread running through the limitations on recovery for emotional distress, consortium, and economic loss is not difficult to identify. . . . [I]t is an age-old concern about extending liability *ad infinitum* for the consequences of a negligent act."[32]

As before, the concern of excessive liability can be depicted by the duty that would exist if the defendant were liable for the physically harmed victim (individual 1) and the $(n-1)$ other individuals who foreseeably suffered pure economic loss, a group that is likely to be larger than those suffering pure emotional harms due to the ripple effect of commercial or economic harms in a market economy:

$$B \circledR P \bullet \{(L_{1:physical} + L_{1:emotional} + L_{1:economic}) + L_{2:economic} + \cdots + L_{n:economic}\}$$

The expanded duty clearly is more burdensome, but limiting the duty solely out of concern for the negligent defendant's interests is subject to the same critique that undermines that justification in the case of pure emotional harm. The defendant has acted negligently, and an unreasonable liberty interest presumably is subordinate to the interests of those individuals whose liberty has been restricted by the loss of money foreseeably caused by the defendant's unreasonable behavior. Such a priority of interests is inherent in the ordinary duty of care, which enables physically harmed plaintiffs to recover for their consequential economic losses. That priority is also inherent in the tort rules allowing some plaintiffs to recover for pure economic loss, making it even more difficult to justify the limitation of duty exclusively with the defendant's interests.

Until the 1950s, it was "virtually impossible" for a plaintiff to recover for pure economic loss absent privity or a contractual relationship with the defendant.[33] Since then, the bar to recovery has eroded somewhat, so that today plaintiffs may be able to recover for negligently inflicted, stand-alone economic harms in situations lacking privity. Such a duty of care typically is based on the defendant's special relationship with the plaintiff, like that between an attorney and client, or the defendant's voluntary undertaking of the duty.[34] So defined, the duty encompasses a limited number of claimants and governs situations, such as legal or accountant malpractice, that usually do not involve physical harms. By allowing a limited number of plaintiffs to recover for pure economic loss, these tort rules give the economic interests of those plaintiffs legal priority over the economic interests of negligent defendants. That priority is not unique to plaintiffs of this type, however, because "economic loss cases lacking [the specter of widespread tort liability] do not receive distinctive treatment" from the courts.[35]

In light of the various instances in which a defendant incurs liability for pure economic loss, why is such liability unfair for the defendant in other cases? Rather than rely on the claim that such liability is somehow unfair for the defendant, a more persuasive rationale relies on the security interest of physically harmed individuals. As a categorical matter, an individual's ability to act in the world is more restricted by physical harm than pure economic loss. Each matters, but physical harms are generally of greater concern. A priority of the security interest, therefore, could explain why the duty of a negligent defendant excludes pure economic loss for the category of cases in which the duty holder's conduct ordinarily creates a risk of physical harm.

Due to the problem of bankruptcy, adequate protection of the security interest can justify limiting the defendant's liability to increase the likelihood that the defendant will have sufficient assets to compensate the physically harmed victims. As compared to extended liability for pure emotional harm, extended liability for pure economic loss is even more likely to bankrupt the ordinary defendant. In both instances, the priority of the security interest justifies a limitation of duty to stave off bankruptcy, thereby giving the physically harmed victims a much higher chance of receiving full compensation for their injuries.

This reasoning is most evident in cases of *medical monitoring*. In these cases, the defendants breached the ordinary duty of care and exposed the plaintiffs to an unreasonable risk of physical harm, such as a substantially increased chance of getting cancer. In light of this risk, these plaintiffs require periodic, costly medical testing, leading them to seek tort recovery for these costs on the ground that the harm was caused by the defendant's negligence. These claims would seem to be barred by the economic loss rule, as the cost of testing is financial and the plaintiffs are not seeking damages for any existing harms to their body or tangible property. Nevertheless, a substantial number of courts allow medical monitoring claims, reasoning that the claim involves the core interest protected by tort law:

> It is difficult to dispute that an individual has an interest in avoiding expensive diagnostic examinations just as he or she has an interest in avoiding physical injury. When a defendant negligently invades this interest, the injury to which is neither speculative nor resistant to proof, it is elementary that the defendant should make the plaintiff whole.[36]

The justification for a medical monitoring award equates the expenditure of money on medical monitoring with the plaintiff's interest in physical security. The plaintiff needs to undergo the costly tests to protect against future physical harm, making these purely monetary expenditures a means of protecting the security interest that can be encompassed by the ordinary tort duty. Protection of the security interest explains why plaintiffs can recover for these pure economic losses.

That same concern has recently caused some courts to reject medical monitoring claims on the ground that "[l]itigation of these preinjury claims could drain resources needed to compensate those with manifest physical injuries and a more immediate need for medical care."[37] As these cases show, courts prioritize claims when the available assets are not sufficient to compensate all tort claimants, leading them to adopt no-duty rules that increase the likelihood that the physically harmed claimants will receive full compensation.

For these same reasons, plaintiffs can recover for pure economic loss in other types of cases.* In accountant or legal malpractice cases, for example, the negligent misconduct does not threaten physical harm (again, as a categorical matter), so the duty can be limited to protect the most important set of economic interests. By limiting duty to the third-party beneficiary of an audit or will, this rule ameliorates the concern that more widespread liability would bankrupt the negligent defendant and leave the most important set of economic interests without adequate recourse to compensation. As in the context of stand-alone emotional harms, duty limitations for economic loss can be justified by a priority of interests involving potential claimants rather than the negligent defendant.[†]

This rationale complements the conventional rationale that duty must be limited to protect a negligent defendant from excessive liability. Consider a driver who negligently causes a minor fender bender on a crowded freeway. These accidents

---

* In most jurisdictions, plaintiffs can recover the financial costs of removing asbestos from public buildings, a liability rule substantively equivalent to the one that allows plaintiffs to recover the financial costs of medical monitoring. *See* Mark Geistfeld, *The Analytics of Duty: Medical Monitoring and Related Forms of Economic Loss*, 88 Va. L. Rev. 1921, 1944–1945 (2002).

† Indeed, most duty cases not involving a special relationship can be conceptualized as involving third-party contract beneficiaries. *See* Dobbs on Torts § 452, at 1286.

routinely cause hundreds of other motorists to lose significant amounts of time as they sit in the ensuing traffic jam, a form of pure economic loss. A duty encompassing these intangible economic harms could easily bankrupt many motorists who inadvertently bump into another car. By substantially increasing the likelihood of bankruptcy, the more expansive duty can substantially restrict the liberty interests of drivers. By itself, the burden does not justify a limitation of duty, but an equal concern for autonomy — protection of the right holder's security interest and the duty holder's liberty interest — can justify a duty excluding most stand-alone economic harms.

F. Special Relationships and the Enabling Torts

Tort law originated as a means of compensating the victims of criminal wrongdoing, so there is nothing controversial about predicating tort liability on the defendant's criminal conduct. A more controversial issue is whether the defendant can incur liability for crimes committed by someone else. If a third-party criminal caused the plaintiff's injury, should the plaintiff be able to recover from a noncriminal defendant who could have prevented the harm by exercising reasonable care?

Protecting someone from a criminal attack is no different than "rescuing" that person from the criminal, and tort law does not recognize a duty to rescue. An important exception is created by a *special relationship*:

> There is no duty so to control the conduct of a third person as to prevent him from causing physical harm to another unless
>
> (a) a special relation exists between the actor and the third person which imposes a duty upon the actor to control the third person's conduct, or
>
> (b) a special relation exists between the actor and the other which gives the other a right to protection.[38]

In a special relationship, the duty holder is often in the best position to protect the right holder from criminal attack. For example, a university has a duty to protect its students from criminal attacks while they are on campus. Students are also able to protect themselves, but the university can take many preventive measures that are impractical for a student, like hiring guards. Other relationships of this type include carriers and passengers, hotels and guests, landlords and tenants, prisons and inmates, and landowners and business visitors. Based on this formulation of duty, a noncriminal defendant (like a university) can incur liability for unreasonably inadequate protection that enables a criminal to injure the plaintiff (a student).[39]

The *enabling torts* also encompass cases in which the noncriminal defendant had a preexisting relationship with the third-party criminal who caused the plaintiff's harm. The relationship typically gives the noncriminal defendant the opportunity to control the criminal impulses of the third party, thereby creating a tort duty to those foreseeable individuals who might be harmed by the criminally disposed third party. For example, those in charge of persons with dangerous propensities, such as criminals or the insane, have a duty to reasonably restrain their charges from harming others.[40]

The enabling torts define duty in terms of the risk threatened by third-party unlawful behavior. The duty is based on the social fact that unlawful behavior frequently occurs. The prevalence of such behavior shows that the threat of criminal and tort liability does not always force individuals to act lawfully. The "inability to effectively reach the putative wrongdoer himself, either through criminal or tort sanctions," creates a "deterrence gap" that provides the basis for the tort duty.[41]

This aspect of the duty relies on an important assumption about how individuals respond to legal rules, an assumption that is critical for the formulation of liability rules.* Anyone who contemplates engaging in criminal conduct presumably considers the cost of criminal and civil sanctions. Those sanctions ordinarily are high enough for deterrence purposes under situations of perfect enforcement, so that criminally disposed actors who know they will be caught and sanctioned will usually act lawfully. Situations of underenforcement, which involve any circumstance that reduces the likelihood a criminal will be caught and sanctioned, reduce the cost of crime and can foreseeably lead a self-interested person to act unlawfully. By making the risk of unlawful behavior foreseeable, tort law assumes that individuals predictably ignore their legal obligations for selfish reasons.[42]

Unlocked doors, for example, make it easier for someone to enter the building and steal things from tenants without getting caught. By increasing the likelihood of detection, the landlord can reduce the incidence of such illegal behavior. The landlord's ability to reduce risk in this manner, created by the pre-existing special relationship with the tenant, supplies the basis for imposing a tort duty on the landlord to protect the tenant from the criminal or tortious misconduct of a third party.

G. Policy-Based Limitations

Any limitation of duty will "cede control over the conduct at issue to some other legal field . . . or leave that conduct legally unregulated."[43] In limiting duty, courts can rely on the policy rationale that the conduct in question should be regulated by another body of law or left unregulated altogether.

---

* *See* Chapter 4, section I (explaining why liability rules must make assumptions about how individuals respond to legal obligations); Chapter 12, section II (showing how the enabling torts rely on a behavioral assumption inconsistent with the assumption that courts have made when applying the rule of strict liability for abnormally dangerous activities).

As we found earlier, liability for the failure to undertake an easy rescue is probably best ceded to the criminal law, explaining why the tort duty is limited by the requirement of feasance.* Another type of duty limitation involves reliance on the contractual relationship.

In *Strauss v. Belle Realty Company*, for example, the plaintiff tenant of an apartment building was seeking compensation for his bodily injuries caused by the defendant utility's gross negligence that left most of New York City without power for 25 hours. The plaintiff was injured in a common area of the building, and electricity for the area was supplied by the defendant utility pursuant to a contract it had with the plaintiff's landlord. According to the New York Court of Appeals, the utility's duty did not extend to individuals like the plaintiff with whom it did not have a contractual relationship. In limiting duty, the court invoked the policy concerns involving the need to limit liability to "manageable levels" due to "the obvious impact of a city-wide deprivation of electric power, or to the impossibility of fixing a rational boundary once beyond the contractual relationship, or to the societal consequences of rampant liability."[44]

Limiting duty to the contractual relationship is defensible in cases involving the negligence liability of a public utility. The widespread use of electricity (or water) means that virtually everyone in the community pays for the service in one form or another, either directly as customer or indirectly in the form of higher prices. A tenant of an apartment building, for example, indirectly pays for the building's electricity in the monthly rent. From the individual's perspective, the liability faced by a utility creates both a burden (via higher prices) and a benefit (via risk reduction and, potentially, damages compensation). Under these conditions, the individual's full set of interests is best protected by a rule for which the benefits of

---

* *See supra* section A.

liability exceed the costs.* Tort liability passes this cost-benefit test only when it would deter or reduce risk, so the liability of a public utility can be defensibly limited to the minimal amount needed to produce the desired amount of deterrence.† A utility would have a sufficient financial incentive to exercise reasonable care if it could be sued by its direct customers. The additional suits brought by indirect customers would only increase the likelihood that the utility will be driven into bankruptcy, and any disruption of service would be detrimental for both direct and indirect customers. Bankruptcy would also prevent the direct customers from receiving full compensation for their injuries. A duty limited to the contractual relationship defensibly prioritizes the claims of direct customers over indirect customers in a manner that can be easily administered by courts, while permitting the amount of liability required for deterrence purposes.

A limitation of duty can also leave the conduct unregulated, making other policy considerations relevant. A good example is provided by the limited duty a landowner owes to trespassers. Under the general rule,

> The landowner owed no duty of reasonable care to trespassers. Instead, the duty was merely not to cause intentional injury, to set a trap, or to cause wanton injury. The landowner

---

* A liability rule can be formulated in cost-benefit terms for cases involving an *intrapersonal* conflict of the right holder's interests, even if such a liability rule is unfair for cases involving an *interpersonal* conflict between the right holder's security interest and the duty holder's liberty interest. *See infra* section II.B. *See also* Chapter 7, section II.B (discussing the issue in the context of private necessity).

† *See* Chapter 4, section I (discussing the properties of efficient liability rules). For this reason, optimal deterrence does not require a limitation of liability to the contractual relationship in all cases. The issue depends on the extent to which a particular formulation of duty is likely to induce the desired forms of safe behavior. For example, the claims that could be filed by direct customers provide substantially more enforcement of the duty for utilities as compared to product sellers, explaining why the two types of cases involve different duties. *Compare* Chapter 1, section III.A (discussing rejection of privity requirement in products liability).

was thus free to maintain dangerous conditions like excavations and also free to carry on dangerous operations such as high speed trains.[45]

The limited duty leaves risky activity unregulated, but it is "slightly less harsh tha[n] it might sound because in many cases to which it would apply, the landowner probably was not negligent even under an ordinary care standard."[46]

Duty is a categorical rule, so a limitation of duty forecloses entire classes of tort claims, including some that would otherwise be meritorious. Suppose that for every 100 cases in which a trespasser suffered injury, only two involved negligence on the landowner's part. A duty to exercise reasonable care would subject the landowner to liability in those two cases — a desirable outcome — but the landowner would not necessarily be sued only twice. Any trespasser who was injured on the property could potentially file suit, and defending only one suit can still be quite burdensome for a landowner who prevails at trial. The burden of legal defense factors into duty analysis, which considers the landowner's interests for the entire class of cases and not merely those involving meritorious claims. A duty that results in too many lawsuits relative to the number of meritorious claims can be disproportionately burdensome for the duty holder, justifying a limitation of the duty.[47]

Important social interests can also justify a limitation of duty. For example, rather than face the prospect of being sued, a landowner could fence the property to keep people off the land. This outcome is problematic insofar as the community would like to have limited access to private lands for recreational use. To make private lands more accessible for this purpose, the majority of states have limited a landowner's liability with recreational-use statutes.* These statutes typically

---

* Largely enacted since the 1960s, 42 states now have such statutes "passed for the purpose of encouraging landowners to hold open to the public their lands and waters for recreational use." Prosser and Keeton on Torts § 60, at 415–416.

limit the duty to instances of wanton or willful misconduct, illustrating how duty can be limited as a quid pro quo for the creation of an important public benefit.*

Moreover, any category can be refined, enabling courts to reformulate a limited duty to make it even less likely that it would bar desirable claims. Courts have adopted numerous exceptions to the rule of no duty for landowners, extending the duty of reasonable care to discovered or known trespassers, reasonably anticipated trespassers, and children who are drawn onto the land by an attractive nuisance. For the remaining class of cases, there is a very low likelihood of anyone trespassing on the land and an even lower likelihood of a trespasser suffering injury. Within this refined category of no-duty cases, reasonable care will hardly ever require the landowner to reduce such a small chance of injury, a very slight safety benefit for right holders that is disproportionate to the categorical burden that the duty would otherwise impose on the occupiers of land.

This dynamic, however, has caused problems. Because a category can always be refined, at some point it can become so narrow that it does not sufficiently generalize beyond the facts of a particular case. These formulations of duty are inappropriate. As one court explained:

> [W]here, as here, the applicable duty relationship is well established, we do not believe New York law condones the limitation of a familiar liability rule simply to avoid placing a disproportionate burden on a defendant in a particular case. The law deals with that problem not by redefining

---

* An analogous outcome occurs with respect to the *charitable immunity*, a rule adopted by the common law that fully limited the liability of charitable or nonprofit organizations. The conventional rationales for the immunity were unpersuasive, leading most states to abolish it. A number, though, allow tort claims to be brought against charities, but deny "recovery to beneficiaries of the charity for injuries caused by the negligence of its ordinary employees, and most states having such a rule draw no distinction between paying and nonpaying beneficiaries." 5 Harper, James and Gray on Torts § 29.17, at 765.

the defendant's duties in each case, but by asking whether —
considering all the circumstances of the particular case — the
defendant breached its duty of care.[48]

The element of breach depends on the particular circumstances of the case and is an issue for the jury, unless the judge
decides as a matter of law that a reasonable juror could reach
only one conclusion about the matter. Nevertheless, some
courts have used the rubric of duty to limit liability as a matter
of law, independent of the reasonable-juror standard, even
though the holdings do not extend beyond the facts of the
case. These legal rulings "abuse" duty by inappropriately taking
issues from the jury.[49] To justify a limitation of duty, judges
must rely on "categorical considerations" sufficiently general to
govern a meaningful group of cases.[50]

II. THE STANDARD OF REASONABLE CARE

The typical jury instruction first defines negligence as the
failure to exercise ordinary care, and then defines "ordinary
care" in terms of the conduct of the reasonably careful or reasonably prudent person. The standard reduces to one of reasonable care, as "a 'reasonably careful person' (or a 'reasonably
prudent person') is one who acts with reasonable care."[51] To
recover, the plaintiff must prove that the defendant breached
this duty to exercise reasonable care — the second element of
a negligence claim.

So far, we have expressed the standard of reasonable care as
some sort of legal requirement, represented by an unspecified
logical operator ®, for the duty holder to incur the burden B of
taking a precaution to eliminate a foreseeable risk consisting of a
probability P that someone in the relevant category of right
holders would suffer harm or loss L. As this formulation B ®
PL implies, the standard of reasonable care has two components.

The first involves measurement of the precautionary burden B and the associated risk that would be eliminated by the precaution, PL. The burden of a precaution routinely varies across individuals. As compared to someone with more experience, for example, a beginner usually has a much harder time driving an automobile carefully. The measure of foreseeable risk can also differ across individuals. Although an omniscient being would know how everything always turns out, such knowledge is not required of us mere mortals, illustrating how the foreseeability of risk depends on the actor's knowledge of the relevant causal processes. The frame of reference, therefore, determines both the burden of a precaution and the foreseeable risks that would be eliminated by such a precaution. For purposes of reasonable care, tort law determines both factors by reference to the legal construct of a hypothetical *reasonable person.*

Once the characteristics of the reasonable person have been defined, tort law must then determine how much of a burden B such an actor would incur to eliminate the foreseeable risk PL. Are the requirements of reasonable care (the unspecified operator ®) fully captured by cost-benefit analysis, obligating the duty holder to take only those precautions for which the burden or cost is less than the reduced risk or safety benefit, $B < PL$? Or does B ® PL mean something else? To evaluate the defendant's conduct, tort law must determine what the standard of reasonable care actually requires of duty holders in particular circumstances, an issue that depends on the characteristics of the reasonable person.

A. The Reasonable Person

The reasonable person can have objective qualities, like ordinary or average traits within the community, or subjective qualities corresponding to the actor's personal traits. The policy issue is one of determining the extent to which negligence liability should account for individual differences. The common law's initial adoption of the purportedly generic "reasonable man" standard has evolved into the reasonable person standard. Why not instead formulate the rule in gender-specific terms, with a reasonable man standard for males, and a reasonable woman standard for females?[52] As this question suggests, the liability rule can be exclusively formulated in objective terms of the reasonable person, it can be formulated solely by reference to the subjective traits of the actor, or it can involve some mix of objective and subjective characteristics.

> By and large the law has chosen external, objective standards of conduct. The reasonably prudent [person] is, to be sure, endowed with some of the qualities of the person whose conduct is being judged, especially where the latter has greater knowledge, skill, or the like, than people generally. But many of the actor's shortcomings such as awkwardness, faulty perception, or poor judgment, are not taken into account if they fall below the general level of the community. This means that individuals are often held guilty of legal fault for failing to live up to a standard which as a matter of fact they cannot meet. Such a result shocks people who believe in refining the fault principle so as to make legal liability correspond more closely to personal moral shortcoming.[53]

Under an objective standard, one can act with no "personal moral shortcoming" and still be subject to negligence liability. For example, the reasonable person always complies perfectly with the requirements of reasonable care, unlike the ordinary person who can be inattentive or inadvertently make mistakes.[54] The reasonable person is a hypothetical legal construct that does not have to realistically describe the actor in question. Someone who does not comply with an unrealistic demand is not personally blameworthy or at fault, making the objectively defined rule of negligence liability "strict" in this particular way.

By recognizing how an objective standard creates pockets of no-fault or strict liability within the negligence rule, we can understand how tort law selects between objective and subjective formulations of the reasonable person standard. An approach that does not recognize this important attribute of negligence liability will find many of these rules to be puzzling.

> The problem is this. The law of negligence takes into account the personal characteristics of a child actor: the standard for judging whether a child's conduct was negligent is the conduct of a reasonably prudent child of the same age, intelligence, and experience. Similarly, the law of negligence takes into account the limitations of the physically disabled: the standard for judging whether a blind man's conduct was negligent, for example, is the conduct of a reasonably prudent blind person, and the standard is specially tailored in the same way for actors with other disabilities. Moreover, an actor suddenly stricken by an unforeseeable physical illness, such as a fainting spell or a heart attack, that makes it impossible for him to act voluntarily is held not liable in negligence for the harmful consequences. But the law of negligence steadfastly refuses to take into account the limitations of the mentally ill: the standard for judging whether the mentally ill actor's conduct was negligent is the conduct of the reasonably prudent sane person, and that standard is applied even when the actor was suddenly stricken by an unforeseeable mental illness.
>
> . . . What can possibly justify judges treating the mentally ill differently than they treat children and the physically disabled? Surely mental illness is just as cogent an excuse for otherwise blameworthy conduct as infancy or physical disability. Surely some forms of mental illness, just like infancy and physical disability, may make it practically impossible for the actor to conform his conduct to the ordinarily required standard. The different treatment of the mentally ill seems to be an unjustifiable anomaly in the law.[55]

Insofar as negligence liability should correspond to personal fault or blameworthiness, the distinctive treatment of the mentally ill is clearly an "unjustifiable anomaly." By requiring the mentally ill to act like reasonable people with normal mental capabilities, tort law has adopted a form of negligence liability that functions as a rule of no-fault or strict liability, for the insane obviously cannot satisfy this unrealistic behavioral demand. One simply incurs liability when his or her mental illness causes harm to another; personal fault or blameworthiness is irrelevant. Tort law does not impose such an unrealistic behavioral demand on children or the physically disabled, because it evaluates their conduct with a reasonable person standard that accounts for their subjective traits of age and physical capabilities. The subjective standard for children and the physically disabled makes negligence liability more dependent on personal fault or blameworthiness, unlike the objective standard for the mentally ill that functions as a form of strict liability, creating an anomaly that requires explanation.

The objective standard applies to the mentally ill because tort law is indifferent to the actor's motivations or reasons. "The standard which the community demands must be an objective and external one, rather than that of the individual judgment, good or bad, of the particular individual. It must be the same for all persons, since the law can have no favorites. . . ."[56] Due to this objective component of the reasonable person standard, the negligence inquiry does not evaluate the actor's state of mind. "A bad state of mind is neither necessary nor sufficient to show negligence. . . ."[57] Because the actor's state of mind is excluded from the liability inquiry, his or her motives for acting, whether deluded or otherwise, are not relevant. As long as the behavior violates the objective standard, actors with crazy motives or good motives are equally subject to negligence liability.

Unlike the objective standard, a pure subjective standard would let the duty holder define the law's requirements by exercising his or her "best judgment," even when doing so would be detrimental to the right holder's protected interest in physical security. To prevent the duty holder's state of mind from unilaterally determining the extent to which tort law protects the right holder's security interest, tort law relies on the objective standard.*

The objective standard also has a behavioral explanation. In deciding how to interact with strangers, an individual cannot realistically accommodate the subjective idiosyncrasies of everyone else. Instead, the individual considers various objective factors like average or ordinary skills and customary rules of behavior. Based on these objective considerations, individuals develop reasonable expectations of how others behave. The protection of those reasonable expectations can explain why tort law defines the duty in objective terms, because an objectively defined duty requires individuals to act in the manner that is reasonably expected by others.[58]

The objective standard is also easily administered by courts, unlike a subjective standard that requires a potentially unverifiable inquiry into the actor's state of mind. If the defendant could avoid liability by testifying that he or she acted with his or her "best judgment," how could the plaintiff disprove that testimony other than by reference to some external standard of behavior? The credibility of the defendant's testimony is likely to turn on how the defendant's behavior compared to others. As a practical matter, the objective standard might be the only administrable rule.

An objective standard, though, will not always correspond to the subjective traits of the actor, creating pockets of no-fault or strict liability within the negligence rule. Some actors who were motivated by nonblameworthy reasons, like mental

---

* *See* Chapter 5, section III (explaining why the unilateral decisions of a right holder or duty holder cannot alter the liability rule in a manner that would be detrimental to the other's autonomy).

illness, will incur (strict) liability. Any justification for the objective standard must explain why these actors are fairly subject to strict liability, unlike children and physically disabled actors who are subject to a less demanding reasonable person standard that accounts for their subjective traits of age and physical capabilities.

By departing from an objective standard of conduct, the actor creates a nonreciprocal risk. As a matter of equality or fairness between the interacting parties, one who creates a nonreciprocal risk is fairly subject to liability for the ensuing injuries, regardless of personal fault or blameworthiness. Insanity is an extreme example, but the behavior is fully analogous to any other abnormally dangerous activity that is subject to strict liability. The inequality of risk, and not personal fault, supplies the rationale for (strict) liability.*

As applied to children, this reasoning leads to a different conclusion. Everyone is a child at some point, and so any risks specific to children are reciprocal or common within the community and not subject to liability. To create a nonreciprocal risk, the child must behave more dangerously than would a reasonable child of similar age, explaining why the reasonable person standard accounts for the subjective quality of young age.

Regardless of reciprocity, strict liability can also be justified by the need to reduce a risky activity that is not adequately regulated by fault-based liability.† This deterrence rationale, though, would produce indefensible results when applied to children.

By requiring children to conform to an objectively defined adult standard of reasonable care, tort law could impose negligence liability on a child who violated that standard, even though the child acted reasonably by reference to his or her

---

* *See* Chapter 3, section III (explaining why nonreciprocal risky activities are subject to strict liability).

† *See* Chapter 3, section II (explaining how strict liability can deter risky activities).

age and experience. The child cannot be blamed for not acting like an adult, making the liability strict in this respect. Insofar as this pocket of strict liability could alter the behavior of children (a dubious premise), it could reduce risk only by increasing the cost of the activity, thereby causing children to engage in the activity less frequently. This outcome is indefensible. The activity in question involves children behaving like (reasonable) kids rather than adults. Any attempt to deter that activity—to force children to act like adults—would "burden unduly the child's growth to majority."[59] Even if strict liability could reduce the risky activity of childlike behavior, a concern for the autonomy or self-determination of children would justify an immunity from such liability.*

The importance of this analysis is apparent in cases involving children who engaged in an "adult" activity. In these cases, tort law requires the child to behave like a reasonable adult. The rule might seem straightforward—anyone who engages in an "adult" activity should behave like a reasonable adult—but courts have had a hard time identifying the distinguishing characteristics of such an activity. The conventional approach relies on the dangerousness of the activity.[60] The dangerousness of the activity, however, does not explain why courts have divided on the issue of whether an adult standard applies to the use of firearms. "A number of cases have applied a child standard of care to the handling of firearms."[61] If an "adult" activity is necessarily one that is dangerous, then the handling of firearms should be governed by the objective standard applicable to adults, contrary to the result reached by a number of courts. Rather than rely on the dangerousness of the activity, a better resolution of the issue is supplied by the underlying principles that govern the choice between negligence and strict liability.

As we found earlier, tort law cannot fairly impose strict liability on children for creating the reciprocal risks characteristic

---

* *See* Chapter 5, section III (explaining immunities from liability).

of childlike behavior in the community, explaining why the conduct is governed by a reasonable child standard. This ratio-nale does not apply to "adult" activities. Even if the child acted reasonably by reference to his or her age and abilities, the con-duct could still create a nonreciprocal risk for any activity that is uncommon for children in the community. By engaging in such an activity in a manner that also violates the objective adult standard, the child would create a nonreciprocal risk subject to (strict) liability. Insofar as this form of strict liability reduces risk, it would not "burden unduly" the growth of children. Kids do not need to engage in "adult" activities to mature properly. The issue does not depend on the dangerousness of the activity, explaining why the conventional approach does not satisfactorily explain the case law. Dangerous activities are often "adult" activities, but not necessarily so. Whether an activity is one for adults and governed by the objective standard instead depends on a policy determination that the activity is not an important component of childhood development within the community.

The cases that applied a child standard of care to the use of guns, for example, were all decided in the 1970s in jurisdictions where hunting quite plausibly was important for childhood devel-opment (Arkansas, New Mexico, Oregon, and Tennessee). Com-munities have changed significantly in this respect over time, and the more recent cases hold children to an adult standard of care when using firearms.[62] The evolving standard illustrates the social construction of tort law, a concept that explains why different communities can adopt different liability rules while still relying on the same underlying principle of liability.*

Reciprocity, however, does not explain why the reasonable person standard accounts for the actor's known physical lim-itations, such as blindness. Any heightened risks created by mental disabilities are nonreciprocal, so the same must be true

---

* *See* Chapter 6.

of physical disabilities. A nonreciprocal risk justifies liability regardless of personal blameworthiness, as in the case of insane actors who are required to comply with the objective standard of the reasonably sane person. Consequently, the nonreciprocal risks created by physical disabilities can also be subject to strict liability under an objective standard.

As we have found, an actor who injures another by a nonreciprocal risk can be immunized from liability when doing so is required as a matter of autonomy.* By formulating the reasonable person standard to account for the actor's physical disabilities, tort law has effectively adopted such an immunity. Any heightened risks caused by the disability are nonreciprocal (as in the case of mental disabilities), but tort law has immunized this behavior from (strict) liability by departing from the objective standard and incorporating the actor's physical traits into the standard of reasonable care.

Whether the immunity can be justified in these terms involves a series of related policy questions:

> Does the law assure the physically disabled, to the degree that they are physically able to take advantage of it, the right to leave their institutions, asylums, and the houses of their relatives? Once they emerge, must they remain on the front porch, or do they have the right to be in public places, to go about in the streets, sidewalks, roads and highways . . . ? If so, under what conditions? What are the standards of care and conduct, of risk and liability, to which they are held and to which others are held with respect to them? Are the standards the same for them as for the able-bodied? Are there legal as well as physical adaptations; and to what extent and in what ways are these concepts tied to custodialism or integrationism?[63]

By accommodating the actor's physical disabilities within the reasonable person standard, tort law recognizes that the

---

* *See* Chapter 5, section III.

disabled are "entitled to live in the world and to have allowance made by others for [their] disability."[64] A blind person must exercise more precaution because of the disability, but others must also act in recognition of the fact that the community contains blind people. A reasonable person standard formulated in these terms is essential for the disabled to participate meaningfully in society, the required autonomy rationale for an immunity from liability.

The reasonable person standard, however, does not accommodate an automobile driver's physical disabilities associated with old age, such as slower reflexes and so on. Once again, the objective standard functions as a form of strict liability. An elderly driver cannot be blamed for being physically unable to drive like a younger person. Why is this particular physical disability subject to strict liability, unlike others like blindness?

Any risk solely attributable to age must be reciprocal to make the liability rule consistent with the one governing the conduct of children. To subject a reciprocal risk to (strict) liability, tort law can rely on a deterrence rationale.* According to this rationale, the objective standard functions as a limited form of strict liability that gives elderly drivers an incentive to avoid situations in which their slower reflexes subject others to a heightened risk of harm, a rationale recognized by courts.[65] As a form of strict liability, this rule of negligence liability can reduce risk without prohibiting the elderly from driving, an outcome that would substantially undermine their autonomy in most communities.† Consequently, tort law can defensibly require elderly drivers to conform to the standard of a reasonably prudent driver with ordinary physical capabilities, even though the reasonable person standard otherwise accounts

---

* *See* Chapter 3, section II (describing rule of strict liability that depends only on deterrence).

† *Compare* Chapter 5, section III (explaining why tort law does not prohibit negligent behavior that does not involve personal fault or blameworthiness).

for the actor's physical disabilities, such as blindness, that are unrelated to age.

We can now reconsider the liability rule governing the mentally ill. The "right to participate in the world" makes the actor responsible for his or her choices. Unless mental illness leaves the individual without any capacity for self-control, he or she has at least some capability for self-determination. The ensuing responsibility for those autonomous choices provides a defensible basis for liability, distinguishing mental disabilities from physical disabilities.

An individual's autonomous choices are based on his or her actual knowledge and skills (even if partially impaired by mental disability), so tort law can also require individuals to exercise any above-average knowledge or skills. One who has the exceptional capacity to reduce risk and fails to do so can be held accountable for the consequences of that autonomous choice, explaining why the reasonable person standard accounts for the actor's above-average skills and knowledge. The reasonable person standard is formulated differently for the mentally impaired and the mentally gifted, but each is governed by the same concept of responsibility.

The reasonable person standard turns out to be a provocative issue for understandable reasons. Tort law defines the reasonable person in the objective terms of normal physical skills and mental abilities, but incorporates the actor's subjective traits into the objective standard for cases involving children, the physically disabled, and individuals with above-average knowledge or skills. Even these rules are subject to exceptions. Old people must drive like young people, and kids sometimes have to behave like reasonable adults. Unless there is some reason why tort law accounts for some individual differences but not others, tort law is vulnerable to claims of discrimination.

The rationale for these rules is obscured by the way in which they can create hidden strains of no-fault or strict liability within negligence liability. Due to the mismatch between the objective standard and the actor's subjective traits, the objective standard often creates pockets of strict liability within the negligence rule. When the objective standard is analyzed as a form of strict liability, the varied formulations of the reasonable person standard are defensible. The reasons for subjecting the mentally ill to strict liability, for example, do not apply to children and physically disabled actors, explaining why an objective standard applies to the mentally ill and a subjective standard to children and the physically disabled. Rules that look like they discriminate against the mentally ill turn out to be defensible. The rules are all ones of negligence liability, but their particular rationale depends on the underlying principles that govern the choice between negligence and strict liability.

B. The Requirements of Reasonable Care

The scope of duty and the characteristics of the reasonable person are matters of law to be determined by the judge, unlike the issue of whether the defendant breached the duty to exercise reasonable care.

> At the heart of negligence law is a standard of conduct of the reasonably prudent person. The jury administers this standard by making a normative determination of what constitutes appropriate conduct in a given situation along with a factual determination as to whether the defendant's conduct met the standard. The jury has a great deal of normative discretion in deciding what is reasonably prudent conduct.[66]

Due to the normative nature of the decision, the jury is not merely determining factual issues. Even "in a case where the facts are undisputed but breach is contested," the "issue of breach goes to the jury."[67] The jury must resolve factual questions and legal or normative questions to determine what reasonable care requires in a particular case. The issue is not exclusively one of fact or law, but instead provides the paradigmatic example of a *mixed question of law and fact.*[*]

For this reason, we have characterized the standard of reasonable care as a legal requirement, represented by an unspecified logical operator ®, for the duty holder to incur the burden B of taking a precaution to eliminate a foreseeable risk consisting of a probability P that someone in a class of right holders would suffer harm or loss L. Even if the burden B of the precaution and the associated risk PL are not disputed, the jury must still determine the requirements of reasonable care ®.

Because the jury's exercise of normative discretion resolves this issue, it might seem pointless to make further inquiry. The matter, however, cannot be so simply resolved. Without some idea of what reasonable care requires, attorneys would be unable to make arguments to the jury. Without some idea of what reasonable care requires, judges could never review jury verdicts on the matter. Attorneys make arguments about reasonable care all the time, and judges routinely evaluate jury verdicts in negligence cases. These practices imply that we can identify the requirements of reasonable care to a considerable degree, even though resolution of the matter requires a normative decision by the jury.

Conceptualizing Reasonable Care　　Reasonable care is defined by the conduct of the reasonable person in the circumstances confronted by the allegedly negligent actor at the time

---

　　[*] Questions of fact are for the jury and questions of law for the judge, whereas a mixed question of law and fact could be determined by either decision maker. The allocation of decision making for such issues typically depends on whether the issue involves categorical considerations (appropriate for judges) or case-specific matters (appropriate for the jury). *Compare Restatement (Third) of Torts: Liability for Physical Harms* § 8 cmt. c ("Tort law has . . . accepted an ethics of particularism, which tends to cast doubt on the viability of general rules capable of producing determinate results and which requires that actual moral judgments be based on the circumstances of each individual situation. Tort law's affirmation of this requirement highlights the primary role necessarily filled by the jury.").

of the relevant safety decision. The reasonable person gives "impartial consideration to the harm likely to be done to the interests of the other as compared to the advantages likely to accrue to [the actor's] own interests."[68] An actor who "impermissibly ranks personal interests ahead of others" violates "an ethical norm of equal consideration" and is fairly subject to liability for injuries caused by such unreasonable conduct.[69]

The impartial consideration of interests reflects the moral principle known as the Golden Rule: "Treat others as you would like to be treated." At minimum, this principle requires the actor to give others the same protection that he or she would provide for his or her own safety, so we can proceed by figuring out how an actor would make personal safety decisions.

Suppose that each time the individual drives an automobile, there is a 1 percent chance that he or she will suffer injuries totaling $100. In light of this risk, what types of safety decisions would the driver make? For each 100 trips, the driver on average will suffer one accident causing $100 of injury costs, making the average cost of each trip $1. The driver, therefore, will rationally estimate the injury cost at $1 per trip, an amount equal to the expected cost of injury*:

$$P \bullet L = (1/100) \bullet \$100 = \$1.$$

To determine whether it is worth taking any precautions to reduce or eliminate the risk, the driver would consider the cost or burden B of exercising care. Suppose the driver could purchase a device that would fully protect him or her from this injury. The cost of the device is $2 per trip. Without the device, the driver would face the expected accident costs of $1. The device would cost the driver more per trip ($2) than it

---

* For more extensive discussion of why individuals rationally evaluate risk in terms of expected value, *see* Chapter 3, section II.

would save in reduced accident costs ($1), so he or she would save money by facing the risk. The driver, more generally, would forgo any precaution and instead face the associated risk whenever the cost of the precaution exceeds the expected injury costs, or $B > PL$. By contrast, if the cost of the device were only $0.50 per trip, the driver would save money by taking this precaution to eliminate the more costly risk ($1). The driver, therefore, would take any precaution costing less than the expected accident costs that he or she would otherwise incur by facing the risk, precautions satisfying the condition $B < PL$.

As this example illustrates, an actor's personal safety decisions correspond to the well-known Hand formula for reasonable care: "[I]f the probability [of injury] be called P; the injury, L; and the burden [of a precaution that would eliminate this risk] B; liability depends upon whether B is less than L multiplied by P: i.e., whether $B < PL$."[70] Indeed, the Hand formula was first adopted in a case involving the issue of whether the actor exercised reasonable care for purposes of self-protection.[71]

Because an individual makes personal safety decisions by reference to a cost-benefit calculus, perhaps a duty holder like an automobile driver could defensibly rely on that same decision rule when making safety choices for the protection of others. A driver would take only those precautions for which $B < PL$ to protect his or her own interests, so how would the driver be impermissibly ranking personal interests ahead of a pedestrian's interests if that same cost-benefit calculus governed the safety decision? The Golden Rule would seem to require only those precautions for which $B < PL$, thereby justifying the Hand formula for reasonable care.

The argument in favor of the Hand formula finds further support in the safety decisions of a strictly liable actor. If the driver is strictly liable for having caused the pedestrian to suffer a $100 injury, the driver's safety decision is equivalent to one of self-protection. He or she can either spend money on precautions to reduce the risk of injury (and the likelihood of being sued), or create the risk and incur any ensuing accident costs (via the imposition of strict liability). As in the case of self-protection, strictly liable actors make safety decisions by reference to a cost-benefit calculus.* Why should negligence liability require otherwise?

The practical concerns of administrability and fair notice may also favor the Hand formula. Unlike the open-ended standard of reasonable care $B \circledR PL$, the Hand formula $B < PL$ gives concrete expression to the general requirements of reasonable care, providing a method for juries and judges to evaluate the defendant's conduct. The Hand formula also makes it clear to duty holders that they must make safety decisions by comparing the costs and benefits, whereas a vaguely specified standard might not give them fair notice of how tort law expects them to behave.

Indeed, the Hand formula provides sound guidance for required forms of safe conduct. Under this formulation of reasonable care, when all other factors are held constant:

- as the probability of injury increases, more care is required;
- as the severity of injury increases, more care is required; and
- as the burden or cost of precaution increases, less care is required.

This last condition is controversial for those who claim that the cost of exercising care is not relevant to the negligence inquiry.[72] The practice of tort law, though, decisively shows otherwise. Automobile accidents, for example, kill more than 40,000 individuals every year. The risk could be eliminated by a ban on driving, but the cost of such an extreme safety measure

---

* This point is more extensively developed in Chapter 3, section II.

is prohibitive, illustrating the general point that the cost of precaution affects the required amount of reasonable care.

Rather than reject the relevance of cost, a more persuasive criticism is that the Hand formula does not fairly balance the cost of precaution against the cost of injury. Cost-benefit analysis gives the same weight to the liberty interest of the duty holder (the burden of precaution B) and the security interest of the right holder (the risk of injury PL), absolving the duty holder of any obligation to take care when the burden on liberty exceeds the threat to physical security, $B > PL$. To prioritize the security interest, tort law can require reasonable precautions in excess of the cost-benefit amount.*

To be sure, the Hand formula corresponds to safety decisions in cases of self-protection and strict liability, but those cases are distinguishable from many negligence cases. An automobile driver makes personal safety decisions by reference to a cost-benefit calculus $B < PL$ and receives a personal benefit from the trip in question. Requiring safety precautions for which $B < PL$, therefore, does not necessarily give equal treatment to a pedestrian who does not benefit from the driving trip. A similar difference applies to the comparison between strict liability and negligence. The rule of strict liability enables the driver to exercise cost-benefit care while benefiting the pedestrian with a damages remedy in the event of injury. If the rule were instead one of negligence liability requiring cost-benefit care, the driver would be required to act the same way, but a pedestrian who was injured by such conduct would no longer have the benefit of a damages remedy. Neither self-protection nor strict liability is fully analogous to negligence liability governed by the Hand formula for reasonable care.

The issue requires more case-specific analysis. As we have found, the fair mediation of conflicting interpersonal interests

---

* *See* Chapter 4, section II (explaining why rights-based liability rules prioritize the security interest in a manner not recognized by cost-benefit analysis).

in physical security and liberty is highly context dependent, so we need to consider how different types of risky interactions affect the requirements of reasonable care.*

Reciprocal Risks   As two automobiles go past one another on the road, each driver simultaneously imposes a risk of physical harm on the other. Each driver is both a right holder and duty holder with respect to the other, an attribute of the risky interaction that is accounted for by the concept of reciprocity.†

In the extreme case of perfect reciprocity, the interacting individuals are identical in all relevant respects, including the degree of risk that each imposes on the other, the severity of injury threatened by the risk, and the liberty interests advanced by the risky behavior. When there are no relevant differences between the two parties, each is equally both a right holder and duty holder with respect to the other. Each driver has the identical right against the other, and each owes an identical duty to the other. When each individual is simultaneously a right holder and duty holder to the same extent, there is no meaningful distinction between the two categories. The *interpersonal* conflict of the right holder's security interest and the duty holder's liberty interest collapses into an *intrapersonal* conflict of these interests for each individual as simultaneous right holder and duty holder.

In these circumstances, neither the right holder nor duty holder prioritizes the security interest over the liberty interest. Each interacting individual would prefer a tort duty that requires a safety precaution only if the benefit of risk reduction

---

* *See* Chapter 5 (discussing how a priority of the security interest can yield rules of negligence liability, strict liability, or immunity from liability, depending on the circumstances of the risky interaction).

† *See* Chapter 3, section III (explaining the concept of reciprocity and describing how courts have relied on the concept to choose between negligence and strict liability).

(fully accruing to the individual as reciprocal right holder) exceeds the burden or cost of the precaution (also fully borne by the individual as reciprocal duty holder). A tort duty that prioritized the security interest would be detrimental to the interests of both parties to the risky interaction.

When the right holder and duty holder each give equal weight to security and liberty interests, tort law can defensibly do the same. The equal weighting of liberty and security interests is embodied in the Hand formula, which requires only those precautions that burden the interest in liberty (B) by less than the associated threat to physical security (the risk PL). For this class of cases, the fair mediation of interests yields the cost-benefit formulation of reasonable care.

Contractual Relationships   The same analysis applies to cases in which the right holder and duty holder have a contractual relationship, as in product cases involving a consumer and manufacturer. In the vast majority of product cases, the right holder can be analyzed as a consumer who both pays for and benefits from the tort duty of a product seller.* Any tort burdens incurred by the manufacturer or other product sellers, including the cost of product safety improvements and liability for injury compensation, are passed on to the consumer in the form of higher prices. These cases only implicate consumer interests, so the liability rule recognizes that "it is not a factor . . . that the imposition of liability would have a negative effect on corporate earnings or would reduce employment in a given industry."[73] In comparing his or her own security and liberty interests, the consumer gives no special priority to either

---

* A consumer for this purpose includes one who uses the product with the purchaser's permission, such as family and friends. The purchaser presumably fully accounts for the user's interests, making it appropriate to conceptualize both types of individuals as right holders who fully internalize the benefits and burdens of tort liability. *See* Mark A. Geistfeld, *Principles of Products Liability* 39–40 (Foundation Press 2006) (also explaining why the analysis covers products purchased by employers for use by employees).

one. As in the case of self-protection, the consumer prefers to pay for product safety only if the benefit of risk reduction (fully accruing to the consumer) exceeds the cost of the safety investment (also fully borne by the consumer in the form of higher prices). The ordinary consumer reasonably expects these safety decisions to satisfy cost-benefit analysis, a difference recognized by courts. Unlike other cases in which the judge tells the jury to evaluate the defendant's conduct under the reasonable person standard, in product cases jurors are instructed to consider the issue of reasonable care in cost-benefit terms.*

product
liability
use
cost-
benefit

Risk-Risk Trade-Offs   In some cases, the only form of precaution involves behavior that exposes the actor to the risk of physical harm, creating a *risk-risk trade-off*. Each risk threatens the security interest of one of the interacting individuals, and so the burden of precaution (the risk of physical harm faced by the actor) should have the same normative weight as the risk that would be eliminated by the precaution (the harm threatened to the other), yielding the balancing embodied in the Hand formula for reasonable care.

A good example is provided by *Eckert v. Long Island Railroad*, in which the court had to determine whether it was unreasonable for the actor to attempt saving a young child, who "was sitting or standing upon the track of the defendant's road as the train of cars was approaching, and was liable to be run over." The actor, "seeing the danger of the child, ran to it, and seizing it, threw it clear of the track on the side opposite to that from which he came; but continuing across the track himself, was struck by the step or some part of the locomotive or tender, thrown down, and received injuries from which he died that night." In the plaintiff's wrongful-death suit, the

---

* *See* Chapter 13 (discussing the *risk-utility* test for defective designs and warnings and explaining why it is substantively equivalent to the consumer expectations test).

defendant railroad claimed that the plaintiff was barred from recovery because the decedent's "negligence contributed to the injury." The jury rejected this argument, and the appellate court affirmed the jury verdict for plaintiff.[74]

The rationale for this decision can be readily expressed in terms of the Hand formula, illustrating how the formula can aid legal analysis. Had the deceased not attempted the rescue, the child was virtually certain to be severely injured or killed by the oncoming train. To eliminate this risk, the deceased had to incur the burden of risking his own life. In algebraic terms, the burden B is comprised of a risk term PL, where P is the probability that the deceased would be hit by the train, and L the loss he would suffer in that event. Even if the deceased were virtually certain to die by attempting to rescue the child ($P = 1$; L = loss of the rescuer's life), the risk faced by the child was of comparable magnitude ($P = 1$ and L = loss of the child's life). Consequently, the railroad could not prove that the decedent rescuer had acted unreasonably. Such proof would entail the following conclusions:

$$B > P \bullet L$$

$$P_{rescuer\ injured} \bullet L_{injury\ suffered\ by\ rescuer} > P_{child\ injured} \bullet L_{injury\ suffered\ by\ child}$$

$$1 \bullet (\text{loss of rescuer's life}) > 1 \bullet (\text{loss of child's life})$$

This condition cannot be satisfied. Tort law does not value one life more greatly than another, explaining why the railroad could not prove that the deceased's effort to save the child was unreasonable.*

---

* To be sure, damages for wrongful death varies for individuals. The amount of damages, however, is not equivalent to the legal valuation of the harm. *See* Chapter 5, section II (using this distinction to explain why negligence liability ordinarily provides better protection of the security interest than strict liability). When the threatened lives have equal legal value and each faces an equal risk, only an equality obtains in the standard of reasonable care. When the evidence on an element is in equipoise, the party bearing the burden of proof loses. The defendant railroad was raising the affirmative defense of contributory negligence, so it failed to satisfy its burden of proving that the deceased acted unreasonably in attempting to save the child.

As *Eckert* illustrates, the jury will naturally compare one risk of harm directly with another risk of harm in the manner required by the Hand formula, making that formulation of reasonable care indistinguishable from the reasonable person standard.

Nonreciprocal Risks Evaluating safety decisions in the cost-benefit terms of the Hand formula is not unfair to a right holder who pays for the burdens of tort liability (as a reciprocally situated duty holder or consumer in a contractual relationship), nor is the method unfair for evaluating how one risk of physical harm should be traded off against another. The only remaining class of cases involves those in which the right holder neither sufficiently benefits from the risky activity nor pays for the burden of tort liability, as in the case of a factory that discharges carcinogens into the drinking water of nearby residents. These cases would also be governed by the Hand formula if the purpose of tort liability were to further the objective of allocative efficiency, but in a rights-based tort system, the Hand formula might not adequately protect the right holder's interest in physical security when threatened by a nonreciprocal risk.[*]

Consider a compensatory tort right. Under ideal conditions in which the right holder could always be fully compensated for his or her injuries, a compensatory tort system would rely on strict liability. Duty holders would voluntarily make safety decisions in the cost-benefit terms of the Hand formula, and the strictly liable duty holders would be obligated to pay fully compensatory damages to right holders for their injuries.[†]

Duty Holder's Obligations = Cost-Benefit Precautions
+ Fully Compensatory Damages

---

[*] *See* Chapter 4, section II (discussing differences between rights-based and efficient liability rules).

[†] *See* Chapter 5, section I (defining attributes of a compensatory tort right).

Under actual conditions, however, the compensatory damages remedy does not always fully compensate an injured right holder. In the event of a fatal accident, monetary damages cannot compensate the deceased right holder for the loss of life's pleasures. Due to this inherent inadequacy of the damages remedy, strict liability cannot adequately protect the compensatory tort right. Instead, tort law must directly control risky behavior by imposing a duty to exercise reasonable care on those who expose others to the risk of physical harm.[*]

This rationale for negligence liability has implications for the standard of reasonable care. If tort law formulated the standard of reasonable care in cost-benefit terms, duty holders would not incur their full compensatory obligations to right holders. A duty holder would spend the same amount of resources on safety precautions as under ideal compensatory conditions (the rule of strict liability with fully compensatory damages), but would not have to pay the right holder for the loss of life's pleasures in the event of a fatal accident. The cost-benefit standard of reasonable care, therefore, requires a duty holder to expend fewer resources than required by the compensatory tort right.

Duty Holder's Obligations > Cost-Benefit Precautions
+ Limited Compensatory Damages

To eliminate this windfall, tort law can require the duty holder to expend those resources on injury prevention.

Duty Holder's Obligations = Precautions Exceeding
Cost-Benefit Amount
+ Limited Compensatory
Damages

---

[*] *See* Chapter 5, section II (relying on the inadequacy of the compensatory damages remedy to justify negligence liability).

The added safety expenditures exceed the amount required by cost-benefit analysis, but reduce risk.* The rationale for requiring these added safety expenditures is not obscure. Dollar for dollar, the prevention of premature death or severe bodily harm provides better protection of the right holder's interest in physical security than does an award of monetary damages for these injuries.

Consistent with this reasoning, empirical studies have found that judges and jurors do not treat reasonable care as a form of cost-benefit analysis, but instead require safety precautions in excess of the cost-benefit amount when the risky conduct threatens serious bodily harm.[75]

This formulation of reasonable care can be quantified to the same degree as the Hand formula. Each requires some method for quantifying the amount of loss L in a case of premature death or severe bodily injury. Presumably, life is infinitely precious. If L is infinity, however, then duty holders must take *any* precaution, no matter how burdensome, to eliminate *any* risk of premature death, however slight ($B < PL = $ infinity). Such a rule would prohibit most automobile driving to eliminate any probability of a fatal accident. Reasonable care does not demand such onerous safety precautions of duty holders, implying that jurors must somehow evaluate the risk of premature death at less than infinity. The cost of these injuries can be measured in a defensible way, but we defer that issue for later discussion.† We can do so because this measure corresponds to the windfall that a duty holder would receive under a cost-benefit negligence standard. By requiring the duty holder to expend those resources on precautions, the standard of reasonable care entails total precautions in excess of the

---

* *See* Chapter 3, section II (explaining why negligence liability can induce precautionary expenditures beyond the amount required by cost-benefit analysis).

† *See* Chapter 14, section III (discussing the measurement of compensatory damages for nonmonetary injuries such as the loss of life's pleasures).

cost-benefit amount required by the Hand formula. The additional safety precautions reduce the risk of injury and directly protect the security interest, providing the right holder with some benefit under the negligence rule that is otherwise absent as compared to cases of self-protection and strict liability.*

Reasonable Care in the Courtroom As we have found, the requirements of reasonable care involve two distinctive normative decisions by the jury. The first is whether reasonable care is equivalent to or more demanding than cost-benefit care. Having resolved this question, the jury then needs to figure out how to compare the burden of a precaution to an injury having no obvious monetary counterpart. How does spending money on a precaution compare to the risk of premature death or severe bodily injury? These hard normative questions are masked by the standard jury instruction that first defines negligence as the failure to exercise ordinary care, and then defines "ordinary care" in terms of the conduct of the reasonable person.

The jury, though, does not have unfettered discretion. The decision involves identifiable forms of normative judgment that make it possible for attorneys to make persuasive arguments about reasonable care and for judges to review jury verdicts of negligence.

For cases involving reciprocal interactions (like two automobile drivers) or contractual relationships (as in products liability or medical malpractice), cost-benefit care corresponds to reasonable care. An attorney who understands this point will be more effective. For example, by emphasizing the bilateral nature of the risky interaction in an automobile accident — the

---

* For more rigorous analysis, *see* Mark Geistfeld, *Reconciling Cost-Benefit Analysis with the Principle That Safety Matters More Than Money*, 76 N.Y.U. L. Rev. 114 (2001). For an alternative argument that reasonable care can require precautions above the cost-benefit amount, *see* Gregory C. Keating, *Pressing Precaution Beyond the Point of Cost-Justification*, 56 Vand. L. Rev. 653 (2003).

manner in which the plaintiff driver was both exposed to risk and imposed risks on other drivers like the defendant — the attorney for the defendant can establish a relationship of equality between the parties, making it easier for the jury to understand why the plaintiff's interest in physical security should be treated equally with the defendant's interest in liberty. "The plaintiff as a driver would not want to be obligated to exercise that much care, so why would it be fair to require the defendant to drive in that manner?"

This argument does not work in all cases. For nonreciprocal interactions, reasonable care can require precautions in excess of the cost-benefit amount, making it important for the attorney to distinguish those cases from the others.

In a products case, for example, the plaintiff's attorney often portrays the product manufacturer as a powerful entity that furthers its own interests (profits) by unilaterally imposing risk on powerless consumers. The argument effectively characterizes the case as one involving a nonreciprocal risk, leading jurors to reject cost-benefit analysis as the appropriate method for evaluating the manufacturer's safety decisions. "Business should not place profits above the safety of consumers!"

To counter this argument, the defendant's attorney needs to tell the jury why these cases do not involve nonreciprocal risks. Like any other increase in cost, the manufacturer's safety investments will increase product price and be borne by consumers. The issue is not one of profits, but of determining the amount of product safety that is preferred by consumers. "Consumers benefit from low prices and only want manufacturers to make cost-effective investments in safety!"

Whether attorneys make these arguments, of course, depends on whether they understand how the requirements of reasonable care depend on the nature of the risky interaction. Perhaps more than any other issue in tort law, the element of reasonable care illustrates the importance of conceptual analysis for effective lawyering.

The same considerations explain how judges can review jury verdicts of negligence. To uphold a jury verdict of negligence, for example, a reviewing court could find that the evidence enabled a reasonable juror to conclude that the defendant did not take some precaution required by the Hand formula. As we have found, the Hand formula adequately expresses the requirements of reasonable care, except for nonreciprocal risky interactions, in which case reasonable care can involve precautions above the cost-benefit amount. When considered across the full spectrum of cases, the Hand formula identifies the minimal amount of required care, making it possible for judges to employ that standard when evaluating jury verdicts of reasonable care.

III. PROOF OF NEGLIGENCE

As part of the prima facie case, the plaintiff must prove that the defendant breached the duty to exercise reasonable care. Typically, the plaintiff proves the element of breach by identifying some precaution that the defendant failed to take. Whether that precaution was required as a matter of reasonable care can depend on customary safety practices or statutory safety requirements. In some cases, the plaintiff cannot even identify how the defendant behaved other than being involved in the accident, requiring resort to circumstantial evidence. These varied forms of proof give further content to the requirements of reasonable care, but the determination still often turns on the jury's "own general normative sense of the situation."[76]

A. The Untaken Precaution

The plaintiff ordinarily proves that the defendant breached the duty to exercise reasonable care by not taking some specific safety precaution that a reasonable person would have taken in the circumstances confronted by the defendant at the time of the safety decision.

> For practicing lawyers, the critical choice is properly identi-
> fying *which* untaken precaution will be the gist of the plain-
> tiff's case. The point is critical not only because it influences
> the chances that the plaintiff will prevail on the threshold
> issue of negligence but also because the choice of negligence
> allegations shapes the remaining issues such as proximate
> causation and contributory negligence.[77]

For example, suppose the plaintiff claims that the defendant negligently used a handheld cell phone while driving. The untaken precaution involves the defendant's driving without using the cell phone, creating a cost or burden B of that lost usage. The risk terms PL then consist of those foreseeable risks that would be eliminated by the untaken precaution. Suppose that by not using the cell phone while driving, the defendant would only eliminate any increased risk of accident attributable to inattention. The allegation of unreasonable care then takes the following form:

$$B_{lost\ usage\ of\ cell\ phone} \circledR (P \bullet L)_{foreseeable\ accidents\ caused\ by\ inattention}$$

The risk term PL can then be decomposed into the separate categories of foreseeable accidents faced by other drivers, pedestrians, and property owners. To satisfy the *Palsgraf* duty requirement, the plaintiff must be within one of these foreseeable categories of accident.[*] To prove that reasonable care required the defendant to forgo talking on the handheld cell phone while driving, the plaintiff could show that $B < PL$ or rely on other forms of proof to be discussed later.[†] To establish

---

[*] *See supra* section I.B.

[†] As established in the prior section, the requirements of reasonable care can equal or exceed those required by the Hand formula, depending on the nature of the case, and so a defendant who failed to take some precaution required by the Hand formula necessarily acted unreasonably.

causation, the plaintiff must prove that he or she was injured in an accident that would not have occurred if the defendant had not been talking on the cell phone.* This requirement means that the accident must be within the category governed by the standard of reasonable care, which is symbolically represented by the term $(P \bullet L)_{foreseeable\ accidents\ caused\ by\ inattention}.$

As this example illustrates, "each element of a plaintiff's specific negligence case depends on how his or her lawyer has specified the untaken precaution. This essentially creative choice determines how the rest of the elements will be analyzed and heavily influences whether the plaintiff will win or lose."[78]

Under modern pleading rules, a plaintiff is not limited to one claim against a defendant. Plaintiffs frequently allege more than one count of negligence in a complaint. These multiple allegations of negligence merely increase the plaintiff's chance of recovery; the plaintiff cannot recover more than once for the injuries in question.

Each negligence claim is framed by a particular untaken precaution. The plaintiff must prove that one such untaken precaution is required by the standard of reasonable care. (The exception, discussed later, involves proof of general negligence by circumstantial evidence.)

This aspect of the negligence claim requires a comparison of the defendant's behavior to some norm of required behavior. Potential sources of the norms of reasonable care include customary safety practices and those specified by law.

B. Custom

Under the early common law, customary safety practices largely determined the requirements of reasonable care. As one court explained:

> No one is held by law to a higher degree of care than the *average* in the trade or business in which he is engaged. . . . A

---

* *See* Chapter 9.

man, in conducting his business in the way that everyone else in a like business does, has measured up to the standard demanded by the law and has exercised the *ordinary* care of prudent men engaged in the business.[79]

During the twentieth century, judges questioned whether customary safety practices were necessarily reasonable. These doubts produced a new rule that was famously articulated by Judge Learned Hand in *The T.J. Hooper*:

[I]n most cases reasonable prudence is in fact common prudence; but strictly it is never its measure; a whole calling may have unduly lagged in the adoption of new and available devices. It never may set its own tests, however persuasive be its usages. Courts must in the end say what is required; there are precautions so imperative that even their universal disregard will not excuse their omission.[80]

The new rule did not render custom irrelevant. A customary safety practice can operate as a shield by helping a defendant prove that the conduct in question was reasonable, or it can operate as a sword by helping the plaintiff prove that the defendant acted unreasonably.

Custom as a Shield "An actor's compliance with the custom of the community, or of others in like circumstances, is evidence that the actor's conduct is not negligent but does not preclude a finding of negligence."[81]

Compliance with custom does not completely shield the defendant from negligence liability, because a customary safety practice can omit reasonable safety precautions. In *The T.J. Hooper*, for example, the alleged customary practice involved equipping tugboats with radio equipment. This untaken precaution had a burden B — the cost of the radio equipment — that was substantially less than the risks PL a tugboat would face if a crew out at sea were unable to learn about impending storms, $B < PL$. Insofar as tugboats were not customarily equipped with radios — a disputed issue in the case — the practice was inefficient and unreasonable. Compliance with custom does not conclusively prove reasonable care.

In light of this rule, one might wonder why courts even bother with custom. When custom is at issue, the court first determines the requirements of reasonable care and then compares those requirements to the customary safety practice. Liability turns entirely on whether the actor's conduct complied with the requirements of reasonable care, not on whether the actor complied with custom. Why even rely on custom at all?

Although custom does not define reasonable care, it still has evidential value. As the *Restatement (Third)* explains:

> Evidence that the actor has complied with custom in adopting certain precautions may bear on whether there were further precautions available to the actor, whether these precautions were feasible, and whether the actor knew or should have known of them. In assessing such evidence, the jury can take into account the fact that almost all others have chosen the same course of conduct as has the actor: "ordinary care" has at least some bearing on "reasonable care." Furthermore, if the actor's conduct represents the custom of those engaging in a certain line of activity, the jury should be aware of this, for it cautions the jury that its ruling on the particular actor's negligence has implications for large numbers of other parties.[82]

As the leading scholarly exposition on the matter further explains, "In these ways evidence of conformity promotes better solutions of negligence problems. Such proof can enter into the process of solving negligence problems without being, in and of itself, the solution."[83] Compliance with custom provides some proof of reasonable care, even though the customary practice does not completely shield the defendant from negligence liability.

In one important context, compliance with custom conclusively establishes reasonable care: "[I]n medical malpractice cases failure to establish nonconformity is fatal to the plaintiff, and the defendant who establishes conformity is entitled to a directed verdict."[84]

The conventional rationale for this rule is that "no other standard is practical. Our judges and juries are usually not competent to judge whether or not a doctor has acted reasonably."[85]

This rationale is unpersuasive. In product cases, courts do not measure reasonable care solely by reference to customary safety practices. Judges and juries independently evaluate the reasonableness of automobile designs, for example, to determine whether the product is defective in this respect. Can courts competently evaluate these complex engineering decisions while being incompetent with respect to medical decisions?*

To avoid such an arbitrary distinction, the rationale for these rules must explain why custom can be unreasonable in one market (products) and not the other (health care). In any market, customs are created by the safety practices agreed on by buyers and sellers. To employ the language of economics, custom is the *market equilibrium*. If the market equilibrium produces the amount of safety required by reasonable care, then the defendant's compliance with custom (or equilibrium safety practices) should be conclusive proof that the defendant did not act negligently. Otherwise, compliance with custom should provide only some evidence of reasonable care. The question, then, is whether such a distinction can be drawn between ordinary product markets and the market for health care.

Consider a manufacturer's decision about whether to install a costly safety device to eliminate an unreasonable product risk of which the ordinary consumer is unaware. By installing the safety device, the manufacturer increases cost (the term

---

* In both types of cases, the court often needs to rely on expert testimony regarding the safety practices in question, so the cases cannot be distinguished in this manner.

B in the standard of reasonable care) and the price of the product. Without the device, the product would expose consumers to the associated risk of injury (the term *PL*). Unless consumers have adequate knowledge of this risk, they will not be willing to pay for the safety device, leading them to purchase the lower priced product without the device. Why spend money on safety if one is unaware of the need to do so? Manufacturers will not tell consumers about these risks, as doing so would only increase product prices and decrease sales. What is the point of advertising negative product attributes to the consumer? The process of price competition predictably forces manufacturers to forgo these types of safety investments, resulting in unreasonably dangerous products. The ensuing safety problem both justifies the tort duty and explains why customary product safety practices can be unreasonably dangerous.[86]

During the 1920s, for example, the president of the automobile manufacturer General Motors "insisted that the company could not make windshields with safety glass because doing so would harm the bottom line." The automobile manufacturers were simply responding to misinformed consumer demand. "G.M. believed that consumers weren't prepared to pay more for cars with safety glass." The same dynamic has occurred throughout the history of automotive safety. During the 1950s, "auto executives told Congress that making seat belts compulsory would slash industry profits." The industry had the same response to air bags. As the president of the Chrysler Motors lamented, "safety has really killed all our business."[87] Without the intervention of tort law or other forms of safety regulation, the market would have adopted customary practices (no safety glass, no seat belts, no air bags) that were unreasonably dangerous.

The market for health care has fundamentally different safety characteristics. The doctor must prescribe care that is in the "best interests of the patient," but this obligation only encompasses the risks of the prescribed treatment, such as side effects, and not its financial cost.* Unconstrained by cost concerns, doctors (the sellers) have an incentive to oversupply care. Doctors generate more revenues and profits by providing more medical treatment — a form of care that reduces risk for the patient. The ordinary patient (consumer) benefits from this treatment and does not fret about the excessive cost, because he or she typically pays for only a fraction of the treatment and passes most of the cost onto the health insurer. As a consequence of these incentives, customary practices in the health-care market are likely to involve too much care, an outcome reflected in the long-running policy concern about the escalating costs of health care.[88] Customary practices involving too much care cannot be unreasonably dangerous, so compliance with these customs should conclusively prove that the defendant physician did not breach the duty to exercise reasonable care.

This rule is under pressure. Due to recent developments within the market for health care, customary practices may no longer involve excessive care. The rise of managed care organizations has led to the increased use of cost-cutting measures that can be unreasonable. It can be cheaper for a health insurer to deny coverage for costly life-saving treatment than to reimburse a sick individual in desperate need of the care. The operative incentives no longer predictably produce too much treatment, explaining why an increasing number of courts are rejecting medical custom as the definition of reasonable care.†

---

* The rationale for this rule is that the patient should decide whether the proposed treatment is worthwhile in light of its financial costs. To enable the patient to make such a decision, tort law requires the doctor to disclose to the patient any information that would be material to his or her decision. Failure to disclose such information subjects the doctor to liability for breach of the *duty to obtain informed consent* for the procedure.

† *See generally* Philip G. Peters, Jr., *The Quiet Demise of Deference to Custom: Malpractice Law at the Millennium*, 57 Wash. & Lee L. Rev. 163 (2000) (identifying 12 states that have rejected custom as definition of reasonable

The decisive role of customary safety practices in the traditional market for health care, therefore, can be explained in terms of its distinctive safety incentives. Outside of the health care market, the pressure to reduce costs predictably leads most sellers to cut back on safety whenever possible, producing customary practices that can be unreasonably dangerous. Within the traditional market for health care, by contrast, the profit incentive leads to the oversupply of medical treatment, producing customary safety practices that cannot be unreasonably dangerous. This dynamic, however, has fueled the rising cost of health care, causing health insurers to adopt cost-cutting practices. The evolving market for health care may ultimately end up with the same safety incentives characteristic of other markets, in which case custom should no longer define the requirements of reasonable care for the medical profession. The rule depends on market incentives, and not on any special difficulties that a court would face in evaluating medical decisions.

Custom as a Sword "An actor's departure from the custom of the community, or of others in like circumstances, in a way that increases risk is evidence of the actor's negligence but does not require a finding of negligence."[89]

As compared to cases in which the defendant uses conformance with custom to defend the reasonableness of the conduct, the role of custom is more decisive for cases in which the

---

care for malpractice and claiming that others are moving in that direction). The courts have not explained this shift other than by noting that customary business practices do not ordinarily define the requirements of reasonable care. *Id.* at 191–192. On one view, the rationale for the change involves the public's loss of trust in the medical profession based on its recognition that doctors are in the business of making profits. *Id.* at 196–201. The profit incentive, however, explains why medical custom is a defensible definition of reasonable care in the traditional market for health care. Any persuasive rationale for the demise of custom must instead involve a change in the market itself, such as the increasingly prevalent measures for cutting costs, typically required by health insurers, that can reduce health care to unacceptably low levels.

plaintiff alleges that the defendant acted unreasonably by not adopting a customary safety practice.

> Conformity evidence only raises questions, but sub-conformity evidence tends to answer questions. If virtually all other members of the defendant's craft follow safer methods, then those methods are practical; the defendant has heedlessly overlooked or consciously failed to adopt common precautions. Super-cautious industrial usages are conceivable, but the self-interest of businessmen checks milquetoastish fears.[90]

Just as price competition can predictably force businesses to cut costs by forgoing reasonable safety precautions, the same dynamic forces businesses to adopt only those precautions that are cost-effective. A customary practice engaged in by profit-maximizing actors has a very low chance of involving care in excess of the cost-justified amount — the "self-interest of businessmen checks milquetoastish fears." A business enterprise that takes less than the customary amount of care, more likely than not, also takes less care than is required by cost-benefit analysis, a clear violation of reasonable care as per the Hand formula.

To avoid liability, such a defendant could argue that the custom is inapplicable. The defendant can avoid liability by showing "its operation poses different or less serious risks than those occasioned by others engaging in seemingly similar activities, or by showing that it has adopted an alternative method for reducing or controlling risks that is at least as effective as the customary method."[91] After all, "[w]hen the defendant must practice his craft under conditions significantly different from others in the same business, there is no customary way of acting-under-the-circumstances."[92]

These kinds of cases explain why the influence of custom has dramatically waned over time. The early common law developed within close-knit communities of individuals engaged in similar activities (like farming) conducted under comparable conditions, creating salient customary practices with considerable appeal. The relationships were reciprocal and individuals repeatedly interacted with one another, the conditions most conducive to reasonably safe customary practices.[93] As society has evolved from localized agrarian communities into a highly industrialized global economy, it has become increasingly more difficult to generate customary practices. Those customs that do emerge do not always occur in close-knit communities of reciprocally situated individuals engaged in roughly the same types of risky activity. Customs today are much more likely to be unreasonably dangerous or inapplicable to the conduct of differently situated actors. Unlike the time of medieval England when custom largely defined the common law, custom now narrows the negligence inquiry in only a few important ways.

C. Safety Statutes and Regulations

In stark contrast to the declining influence of custom, negligence law has been increasingly shaped by legislatively enacted statutes and the administrative regulations promulgated thereunder.

> We live in the "Age of Statutes." Even the venerable common law area of torts is not immune from the pervasive influence of statutes. For example, in Oregon, statutes control civil liability areas including wrongful death, caps on damages, comparative negligence, products liability, informed consent, and landlord/tenant issues. . . . Such statutes may create, modify, or prohibit tort actions, or be the basis for courts providing or changing common law tort actions. Statutes may relate to one or more of the elements that are required for tort liability: a duty to act in a particular way, a standard of conduct (intent, recklessness, negligence, or liability without fault) that determines whether the duty is violated, the nature of the interest

that must be invaded (physical injury, economic harm, etc.), causation, and the kind of remedy provided (compensatory damages, punitive damages, injunctive relief, etc.).[94]

A statute can create a new *cause of action* or legal basis for the plaintiff to recover from the defendant under a given set of facts. Statutes expressly create a new cause action when they "declare conduct unlawful, impose a public-law penalty on the person whose conduct violates the statute, and also specify that the violator is civilly liable in damages to the victim of the violation."[95] Even if the statute does not expressly provide for civil liability, it may create an implied cause of action under certain conditions.* In either case, the new cause of action is based on the statute and not tort law.

Regardless of whether a statute creates its own cause of action, it can prohibit a cause of action based on tort law. Conduct complying with a statutory requirement is immune from tort liability whenever the statute *preempts* tort law in this respect. Due to the supremacy of legislative law over the state common law of torts, these statutes (or any regulations promulgated thereunder) entirely displace any tort rules governing such conduct.† Whether a statute preempts tort law depends on the purpose of the statute. Did the legislature intend to displace the requirements of tort law with the statutory provisions? The issue is wholly one of statutory interpretation.‡

---

* To determine whether a federal statute creates an implied federal statutory cause of action, courts must apply the factors set forth in *Cort v. Ash*, 422 U.S. 66 (1975). Whether a state statute creates an implied state statutory cause of action depends on different considerations. *See, e.g.,* Forell, note 94 (describing approach of Oregon courts).

† A federal statute, for example, has supremacy over any form of state law pursuant to the Supremacy Clause in Article VI of the U.S. Constitution.

‡ The statutory question, though, can turn on institutional considerations. *See* Catherine M. Sharkey, *Products Liability Preemption: An Institutional Approach*, 76 Geo. Wash. L. Rev. 449 (2008).

Even if a statute does not preempt state tort law, it can still be relevant for resolving a tort dispute. <u>Proof that an actor violated a statute</u> can establish *negligence per se*:

> An actor is negligent if, without excuse, the actor violates a statute that is designed to protect against the type of accident the actor's conduct causes, and if the accident victim is within the class of persons the statute is designed to protect.[96]

This doctrine reflects the simple idea that the reasonable person complies with a safety statute unless there is a good excuse for not doing so. This simple idea, though, masks a number of issues.

To see why, suppose the defendant automobile driver had been exceeding the statutory speed limit on the highway when he or she was involved in an accident with the plaintiff, another driver. By proving the statutory violation, the plaintiff establishes negligence per se:

1. The statute has a safety purpose — the speed limit is designed to reduce accidents caused by those who drive at excessively high speeds.
2. The plaintiff was a driver on the highway and within the class of persons protected by the safety statute.
3. The plaintiff was injured by the type of accident that the statute seeks to avert — a car crash caused by high speed.
4. The defendant had no excuse for speeding.

On these facts, the statute reflects a legislative determination that the defendant's burden of complying with the speed limit is justified by the reduced risk of automobile accidents faced by other drivers like the plaintiff. The statute does not expressly address the requirements of reasonable care, but the legislature has implicitly determined that compliance with the speed limit is a reasonable means of reducing automobile accidents caused by higher speeds:

$$B_{complying\ with\ speed\ limit} ® (P • L)_{exceeding\ speed\ limit}$$

The statutory violation accordingly proves that the defendant breached the tort duty to exercise reasonable care. <u>The statutory violation, in other words, constitutes negligence per se.</u>

As this example illustrates, the statute does not have to expressly state that its safety requirements are reasonable or must be incorporated into the duty of reasonable care. The court instead adopts that conclusion as a matter of tort law. "When the court accepts the standard it rules in effect that defendant's conduct falls below that of a reasonable man as the court conceives it. It does no more than it does in any ruling that certain acts or omissions amount as a matter of law to negligence."[97]

> There are several rationales for this common-law practice. First, . . . as a matter of institutional comity it would be awkward for a court in a tort case to commend as reasonable that behavior that the legislature has already condemned as unlawful. . . . [Second,] when the legislature has addressed the issue of what conduct is appropriate, the judgment of the legislature, as the authoritative representative of the community, takes precedence over the views of any one jury. [Third, in] general, statutes address conduct that conspicuously recurs in a way that brings it to the attention of legislatures. Negligence per se hence replaces decisionmaking by juries in categories of cases where the operation of the latter may be least satisfactory [due to the possibility of inconsistent jury verdicts across recurring cases and the associated problems of] inequality, high litigation costs, and failing to provide clear guidance to persons engaged in primary activity.[98]

These institutional considerations also give courts discretion to reject a statutory requirement when its application in a particular case would be inconsistent with reasonable care. Suppose that the defendant driver in our example was speeding only because he or she was transporting someone in desperate need of immediate medical treatment to a nearby emergency room. In cases like this, the defendant claims that there was a legitimate safety reason for violating the speed limit.

By allowing the defendant to make an argument of this type, courts recognize that noncompliance with a safety statute may be reasonable in extraordinary conditions. Sometimes it is safer to violate a statute than to comply with it. The excuse of such violations allows courts to exercise the same type of discretion as exercised by other public officials "in determining which violations of the statutes warrant the initiation of public proceedings."[99]

The role of excuse is even broader, encompassing so-called "technical" violations of statutes or situations in which the actor violated the statute despite exercising reasonable care. For example, "if a statute imposes a strict-liability obligation on motorists to remain on the right side of the road, the motorist whose car crosses the middle of the road because of a sudden tire deflation is excused from negligence per se if the tire deflates despite the motorist's reasonable efforts to prevent this result."[100] The standard of reasonable care is formulated to promote safety, and so if there is no safety purpose that would be furthered by enforcing the statutory requirement, the violation will be excused.

As is true in other respects, the actor does not get to determine the requirements of reasonable care.* "The violation of a safety statute is not excused by the fact that the person sincerely or reasonably believes that the requirement set by the statute is excessive or unwise; nor is it an excuse if the person is unaware or ignorant of the statutory requirement." And because customary practices can be unreasonable, it is not "an excuse if there is a custom to depart from the statutory requirement."[101] Speeders and jaywalkers beware!

The black-letter rule of negligence per se applies only when the statute in question is "designed to protect against the type of accident the actor's conduct causes." The implications of this requirement depend on the type of case.

---

    * *See supra* section II.A (describing objective characteristics of the reasonable person).

Jaynasfkný

The Statute Has No Safety Rationale   Statutes can regulate risky conduct for reasons having nothing to do with safety. A statute forbidding the sale of alcohol to minors, for example, could have the sole purpose of promoting good morals. Lacking a safety purpose, the statute is not designed to protect against *any* type of accident. A defendant who violated the statute by selling beer to a minor would not commit negligence per se in the event that the minor caused an automobile accident while driving home drunk.

The Statute Only Promotes Safe Practices in General
For negligence per se to apply, the statute must regulate particular forms of safe conduct and not merely promote safe practices in general. This requirement is illustrated by cases involving defendants who violated a statute by driving or practicing medicine without a license. A licensing statute typically promotes safety by educating individuals about safe practices and ensuring that they have the minimal skills necessary for engaging in the activity. The licensing statute, however, does not require particular forms of safe behavior other than procurement of the license. The mere fact that someone has a license does not mean that he or she necessarily exercised reasonable care, and someone without a license can be a much safer driver or effective doctor than a licensed actor. The issue depends on the individual's conduct, not on the license. Consequently, the court must evaluate the unlicensed defendant's conduct by reference to the behavior of the reasonable person. To be sure, the reasonable person has a license and the associated knowledge and skills one gains from procuring the license. Whether the defendant exercised such care on a particular occasion, however, has nothing to do with possession of the license. The violation of such a safety statute does not constitute negligence per se.

The Statute Has a Safety Rationale Different from the One Implicated by the Negligence Claim   In some cases, the defendant violated a statute with a safety purpose of reducing a particular type of risk, but the plaintiff was injured by a different type of risk. Even though the black-letter rule of negligence per se does not apply — the statute must be "designed to protect against the type of accident the actor's conduct causes" — the statutory violation can still serve as proof of negligence in some cases. The traditional formulation of negligence per se does not fully explain cases of this type.

A good example is provided by statutes known as *dram shop acts*, which typically prohibit the commercial sale of alcohol to a minor or an intoxicated person. Tort cases involving violations of these statutes have produced three different outcomes. In some jurisdictions, courts have held that a violation of the statute does not create any tort cause of action. In other jurisdictions, courts have held that such a violation can constitute negligence per se in claims involving the victim of a drunk-drunk driving accident. Within these jurisdictions, courts have split over the issue of whether negligence per se applies to claims the inebriated patron filed against the tavern.

These cases have produced three different outcomes for an identifiable reason. A statute can have three different relations to the element of duty, and each has a different implication for the relevance of the statutory violation with respect to the issue of breach.

First, the statutory violation can involve a defendant who did not owe any duty of care to the plaintiff. "At common law, third-party dispensers of alcoholic beverages were not liable for injuries and deaths caused by their drunk customers."[102] Against this existing no-duty rule, a newly enacted dram shop statute could be the source of a new tort duty, depending on how the court interpreted the statutory purpose. Some courts determined that the dram shop act did not create a new tort duty, making negligence per se irrelevant. Unless the defendant otherwise owed a duty of care towards the plaintiff with respect to the conduct in question, the issue of breach (the statutory violation) does not matter.

Other courts, by contrast, determined that the dram shop act created a new tort duty and source of liability. Many of these statutes expressly provided for a private right of action. A statute, therefore, can affect a negligence claim by creating a new duty that had not previously been recognized by tort law.[103]

Statutes of this type are addressed by the black-letter rule of negligence per se. To create a new duty of reasonable care that would not otherwise be recognized by the common law of torts, the statute must have a safety purpose as required by the black-letter rule. The element of duty, after all, defines the risks of harm that the duty holder must eliminate by exercising reasonable care, and so a duty cannot exist unless there is a safety purpose for the required conduct.*

Having created a new duty, the statute also fully determines the risks governed by the duty:

$$B_{complying\ with\ the\ statute} ® (P • L)_{risks\ regulated\ by\ statute}$$

To recover for the breach of such a duty (the statutory violation), the plaintiff must show that the accident in question is encompassed within this duty (the accident must be within the category $(P • L)_{risks\ regulated\ by\ statute}$).† The plaintiff, in other words, must be within the class of persons protected by the safety statute, and be injured by the type of accident that the statute seeks to avert — the remaining requirements of negligence per se.

Based on this type of duty, some courts have concluded that a tavern can incur negligence liability for violating a dram shop act by serving an obviously intoxicated patron who subsequently injured the plaintiff in a drunk-driving accident. These acts have the safety purpose of protecting the public from drunk drivers.

---

* *See supra* Part I (explaining why the element of duty defines the risks governed by the standard of reasonable care).

† Recall the prior discussion in this section concerning the manner in which the untaken precaution affects every element of the plaintiff's negligence claim.

The plaintiff was a member of the class and injured by the type of accident that the statute was designed to avoid, satisfying the requirements of negligence per se.

Having adopted this rule of negligence per se, courts then had to determine whether an intoxicated patron could sue the tavern for injuries suffered as a result of his or her inebriated state. A majority of courts have rejected these claims. As one court explained, dram shop acts "were created to protect the general public from drunk driving accidents, not to reward intoxicated liquor consumers for the consequences of their voluntary inebriation."[104] The defendant tavern simply owed no duty to the plaintiff patron. By violating the dram shop act and breaching the associated duty of reasonable care, the defendant tavern incurred tort responsibility for only those risks encompassed by the tort duty. Because the duty is created by a statute that is designed to protect members of the public from drunk drivers, the risk that an inebriated patron will cause injury to himself or herself is not encompassed within the tort duty. An intoxicated patron is not a member of the class protected by the statute (or within the category $(P \bullet L)_{risks\ regulated\ by\ statute}$) as required by the black-letter rule of negligence per se, explaining why the majority of courts have rejected claims of negligence per se in drunk-driving suits brought by an injured patron against the tavern.

In contrast, "a significant minority of jurisdictions has imposed a common law duty . . . to allow a suit by an injured liquor consumer against the parties who furnished the liquor."[105] These courts base the duty on the common law of torts. Although the traditional common-law rule did not impose a duty on the providers of alcohol, "the courts began reversing themselves about 1960. Most courts without a Dram Shop statute now recognize a common law duty of reasonable care and impose liability when the licensed seller of alcohol negligently sells to a minor or intoxicated person who, as a result, causes injury to the plaintiff."[106] As these cases show, common-law principles can be sufficient to justify imposing a tort duty on the providers of alcohol; a dram shop act is not needed for that purpose.

Because the common law can be the source of a duty running from a tavern to its patron, those courts in jurisdictions with a dram shop act now face a new question. In the event that a defendant violates the dram shop act, how would the statutory violation affect a negligence claim predicated on a breach of the common-law duty that exists independently of the statute? This issue illustrates the third way in which a statute can affect a negligence claim.

<u>When a statute is not the source of a duty, it does not necessarily define the scope of the duty</u>. The source of the duty resides in the common law of torts, enabling courts to rely on ordinary tort principles to define the risks encompassed by the duty. The common law ordinarily extends duty to encompass the foreseeable risks of physical harm caused by the duty holder's failure to take the safety precaution in question.* This general or ordinary duty of care typically requires many forms of precautionary behavior. Due to the general nature of the duty, it can incorporate any safety behavior required by statute in order to reduce those risks regulated by the statute. The preexisting tort duty, however, also makes the duty holder responsible for any other risks encompassed within the common-law duty to exercise reasonable care.†

For this type of duty, the violation of a dram shop act can subject a defendant tavern to negligence liability for selling alcohol to a visibly intoxicated patron who was subsequently injured in a drunk-driving accident. The risk is different from the one regulated by the dram shop act, but it is still governed by the common-law duty. The reasonable person would foresee

---

* *See supra* Part I.B.

† The duty holder's responsibility for risks in addition to those regulated by the statute explains why a statutory requirement can serve as a minimum standard of care, a possibility often recognized by courts. *E.g., Vance v. U.S.*, 355 F. Supp. 756, 760 (D. Alaska 1973).

that the provision of alcohol to such a person increases the risk that he or she will be involved in a drunk-driving accident. The breach of this common-law duty is then proven by the statutory violation.

As the statute establishes, it would be unreasonable for a duty holder to violate the statute with respect to those risks governed by the statute:

$$B_{complying\ with\ the\ statute} \circledR (P \bullet L)_{risks\ regulated\ by\ statute}$$

By implication, the statutory violation also proves that the defendant's conduct was unreasonable when considered in relation to the other risks encompassed by the common-law duty:

$$B_{complying\ with\ the\ statute} \circledR (P \bullet L)_{risks\ regulated\ by\ statute}$$
$$+ (P \bullet L)_{other\ foreseeable\ risks\ of\ physical\ harm}$$

The statutory violation can prove that the defendant tavern acted unreasonably, even if the plaintiff was injured by a risk different from the one regulated by the statute (those in the category $(P \bullet L)_{other\ foreseeable\ risks\ of\ physical\ harm}$). Under this approach, courts incorporate the statutory provisions into an existing common-law duty, and then recognize that the statutory violation implies that the defendant acted unreasonably with respect to all other risks encompassed within the duty, such as the foreseeable risk that an inebriated patron will injure himself or herself while driving home from the tavern.*

Courts have not taken this approach in cases involving violations of a dram shop act, although some have done so in other types of cases.† These cases depart from the black-letter

---

* In order to limit the duty to those risks regulated by the statute, the court would have to conclude that the statute preempts the common-law duty that would otherwise exist.

† Courts allowing the inebriated patron to recover from the tavern have interpreted the governing dram shop act to include the patron within the class of persons protected by the statute. These statutory interpretations, however, are

requirements of negligence per se, leading these courts to treat the statutory violation as evidence of negligence.[107]

The statutory violation should have the same evidential weight as it does in the ordinary case of negligence per se. When the statute is incorporated into an existing tort duty, it partially determines the requirements of reasonable care within a duty defined by principles of the common law. The black-letter rule on negligence per se no longer applies, but the value of the legislative determination of reasonable care remains the same, justifying an equivalent evidential weight.

Like the other types, these cases require one to look carefully at how a statute interacts with the common law of torts. A statute does not always have to create a new duty, nor does tort law necessarily recognize a duty in all cases. Lacking the element of duty, the issue of breach (the statutory violation) is irrelevant. A statute can create a new duty, though, in which case the statute also fully determines the requirements of reasonable care. These cases are appropriately governed by the doctrine of negligence per se. A statute can interact with tort law in other ways. It can preempt an existing tort duty and eliminate tort liability altogether, or it can preempt an existing tort duty by fully specifying the required forms of reasonable care. A statute can also supplement an existing tort duty, in which case courts can depart from the black-letter rule of negligence per se. In these cases, courts are still complying with the underlying rationale of negligence per se by relying on the legislative determination of what reasonable care requires for the conduct in

---

often questionable. *E.g., Smith v. Sewell,* 858 S.W.2d 350, 356 (Tex. 1993) (Gonzales, J., dissenting). Courts can avoid that issue of statutory interpretation by recognizing that the statutory violation can establish the requirements of reasonable care within a common-law duty, even if the plaintiff is not within the class protected by the statute. *Compare Kernan v. American Dredging Co.,* 355 U.S. 424, 438 (1958) (rejecting the tort "rule that violation of a statutory duty creates liability only when the statute is intended to protect those in position of the plaintiff from the type of injury that in fact occurred").

question. The different ways in which a statute can interact with the common law of torts explain the different rules.

D. Precedent

Like a safety statute, precedent established by the case law can define the requirements of reasonable care. A prior finding of negligence by a jury, however, cannot serve this function. "A jury decision on the negligence issue is not a precedent for later cases involving different parties and is not even admissible in such later cases as a possible guide to later juries."[108] Only judges can establish binding precedent by formulating the requirements of reasonable care as a rule of law that governs a general category of cases.

We have previously found that judges can determine the requirements of reasonable care by adopting no-duty rules, which absolve actors of the duty to exercise reasonable care in recurring sets of circumstances.* For example, an actor typically has no duty to take precautions reducing the risk of pure economic loss. Our present inquiry involves judges determining the requirements of reasonable care within an established duty. Conduct violating these judicial rules of reasonable care would then be negligent as such, analogous to statutory violations amounting to negligence per se.

According to Holmes, as negligence law evolves, jury determinations of reasonable care on a case-by-case basis will be replaced by judicially adopted rules of reasonable conduct governing categories of cases:

> When a case arises in which the standard of conduct, pure and simple, is submitted to the jury, the explanation is plain. It is that the court, not entertaining any clear views of public policy applicable to the matter, derives the rule to be applied from daily experience, as it has been agreed that the great

---

* *See supra* Part I.

body of the law of tort has been derived. But the court further feels that it is not itself possessed of sufficient practical experience to lay down the rule intelligently. It conceives that twelve men taken from the practical part of the community can aid its judgment. Therefore it aids its conscience by taking the opinion of the jury.

But supposing a state of facts often repeated in practice, is it to be imagined that the court is to go on leaving the standard to the jury forever? Is it not manifest, on the contrary, that if the jury is, on the whole, as fair a tribunal as it is represented to be, the lesson which can be got from that source will be learned? Either the court will find that the fair teaching of experience is that the conduct complained of usually is or is not blameworthy, and therefore, unless explained, is or is not a ground of liability; or it will find the jury oscillating to and fro, and will see the necessity of making up its mind for itself. . . .

If this be the proper conclusion in plain cases, further consequences ensue. Facts do not often exactly repeat themselves in practice; but cases with comparatively small variations from each other do. A judge who has long [presided over negligence trials] ought gradually to acquire a fund of experience which enables him to represent the common sense of the community in ordinary instances far better than an average jury. He should be able to lead and to instruct them in detail, even where he thinks it desirable, on the whole, to take their opinion. Furthermore, the sphere in which he is able to rule without taking their opinion at all should be continually growing.[109]

Holmes was able to confirm this prediction while serving as a Justice on the U.S. Supreme Court in a famous case involving a fatal accident at a rail crossing. The defendant railroad argued that the decedent automobile driver had failed to exercise reasonable care by not stopping before he drove over the tracks. The Court agreed in an opinion authored by Holmes:

When a man goes upon a railroad track he knows that he goes to a place where he will be killed if a train comes upon him before he is clear of the track. He knows that he must stop for the train, not the train stop for him. In such circumstances it seems to us that if a driver cannot be sure otherwise whether a train is dangerously near he must stop and get out of his vehicle, although obviously he will not often be required to do more than to stop and look. It seems to us that if he relies upon not hearing the train or any signal and takes no further precaution he does so at his own risk. . . . [W]e are dealing with a standard of conduct, and when the standard is clear it should be laid down once for all by the Courts.[110]

Like any other rule, the "stop, look, and listen" rule was inevitably subject to litigation pressures. For cases in which the rationale for the rule clearly applied, a driver who failed to "stop, look, and listen" would not find it worthwhile to litigate the issue. Why spend resources fighting an established rule that makes evident sense on the facts? Instead, the rule predictably attracted litigation when its rationale was less compelling as applied to the facts at hand. In particular, the rule of "stop, look, and listen" assumes the driver would get out of the vehicle to look for an oncoming train when required for obtaining an unobstructed view. What if the conditions were such that it would have been unsafe for the driver to leave the automobile, and so after having stopped the car, he instead made his best efforts to look and listen for an oncoming train before crossing the tracks, when he was hit by a train that he could not see due to an obstruction? On these facts, the U.S. Supreme Court decided not to apply the "stop, look, and listen" rule, observing that it "has been a source of confusion in the federal courts to the extent that it imposes a standard for application by the judge, and has had only wavering support in the courts of the states. We limit it accordingly."[111]

This holding looks like it repudiates judicial efforts to define the requirements of reasonable care, although it could instead have the more modest objective of adopting an exception to the rule. For example, a statutory violation is excused under the appropriate conditions, and yet the statute continues to supply a legislatively prescribed rule of reasonable conduct that governs most cases. The same can be true of judicially created rules of reasonable care. For cases in which the rationale for the rule applies, the actor's violation of the prescribed course of conduct will amount to negligence as a matter of law. Otherwise, the violation will be excused. A judicially adopted rule of reasonable care does not have to apply in each and every case.

Consistent with this reasoning, judges have continued to adopt rules of reasonable care. They do so when:

> the need for providing a clear and stable answer to the question of negligence is so overwhelming as to justify a court in withdrawing the negligence evaluation from the jury. . . . [There are also] some intermediate issue[s] that can clearly profit from the clarity and finality of a judicial resolution. For example, in cases involving plaintiffs who are injured by railroad trains at highway crossings, courts have decided on their own that despite motorists' ability to observe approaching trains, the negligence doctrine imposes on railroads the "duty" to give an adequate warning to highway users. Of course, even given this decision by the court, what counts as an adequate warning is often determined by the jury on a case-by-case basis.[112]

In addition to providing a "clear and stable answer to the question of negligence," judicial rulings in prior cases can limit the negligence inquiry without dictating particular outcomes. An open-ended determination about the requirements of reasonable care at a railroad crossing is quite different from the more limited determination about what constitutes an adequate warning to highway users. In these cases, the jury still determines the precise requirements of reasonable care in light of the individual circumstances of the case, but its normative decision is significantly constrained by judicially created precedent. Even if Holmes had been overly optimistic about the extent to which negligence law would become defined by precedent, judges have nevertheless significantly guided the jury's determination of reasonable care.

E. Circumstantial Evidence: *Res Ipsa Loquitur*

So far, we have been addressing specific forms of allegedly unreasonable behavior. The plaintiff identifies some precaution that the defendant failed to take, and then argues that the untaken precaution was required as a matter of reasonable care, perhaps because of a custom, statute, or precedent. Instead of relying on this type of proof, the plaintiff sometimes uses *circumstantial evidence* concerning the nature of the accident to create an inference that it was caused by some unspecified unreasonable behavior of the defendant.

> In the final analysis all proof requires some process of inference, before it can be translated into an actual decision by the trier. We are accustomed, however, to divide proof into direct and circumstantial. When evidence of a fact is in the form of testimony by a purported observer of that fact, we call the evidence direct, *as to that fact.* . . . Where the thing itself, which is one of the facts in issue (such as the torn carpet that caused the accident, or the injured limb), is put before the trier for actual inspection we call the evidence "real evidence." In all other cases proof is called circumstantial and will be seen to require further processes of inference. Typically it involves proof of fact A (which is not itself a fact in issue) as the basis of an inference of the existence of fact B (which is in issue).[113]

Anyone who has read or watched a murder mystery knows about circumstantial evidence. Without the testimony of someone who directly observed the murder, the case is built on circumstantial evidence, such as the bloodied weapon containing the fingerprints of the prime suspect, and so on.

Circumstantial evidence creates a reasonable inference of negligence when it satisfies the doctrine of *res ipsa loquitur*, a Latin phrase meaning "the thing speaks for itself." The doctrine has been formulated in various ways over the years, but the most straightforward version is provided by the *Restatement (Third)*:

> The factfinder may infer that the defendant has been negligent when the accident causing the plaintiff's physical harm is a type of accident that ordinarily happens as a result of the negligence of a class of actors of which the defendant is the relevant member.*

Given the circumstances of such an accident, the jury as fact finder can reasonably infer that the plaintiff's injury, more likely than not, was caused by the negligence of the defendant. The accident "speaks for itself" on the issue, satisfying the plaintiff's burden of proving this element.

By establishing *res ipsa loquitur*, the plaintiff does not have to identify the specific manner in which the defendant acted unreasonably — the doctrine proves *general negligence* as opposed to *specific negligence*. "The Latin phrase is generally saved for cases where many of the important proven facts are pretty general, although the use of the term is far from precise."[114]

---

* *Restatement (Third): Liability for Physical Harm*, § 17. The traditional formulation of *res ipsa loquitur* requires that (1) the accident must ordinarily be of the type that does not occur in the absence of negligence; (2) the defendant had exclusive control of the injury-causing instrumentality; and (3) the plaintiff was not responsible for the injury. As interpreted by the case law, these requirements are more simply stated by the *Restatement (Third)* formulation. The requirement of "exclusive control," for example, requires proof showing that the defendant created or is otherwise legally responsible for the tortious risk that ultimately materialized and injured the plaintiff, regardless of who had possession of the instrumentality at the time of injury. Consequently, *res ipsa loquitur* can apply to a bottler of soda, even if the bottle exploded while being handled by the plaintiff. The *Restatement (Third)* rule yields the same conclusion in a more straightforward manner.

The phrase was first invoked to establish negligence in the 1863 English case *Byrne v. Boadle*, which involved a plaintiff who was walking down the street when he was hit and seriously injured by a barrel that fell from the defendant merchant's second-story storeroom.[115] The plaintiff offered no evidence of how the defendant had handled the barrel. Nevertheless, the court unanimously ruled that the plaintiff had sufficiently proven negligence. As Chief Baron Pollock explained, "[a] barrel could not roll out of a warehouse without some negligence." Because the defendant had exclusive control of the barrel when it fell, the circumstances of the accident sufficiently proved that the defendant had been negligent. The plaintiff's inability to identify the particular form of unreasonable behavior was irrelevant, and courts have continued to absolve the plaintiff of any need to identify the specific way in which the defendant acted unreasonably when the proof otherwise satisfies the requirements of *res ipsa loquitur*.

The plaintiff can also use *res ipsa loquitur* to prove specific negligence. For example, if the plaintiff alleges that the defendant mechanic negligently failed to tighten the bolts when reinstalling an automobile tire, he or she could prove that allegation by showing that the tire fell off the car shortly after he or she drove away from the defendant's garage. This proof of specific negligence is purely circumstantial and can be established by *res ipsa loquitur*. A tire does not ordinarily fall off an automobile shortly after being installed unless the installation was done negligently. Any form of circumstantial evidence that satisfies the plaintiff's burden of proving unreasonable care will also satisfy the requirements of *res ipsa loquitur*, regardless of whether the plaintiff is alleging specific or general negligence.

Nevertheless, the doctrine is associated with general negligence for good reason. When the exercise of reasonable care involves only a few precautions, as with the installation of an automobile tire, the plaintiff can identify a form of specific negligence that can be proven with circumstantial evidence. The claim is not aided by invocation of *res ipsa loquitur*, because the fact that the tire quickly fell off the car otherwise proves that the defendant failed to secure the tire. When reasonable care requires a much larger number of required precautions, and no one other than the defendant could observe whether all of the precautions were taken, the defendant could have acted unreasonably in numerous unidentifiable ways, requiring an allegation of general negligence via *res ipsa loquitur*.

Typically, the two interrelated factors — a large number of behavioral precautions and the slim chance of an unavoidable accident — provide the strongest case of *res ipsa loquitur*.[116]

> Consider the situation in *Byrne v. Boadle* where workers were using a jigger-hoist to move barrels above a public sidewalk. Because the danger rate was high, so was the rate of required precaution. Once the workers had begun, there could scarcely have been a moment when precautions were not required. Was the rope still taut? Was the jigger-hoist still properly rigged? Was the barrel approaching an obstacle that might jar it loose? These were questions that the workers constantly had to ask if the people below were to remain safe. Yet, so long as the workers complied with the negligence standard, it was unlikely that there would be an accident. When people move barrels above sidewalks, the required rate of precaution is so high that little risk is left for unavoidable accidents.[117]

Due to the variety of required behavioral precautions — those involving conduct rather than durable safety technologies like strong ropes that could be directly examined after the accident — there was a high likelihood that the defendant's employees failed to take one or more of them. Due to the variety of required behavioral precautions, there was also virtually no chance of an unavoidable accident — one that occurs despite the exercise of reasonable care. For the entire class of accidents (barrels falling out of windows), most are probably attributable to legal fault or the failure to exercise reasonable care in some unidentified way. In these circumstances, the mere fact of accident, more likely than not, proves that it was caused by unreasonable behavior. If the proof also shows that the injury-causing instrument (barrel) was in the defendant's control at the time when the unreasonable risk was created, then the evidence establishes that the accident, more likely than not, was caused by the defendant's negligence.

Even if the risk of accident is quite low, the fact of an accident does not imply that it was caused by negligence. *Res ipsa loquitur* requires that most of the accidents are caused by negligence or legal fault, with the implication that less than 50 percent of the accidents are unavoidable or caused by no-fault:

F region:
Accidents caused by some form of legal fault or failure to exercise reasonable care

NF region:
Unavoidable accidents

The relevant issue is whether the proportion of accidents caused by legal fault exceeds the proportion of unavoidable accidents. Resolution of the issue depends on the relative number of injuries. It does not depend on the mere likelihood of accident, or on the fact that negligence increases the risk (which is always true).

Consequently, the strongest case for *res ipsa loquitur* involves a large number of behavioral precautions that effectively eliminate the risk of accident, as in *Byrne*. When the defendant is required to act in a variety of ways to reduce risk, the likelihood increases that the defendant will make a mistake at some point. Human behavior is not ordinarily infallible. Most accidents, therefore, will be attributable to negligent mistakes, with only a small proportion involving actors who behaved perfectly and still caused an (unavoidable) accident.

Under the early common law, for example, common carriers were required to exercise the utmost care for the protection of passengers. Compliance with such a standard would virtually eliminate the risk of accident. The demanding standard of reasonable care also involved a large number of required behavioral precautions that could not be observed by anyone other than the defendant. Trains and tracks had to be maintained properly, the tracks kept clear of obstructions, signals in good working order, and personnel in a state of constant vigilance. The variety and number of required behavioral precautions created numerous opportunities for negligent behavior. The variety and number of required precautions also virtually eliminated the risk of unavoidable accident. The combination of these two factors explains why the early cases of *res ipsa loquitur* typically involved negligence claims brought by a passenger against a railroad or other common carrier.[118]

Because *res ipsa loquitur* is particularly well-suited for cases involving a demanding standard of reasonable care, the doctrine reduces the role of strict liability. Recall that a demanding standard of reasonable care is justified by the importance of reducing risk to protect the individual interest in physical security.* The extent to which negligence liability actually reduces risk, however, depends on the plaintiff's ability to prove that the defendant breached the duty to exercise reasonable care.

> One argument favoring strict liability is that the unavailability of evidence in some cases renders the plaintiff unable to establish what may well have been the defendant's actual negligence. By providing the plaintiff in such cases with an

---

* *See* Chapter 5, section II.

alternative method of proving the defendant's negligence, res ipsa loquitur reduces the need for strict liability.[119]

Res ipsa loquitur provides yet one more example of how the standard of reasonable care is integrally related to the fundamental choice between negligence and strict liability.*

---

* *See* Chapter 3, section I.

~ 9 ~

Causation

[handwritten: cause connects right and duty]

Whether the claim involves an intentional tort, negligence, or strict liability, the prima facie case for liability requires the plaintiff to prove that his or her injury was caused by the defendant's tortious conduct. The element of causation ties the violation of the plaintiff's tort right to the defendant's breach of duty, entitling the plaintiff to receive compensation from the defendant wrongdoer. Causation establishes the right-duty nexus that is essential to tort liability.

The element of causation involves two distinctive issues that courts have traditionally lumped together under the rubric of *proximate cause*. Today these issues are treated separately, with one pertaining to the factual cause of the injury, and the other to a policy-based determination of legal or proximate cause that defines the appropriate scope of liability. Both of these causal issues are jury questions.

[handwritten: Two causes: · factual question for jury · policy determ. of proximate causality]

I. FACTUAL CAUSE

A. The But-For Test

Factual cause ordinarily is evaluated under the *but-for test*, which requires the plaintiff to prove that but for the defendant's tortious conduct, the injury would not have occurred.

If the defendant committed a battery by punching the plaintiff in the face, for example, the causal connection between the punch and facial injuries is evident. But for the punch, the plaintiff would not have suffered the facial injuries, making the punch a factual cause of the injuries.

When fully analyzed, the but-for test involves four steps that are necessary to frame the causal question properly:

First, one must identify the injury or injuries for which redress is sought. This step rarely presents any difficulty. . . .

Second, one must identify the defendant's wrongful conduct. Care is required here. It is not enough for the plaintiff to show that her injuries would not have occurred if the defendant had never been born; the plaintiff must show that her injuries probably would not have occurred if the defendant had not engaged in the particular conduct alleged (and ultimately proved) to have been wrongful. . . .

The third step is the trickiest. It involves using the imagination to create a counterfactual hypothesis. One creates a mental picture of a situation identical to the actual facts of the case in all respects save one: the defendant's wrongful conduct is now "corrected" to the minimal extent necessary to make it conform to the law's requirements. . . .

The fourth step asks the key question whether the injuries that the plaintiff suffered would probably still have occurred had the defendant behaved correctly in the sense indicated.[1]

In a negligence case, we can precisely frame this causal inquiry within the standard of reasonable care, $B \circledR PL$. For example, suppose the plaintiff proves that the defendant driver committed negligence per se by exceeding the statutory speed limit when he or she crashed into the plaintiff's car. The plaintiff's proof of negligence per se means that:

$$B_{complying\ with\ speed\ limit} \circledR (P \bullet L)_{foreseeable\ accidents\ caused\ by\ exceeding\ speed\ limit}$$

By exercising reasonable care, the defendant would eliminate all *tortious risks* (those in the category $(P \bullet L)_{exceeding\ speed\ limit}$).

The precaution would also eliminate other collateral risks excluded from the duty, such as unforeseeable risks and most risks of pure economic or emotional harms:

$$B_{complying\ with\ speed\ limit} ® (P • L)_{tortious\ risks} \\ + (P • L)_{collateral\ risks} \Bigg]$$

To prove but-for causation, the plaintiff must first identify his or her injury or loss L, and then show that it was caused by a tortious risk or one of the collateral risks that would have been eliminated by the untaken precaution: But for the defendant's speeding, these risks would not have been created and could not have injured the plaintiff. The element of causation, therefore, can be described by reference to the inquiry framed by the standard of reasonable care.*

This inquiry is more complicated than our earlier example of battery. By complying with the statutory speed limit, the driver would only prevent accidents caused by exceeding the speed limit. The driver could comply with the speed limit and an accident could still occur. Despite the exercise of reasonable care, some accidents are unavoidable. Because we do not know what would have happened if the driver had not been speeding, the element of causation is necessarily counterfactual in nature. How can the jury determine whether a particular accident was caused by excessively high speed or was otherwise unavoidable?

According to Judge Guido Calabresi:

> The problem of linking defendant's negligence to the harm that occurred is one that many courts have addressed in the past. A car is speeding and an accident occurs. That the car was involved and was a cause of the crash is readily shown. The accident, moreover, is of the sort that rules prohibiting

---

* *Compare* Chapter 8, section III.A (describing how the plaintiff's allegation of breach — the untaken precaution — affects other elements of the negligence claim, including causation).

Difference between def. as but-for cause and defs. negl. as but-for cause

speeding are designed to prevent. But is this enough to support a finding of fact, in the individual case, that *speeding* was, in fact, more probably than not, the cause of the accident? . . . To put it more precisely — the defendant's negligence was strongly causally linked to the accident, and the defendant was undoubtedly a *but for* cause of the harm, but does this suffice to allow a fact finder to say that the defendant's *negligence* was a *but for* cause?

At one time, courts were reluctant to say in such circumstances that the wrong could be deemed to be the cause. They emphasized the logical fallacy of *post hoc, ergo propter hoc*, and demanded some direct evidence connecting the defendant's wrongdoing to the harm.

All that has changed, however. And, as is so frequently the case in tort law, Chief Judge Cardozo in New York and Chief Justice Traynor in California led the way. In various opinions, they stated that: if (a) a negligent act was deemed wrongful *because* that act increased the chances that a particular type of accident would occur, and (b) a mishap of that very sort did happen, this was enough to support a finding by the trier of fact that the negligent behavior caused the harm. Where such a strong causal link exists, it is up to the negligent party to bring in evidence denying *but for* cause and suggesting that in the actual case the wrongful conduct had not been a substantial factor.[2]

paraphy of the statt point

For ease of exposition, we will call this the *liberal rule of but-for causation*. The liberality of the rule is most apparent in cases involving the defendant's negligent failure to provide emergency equipment, such as a lifesaving device on board of a boat. In one representative case, the court let the jury decide whether this type of negligence caused the decedent to drown, even though the failure to install the device could have caused the death only if "there was time for a crew member to go to the hypothetical storage location, obtain the hypothetical line-throwing appliance, move it to the appropriate firing location, and fire the appliance — all before [the decedent] went limp in the water."[3] The jury cannot determine factual causation by speculation or conjecture, and yet the court, like others in analogous cases, submitted the issue to the jury because there was some chance that the safety device would have prevented the drowning. Given the exigencies of an emergency situation, the likelihood of a successful lifesaving operation would seem to be far less than 50 percent. By routinely submitting these cases to the jury, courts appear to be relaxing the plaintiff's burden of proving factual causation with a preponderance of the evidence. The circumstances in which courts take this approach are fully captured by the liberal rule of but-for causation, explaining why the rule is often characterized as one that relaxes the plaintiff's burden of proof.

> The reason seems fairly obvious. It would be futile for the courts to recognize a duty to provide emergency equipment and to impose an obligation to proceed promptly to the rescue if the defendant could successfully seize upon the uncertainty which nearly always attends the rescue operation as a reason for dismissing the claim. In such situations an insistence on proof by probabilities or better has no place. The ever-present chance that the rescue might fail is a part of the risk against which the rule protects.[4]

Despite the apparent way in which these cases reduce the plaintiff's burden of proving causation, there are good reasons for concluding otherwise. Courts often find for the defendant on the ground that the plaintiff could not prove factual causation by a preponderance of the evidence, even if doing so effectively prevents the entire class of plaintiffs from recovering.

For example, suppose the defendant negligently polluted an aquifer in a manner that increased the incidence of some disease in the population exposed to the contaminated drinking water. Suppose that for every three such injuries, two would be caused by the existing background risk and one by the defendant's negligence. Because the defendant's tortious misconduct did not at least double the risk of disease, no one suffering from the disease can prove that the defendant, more likely than not, caused the injury (for every three victims of the disease, only one was injured by the defendant). The defendant avoids liability altogether, even though the pollution undoubtedly injured someone (one of every three victims). Enforcing the requirement of causation would seem to make it "futile" to recognize such a duty in the first instance, and yet courts regularly do so. What distinguishes the cases governed by the liberal rule of but-for causation?

In describing the rule as a more liberal approach to the causal problem, Judge Calabresi explained that it replaced a strict rule requiring "some direct evidence" of factual causation. Consequently, the rule can be liberal in the limited sense that it does not require direct evidence and allows the plaintiff to prove factual causation solely by circumstantial evidence. As illustrated by *res ipsa loquitur*, a doctrine of circumstantial evidence does not necessarily reduce the plaintiff's burden of proving the prima facie case, indicating that the liberal rule of but-for causation also does not necessarily reduce the plaintiff's burden of proof.*

Consider the New York case cited by Judge Calabresi in which the defendant, whose vehicle did not have headlights as statutorily required, was involved in a nighttime accident with the plaintiff.[5] For this class of accidents, most are probably attributable to the absence of headlights:

F region: Nighttime accidents caused by lack of headlights on one of the colliding vehicles	**NF region:** Accidents not caused by such legal fault

---

* *See* Chapter 8, section III.E (discussing *res ipsa loquitur*).

In effect, a nighttime accident involving a vehicle without headlights "speaks for itself" on the issue of whether the absence of the headlights caused the accident. The plaintiff's causal proof is entirely circumstantial, making it similar to *res ipsa loquitur* in that limited respect. The claim, though, is not one of *res ipsa loquitur*, because the plaintiff used direct evidence to prove that the defendant was specifically negligent for not having working headlights on the vehicle. The plaintiff instead satisfied the ordinary burden of proving factual causation with circumstantial evidence, thereby shifting the burden of disproving factual causation to the defendant.

As Judge Cardozo explained in the case, the defendant could rebut the plaintiff's causal proof by showing, "for example, that in the particular instance the presence of very bright street lights or of a full moon rendered the lack of lights on the vehicle an unlikely cause." Such evidence would turn the class of relevant accidents from "nighttime accidents caused by a vehicle without headlights" into "nighttime accidents on brightly lit streets caused by a vehicle without headlights." For this class of accidents, the defendant's negligent failure to have working headlights was not the probable cause of the accident.

F region: Nighttime accidents on brightly lit streets caused by lack of headlights	NF region: Accidents not caused by the legal fault of driving at night without headlights

The issue of factual causation accordingly depends on the circumstances of the nighttime accident. Was it on a darkened road or one that was lit by streetlamps or a full moon? Resolution of this issue does not require any reduction in the plaintiff's burden of proof.

The circumstances of the accident satisfy the plaintiff's burden of proving factual causation only if most accidents of this type are caused by the tortious risk in question. This particular issue can be resolved without detailed evidence of the probabilities or expert testimony. Based on our experience, we know that the absence of headlights is the most likely cause of a collision on a darkened highway, explaining why courts have long recognized that the causal issue "is ordinarily a question of fact for the jury, to be resolved by the exercise of good common sense in the consideration of the evidence of each particular case."[6]

In resolving this causal question, the jury could reasonably consider the nature of the underlying tort duty. The counterfactual inquiry required by the but-for test frequently involves assumptions about human behavior. Would headlights on an oncoming vehicle help other drivers avoid a collision? Would compliance with the speed limit give the driver enough time to avoid an accident? Would a lifesaving device on a boat save someone from drowning? In each of these cases, the duty to take the precaution in question — to have working headlights on vehicles, to comply with the speed limit, or to have lifesaving devices on boats — assumes that the precaution would prevent a significant number of accidents. This attribute of the duty can help the jury resolve the issue of causation.

Because the precaution would enable the relevant actors to prevent a significant number of injuries, a jury could reasonably conclude that if there was some opportunity for rescue, a lifesaving device would have made a difference in this particular case by helping those on board to save the decedent from drowning. Such a finding would not involve conjecture or speculation, as it stems from the reasonable behavioral assumption embodied in the duty to install lifesaving devices on boats.

A judge who submits such an issue of factual causation to the jury is applying our so-called liberal rule of but-for causation. The lifesaving device ordinarily would not make a difference, but the rule provides a reasonable basis for distinguishing the ordinary case from the case at hand. As implied by the duty, the relevant actors could use the precaution to prevent injury in a significant number of cases. If that outcome could have occurred in the present case, the jury has a reasonable basis (the duty) for concluding that the precaution would have prevented the injury in question. Such a finding by the jury satisfies the liberal rule of but-for causation, but the rule turns out to be liberal only insofar as it permits the jury to draw reasonable behavioral inferences from the nature of the underlying duty.

So conceptualized, the liberal rule of but-for causation can be squared with the plaintiff's ordinary burden of proving causation. In some cases, for example, there will be no chance of saving the decedent. The behavioral inference is irrelevant. The same outcome occurs whenever the causal question does not involve human behavior, as in the prior example of the polluted aquifer. After the defendant had created the unreasonable risk of injury by contaminating the drinking water, the issue of whether that risk materialized and injured the plaintiff only depends on how the polluting chemicals interact with the human body. A behavioral inference would not help the plaintiff prove that his or her injuries were caused by the chemical, making the liberal rule of but-for causation inapposite for cases of this type. Cases applying the ordinary rule of but-for causation, therefore, can be harmonized with those applying the liberal rule.*

Whether the risk in question depends on human behavior or other forces is not always clear, an ambiguity that can

---

* An important exception is *Zuchowicz*, in which the court applied the liberal rule to a defendant who negligently gave the plaintiff a double dosage of prescribed medicine. The causal issue did not require behavioral inferences, making the liberal rule inapposite for reasons evident in the case. If a double dosage would more than double the risk of injury, then the overdose, more likely than not, caused the plaintiff's injury. This factual issue can be directly proven by scientific evidence, making it unnecessary to rely on a behavioral presumption of any sort. Doubling the dosage of a drug does not ordinarily double the risk of side effects, and so there was not a sufficient basis for concluding that the defendant's negligence, more likely than not, caused the harm.

explain the otherwise puzzling doctrine known as *loss of a chance*. This doctrine addresses a causal problem that frequently exists in medical malpractice cases. For example, if someone enters the hospital with cancer that is likely to kill him or her, and the doctor misdiagnoses the disease and fails to treat it, the resulting death would not have been caused by the malpractice: More likely than not, the patient would have died anyway due to the cancer. For this category of cases, the element of factual cause forecloses an entire class of very sick patients from being protected by malpractice liability at a time when the tort right is of critical importance for them. To address this problem, the Washington Supreme Court in the seminal case *Herskovits v. Group Health Co-operative of Puget Sound* decided to recognize a claim that the defendant's negligence caused the patient to lose a significant chance of recovery. If the malpractice, more likely than not, reduced the patient's chances of recovery, then the liability rule provides recovery for that lost chance.*

In the two decades that have elapsed since the *Herskovits* decision, courts around the country have struggled when faced with loss-of-a-chance cases. A number of jurisdictions strictly abide by traditional rules of causation in allowing recovery only for the loss of better-than-even odds. Courts in a handful of states have adopted a relaxed standard of causation in these cases, allowing potentially full recoveries where a "substantial possibility" existed that the negligent conduct brought about the harm even though the likelihood that the defendant caused the injury did not exceed 50%. Several jurisdictions have decided to recognize loss-of-a-chance claims involving less-than-even odds and allow recovery of proportional damages (either discounting by the

---

* 664 P.2d 474 (Wash. 1983) (plurality). The court's opinion was deeply influenced by a law review article that first developed the doctrine. *See* Joseph H. King, Jr., *Causation, Valuation, and Chance in Personal Injury Torts Involving Preexisting Conditions and Future Consequences*, 90 Yale L.J. 1353 (1981).

percentage lost or allowing the jury to use its discretion in setting an appropriate lump-sum award). . . . Those jurisdictions that recognize claims for the loss of less-than-even odds generally have not extended the theory beyond the medical malpractice context.[7]

It is not apparent, however, why the doctrine is limited to medical malpractice cases.

In reality, the loss of a chance theory can have an exceedingly broad application. . . . Even in its narrow formulation the theory potentially applies to several very large categories of cases, including legal malpractice cases, and cases involving failures to rescue, to warn, to provide safety devices, and to give informed consent to medical procedures. In its broad formulation, the theory can apply to all cases where a tortfeasor creates a risk of harm and it is uncertain whether the harm has already occurred or will occur in the future. In this broad formulation, the "loss of a chance" theory provides a basis for largely substituting "probabilistic causation" for the traditional "all or nothing" approach to causation.[8]

The doctrine would have these potentially widespread implications if it redefines the element of damages or compensable harm. For cases in which the malpractice did not cause the wrongful death of the patient, the facts can still show that the defendant, more likely than not, caused the patient to suffer a significant lost chance of survival. By converting the damages claim from one of wrongful death into one of a lost chance, courts solve the causal problem. By doing so, however, courts could be adopting a rule of "probabilistic" causation that allows any injured plaintiff to recover merely by proving that he or she had been exposed to an unreasonable risk of harm by the defendant. "If, for example, defendant exposes plaintiff to radiation that creates a 10 percent chance of causing plaintiff to get cancer, defendant has deprived plaintiff of a 10 percent chance of avoiding cancer."[9] A risk of harm can always be recharacterized as a lost chance of avoiding injury, so the doctrine could radically alter tort law, absent some limiting principle.

The doctrine does not have to be interpreted in this manner. It has an obvious connection to the rescue cases — the negligence in each case clearly robs the right holder of a significant chance to escape from an impending peril — thereby implicating our so-called liberal rule of but-for causation. Insofar as that rule is best interpreted as one that allows the jury to draw reasonable behavioral inferences from the nature of the underlying duty, it provides a rationale for limiting the loss-of-a-chance doctrine to medical malpractice cases in a manner that does not depend on a rule of probabilistic causation.

Consider someone who has cancer and seeks medical attention. The statistics show that for this type of cancer, the patient is unlikely to survive. Beyond the provision of ordinary medical treatment, is the chance of survival entirely independent of human behavior, or are the patient's prospects dependent on his or her behavior and that of the doctor? Individuals commonly believe that they can "fight" diseases in various ways, including diet, exercise, positive thought, and prayer: "The cancer will kill most people, but not me. I am different. I will prevail." In seeking out medical attention, individuals often believe that the odds are not fixed and that the choice of doctor matters in this respect. Consequently, a court could defensibly incorporate a behavioral component into the doctor's duty to provide reasonable medical care. Such a duty assumes that patients can survive despite the odds, and that the physician will help the patient do so. In light of this behavioral assumption, a jury could reasonably conclude that the patient would have survived if the physician's malpractice had not taken away a significant chance of doing so. Such a finding would not involve conjecture or speculation, as it stems from the reasonable behavioral assumption embodied in the physician's duty — the same type of finding made by the liberal rule of but-for causation.

So, too, a court could decide that the odds of survival do not largely depend on individual behavior. Without question, patients often believe that they will beat the odds, but such a belief does not necessarily provide a reasonable basis for liability: The cold, hard truth is in the numbers. Courts adopting this view will rely exclusively on the medical probabilities of survival, leading them to reject claims whenever the statistics show that the patient would probably have died anyway.

As illustrated by these cases, the issue of factual causation often implicates statistical evidence, requiring courts to interpret the meaning of probabilities. In these kinds of cases, courts regularly disagree about the appropriate outcome. Perhaps the nature of probabilistic reasoning has led some courts to adopt probabilistic liability rules that depart from the traditional "all or nothing" rule of factual causation. Such a departure from an established rule will inevitably be controversial. Alternatively, courts could be disagreeing about the relevance of probabilities derived from the common experience of large numbers of individuals. For some, the statistical evidence is dispositive of the individual claim. Others, though, could question whether it is fair to treat the plaintiff (or defendant) merely as an undifferentiated member of a statistical group. Does fairness require more individualized treatment? If so, the fact that most people would die from a disease does not necessarily prove that the plaintiff faced the same fate. Differing interpretations of probabilistic evidence can explain why some courts deny recovery under circumstances in which others submit the issue to the jury. The interpretation of probabilistic evidence is not limited to causal questions, but it recurs with enough frequency to place the issue of factual causation at the center of many disputes involving scientific or statistical evidence.[10]

B. Multiple Tortious Causes

Courts do not use the but-for test of causation in cases involving multiple tortious causes, each of which was independently sufficient to cause the plaintiff's injury. The classic example involves two independent tortfeasors who negligently started separate fires that subsequently merged and destroyed the plaintiff's property. Each fire was sufficient to cause the entirety of the plaintiff's damage, and so the plaintiff cannot prove that either fire was a but-for cause of the injury. Defendant 1 can say, "Even if I had not negligently started a fire, the plaintiff's property still would have been burned by the other fire, so my negligence was not a but-for cause of the plaintiff's harm." Defendant 2 can then say the same thing by relying on the fact that the fire of Defendant 1 would have independently destroyed the plaintiff's property. The but-for test would deny the plaintiff recovery altogether, even though his or her property was destroyed by the combined negligence of the two defendants. In these cases, "all courts impose liability on both tortfeasors without requiring 'but for' causation [as applied to each defendant individually]. Courts do this to avoid the obvious injustice of allowing each culpable tortfeasor to escape liability to an innocent victim by hiding behind the negligence of the other tortfeasor."[11]

The same problem exists in many cases involving toxic substances and diseases. In asbestos cases, for example, the plaintiff can prove that his or her injury was caused by exposure to asbestos products supplied by multiple defendants. Based on this evidence, each defendant asbestos supplier can argue that the injury, more likely than not, was caused by the other defendants' asbestos products. This defense, when employed by each defendant asbestos supplier, would deny the plaintiff's recovery under circumstances in which the plaintiff has proven that the injury was caused by the defendants' asbestos products. The causal problem is similar to the one created by the two-fires cases, and courts apply the same causal rule in both instances.

As the Maryland Court of Appeals explains:

> In products liability involving asbestos, where the plaintiff has sufficiently demonstrated both lung disease resulting from exposure to asbestos and that the exposure was to the asbestos products of many different, but identified, suppliers, no supplier enjoys a causation defense solely on the ground that the plaintiff would probably have suffered the same disease from inhaling fibers originating from the products of other suppliers.[12]

An asbestos defendant cannot avoid liability merely because the injury, more likely than not, was caused by the defective asbestos products sold by the other defendants. This rule is adopted by the *Restatement (Third)* for all cases involving toxic substances and diseases.[13]

Because the but-for test does not work in these cases, courts determine factual causation by asking whether the actor's negligent conduct was "a substantial factor in bringing about the harm."[14] Each of the two negligently started fires was a substantial factor in causing the destruction of the plaintiff's property, and so the substantial-factor test satisfactorily addresses the cases involving multiple tortious causes.

In practice, courts have not always limited the substantial-factor test to cases of multiple tortious causes, with some using it as the exclusive test for factual causation in all tort cases. However, when the test governs cases not involving multiple tortious causes, it can create problems due to the way in which it apparently reduces the plaintiff's burden of proof. Even if the defendant's tortious conduct was not the probable cause of the injury, the jury could deem it to have been a substantial factor. The concept of a substantial factor is not well-defined, making it particularly vulnerable to misapplication.

To avoid this problem, the *Restatement (Third)* has jettisoned the substantial-factor test. It has instead adopted the NESS test of causation, which deems the tortious conduct to have been a cause of the accident whenever it is a **n**ecessary **e**lement of a **s**ufficient causal **s**et:

> A useful model for understanding factual causation is to conceive of a set made up of each of the necessary conditions for plaintiff's harm. Absent any one of the elements of the set, the plaintiff's harm would not have occurred. Thus, there will always be multiple (some say, infinite) factual causes of harm, although most will not be of significance for tort law and many will be unidentified.[15]

For example, the NESS test readily identifies each of the two negligent fires as a tortious cause: "Each fire was necessary for the sufficiency of a set of existing antecedent conditions that contained it but not the other fire."[16] The logic of this conclusion, in turn, generates the *Restatement (Third)* rule for multiple tortious causes:

> If multiple acts exist, each of which . . . alone would have been a factual cause of the physical harm at the same time in the absence of the other act(s), each act is regarded as a factual cause of the harm.[17]

This rule straightforwardly resolves the two-fire cases, but resolution of the asbestos cases requires further analysis. When multiple defendants each supplied different asbestos-containing products onto the site where the plaintiff inhaled the asbestos fibers that caused his or her cancer, the plaintiff cannot prove that the asbestos supplied by any one defendant was sufficient to cause the harm.* Yet the courts impose

---

* Based on existing scientific knowledge, we do not know whether asbestos causes cancer by cumulative exposure or a single exposure. Given this indeterminacy, the plaintiff cannot prove the minimal amount of asbestos exposure that would be sufficient to cause the harm.

liability on all these defendants. To cover these cases, the *Restatement (Third)* states that the rule for multiple tortious causes applies even if "an actor's conduct requires other conduct to be sufficient to cause . . . [the] harm."[18] This result follows from the NESS test, which constructs causal sets in terms of the antecedent conditions that existed at the time of injury. Given the total amount of asbestos fibers at a particular site, a causal set can be constructed for which the defendant's asbestos is an element needed to make the total amount of asbestos sufficient for causing the cancer. Each asbestos defendant will be contained in some such set, making each one a factual cause of the plaintiff's cancer.

As the asbestos cases illustrate, the issue of factual causation can be complex when the injury was caused by multiple tortious causes. Other cases of this type involve even harder causal questions addressed by the doctrines of alternative liability and market-share liability, issues to which we return once the foundation for analysis is fully in place.*

II. PROXIMATE CAUSE AND THE SCOPE OF LIABILITY (A REPRISE OF DUTY)

An old proverb illustrates how an isolated instance of wrongdoing can have widespread consequences:

> For want of a nail, the shoe was lost; for want of a shoe, the horse was lost; for want of a horse, the rider was lost; for want of a rider, the battle was lost; for want of a battle, the kingdom was lost; and all for the want of a horseshoe nail.

The defendant who negligently put the shoe on the horse was a factual cause of the kingdom being lost. Should he or she be liable for that loss? The question is not factual, but instead

---

* *See* Chapter 10, section III.

involves a policy judgment concerning the appropriate scope of liability for injuries that were caused by the defendant's tortious conduct.

Tort law has determined that some limitation of liability is warranted. To recover, the plaintiff must prove that the defendant's tortious act or omission was a *legal* or *proximate* cause of the injuries in question. The element of proximate cause limits the liability of a defendant whose tortious conduct was a factual cause of the plaintiff's harm.

Courts have had a hard time identifying the policy rationales for this limitation of liability. "There is perhaps nothing in the entire field of law which has called forth more disagreement, or upon which the opinions are in such a welter of confusion."[19]

The difficulty stems from the writ system, which forced courts to rely on the rubric of causation to resolve difficult policy questions. After the writ system was abolished, courts continued to use the language of causation to resolve policy questions. Courts, for example, ruled that stand-alone emotional and economic harms are never proximately caused by negligence. This legal conclusion was based solely on policy concerns having nothing to do with the governing principles of causation. Today these issues are addressed by duty analysis, which limits liability for pure emotional harms due to policy concerns about financially crushing liability, the administration of a large number of claims, and so on.* Much of the history of proximate cause involves efforts to disentangle that element from the element of duty.

Both elements define the defendant's scope of liability, but nevertheless are distinctive. The element of duty involves a determination of whether a defined class of actors should be legally responsible for accidents caused by certain types of risks

---

* *See* Chapter 8, section I.D (discussing the limitation of duty to exclude most cases of stand-alone emotional harms).

(like foreseeable risks of physical harm and so on). The categorical nature of the decision makes it an issue of law to be determined by judges. Having defined the scope of duty as a matter of law, courts must then address the separate issue of whether the categorical duty encompasses the particular risk that caused the plaintiff's injury. This issue is case-specific, making proximate cause an evaluative decision for the jury.

In defining the appropriate scope of liability for purposes of proximate cause, two types of approaches are possible. One relies on hindsight to trace the causal sequence directly backward from the injury to the defendant's misconduct. The other approach is forward looking and determines proximate cause from the perspective of the reasonable person at the time of the tortious misconduct. Each has merit, which is why there has been so much debate about the proper specification of proximate cause.

A. The Directness Test

Lest there be any doubt about the continued influence of the writ system, one only has to consider the element of proximate cause. The writ of trespass let the plaintiff recover for physical harms "directly" caused the defendant, whereas the writ of trespass on the case provided recovery for "indirect" physical harms caused by the defendant in specific circumstances.* With the abolition of the writ system, courts were supposed to rely on the substantive bases of liability inherent in these (and other) writs. The combined logic of the two writs suggests that a defendant is liable for all physical harms directly caused by the tortious misconduct and can also incur liability for having indirectly caused harms in specific circumstances, most notably, when the defendant could reasonably anticipate or foresee that such harms would occur. A direct cause is always

---

* *See* Chapter 1, section I (discussing the writ system).

proximate, whereas an indirect cause is proximate only when it foreseeably brings about the harm — a formulation known as the *directness test*.

The directness test was famously adopted in *Polemis*, which subjected the defendant to liability for the unexpected, direct consequences of the negligent misconduct. The defendant's employees negligently dropped a plank into the hold of a ship. The employees should have foreseen that the dropped plank could have damaged persons or cargo in the hold below or even the ship itself by denting the hold. The plank instead unexpectedly threw a spark that ignited petroleum vapors, causing a fire that destroyed the ship. The fire was not reasonably foreseeable, forcing the court to choose between an approach based on foresight and one based on hindsight. It opted for the latter. As one of the justices concluded, "If the act would or might probably cause damage, the fact that the damage it in fact causes is not the exact kind of damage one would expect is immaterial, so long as the damage is in fact directly traceable to the negligent act. . . ."[20]

The requirements of the directness test in *Polemis* are unclear. Does liability extend to *any* direct consequences of the negligent act? Although *Polemis* suggests as much, that interpretation of the directness test presents a widely recognized problem for a recurring class of cases.

The problem is illustrated by the well-known case *Berry v. Sugar Notch Borough*, in which the defendant railroad was negligently speeding when its train was struck by a falling tree, injuring the plaintiff.[21] If the train had been operating at a reasonable speed, it would not have been located on the track at the point where the tree fell, establishing factual causation. The circumstances of the accident also satisfy the directness test articulated in *Polemis*. As a direct consequence of speeding, the train was involved in a crash, although in an unexpected manner. The directness test for proximate cause appeared to be satisfied, but the *Berry* court found otherwise. "The same thing might as readily have happened to a car running slowly, or it might have been that a high speed alone would have carried him beyond the tree to a place of safety." It was merely a coincidence that the tree fell on the speeding train, severing the necessary causal link between the defendant's negligence and the plaintiff's injury.

Cases like this have led courts to adopt the *risk rule*, a "principle which excludes liability where the injury sprang from a hazard different from that which was improperly risked."[22] The injury in *Berry* was caused by the hazard of falling trees, a hazard different from that which the defendant railroad had improperly risked by speeding. By limiting liability to injuries caused by a tortious hazard or risk (the speeding train), the risk rule absolves the defendant of liability for injuries that were only coincidentally connected to the tortious behavior (a falling tree).

When supplemented by the risk rule, the directness test has wide support. "The weight of authority in this country rejects the limitation of damages to consequences foreseeable at the time of the negligent conduct when the consequences are 'direct,' and the damage, although other and greater than expectable, is of the same general sort that was risked."[23]

To apply the test, courts must distinguish direct causes from other causes. An injury is not directly caused by the defendant's misconduct when a force intervenes between the defendant's conduct and the harm:

> By and large external forces will be regarded as intervening if they appear on the scene after the defendant had acted unless perhaps their pending inevitability at the time of the defendant's negligent act or omission is made crystal clear. And when a new force (for which the defendant is not responsible) "intervenes" in this crude sense to bring about a result that the defendant's negligence would not otherwise have produced, the defendant is generally held [liable] for that result only

where the intervening force was foreseeable. As many cases put it, a new and unforeseeable force breaks the causal chain.[24]

An unforeseeable intervening force is a *superseding cause* that eliminates the defendant's negligence as a proximate cause of the injury. For example, suppose the defendant negligently started a fire that smoldered for a few days. The fire was then widely spread by an unexpected storm with exceptionally high winds, causing damage to the plaintiff's property. An unforeseeable storm supersedes the defendant's prior negligent conduct and cuts off liability for the ensuing harms. If that same storm, though, had been blowing at the time when the defendant first set the fire, the fire would have been a direct, proximate cause of the ensuing damage. The timing of the causal forces determines whether they supersede the defendant's negligence, and an intervening force must be foreseeable for the negligence to be a proximate cause.

Consistent with the causal rules embodied in the writs of trespass and trespass on the case, proximate cause is established under the directness test for injuries that were either directly or foreseeably caused by the tortious risk.

B. The Foreseeability Test

The directness test critically depends on the distinction between direct and intervening causes, and dissatisfaction with that distinction motivated courts to consider other formulations of proximate cause. Consider the required distinction for an unexpected storm that entered the accident scene after the defendant's negligent conduct. For the storm to be an intervening cause, the court must conclude that its force came into existence after the negligent conduct. How can the court make such a determination? As chaos theory shows, the movement of a butterfly in Africa can set in motion forces that ultimately cause a hurricane to cross the Atlantic

Ocean. The "force" of such a storm can be in place long before the negligent defendant's conduct occurred, even if the storm entered the scene of the accident after the defendant had acted. The timing of the causal forces is all that matters for distinguishing between direct and intervening causes, and yet there is no good way to determine reliably when the force was initiated. Why not when the earth was first formed? None of these questions have any apparent connection to the underlying policy issue about the appropriate scope of the defendant's liability, a severe problem for the directness test.

For essentially these reasons, the court in the case known as *Wagon Mound I* rejected *Polemis* with such forceful argument that the directness test thereafter effectively ceased to be good law in the British Commonwealth. As the court scathingly concluded in its evaluation of the directness test, "The impression that may well be left on the reader of the scores of cases in which liability for negligence has been discussed is that the courts . . . were at times in grave danger of being led astray by scholastic theories of causation and their ugly and their barely intelligible jargon. . . ."*

Having rejected the directness test, the court then considered whether proximate cause should instead be defined in terms of the "natural or necessary or probable consequences" of the negligent act, a definition used by "scores" of courts "feeling their way to a coherent body of doctrine."

> For, if it is asked why a man should be responsible for the natural or necessary or probable consequences of his act (or any other similar description of them) the answer is that it is not because they are natural or necessary or probable, but

---

* *Overseas Tankship (U.K.) Ltd. v. Morts Dock & Eng'g Co., Ltd.* [1961] A.C. 388 (P.C. Aust.). The case is known as *Wagon Mound I* because it involved a vessel known as the Wagon Mound that negligently discharged oil that subsequently caught fire while floating on the water, causing destruction of the plaintiff's dock. Another case, *Wagon Mound II*, involved a different plaintiff seeking recovery for injuries caused by the same fire.

because, since they have this quality, it is judged by the standard of the reasonable man that he ought to have foreseen them.[25]

Proximate cause had long been defined in terms of foreseeability with good reason:

> For, if some limitation must be imposed upon the consequences for which the negligent actor is to be held responsible — and all are agreed that some limitation there must be — why should that test (reasonable forseeability) be rejected which, since he is judged by what the reasonable man ought to foresee, corresponds with the common conscience of mankind, and a test (the "direct" consequence) be substituted which leads to nowhere but the never-ending and insoluble conundrum of causation.[26]

Under the *foreseeability test*, the defendant's negligence is a proximate cause of only those types of accidents that the reasonable person would have foreseen at the time of the conduct in question. Due to the compelling logic of foreseeability and the "insoluble" problems of direct causation, foreseeability has become the dominant test for proximate cause. "It is very doubtful that liability unlimited by foreseeability has much contemporary support."[27]

The triumph of the foreseeability test has not been complete, however, due to the continued influence of the directness test. "Even when a foreseeability standard is employed for the scope of liability, the fact that the actor neither foresaw nor should have foreseen the extent of harm caused by the tortious conduct does not affect the actor's liability for the harm."[28] This principle is colloquially known as the *eggshell-skull rule*. According to this rule, even if the defendant could not foresee that the plaintiff had some pre-existing susceptibility to physical harm (the eggshell skull), the defendant incurs responsibility for the full extent of the physical harm directly caused by the negligent conduct (a crushed skull from an impact that ordinarily would cause minor harm). As long as the nature of the harm was reasonably foreseeable (like some bodily injury caused by the tortious risk), proximate cause is established; the extent of harm (the crushed skull) does not have to be foreseeable when directly caused by a foreseeable injury (a blow to the head).

This universally adopted rule has not been adequately squared with the logic of the foreseeability test. The *Restatement (Third)* recognizes that the rule is "difficult to reconcile" with foreseeability, but nevertheless justifies it on the grounds that such cases "rarely arise" and it is "administratively convenien[t]" to avoid the "sometimes uncertain and indeterminate inquiry into whether the extent of harm was unforeseeable."[29] The tension between the directness and foreseeability tests continues to persist.

C. Foreseeability and Directness Combined: Distinguishing the Prima Facie Case from the Extent of Damages

Whether the majority of courts rely on the directness test or the foreseeability test is a surprisingly hard question. On one view, "The weight of authority in this country rejects the limitation of damages to consequences foreseeable at the time of the negligent conduct when the consequences are 'direct,' and the damage, although other and greater than expectable, is of the same general sort that was risked. . . ."[30] According to the other view, "It is very doubtful that liability unlimited by foreseeability has much contemporary support."[31] Which is correct?

Despite their apparent differences, the two views can be reconciled. When fully analyzed, the directness and foreseeability tests for proximate cause turn out to be equivalent for reasons that have not been adequately identified by the courts.

The issue requires closer consideration of the plaintiff's proof. The element of proximate cause only matters if the plaintiff can establish all other elements of the prima facie case. Consider the plaintiff's proof that the defendant breached the duty to exercise reasonable care. As implied by this evidence, the defendant's failure to take the reasonable precaution with a burden B created both tortious risks and other collateral risks not encompassed by the duty, including unforeseeable risks:

$$B \circledR (P \bullet L)_{tortious\ risks}$$
$$+ (P \bullet L)_{collateral\ risks}$$

To satisfy the element of factual causation, the plaintiff must have been injured either by a tortious or collateral risk: But for the defendant's failure to take the precaution, these risks would not have been created and could not have injured the plaintiff. Having fully specified the nature of the plaintiff's proof, we can now reconsider the element of proximate cause.

The directness test has widespread support only when supplemented by the risk rule, "which excludes liability where the injury sprang from a hazard different from that which was improperly risked."[32] The defendant's negligent conduct improperly risked only those accidents caused by tortious risks; accidents caused by collateral risks necessarily spring from a different hazard and cannot be a proximate cause of the plaintiff's injuries. When the directness test is supplemented by the risk rule, the plaintiff cannot recover if the accident was directly caused by a collateral risk.

The same result is attained by the foreseeability test. The category of tortious risks necessarily includes only foreseeable risks, whereas any collateral risks of physical harm must be unforeseeable to fall outside of the duty.* Like the directness

---

* *See* Chapter 8, section I.C (describing the ordinary duty of care). The risk rule then further limits the category of tortious risks to those foreseeable risks encompassed by the duty, thereby excluding most foreseeable risks of pure emotional harm and so on.

test, the foreseeability test limits liability to accidents caused by a tortious risk.

To clarify the nature of this inquiry, the *Restatement (Third)* adopts new terminology called the *risk standard*: "An actor's liability is limited to those physical harms that result from the risks that made the actor's conduct tortious."[33]

For cases in which the risk standard is satisfied, the tortious risk must have proximately caused the plaintiff *some* physical harm, completing the plaintiff's prima facie case for liability (duty, breach, causation, and damage). Having established the prima facie case, the plaintiff must then prove the amount of damages to which he or she is entitled.

Like the element of proximate cause, the damages inquiry involves a causal question: Did the defendant's tortious conduct cause the full extent of damages claimed by the plaintiff? The causal question for determining the extent of damages importantly differs from the element of proximate cause in the prima facie case, and that difference explains the continued vitality of the directness test.

Tort law could not fairly determine the amount of damages by relying on the foreseeability test. Compensatory damages are limited to the amount of harm for the injury in question, so a defendant who caused an unforeseeably low amount of damages would have to pay only that amount. A blow that would crush an ordinary skull, for example, could cause only minor injury to a hard-headed plaintiff, yielding a damages award substantially less than the foreseeable amount. The foreseeability test would only be operative, then, for cases in which the plaintiff suffered unforeseeably high damages (like the severe head injuries incurred by a plaintiff with an eggshell skull). The foreseeability test would prevent the defendant from paying unforeseeably high damages while permitting the defendant to pay unforeseeably low damages, a one-sided advantage that is unfair for the plaintiff.

By contrast, the directness test is a more fair method for determining the extent of damages. The test can be justified by a widely adopted evidentiary principle for determining damages.

Consider a case involving a promising first-year law student who was permanently disabled by the defendant's tortious misconduct, leaving him or her unable to practice law. As part of the damages award, the plaintiff can collect the future earnings he or she will lose as a result of the tortious injury. Various types of evidence show how much a law student is likely to earn in the future. Even the best evidence of projected future earnings, however, cannot establish that this particular student, more likely than not, would in fact receive these earnings 30 or 40 years from now had he or she not been permanently disabled. Such certainty is not possible for damage calculations extending far into the future. The more-likely-than-not evidentiary standard would bar many claims for lost future earnings.

Barring the plaintiff from recovery would be unjust, though, because the evidentiary problem was created by the defendant's tortious wrongdoing. Had the defendant's tortious conduct not permanently disabled the student, there would be no need to estimate the student's lost future earnings. Hence it would be "a perversion of fundamental principles of justice" if the uncertainty created by the defendant's tortious misconduct were to bar the plaintiff from recovering damages.[34] To avoid this injustice, tort law reduces the plaintiff's burden of proof regarding causal questions in the damages phase. The plaintiff is only required to establish the amount of damages with "as much certainty as the nature of the tort and the circumstances permit."[35]

In some cases, this principle can reduce the plaintiff's burden of proof, but the circumstances do not always require that outcome. Regardless of how it affects the burden of proof, the principle allocates the burden of any inherent factual uncertainty to the defendant in the damages phase of the case. For this reason, the principle can explain why courts determine the extent of damages by relying on the directness test.

To establish the prima facie case, the plaintiff must prove that the defendant is responsible for a tortious risk that proximately caused the plaintiff some compensable damage (typically physical harm). By proving that he or she suffered other injuries that were directly caused by the tortious risk, the plaintiff has proven these additional damages with "as much certainty as the nature of the tort and the circumstances permit." The defendant might not have been able to foresee the full extent of these damages, but any inherent uncertainty concerning the extent of damages must be borne by the defendant.

This reasoning explains why "[t]he weight of authority in this country rejects the limitation of damages to consequences foreseeable at the time of the negligent conduct when the consequences are 'direct,' and the damage, although other and greater than expectable, is of the same general sort that was risked."[36] The plaintiff can also suffer other harms that were indirectly caused by the tortious risk, but the defendant's liability cannot extend into the indefinite future. Lacking the limitation of direct causation, the only other defensible way for courts to limit liability is by relying on foreseeability. The extent to which the defendant's tortious conduct caused the plaintiff's damages, therefore, encompasses both direct harms and indirect, foreseeable harms — a rule corresponding to the directness test.

To be sure, this rule is one of proximate cause. The quantification of damages, though, only occurs after the plaintiff has established the prima facie case for liability. The directness test, therefore, does not determine the element of proximate cause in the prima facie case.

Consider how this interpretation of the directness test applies to *Polemis*. The defendant created a tortious risk of damaging the ship by the concussive force of the dropped plank. On landing in the hold below, the plank presumably caused some damage to cargo or the ship itself, however slight. The plaintiff's proof accordingly established the prima facie case — the defendant had breached the duty to exercise reasonable care in a manner that foreseeably caused the plaintiff to suffer some physical harm. The only remaining issue involved the extent of damages. In addition to causing some physical harm to the ship or cargo, the tortious risk (concussive force) directly caused an unforeseeable fire that destroyed the ship. Under the evidentiary principle embodied in the directness test, the unforeseeable extent of these damages is properly placed on the defendant wrongdoer and not the plaintiff accident victim. In effect, the ship's unexpected vulnerability to fire from a blow to the ship's body was just like a thin-skulled individual's unexpected vulnerability to injury from a blow to the head.[37] The outcome in *Polemis* can be supported by the directness test limited to the determination of damages, even though the case did not expressly limit the test and has been widely rejected for that reason.

When the directness test is limited to causal questions in the damages phase of the case, it is not relevant to the issue of proximate cause that is part of the plaintiff's prima facie case. The defendant cannot incur any liability without having proximately caused some compensable damage, requiring satisfaction of the foreseeability test or the substantively equivalent risk standard in the *Restatement (Third)*. Having established liability on this basis, the plaintiff must then prove the extent to which the defendant caused damage. Unlike the issue of proximate cause in the prima facie case, the causal question in the damages phase of the case cannot be fairly resolved by the foreseeability test. The directness test is the appropriate method for determining the amount of damages, but the plaintiff must first establish the prima facie case.

D. The Characterization of Tortious Risk

Proximate cause requires proof that the plaintiff suffered some foreseeable damage, like bodily injury, caused by the type of risk that made the defendant's conduct negligent. Resolution of this issue critically depends on how the court characterizes the tortious risk.

The plaintiff would like to define the tortious risk as broadly as possible. The broadest definition is "the risk of harm," because the fact of harm would establish proximate cause, regardless of the type of injury or how it occurred. This definition of the tortious risk would encompass harms excluded from the duty, like many forms of pure emotional or economic loss, and would also include nonforeseeable risks of physical harm, making the definition much too broad.

The defendant, by contrast, prefers narrow definitions of the tortious risk. An extremely narrow definition would include all details of the accident, turning the tortious risk into the prospect that the particular plaintiff would suffer the particular injury on a particular date at a particular location. That characterization requires perfect foresight, effectively eliminating the less demanding requirement of reasonable foreseeability.

Between these two extremes lies the appropriate formulation of the tortious risk. "No specific rule can be provided about the appropriate level of generality or specificity to employ in characterizing the type of harm for purposes" of establishing proximate cause.[38]

A tortious risk must be foreseeable, and so the appropriate characterization of tortious risk can be derived from the concept of foreseeability. As previously discussed, duty is limited to the foreseeable risks of harm because the defendant can make safety choices only for risks that can be foreseen.*

---

* *See* Chapter 8, section I.B.

Lacking the ability to choose, the defendant cannot fairly be subject to liability. The concept of foreseeability is behavioral.

The reasonable person makes safety decisions by reference to types of accidents that threaten foreseeable classes of potential victims. An automobile driver, for example, decides how safely to drive by considering the risk of an automobile accident in relation to other drivers, pedestrians, and nearby property owners. In light of these risks, the reasonable driver takes certain precautions to prevent these foreseeable types of accidents. A defendant who failed to take such a precaution created tortious risk.

To be injured by tortious risk, the plaintiff must be within a class of potential victims who were foreseeably threatened by the conduct (the *Palsgraf* rule), and the injury must have been caused by the type of accident that at least partially motivated the need for the precaution in the first instance. A behavioral conception of foreseeability, provides a method for determining whether the plaintiff was injured by a tortious risk.

To be sure, many doubt that the concept of foreseeability provides an adequate method for limiting liability. According to the U.S. Supreme Court, "If one takes a broad enough view, *all* consequences of a negligent act, no matter how far removed in time or space, may be foreseen. Conditioning liability on foreseeability, therefore, is hardly a condition at all."[39]

The concept of foreseeability is vulnerable to such criticism for historical reasons. Before courts and scholars refined negligence liability by distinguishing the element of duty from other aspects of the claim, much of the work done by duty analysis occurred within the element of proximate cause. Courts, for example, limited liability for pure emotional harms by concluding that such harms were simply not foreseeable, even though a negligent actor knows that the physical harms suffered by an accident victim will ordinarily cause emotional distress to family and friends. When employed in this manner, foreseeability merely expresses a legal conclusion, eliminating any analytic purpose it might otherwise have.

Now that the element of duty has been disentangled from the element of proximate cause, courts no longer need to invoke foreseeability in conclusory terms. Understood as a behavioral concept for the safety decision in question, foreseeability provides a defensible method for identifying the proximate cause of an injury.

To illustrate how the concept of foreseeability makes it possible to resolve issues of proximate cause, consider the tort claims stemming from the September 11, 2001 terrorist attacks on the World Trade Center. The victims of the attack, or their survivors, were entitled to receive compensation from a statutorily created federal fund in exchange for waiving their tort rights.[40] A number of victims chose instead to assert their tort rights against various defendants, including both the owner and operator of the World Trade Center.

The plaintiffs' tort claims would seem to be barred on grounds of foreseeability, and the defendants moved to dismiss the claims for this reason (and others):

> Defendants argue that the ground victims lost their lives and suffered injuries from an event that was not reasonably foreseeable, for terrorists had not previously used a hijacked airplane as a suicidal weapon to destroy buildings and murder thousands. Defendants contend that because the events of September 11 were not within the reasonably foreseeable risks, any duty of care that they would owe to ground victims generally should not extend to the victims of September 11.*

Despite the force of this argument, the plaintiffs had an even stronger response, one that fully illustrates how the plaintiff's proof of breach — the identification of the reasonable

---

* *In Re September 11 Litigation*, 280 F. Supp. 2d 279, 295 (S.D.N.Y. 2003). In the interest of full disclosure, I provided legal advice on this matter, so my role in that capacity might bias the following discussion.

safety precaution that the defendant failed to take — frames the analysis of every element of negligence liability, including foreseeability.

> The WTC Defendants contend that they owed no duty to "anticipate and guard against crimes unprecedented in human history." Plaintiffs argue that defendants owed a duty, not to foresee the crimes, but to have designed, constructed, repaired and maintained the World Trade Center structures to withstand the effects and spread of fire, to avoid building collapses caused by fire and, in designing and effectuating fire safety and evacuation procedures, to provide for the escape of more people.

By selecting untaken precautions that would reduce the risk of fire faced by the tenants and occupants of densely populated, high-rise commercial buildings, the plaintiffs were able to satisfy the requirement of foreseeability. The plaintiffs' negligence claims effectively defined the tortious risk as "the risk of being injured by a fire in a building lacking adequate fire-safety protections." This tortious risk caused the injuries for which the plaintiffs sought compensation. Most obviously, a fire can foreseeably burn victims. A fire can also foreseeably cause the collapse of a building, the cause of injury for most victims.

To be sure, the fire that destroyed the World Trade Center was not an ordinary fire. It was caused by an unprecedented criminal act of terrorism. This detail, however, does not factor into the definition of tortious risk. As the enabling torts establish, those who own and operate buildings have a duty to protect tenants and other occupants from criminal attack.* One foreseeable form of criminal attack involves fire (arson), so the duty to protect tenants and occupants from fire includes the risk of arson. Fires can be caused

---

* *See* Chapter 8, section I.F.

by various other sources as well, creating a duty to protect those in a building from a fire, regardless of its origin (electrical problems, arson, or whatever). The general threat of fire, for example, motivates the adoption of reasonably safe procedures for evacuating the building; the procedures aren't implemented to provide safe escape from fires only originating from certain sources. The particular source of the fire, including the motives of the arsonists, is an irrelevant detail for purposes of defining the tortious risk.

All that remains is the fact that the arson caused an unforeseeably high toll of death and destruction, the most salient and disturbing aspect of the fires. The extent of damages, however, does not have to be foreseeable.[*] The tortious risk, therefore, could properly be defined as "the risk of being injured by a fire in a building lacking adequate fire-safety protections," so any victim who was injured by that risk was foreseeably harmed by the defendants' alleged negligence.[†]

This definition of tortious risk does not unilaterally favor every potential tort claimant. Once the tortious risk is defined as "the risk of being injured by fire in a building lacking adequate fire-safety protections," the claims involving victims who were killed by the initial plane crashes do not satisfy the element of factual causation. The same is true of any claims involving victims who could not have escaped the buildings had they been equipped with reasonable fire-safety protections. This definition of tortious risk solves the problem of foreseeability for most plaintiffs in the case, but can do so only by limiting the number of successful claimants.

---

[*] *See supra* section C.

[†] The court never expressly adopted this definition of tortious risk, and it also left open the possibility that the defendants could prove the absence of proximate cause. As the foregoing analysis suggests (while perhaps revealing an adversarial bias), it is hard to see how the defendants could avoid liability on this basis, for doing so would require a definition of tortious risk that distinguishes between different types of criminal motives for committing arson.

The World Trade Center case shows how the plaintiff's choice of an untaken precaution frames the proximate cause inquiry. Any given untaken precaution creates a tortious risk of definite character. The alleged negligence of the World Trade Center defendants involved their failure to take various fire-safety precautions that would have protected those in the building from being harmed by fire. The risk of fire involves a variety of individuated risks, including the risk of fire by electrical malfunction, the risk of arson, and even the risk of arson caused by terrorists. The particular source of the fire does not matter, though, because the reasonable building owner or operator would consider the safety precautions at issue by reference to the general threat of fire as opposed to fires originating from specific sources. The manner in which the defendants allegedly breached the duty to exercise reasonable care determines the tortious risk, so in this important respect, the element of proximate cause involves a reprise of duty.

✗ 10 ✗

Multiple Tortfeasors

Different actors can each tortiously cause the plaintiff's injury. For example, terrorists can set fire to a building, trapping many occupants who were unable to escape in time due to the inadequate fire-protection measures taken by the building's owner or operator. Had the terrorists not set fire to the building, its occupants would not have been harmed. Had the building's owner or operator adopted reasonable fire-safety precautions, many or most of the occupants could have safely escaped from the burning building. Those who suffer injury as a result can establish a prima facie case for liability against the terrorists, the owner of the building, and the operator of the building. Each of these defendants is independently responsible for the plaintiff's injury, requiring special rules for addressing the liability of multiple tortfeasors.

I. JOINT AND SEVERAL LIABILITY OF JOINT TORTFEASORS AND OTHERS

When one is responsible for the conduct of another, tort law groups them for liability purposes. If individuals conspire to pursue an illegal objective, for example, then each co-conspirator is liable for the injuries tortiously caused by any other co-conspirator in furtherance of the illegal objective.

Similarly, one who aids and abets a tortfeasor is liable for the resultant injuries. In these cases, the individuals have acted as a group in causing the injury, making each responsible for any injuries tortiously caused by the group.

Even if the group has legitimate objectives, its members are still subject to a joint duty. For example, an owner of a building can be jointly responsible with the operator of the building to ensure that adequate fire-safety precautions are in place. By jointly carrying out the activity, each participant becomes responsible for the conduct of others in the group, subjecting each to liability for injuries tortiously caused by others in the joint enterprise.

> Strictly speaking, the words *joint tort* should be used only where the behavior of two or more tortfeasors is such as to make it proper to treat the conduct of each as the conduct of the others as well. In effect, this requires the existence of a concert of action or the breach of a joint duty. In terms of legal responsibility, the distinguishing feature of a wrong to which the label joint tort has been affixed is that the tortfeasors will be held jointly and severally — or entirely — liable for the harm proximately resulting.[1]

Joint and several liability is a substantive doctrine that makes each tortfeasor legally responsible for the entirety of the plaintiff's damages. The plaintiff's tort claim, however, is not one of joint and several liability. The plaintiff files a claim against an individual defendant and must prove that this defendant tortiously caused the injuries in question, making the substantive basis of liability dependent on the underlying tort (negligence, strict liability, or whatever). Whether the defendant is subject to joint and several liability then depends on whether other tortfeasors are also legally responsible for the same injuries. In the event that another tortfeasor is also legally responsible for the injuries, then the liability of the defendant and the other tortfeasor can be governed by the rule of joint and several liability.

In any case involving multiple tortfeasors subject to joint and several liability, the plaintiff does not have to sue every tortfeasor. The doctrine of joint and several liability gives the plaintiff the option to sue all of the tortfeasors, a single tortfeasor, or some combination thereof. The plaintiff can recover only once for these injuries, but joint and several liability gives the plaintiff the valuable option of choosing which tortfeasor to sue. One of the tortfeasors might be bankrupt or outside the jurisdiction of the court, and so joint and several liability allows the plaintiff to receive full recovery from one or more of the remaining jointly and severally liable defendants. Each defendant is independently responsible for having tortiously caused the plaintiff's damages, and so each can be held fully accountable for those damages.

Consequently, a joint duty is not the only source of joint and several liability. The doctrine also applies to multiple tortfeasors whose independent tortious acts concurred in causing the plaintiff's damage. Examples include the previously discussed cases of multiple independent fires and those involving multiple suppliers of asbestos products.* In these cases, the plaintiff proves a prima facie case against one defendant (like one who negligently started a fire that proximately caused the damage). The liability only takes the form of joint and several liability because other tortfeasors independently violated separate duties that make them responsible for the entirety of the plaintiff's damages (the other who negligently started an independent fire that also proximately caused the plaintiff's damage).

Even if the defendant did not tortiously cause the entire injury, joint and several liability can apply if the harm cannot be apportioned among the respective causes. Consider a plaintiff who was injured in a car crash caused by a drunk (and insolvent) driver. Suppose those injuries were then enhanced

---

* *See* Chapter 9, section I.B.

by a defective seat belt for which the defendant automobile manufacturer is legally responsible. Ideally, "the manufacturer should be liable for that portion of the damage or injury caused by the [defect] over and above the damage or injury that probably would have occurred as a result of the impact or collision absent the [defect in the seat belt]."[2] The ideal outcome is not possible in a case of *indivisible harm*, which involves injuries that are not capable of being apportioned among their respective causes. A plaintiff who was badly injured in a car crash will typically be unable to show which injuries were caused by the crash and which were caused by the defective seat belt. This lack of proof, though, is not fatal to the plaintiff's claim. The issue involves the extent of damages caused by a defect that proximately caused some damage. In determining the extent of damages caused by a tortious risk, tort law places the burden of any inherent factual uncertainty on the defendant.* By proving that the injury is indivisible, the plaintiff has proven the extent of damages with as much certainty as the circumstances permit. The resultant factual uncertainty must be borne by the defendant. Unless the defendant manufacturer can prove which injuries were caused by the defective seatbelt and which were caused by the underlying accident (for which the drunk driver would otherwise be solely legally responsible), it can incur joint and several liability for the entire indivisible harm.†

Having incurred joint and several liability, a defendant who discharged the judgment (such as the automobile manufacturer) can try to recover the payment from another tortfeasor (the drunk driver). In an action for *indemnity*, a jointly and severally liable defendant claims that another jointly and severally liable tortfeasor should pay for the entire amount of the judgment. Under the early common law, indemnity provided

---

* *See* Chapter 9, section II.C.

† For these same reasons, even if the accident were not caused by the negligence of another driver, the defendant would still be liable for the entirety of the indivisible injury.

the only mechanism for shifting the liability from one tortfeasor to another. The common law did not recognize any apportionment of liability, so it only allowed actions that placed the entire burden of liability on a single party.

Today matters are different. The adoption of comparative responsibility (discussed in the next chapter) allows for the apportionment of damages. A jointly and severally liable defendant can now seek *contribution* from another tortfeasor in an action that seeks to recover only a portion of the damages paid or owed to the plaintiff. The amount of each tortfeasor's liability is usually determined by the jury.

For example, if the owner of the World Trade Center were to incur liability for some of the deaths that occurred on September 11, 2001, it could seek contribution or indemnity from the terrorists who destroyed the buildings.* Such a suit, of course, is not practical, so the owner of the buildings would be unable to shift the liability in this fashion.†

Under joint and several liability, the risk that a tortfeasor is insolvent or immune from suit is borne by each of the jointly and severally liable defendants. The plaintiff's right to compensation does not depend on the defendant's ability to recover the judgment from another tortfeasor.‡

---

* More than 90 families filed tort suits against the World Trade Center Defendants, the airlines, and airplane manufacturer, and most of those claims have settled. *See* Anemona Hartocollis, *Settlements Do Not Deter 9/11 Plaintiffs Seeking Trial*, N.Y. Times B1 (Sept. 19, 2007). For discussion of this case, see Chapter 9, section II.D.

† The federal statute that created the Victims' Compensation Fund, however, limits the amount of tort liability to the policy limits of the defendant's liability insurance. *See* 49 U.S.C. § 40101.

‡ In all of the previously discussed scenarios, the defendant would be jointly and severally liable under the common law. As part of the tort reforms enacted since the 1980s, most states have limited joint and several liability, typically for certain types of damages (like pain and suffering) or cases (like medical malpractice). These statutes instead subject a defendant to several liability based on a determination of comparative responsibility (discussed in Chapter 11). In these cases, the plaintiff bears the risk that any tortfeasor will be insolvent.

II. VICARIOUS LIABILITY

Joint and several liability is a substantive rule governing the liability of multiple tortfeasors, so application of the rule depends on some other substantive rule that makes each of these parties a tortfeasor who is legally responsible for the entirety of the injury. An important substantive rule of this type makes a defendant *vicariously liable* for the tort committed by someone else. In practice, cases of vicarious liability are the most common instance in which multiple tortfeasors are subject to the rule of joint and several liability.

Vicarious liability ordinarily is based on the principle of *respondeat superior*, which makes an employer vicariously liable for torts committed by an employee acting within the scope of employment. Many of the cases we have previously discussed involved defendants like railroads or ship owners that incurred vicarious liability for the torts committed by their employees. In these cases, the employer could not be faulted for either hiring or supervising the employee who committed the tort; the liability of the employer, like any other vicariously liable party, is strict.

> Under the fault principle as we know it today there are many situations in which *A* is held liable to *C* for damages that *B*'s negligence has caused *C*, even though *A* has been free of negligence or other fault. In such a case *A* is vicariously liable for *B*'s fault, such liability being imposed because of some relationship between *A* and *B*. . . . There may be reasons for making innocent *A* pay for *B*'s defaults, but they are no part of a philosophy that rests liability on personal moral shortcoming.[3]

Numerous explanations for this rule of no-fault or strict liability have been offered over the years. "[T]hese justifications, while interesting, tend to be incomplete, or persuasive only in part."[4]

Consider the evidentiary rationale for strict liability, which uses strict liability to create a financial incentive for duty holders to adopt reasonable safety precautions that are not effectively governed by negligence liability due to plaintiffs' difficulty of proving legal fault.* Plaintiffs would typically have a hard time proving that an employer used unreasonable systems of worker discipline and control, so strict liability (in the form of vicarious liability) could reduce risk in a manner that cannot be adequately regulated by negligence liability. However, vicarious liability can induce the employer to cover up instances of employee misconduct to reduce liability costs, thereby diluting the safety incentive.[5] Moreover, the employee is also jointly and severally liable for the tortious misconduct. The employee's independent incentive to act reasonably casts further doubt on a deterrence rationale for subjecting the employer to vicarious liability. At best, the objective of risk reduction only partially explains the doctrine.[6]

Vicarious liability is also not persuasively justified by the other commonly accepted rationale for strict liability, which is based on the fairness of providing plaintiffs with compensation for injuries caused by the defendant's reasonable, nonreciprocal risky activity.† As we have found, a defendant engaged in a common activity does not create a nonreciprocal risk subject to strict liability.‡ Employment relationships are common in the community, so how can these relationships routinely create nonreciprocal risks subject to strict liability?

After concluding that none of the common rationales for strict liability are sufficiently persuasive, Judge Henry Friendly in the famous case *Ira S. Bushey & Sons, Inc. v. United States* concluded that vicarious liability is based "in a deeply

---

* *See* Chapter 3, section II (discussing the evidentiary rationale for strict liability).

† *See* Chapter 3, section III (discussing the reciprocity rationale for strict liability).

‡ *See* Chapter 5, section III.

rooted sentiment that a business enterprise cannot justly disclaim responsibility for accidents which may fairly be said to be characteristic of its activities."[7] This rationale has been widely adopted.

The *Bushey* rationale, though, is also problematic or otherwise incomplete:

> The harms of knife cuts are in some sense "characteristic" of the distribution of knives; adverse side effects are "characteristic" of the manufacture of prescription drugs; and injuries to passengers are evidently "characteristic" of the operation of a bus system. Yet our tort system shows no interest in imposing automatic liability on the companies that produce knives and drugs and that operate buses. Whatever our system's rules of strict liability, they exclude such results.[8]

Like vicarious liability, there is another rule of strict liability that has been widely adopted without being well understood. In cases of private necessity, one who acts reasonably by exercising the privilege to use another's property for purposes of self-protection must pay for any ensuing damage to that property. The conventional rationales for strict liability do not explain this doctrine, although we found that strict liability can be justified by the actor's control over the property in question.* This conception of responsibility straightforwardly explains why vicarious liability applies to risks "characteristic" of the business in question.

By creating an employment relationship with another, the employer also creates risks that are characteristic of the business activity in question. The requirement that vicarious liability applies only to "accidents which may fairly be said to be characteristic of its activities," therefore, is simply a requirement that the employer must have created a foreseeable risk of harm by entering into the employment relationship. Having

---

* *See* Chapter 7, section II.B.

created a foreseeable risk of harm that is within its control, the employer can then incur legal responsibility for the ensuing injuries, regardless of whether the employer otherwise acted reasonably. The concept of responsibility is identical to that which justifies the application of strict liability to cases of private necessity, and to that which justifies a compensatory tort duty in general.*

Responsibility justifies the tort duty, whereas liability also requires a breach of that duty. Consequently, vicarious liability only applies when the employee (or any other *agent* of the vicariously liable *principal*) has committed some tort. In these circumstances, the employer or other type of principal becomes responsible for a tortious risk and is (vicariously) liable for damages proximately caused by that risk.

Once the doctrine is interpreted in this manner, its contours become readily understandable. For example, the foreseeable risks created by the working environment include those stemming from the associated social interactions:

> Men do not discard their personal qualities when they go to work. Into the job they carry their intelligence, skill, habits of care and rectitude. Just as inevitably they take along also their tendencies to carelessness and camaraderie, as well as emotional make-up. In bringing men together, work brings these qualities together, causes frictions between them, creates occasions for lapses into carelessness, and for fun-making and emotional flare-up. . . . These expressions of human nature are incidents inseparable from working together. They involve risks of injury and these risks are inherent in the working environment.[9]

So, too, the employer is not responsible for risks attributable to the employee's personal life, a requirement embodied in

---

* *See* Chapter 5 (using this conception of responsibility to justify a compensatory duty that is correlative to a compensatory tort right).

the rule of *frolic and detour*, which absolves the employer of vicarious liability for torts committed by the employee acting outside the scope of work (the "frolic and detour"). As *Bushey* explained, "the activities of the 'enterprise' do not reach into areas where the servant does not create risks different from those attendant on the activities of the community in general." For vicarious liability to apply, the employment relationship must create risks additional to those that would otherwise exist in the community, a requirement that excludes risks created by the employee's personal life.

In *Bushey*, for example, the employee was a seaman who was "returning from shore leave late at night" to a U.S. Coast Guard vessel where he was stationed. The vessel was "being overhauled in a floating drydock," and the employee, "in the [inebriated] condition for which seaman are famed, turned some wheels on the drydock wall," causing the plaintiff's drydock (and the employer's ship) to partially sink. The employee's conduct furthered no business purpose of his employer. The intentional misconduct was still a risk "characteristic" of the business, however, because it had been created by the employment relationship. The risks of drunken misconduct, although general within the community, are foreseeably increased by an employment relationship that places employees on ships at sea for extended periods of time. "[T]he proclivity of seamen to find solace for solitude by copious resort to the bottle has been noted in opinions too numerous to warrant citation." The employer (the U.S. Government) could also foresee the more general risk "that crew members crossing the drydock might do damage, negligently or even intentionally." "Once all of this is granted, it is immaterial that [the seaman's] precise action was not to be foreseen. . . ." The intentional misconduct of the employee was one of the risks characteristic of the business, subjecting the employer to vicarious liability.

By itself, foreseeability is not sufficient to make one legally responsible for a risk. Foreseeability only matters insofar as it enables the actor to control the risk.* Vicarious liability accordingly requires an employment relationship of a certain type. The employee must be a *servant* of the employer as *master*, anachronistic terms that usefully portray control as an integral component of vicarious liability.

Unless the employer has adequate control over the conduct, the employee is an *independent contractor* for whom the employer is not vicariously liable. When you hire a taxi, for example, the driver is an independent contractor. You are not vicariously liable for any traffic accidents negligently caused by the driver. You have only told the cab driver about the objective in question (your destination), but otherwise have exercised no meaningful control over the driving itself. To be vicariously liable, the employer must have adequate control over both the means and ends of the activity, a substantive issue that does not turn on the label the parties otherwise attach to their relationship.

Some risks cannot be delegated in this manner. Someone subject to a *nondelegable duty* is vicariously liable for the torts committed by an independent contractor. The duty is simply so important that it cannot be delegated to another. Such duties are often statutorily created, and can also involve "special risks, peculiar to the work to be done" that does not involve "a normal, routine matter of customary human activity, such as driving an automobile," but instead creates "a special danger to those in the vicinity, arising out of the particular situation created, and calling for special precautions."[10] Examples include demolition and the aerial spraying of pesticides. Like the other rules of vicarious liability, courts determine whether a duty is nondelegable by asking whether the risk can be fairly attributed to the employer.[11]

When based on this rationale, vicarious liability is substantively equivalent to the rule of strict liability in cases of private

---

* *See* Chapter 8, section I.B.

necessity. Each involves a form of liability that does not depend on the two commonly accepted rationales for strict liability. Each rule of strict liability is instead defensible for the same basic reason. Liability in both types of cases can be justified by the principle that an actor can fairly be held responsible for the foreseeable injuries caused by the exercise of autonomy — the "deeply held sentiment in the community" invoked by *Bushey* and widely embraced by courts.

III. ALTERNATIVE AND MARKET-SHARE LIABILITY

Cases involving multiple tortious actors can create an issue that has fascinated tort scholars and caused long-running disputes among courts. What happens when the plaintiff can prove that he or she was injured by someone in a group of independent tortious actors, but cannot identify which one caused the harm?

This line of cases famously begins with *Summers v. Tice*, in which the plaintiff was injured while hunting quail with the two defendants.[12] Each defendant negligently fired his shotgun in the direction of the plaintiff at about the same time from approximately the same distance. The plaintiff was struck in the eye and face by a single shot of pellets, but could not identify which defendant's shot had hit him. The evidence only established that each defendant had an equal likelihood of doing so, leaving the plaintiff unable to prove that either defendant, more likely than not, caused the injury. Nevertheless, the California Supreme Court concluded that it was appropriate to shift the burden of proof to the defendants, requiring each to prove that he was not the cause of the plaintiff's injury. If neither defendant could provide such proof, each would be jointly liable for the plaintiff's injury.

This rule of *alternative liability* has been adopted by the *Restatement (Second)*:

> Where the conduct of two or more actors is tortious, and it is proved that harm has been caused to the plaintiff by only one of them, but there is uncertainty as to which one has caused it, the burden is upon each such actor to prove that he has not caused the harm.[13]

The rationale for alternative liability is based on "the injustice of permitting proved wrongdoers, who among them have inflicted an injury upon the entirely innocent plaintiff, to escape liability merely because the nature of their conduct and the resulting harm has made it difficult or impossible to prove which of them has caused the harm."[14] This justification tracks the reasoning of the *Summers* court.

The rule has gained widespread acceptance. According to the *Restatement (Third)*, the "rationale for shifting the burden of proof to defendants whose tortious conduct exposed the plaintiff to a risk of harm is that, as between two culpable defendants and an innocent plaintiff, it is preferable to put the risk of error on the culpable defendants."[15]

As formulated, the *Restatement* rationales for alternative liability are not fully persuasive. The *Restatement (Second)* invokes the "injustice" of allowing the defendant wrongdoers to escape liability only because their tortious conduct created factual uncertainty about the actual cause of the injury. But tortious conduct routinely creates factual uncertainty regarding causation. A defendant who exposed an injured plaintiff to a 10 percent chance of harm may have been the actual cause of the injury, but our limited knowledge of the relevant causal processes only allows the causal statement to take a probabilistic form. In such a case, the mere fact that the defendant's tortious conduct makes it impossible for the plaintiff to prove causation by a preponderance of the evidence does not ordinarily relieve the plaintiff of the burden of proof. What explains the different rule with respect to alternative liability?

The *Restatement (Third)* does not sufficiently clarify matters by simply asserting that as between the "culpable" defendant and "innocent" plaintiff, the "risk of error" should be put on the defendant. Carried to its logical conclusion, this proposition implies that a single defendant who has acted tortiously should have to disprove causation with certainty, for that rule places the risk of error (liability in cases lacking complete certainty) on the culpable defendant rather than the innocent plaintiff. A defendant responsible for a 10 percent tortious risk of harm would be liable. By not shifting the burden of proof in these cases, courts have rejected the proposition that the "risk of error" should always be borne by a defendant who has acted unreasonably. What makes that proposition valid in cases of alternative liability?

Due to the inadequacy of the *Restatement* rationales, many have interpreted alternative liability as a rule that provides compensation for the exposure to tortious risk, conditional on the occurrence of injury. The plaintiff in *Summers* proved that he had been exposed to a 50 percent risk of injury by each defendant, and that the cumulative risk caused his injury. Each defendant incurred liability for 50 percent of the plaintiff's total damages. The plaintiff received full compensation for the injury from the two defendants, but the liability of each defendant was only based on the risk that he caused injury and not proof that he actually caused the harm. The result in *Summers* reflects the logic of risk-based liability.*

Although alternative liability has some characteristics of risk-based liability, courts do not apply the rule in that manner. The plaintiff in *Summers* was shot by one of the two

---

* *Compare* Chapter 9, section I.A (discussing the risk-based interpretation of the loss-of-a-chance doctrine in medical malpractice cases).

defendants, so the court was certain that the actual tortfeasor would be liable. Consistently with this aspect of *Summers*, "[c]ourts have insisted that all persons whose tortious acts exposed the plaintiff to a risk of harm be joined as defendants as a condition for alternative liability."[16] The joinder requirement is hard to square with a risk-based rule, which would allow the plaintiff to sue only some of the potential tortfeasors and recover an amount of damages proportional to the risk of injury created by these defendants. The plaintiff, for example, could sue one defendant who created a 40 percent chance of tortiously causing the harm and recover 40 percent of the damages. Because such a claim does not satisfy the joinder requirement, alternative liability does not function as a risk-based liability rule.

This limitation of alternative liability became pronounced in cases involving the unpatented drug diethylstilbestrol (DES), a synthetic form of estrogen that was prescribed as a miscarriage preventative. After millions of pregnant women had taken DES, the Food and Drug Administration banned this use of the drug in 1971. Researchers found that the drug could cause vaginal cancer and other reproductive organ anomalies in the offspring of mothers who ingested DES during pregnancy. For decades, medical journals had provided evidence of the drug's hazards, and the manufacturers might also have been able to identify the risks by adequate testing. A warning that did not apprise consumers of any such foreseeable risk would render DES a defective product, subjecting a DES manufacturer to liability for injuries caused by the defective drug.* A plaintiff who was injured by DES, though, usually is unable to determine which manufacturer's product caused the injury. The drug was generic and typically had no meaningful brand identification. Pharmacists routinely filled prescriptions with whatever brand was on the shelf. After

---

* *See* Chapter 13 (discussing warning defects).

the plaintiff's mother purchased and ingested the generic DES, decades passed before the plaintiff offspring suffered injury, making it virtually impossible for a plaintiff to identify the particular manufacturer responsible for the injury.

This evidentiary problem is identical to the one addressed by the rule of alternative liability. Each defendant DES manufacturer exposed the plaintiff to the same tortious risk by supplying the same defective product in the relevant market, just as each defendant in *Summers* exposed the plaintiff to the same tortious risk by negligently firing at him. Only one manufacturer was the factual cause of the plaintiff's harm, just as only one shooter in *Summers* injured the plaintiff. However, the circumstances surrounding the tortious conduct engaged in by each manufacturer (the sale of a generic, defective product) and the resulting harm (cancer or other injury occurring long after exposure to the defect) have made it unreasonably difficult for the plaintiff to identify which particular manufacturer caused the harm — the same type of evidentiary problem confronted by the plaintiff in *Summers*.

As a practical matter, however, a DES plaintiff cannot recover under alternative liability. Due to the large number of DES manufacturers, the fluid nature of the market, and the passage of time, the plaintiff rarely can join all of the potential tortfeasors, unlike the plaintiff in *Summers*. The joinder requirement effectively bars almost all DES plaintiffs from recovery, despite the proof that each one was tortiously injured by someone in the group of DES manufacturers, and that each DES manufacturer injured someone.

To overcome this limitation of alternative liability, the California Supreme Court, in the seminal case *Sindell v. Abbott Laboratories*, held that a plaintiff could recover against a group of DES manufacturers comprising a "substantial share" of the relevant market.[17] Within such a group of defendants, a manufacturer that had 10 percent of the relevant market would be severally liable for 10 percent of the plaintiff's harm.

In a series of influential articles, leading tort scholars argued that market-share liability is best justified by an emergent risk-based conception of tort liability that is formulated to promote deterrence in a fair manner.[18] An actor who faces liability for creating an unreasonable risk has an incentive to act reasonably. This form of liability is also fair. Rather than distinguishing among otherwise identical actors on the contingent basis of whether their unreasonable behavior caused physical harm, tort law can treat each actor equally by making each responsible for his or her own behavior — the unreasonable risk he or she imposed on the injured plaintiff.

A risk-based liability rule, though, fundamentally alters the nature of the tort right, so that it protects against risk exposure and not physical harm. Consequently, market-share liability has been much more controversial than alternative liability. A "number of courts" have adopted market-share liability in these cases, but a "roughly equal number of courts have declined to craft a new theory for DES plaintiffs, expressing concern that to do so would rend too great a chasm in the tort-law requirement of factual causation."[19] The common theme for these courts is that market-share liability "requires a profound change in the fundamental tort principle of causation. [W]e cannot pretend that any such theory is consistent with common law principles of tort liability."[20]

The courts that have adopted market-share liability, though, do not believe that it departs from the fundamental tort requirement of causation. In *Sindell*, the California Supreme Court said that the liability rule is "grounded upon an extension of the *Summers* doctrine."[21] The *Summers* doctrine of alternative liability is widely accepted, presumably because courts believe that it adequately satisfies the requirement of factual causation. Insofar as market-share liability is merely an extension of alternative liability, it also presumably satisfies the fundamental requirement that the plaintiff must prove that his or her injury was caused by the defendant.

Indeed, the sharply divided case law on market-share liability most plausibly stems from a disagreement about whether alternative liability properly extends to market-share liability. Although the California Supreme Court sought to justify market-share liability in these terms, it never clearly explained the rationale, nor has it adequately explained the doctrine of alternative liability, an inadequacy reflected in the previously discussed *Restatement* rationales for the liability rule. Tort scholars have not sufficiently clarified matters either. In rejecting both alternative and market-share liability, one court observed that "none of the cases or commentaries presents a rigorous analysis of why [the doctrines are] 'fair.'"[22] The courts that have rejected market-share liability are understandably wary of the claim that it can be justified by alternative liability.

To determine whether market-share liability is a defensible extension of alternative liability, we must first figure out how alternative liability satisfies the requirement of factual causation. Courts have insisted on the causal requirement in the DES cases, making it highly unlikely that they adopted alternative liability to ease the plaintiff's burden of proving causation. Any plausible rationale for alternative liability will have to explain how it satisfies the traditional tort principle that a plaintiff must prove causation by a preponderance of the evidence.

Alternative liability has this property if the plaintiff's causal proof applies to the group of defendants rather than to each defendant individually. In *Summers*, for example, the plaintiff proved that the two defendants, considered together, more likely than not caused the physical harm. As the *Summers* court concluded, "we believe it is clear that the [trial] court sufficiently found on the issue that defendants were jointly liable and that thus the negligence of both was the cause of the injury or to that legal effect."[23] By permitting the plaintiff to prove factual causation with the combined tortious misconduct of the defendants, the "legal effect" of the proof establishes that "the negligence of both was the cause of the injury," thereby satisfying the element of causation.

According to a leading torts treatise, such a modified rule of but-for causation can explain alternative liability and related forms of liability:

> When the conduct of two or more actors is so related to an event that their combined conduct, viewed as a whole, is a but-for cause of the event, and application of the but-for rule to them individually would absolve all of them, the conduct of each is a cause in fact of the event.[24]

In addition to explaining alternative liability, causal grouping straightforwardly resolves the otherwise difficult cases of multiple independent tortious causes, including the two negligently caused fires that destroyed the plaintiff's property, and the asbestos cases in which the injury, more likely than not, would have occurred even if any particular asbestos defendant had not exposed the plaintiff to its asbestos products.* When causation can be proven by the combined tortious conduct of the defendants, the liability rule is easy to understand. More likely than not, the two tortious fires caused the plaintiff's harm, entitling the plaintiff to receive compensation from the two defendant wrongdoers. More likely than not, the asbestos supplied by the group of defendant manufacturers caused the plaintiff's harm, entitling the plaintiff to receive compensation from the group of defendant wrongdoers. This form of causal proof is also much more intuitive than the only other method for establishing causation in these cases, the so-called NESS test.†

Under this approach, the plaintiff must prove, by a preponderance of the evidence, that he or she was injured by tortious

---

* *See* Chapter 9, section I.B.

† *See id.* (describing how an act is a factual cause of the injury if it is a necessary element in a set of conditions sufficient for causing the injury).

conduct engaged in by the group of defendants, and that each
defendant's tortious conduct may have actually caused or contributed to the injury. Unless a defendant rebuts this evidence,
he or she cannot reasonably deny that the plaintiff was harmed
by one of the defendants, including himself or herself. A
defendant, therefore, cannot avoid liability merely by arguing
that the other defendants, more likely than not, caused the
harm, if that same argument would enable every other defendant
to avoid liability. In these circumstances, the defendant's argument effectively denies that the plaintiff was harmed by *any* of
the defendants, including himself or herself, even though the
defendant's failure to rebut the plaintiff's proof disables the
defendant from denying liability on this basis. A defendant
must instead prove that he or she did not act tortiously or
could not possibly have caused the injury, the only evidence
directly rebutting the plaintiff's proof.[25]

Unlike the liability grouping that occurs for the joint torts and
vicarious liability, causal grouping cannot make a defendant
responsible for the conduct of other tortfeasors. One of the
defendant shooters in *Summers* was not responsible for the
conduct of the other defendant shooter; otherwise the case
would involve a concert of action governed by liability grouping.
Summers required a new rule precisely because one defendant
was not responsible for the conduct of the other.

Because the plaintiff in *Summers* could establish the prima
facie case only against the group of tortious actors, his ability to
recover from any defendant could only depend on the defendant's relation to the group. The group is defined exclusively in
causal terms—the likelihood that it caused the plaintiff's
injury. Each individual defendant is a member of the causal
group only by virtue of his responsibility for an independent
tortious risk that might have injured the plaintiff. Each defendant's contribution to the total risk of injury created by the
group, therefore, defines the extent of his responsibility for
the group's conduct. Consistent with this reasoning, each of

the two defendants in *Summers* incurred liability for 50 percent of the injury, an amount exactly corresponding to the risk that each caused the injury in question. Under this method of apportionment, the interest of the plaintiff who has established a right to receive compensation for the injury from a group of defendants exactly corresponds to the interest of each individual defendant as a member of the causal group.[26]

This reasoning also explains why courts insist that alternative liability requires joinder of all the potential tortfeasors. Alternative liability gives the plaintiff 100 percent compensation for the injury from the defendants. When the joinder requirement has been satisfied, the proportional liability of each defendant adds up to 100 percent. Each of the two defendants in *Summers*, for example, incurred liability for 50 percent of the injury, enabling the plaintiff to receive 100 percent of the damages. The imposition of joint and several liability on the group of all potential tortfeasors lets the plaintiff receive full compensation for the injury without requiring any individual defendant to incur liability in excess of the probability that he or she actually caused the injury.*

For this reason, the California Supreme Court had to modify alternative liability to produce market-share liability. Because the plaintiff could not join all potential tortfeasors as required by alternative liability, *Sindell* held that the plaintiff must instead join a "substantial share" of the market to establish market-share liability. Properly applied, this requirement ensures that the group of DES defendants, more likely than not, caused the plaintiff's injury. By satisfying this

---

* Due to the joinder requirement, any case of alternative liability must involve joint liability. Nevertheless, courts have interpreted alternative liability as involving joint and several liability. For several liability to have any meaning in a case of alternative liability, it must provide the basis for imposing on each defendant its proportionate share of liability when that amount differs from its pro rata share of liability — the same basis for apportionment provided by several liability in market-share cases.

requirement and all of the other remaining requirements for alternative liability, the plaintiff has established a prima facie case against the group of defendants. Alternative liability would make the defendants jointly and severally liable for the entire injury, resulting in an unfairly excessive amount of liability for each individual defendant. For example, a DES defendant that had only 10 percent of the market should be liable for only 10 percent of the plaintiff's injury—the amount representing the defendant's responsibility (individual risk creation) for the group's conduct (the total tortious risk imposed on the plaintiff). To "protect . . . defendants against excessive liability," the court in a later case concluded that market-share liability involves several liability, with the liability of each DES defendant being limited by the probability that it actually caused the plaintiff's injury—an amount defined by its market share.[27] A DES defendant that had 10 percent of the market would be severally liable for 10 percent of the plaintiff's injury.

Having altered the rule of alternative liability in these two respects, *Sindell* could defensibly conclude that market-share liability is "an adaptation of the rule in *Summers* which will substantially overcome [the] difficulties" faced by a plaintiff who cannot join every potential tortfeasor in the lawsuit. Market-share liability does not fully overcome this difficulty, as the plaintiff does not receive full compensation for the injury. The plaintiff's recovery is limited by the rule of several liability, which makes the individual manufacturer responsible only for the defective products it actually sold. This limitation of liability is required, according to the court, to avoid the unfairness that would arise if "one manufacturer would be held responsible for the products of another or for those of all other manufacturers if plaintiff ultimately prevails." The plaintiff can prove causation by reference to the group of manufacturers, but the extent of each defendant's responsibility for the group's conduct is limited by its contribution to the total risk of injury created by the group — the same outcome achieved by alternative liability.*

For alternative or market-share liability to apply, courts typically require that the tortious conduct of each defendant must be fungible or substantially similar. The courts have stringently applied this requirement, sharply limiting application of market-share liability to exclude, for example, cases of asbestos or lead paint exposure.[28]

Under causal grouping, the plaintiff must prove that each defendant created a tortious risk that is fungible only in the sense that the risk may have actually caused the plaintiff's injury, and would subject the defendant to liability if it did cause the harm.

Consider a plaintiff who contracted AIDS from either a tortfeasor who failed to disclose the condition prior to sexual relations or from defective (contaminated) blood purchased from multiple blood suppliers over a period of time. These forms of tortious conduct are not similar, but the plaintiff should still be able to establish alternative liability against both the sexual partner and the blood suppliers (assuming the proof does not otherwise identify one of the defendants as the but-for cause of the disease). Each defendant exposed the plaintiff to a tortious risk that might have caused the injury, and one of them actually caused the harm and would be

---

* Whereas the California rule of market-share liability finds support in alternative liability, the same is not necessarily true of the other forms of market-share liability adopted by other states. *Compare Hymowitz v. Eli Lilly & Co.*, 539 N.E.2d 1069 (N.Y. 1989) (adopting rule of market-share liability based on the national market that does not allow a DES manufacturer to exculpate itself by proving that it could not have caused the plaintiff's injury); *Collins v. Eli Lilly Co.*, 342 N.W.2d 37, 48–49 (Wis. 1984) (adopting rule of market-share liability that lets a DES plaintiff recover full damages for the entire injury from a single manufacturer in the national market, although "a defendant could escape liability if it proved by a preponderance of the evidence that the DES it produced or marketed could not have reached the plaintiff") (footnote omitted).

subject to liability for having done so.* The fact that some defendants otherwise engaged in entirely different forms of behavior is irrelevant.

Once the other requirements for causal grouping have been satisfied, each defendant's liability depends only on the amount of tortious risk for which that defendant is responsible. Liability does not always require market shares, so a more descriptively apt name for the liability rule might be "risk-adjusted" liability.

---

* Numerous jurisdictions have enacted *blood-shield* statutes that immunize the suppliers of blood products from the rule of strict products liability. If the defendant blood suppliers in this example were immune from liability, the plaintiff would lose. Rather than relying exclusively on the other defendants' tortious conduct — the only form of exculpatory proof barred by causal grouping — the blood suppliers instead invoke the blood-shield statute. Once these defendants are removed from the case, the plaintiff can proceed only against the sexual partner, who on these facts did not create more than a 50 percent chance of injuring the plaintiff.

∽ 11 ∽

Defenses Based on the Plaintiff's Conduct

A plaintiff who has proven a prima facie case of negligence liability is not necessarily entitled to full compensation. The defendant may be able to establish an affirmative defense, the most important of which are based on the plaintiff's conduct. Some of the defenses absolve the defendant of liability altogether, whereas others reduce the amount for which the defendant is liable.

I. ASSUMPTION OF RISK

The common law has long recognized the principle expressed in the Latin maxim *volenti non fit injuria*, or "No injury or wrong is done to one who consents."[1] The writ system denied recovery if the defendant acted on the plaintiff's consent.* The principle was then incorporated into the intentional torts, which deny recovery to a plaintiff who had consented to the intentional interference with his or her legally protected

---

* *See* Chapter 1, section I.B.

interests.* With the later development of negligence liability, the principle found expression in the doctrine of *assumption of risk*, which relieves the defendant of responsibility for a risk voluntarily encountered by the plaintiff who had sufficient knowledge of the risk.

Assumption of risk requires choice and knowledge, elements that could be satisfied routinely if they are not sufficiently specified. When you choose to drive a car, for example, you know there is some risk that another driver on the road will be intoxicated. In the event that a drunk driver crashes into you, no court would conclude that you assumed the risk of being injured by a drunk driver. The required elements are more demanding than some choice to face a general risk of which one is aware.

Due to the range of circumstances in which individuals choose to face a known risk, the doctrine of assumption of risk has been divided into different categories, with each having a different implication for the tort inquiry.

A. Express Assumption of Risk

The plaintiff expressly assumes a risk by agreeing to an enforceable oral or written contract that exculpates the defendant from negligence liability. The defense is analogous to the role of consent in the intentional torts. "Any agreement by words or conduct that would constitute consent to an intentional tort constitutes a defense" to negligence liability.[2]

According to the *Restatement (Second)*, an exculpatory agreement is enforceable only if freely and fairly made between parties who are in an equal bargaining position, and it does not interfere with important social interests.[3] An agreement that interferes with important social interests violates public policy

---

* *See* Chapter 7, section I.G.

and is unenforceable, exposing the defendant to liability for the conduct in question.

Due to the vagueness of this inquiry, courts had difficulty determining whether exculpatory agreements violated public policy. In *Tunkl v. Regents of the University of California*, the California Supreme Court synthesized the relevant factors from the case law to produce an inquiry now followed by most jurisdictions:

> In placing particular contracts within or without the category of those affected with a public interest, the courts have revealed a rough outline of that type of transaction in which exculpatory provisions will be held invalid. Thus the attempted but invalid exemption involves a transaction which exhibits some or all of the following characteristics. [1] It concerns a business of a type generally thought suitable for public regulation. [2] The party seeking exculpation is engaged in performing a service of great importance to the public, which is often a matter of practical necessity for some members of the public. [3] The party holds himself out as willing to perform this service for any member of the public who seeks it, or at least for any member coming within certain established standards. [4] As a result of the essential nature of the service, in the economic setting of the transaction, the party invoking exculpation possesses a decisive advantage of bargaining strength against any member of the public who seeks his services. [5] In exercising a superior bargaining power the party confronts the public with a standardized adhesion contract of exculpation, and makes no provision whereby a purchaser may pay additional reasonable fees and obtain protection against negligence. [6] Finally, as a result of the transaction, the person or property of the pur- chaser is placed under the control of the seller, subject to the risk of carelessness by the seller or his agents.
>
> While obviously no public policy opposes private, voluntary transactions in which one party, for a consideration, agrees to shoulder a risk which the law would otherwise have

placed upon the other party, the above circumstances pose a different situation. In this situation the releasing party does not really acquiesce voluntarily in the contractual shifting of the risk, nor can we be reasonably certain that he receives an adequate consideration for the transfer. Since the service is one which each member of the public, presently or potentially, may find essential to him, he faces, despite his economic inability to do so, the prospect of a compulsory assumption of the risk of another's negligence. The public policy of this state has been, in substance, to posit the risk of negligence upon the actor; in instances in which this policy has been abandoned, it has generally been to allow or require that the risk shift to another party better or equally able to bear it, not to shift the risk to the weak bargainer.[4]

Each *Tunkl* factor does not have to be satisfied for a court to invalidate an exculpatory agreement, but the combined logic of the factors yields an inquiry that enables the court to determine whether the plaintiff had sufficient choice and knowledge, the two elements that must be satisfied for the plaintiff to assume the risk.

If the service in question is one of "practical necessity" or otherwise "essential," the plaintiff presumably did not have sufficient choice about the matter, particularly if the defendant did not give the plaintiff any opportunity to "obtain protection against negligence" (factors [2], [4], and [5]). The absence of meaningful choice negates assumption of risk, enabling the court to invalidate the exculpatory agreement on this ground alone.

Even if the plaintiff had a choice about the matter, the exculpatory agreement can still be unenforceable: The choice must also be informed. A plaintiff who did not know the full magnitude of the risk would not fully understand the importance of being protected against the risk, giving the defendant "a decisive advantage of bargaining strength" on the associated safety matters (factors [4] and [5]). Such a plaintiff thought he or she was consenting to something materially different from the actual risk, a sufficient ground for negating any defense based on consent.*

An agreement lacking the requisite choice or knowledge implicates public policy—the risks are "particularly suitable for public regulation"—when the service is generally available to the public, and "the person or property of the purchaser is placed under the control of the seller, subject to the risk of carelessness by the seller or his agents" (factors [1], [3], and [6]). In these circumstances, the exculpatory agreement will expose the plaintiff and similarly situated right holders to unreasonable dangers, a violation of public policy that renders the agreement unenforceable.

So conceptualized, the *Tunkl* inquiry ultimately reduces to the policy question identified by the court: Was the plaintiff a "weak bargainer," and did he or she "really acquiesce voluntarily in the contractual shifting of the risk?" A "weak bargainer" does not have the information required to assume the risk, nor could the defense be established if the element of choice is lacking because the plaintiff did not "acquiesce voluntarily" to the exculpatory agreement.

Under this interpretation, the *Tunkl* inquiry for service contracts is consistent with the rule governing product contracts. According to the *Restatement (Third)*, exculpatory agreements or contractual waivers of tort liability "do not bar or reduce otherwise valid products-liability claims against sellers or other distributors of new products for harm to persons."[5] The reason is that consumers do not adequately understand the magnitude of product risk. "It is presumed that the ordinary product user or consumer lacks sufficient information and bargaining power to execute a fair contractual limitation of

---

* *See* Chapter 7, section I.G (explaining that consent relieves the defendant from liability only if the plaintiff has adequate knowledge of the interaction in question).

rights to recover."[6] Consumers who are not sufficiently informed about product risk will be weak bargainers about safety, with the predictable result that exculpatory agreements will give sellers an incentive to supply unreasonably unsafe products — the same market dynamic that can make customary product-safety practices unreasonable.* These exculpatory agreements interfere with the important social interest in preventing physical harm, making them unenforceable.

This type of inquiry, however, is masked by the *Tunkl* listing of multiple factors, causing some courts to assume that an exculpatory agreement can be invalidated only if the service is essential or highly necessary. For example, the Montana Supreme Court enforced an exculpatory agreement involving a ski resort because "a private recreational business does not qualify as a service demanding a special duty to the public, nor are its services of a special, highly necessary or essential nature."[7] Holdings like this are common and arguably represent the prevailing rule.

By enforcing an exculpatory agreement merely because the service involves a discretionary activity like skiing, a court never considers whether the plaintiff had enough information to be a strong bargainer with respect to the safety issues. Without proof that the plaintiff had sufficient knowledge of the risk, the defendant does not establish assumption of risk. The defense does not solely depend on whether the activity is discretionary, as confirmed by the rule invalidating agreements that exculpate the sellers of new products from tort liability for physical harms caused by defects in their products, whether essential or not.

Indeed, proper application of the *Tunkl* factors will ordinarily invalidate exculpatory agreements involving ski resorts, the result reached by the Vermont Supreme Court.[8] "Whether

---

* *See* Chapter 8, section III.B.

or not defendants provide an essential public service does not resolve the public policy question in the recreational sports context." The policy objective "is to place responsibility for maintenance of the land on those who own or control it, with the ultimate goal of keeping accidents to the minimum level possible." Skiers are not strong bargainers with respect to these safety issues, as they "are not in a position to discover and correct risks of harm." A skier will typically know only about the general risks of skiing, but not risks unique to a particular resort on any given day. Are the ski lifts in good working order? Are the trails properly maintained and marked? Lacking good information about these risks, skiers are weak bargainers who will enter into broad exculpatory agreements, removing "an important incentive for ski areas to manage risk . . . with the public bearing the cost of the resulting injuries." The exculpatory agreement would create a safety problem in violation of public policy, rendering it unenforceable for essentially the same reason that courts invalidate exculpatory agreements in product cases.

When the exculpatory agreement is contained in a service contract between commercial parties, courts regularly enforce the agreement. These kinds of provisions are often in construction contracts. Commercial parties are usually knowledgeable of the associated risks, and the exculpatory agreement presumably affects the contract price. As the *Tunkl* court observed, in these circumstances "no public policy opposes private, voluntary transactions in which one party, for a consideration, agrees to shoulder a risk which the law would otherwise have placed upon the other party." When the contracting parties have an adequate understanding of the risk, their consensual arrangements further the objective of private ordering or self-determination without producing a safety problem in violation of public policy. The required elements of choice and knowledge are satisfied, justifying the enforcement of these kinds of exculpatory agreements.

B. Primary Assumption of Risk

Exculpatory agreements for recreational sports like skiing often seem to be enforceable for the simple reason that participants in these activities surely assume the risks inherent in the activity. A skier assumes the risk of a broken leg caused by a fall on a properly maintained ski trail. An exculpatory agreement to that limited effect would be enforceable, but such a contract is unnecessary. Under the doctrine known as *primary assumption of risk*, the ski resort owes no duty with respect to the inherent risks of skiing, independent of any exculpatory agreement or other disclaimer of liability.

Many activities involve risks that cannot be eliminated without fundamentally altering the activity itself. Recreational sports like football, hockey, skiing, or soccer would not be properly labeled as such if those who participated in these activities had to conduct themselves in a manner that reduced the risks inherent in the sport. By participating in the activity, the actor (primarily) assumes responsibility for its inherent risks.

A risk is inherent in an activity if the ordinary participant would reasonably consent to the risk, and the risk cannot be tailored to satisfy the idiosyncratic needs of any particular participant like the plaintiff. For example, someone who knows nothing about baseball and is hit by a ball while sitting in the outfield bleachers is barred from recovery. The stadium cannot be designed with safety features tailored to each fan; safety decisions must be made by reference to the average or ordinary fan.* The ordinary fan sitting directly behind home plate would want to be protected from foul balls, because the cost of the netting and the partially obstructed view are reasonable in light of the heightened risk. Other areas like the

---

* Similarly, a product seller's tort duty is based on the reasonable safety expectations of the average or ordinary consumer. For cases in which the seller knows of the consumer's particular safety requirements and agrees to satisfy them, liability is governed by a separate contract doctrine known as the *warranty of fitness for a particular purpose*.

outfield bleachers have a much lower risk, and the ordinary fan would reasonably prefer an unobstructed view and an opportunity to catch a ball. Reasonable or objective consent can eliminate the tort duty, just like reasonable or objective consent can absolve a defendant of liability for an intentional tort.* Anyone who participates in an activity assumes the risk in this primary sense, regardless of whether he or she actually consented to the risk.

C. Implied or Secondary Assumption of Risk

The doctrines of express and primary assumption of risk relieve the defendant of any duty with respect to the assumed risks, so the only remaining role for assumption of risk involves cases in which the plaintiff encounters a risk that is encompassed within the defendant's duty to exercise reasonable care. In the event that the defendant breaches the duty and exposes the plaintiff to an unreasonable risk, a plaintiff who knows of the risk and then chooses to face it is subject to the defense of *implied* or *secondary assumption of risk*.

This defense has probably been misapplied more frequently than any other doctrine of tort law. An infamous example involves *Lamson v. American Axe & Tool Company*, an opinion authored by none other than Oliver Wendell Holmes, who was then Chief Justice of the Massachusetts Supreme Court.[9] The plaintiff had been an employee of the defendant for many years. He painted hatchets before placing them on racks to dry. The defendant installed new racks, and the plaintiff complained that they were not safe because the hatchets were prone to falling off. The employer told him "that he would have to use the racks or leave." Because the plaintiff knew of the risk and chose to stay on

---

* *See* Chapter 7, section I.G. As in the case of an intentional tort, reasonable or objective consent does not eliminate the tort duty when the actor knows or should know that the other is not actually consenting and the actor can conform his or her behavior accordingly.

the job, Holmes concluded that he was barred from recovery for injuries he suffered when a hatchet fell off the rack. "He stayed and took the risk." This choice to face the risk, though, was not of the type that should have barred the plaintiff's recovery, illustrating how courts have misapplied the doctrine.

The plaintiff should be denied recovery only if he or she assumed a risk after making the same safety decision involved in the allegation of negligence. For example, suppose the plaintiff in *Lamson* had a choice of using either the old or new racks, and he made an informed decision to use the new, allegedly unsafe ones. Having exercised his autonomy in this manner, the plaintiff would be responsible for the consequences of that choice. His informed choice implies that the burden for him of eliminating the risk (by using the old racks) exceeded the risk he faced by using the new racks ($B_{old\ racks} > PL_{falling\ hatchet}$). Having incurred responsibility for that informed choice, the plaintiff cannot claim that the defendant owed him a duty to make the identical choice in a different manner ($B_{old\ racks} < PL_{falling\ hatchet}$). The plaintiff's informed decision to face a risk and forgo a particular precaution, therefore, relieves the defendant of any tort obligation to eliminate the same risk by adopting the same precaution that had been rejected by the plaintiff.[10]

The plaintiff's safety decision in *Lamson*, however, was different from his allegation of negligence. In deciding to face the risk, the plaintiff presumably considered the cost or burden of quitting the job as compared to the risk of being harmed by a falling hatchet. Because the cost of changing jobs is quite high, the plaintiff decided to face the risk ($B_{quit} > PL_{falling\ hatchet}$). The plaintiff's safety decision differed from his allegation that reasonable care required the employer to use racks comparably safe to the old ones ($B_{old\ racks} < PL_{falling\ hatchet}$). The plaintiff's choice to face the risk provided no defensible reason for limiting the employer's duty, yet the court denied recovery merely because the plaintiff had made some choice to face the risk, a misapplication of the doctrine that recurred in employment cases of the era.*

When assumption of risk only requires some choice to face a known risk, bad results routinely follow. For example, individuals who travel on the roadways and know about the problem of drunk driving would assume the risk of being injured by a drunk driver. The example exaggerates the problem, but courts with unfortunate regularity have concluded that assumption of risk is established merely because the plaintiff made some choice to face a known risk, like the plaintiff in *Lamson*.

In 1956, a leading treatise argued that the doctrine of assumption of risk should be abolished, except for cases of express assumption of risk. "It adds nothing to modern law but confusion."[11] The doctrine did not appear in the *Restatement (First)*, was included in the *Restatement (Second)* only after heated debate, and is now rejected by the *Restatement (Third)*.[12]

The defense can be jettisoned, except for cases involving express assumption of risk, because other doctrines would also bar recovery while avoiding the problems created by the defense:

- Primary assumption of risk relies on objective consent. The rule can bar recovery even if the plaintiff did not in fact subjectively consent (as in the earlier example of the baseball game). Rather than rely on the fiction of subjective consent, the rule can be formulated as one of no duty based on objective consent.
- In cases of implied or secondary assumption of risk, the defense can also be reformulated in terms of objective consent. In these cases, the defendant breached the duty to exercise reasonable care by exposing the plaintiff to an unreasonable risk, and the plaintiff then made an informed choice to face the unreasonable risk. By definition, the reasonable person would refuse to face an unreasonable

---

* *Compare* Chapter 6 (explaining the late nineteenth-century cases in terms of a conception of worker autonomy deeply influenced by the abolition of slavery).

risk. Because the reasonable person would not (objectively) consent to the risk exposure, a plaintiff who (subjectively) consents is acting unreasonably, making his or her assumption of risk a form of contributory negligence that would bar recovery (for reasons discussed in the next section).

Whether the defense is formulated in terms of the plaintiff's subjective consent or the objective consent of the reasonable person, the outcome is the same:

Objective Inquiry	Subjective Inquiry	Outcome
Consent	Consent	No liability (no duty)
Consent	No consent	No liability (no duty)
No consent	No consent	Liability
No consent	Consent	Contributory negligence/ assumption of risk

When scholars first sought to abolish assumption of risk, it did not matter whether the plaintiff assumed the risk or was contributorily negligent. Either defense barred the plaintiff from recovery. Assumption of risk, however, required courts to determine whether the plaintiff adequately appreciated the risk, a more difficult inquiry than one of determining whether a reasonable person would voluntarily face the risk. Rather than apply the troublesome doctrine of implied or secondary assumption of risk, most jurisdictions decided to treat the defense as a form of contributory negligence, the approach taken by the *Restatement (Third)*.

II. CONTRIBUTORY NEGLIGENCE AND LAST CLEAR CHANCE

An accident can be caused by the independent conduct of multiple actors, including the plaintiff. A plaintiff who failed to exercise reasonable care can be legally at fault for the accident under the doctrine of *contributory negligence*, just like a defendant can be legally at fault under the doctrine of negligence liability.

Contributory negligence conventionally dates from *Butterfield v. Forrester*, an early nineteenth-century English case involving a plaintiff who was "riding as fast as his horse could go" when he ran into a pole that the defendant had negligently placed across part of the public road.[13] The plaintiff was thrown from the horse and suffered injury. The trial judge instructed the jury to find for the defendant "if a person riding with reasonable and ordinary care could have seen and avoided the obstruction." The jury verdict for the defendant was upheld on appeal. "One person being in fault will not dispense with another's using ordinary care for himself. Two things must concur to support this action, an obstruction in the road by the fault of the defendant, and no want of ordinary care on the part of the plaintiff." The plaintiff failed to exercise "ordinary care," and the contributory negligence barred recovery — a holding that was widely adopted by other courts.

Courts developed this doctrine in the writ system, which used the concept of causation to resolve substantive issues of policy. Consequently, contributory negligence originated as a rule of proximate cause.

> The doctrine . . . has been referred to as "miscalled" and as "misleading" because there is an unfortunate divergence between its real content and its name. The name . . . would suggest that the ground of the doctrine rests upon the fact that a man who does not take ordinary care for his own safety is to be, in a manner, punished for his carelessness by being denied the right to sue anyone else even though the other's carelessness is concerned in the production of damage. In content, however, the doctrine is posited on the fact that it was the plaintiff's act which was the proximate cause of the injury. His right to recover was not there denied because his

negligence had contributed to the accident for, in those early days, the notion of negligence had not yet arisen. Rather, he failed to recover because his own act had been the direct cause of the accident.[14]

The plaintiff's negligence was not always the direct, proximate cause of the accident. In some cases, the plaintiff first acted negligently, and the defendant then discovered or should have discovered the plaintiff's prior negligence. A defendant who proceeded to negligently cause the plaintiff's injury in these circumstances would be fully liable under the doctrine of *last clear chance*.[15] The defendant's negligent behavior occurred after the plaintiff had acted unreasonably, making the defendant's negligence the direct, proximate cause of the accident that superseded the plaintiff's prior negligence.*

Similar causal reasoning produced the doctrine of *avoidable consequences*, which involves the plaintiff's duty to mitigate damages tortiously caused by the defendant. A plaintiff who chose not to receive adequate medical attention, for example, would be contributorily negligent and barred from recovery for any enhanced injuries attributable to the inadequate treatment — an issue that can raise hard questions about the characteristics of the reasonable person.† The plaintiff's unreasonable conduct was the direct, proximate cause of the enhanced injuries, superseding the defendant's prior negligence.

With the abolition of the writ system and the substantive development of negligence liability, it became necessary to identify a substantive rationale for these doctrines. Each one has a causal rationale rooted in the requirements of the writ system, but do the doctrines otherwise make sense?

---

* *See* Chapter 9, section II.A. (defining direct and superseding causes).

† In some cases, the plaintiff for religious reasons did not seek medical treatment, requiring courts to determine whether the reasonable person standard should incorporate the subjective trait of religious belief. *Compare* Chapter 8, section II.A (discussing policy rationales for incorporating the actor's subjective traits into the otherwise objective standard of the reasonable person).

Various rationales have been proffered for contributory negligence, but none are fully satisfactory. "The reasons that justify providing the victim with a remedy when the injurer has been negligent simply do not suffice to justify limiting the victim's remedy when the victim has been negligent."[16]

For example, negligence liability serves the function of reducing risk, whereas contributory negligence does not ordinarily have that function. In most cases, plaintiffs must make safety decisions without knowledge of how the defendant had behaved. Plaintiffs must instead make their safety decisions based on an assumption of how duty holders like the defendant will behave. When confronted by an adequately enforced rule of negligence liability, duty holders have an incentive to exercise reasonable care. In these circumstances, plaintiffs assume that duty holders will act reasonably, so plaintiffs make safety decisions with the expectation that they will incur the cost of any accidental injuries they might suffer. Plaintiffs have an incentive to protect themselves from uncompensated injury, eliminating deterrence as a persuasive rationale for contributory negligence.*

The doctrine of contributory negligence has also eluded justification as a matter of fairness. The plaintiff's unreasonable conduct caused the injury, but the same is true of the defendant's unreasonable behavior. As a matter of equality, why is it fair to place the entire burden of injury on the plaintiff in a case of contributory negligence, or the defendant in a case of last clear chance?

We can better understand the doctrines by conceptualizing them in causal terms, an approach suggested by their historical origins as rules of proximate cause. The abolition of the writ

---

* Even if the plaintiff expects to recover tort damages in the event of injury, a damages award is not fully compensatory for serious bodily injury, giving the plaintiff an incentive for avoiding the accident. *Compare* Chapter 5, section II (discussing the inadequacy of compensatory damages in relation to negligence liability).

system allowed courts to develop the substantive rationales for liability rules, but as we have found in other contexts, the substantive logic of the writ system was framed in causal terms that continued to influence the courts.* When placed within this historical context, the doctrines coherently work together in a manner that is not otherwise apparent.

Consider the conditions that ordinarily exist in these cases. To establish negligence, the plaintiff must prove that the defendant's failure to exercise reasonable care was a factual cause of the injury. In *Butterfield*, for example, if the defendant had acted reasonably and not placed the pole in the road, the plaintiff would not have been injured, even though he was riding the horse as fast as possible. Likewise, to establish the affirmative defense of contributory negligence, the defendant must prove that the plaintiff failed to exercise reasonable care, and that the unreasonable conduct was a factual cause of the injury. In *Butterfield*, for example, if the plaintiff had exercised reasonable care, he would have seen the obstruction in the road and avoided the injury (as the jury found). In a case of negligence and contributory negligence, the following conditions necessarily exist:

Defendant's Conduct	Plaintiff's Conduct	Outcome
Unreasonable	Unreasonable	Accident
Unreasonable	Reasonable	No accident
Reasonable	Unreasonable	No accident

When evaluated in these causal terms, the conduct of the plaintiff is indistinguishable from the conduct of the defendant. For example, the plaintiff in *Butterfield* could argue that he reasonably assumed that the road would be

---

* *See* Chapter 9, section II (discussing influence of the writ system on the doctrine of proximate cause).

clear, which is why he rode his horse so fast.* Based on that reasonable assumption, the plaintiff could credibly argue that the defendant should be liable (compare the first and third rows in the preceding table). The defendant, though, could make the identical argument. He placed the pole in the road after assuming that anyone riding a horse would be going at a reasonable speed that would enable him or her to see the pole and stop in time. Based on that reasonable assumption, the defendant could credibly argue that the plaintiff is responsible for the accident (compare the first and second rows in the table). Any assessment of the conduct of one party applies equally to the conduct of the other.

In a case of contributory negligence, the plaintiff and defendant have each exercised their liberty in an unreasonable manner, and their unreasonable liberty interests are normatively indistinguishable. Without any normative distinction between the conflicting interests of the parties, tort law has no basis for shifting the loss from one party (having a subordinate interest) to the other (having a prioritized interest). The loss must lie where it fell, on the plaintiff as accident victim.†

This same reasoning explains the doctrines of assumption of risk and last clear chance. The plaintiff can only assume a known risk, so the plaintiff necessarily knows that the defendant has acted unreasonably. In these circumstances, the plaintiff cannot reasonably assume that the defendant exercised reasonable care (the third row is eliminated), leaving

---

* *Compare Haugh v. Jones & Laughlin Steel Corp.*, 949 F.2d 914, 920 (7th Cir. 1991) (Posner, J.) ("Ordinarily a person is not deemed contributorily negligent for failing to take precautions against the negligence of others."). The rule is not absolute because in some cases an individual can foresee that others will act unreasonably. *See* Chapter 8, section I.F (describing how a special relationship can create a duty to protect against foreseeable third-party criminal harms).

† *See* Chapter 5, section I (explaining why tort law can shift the loss from the plaintiff to the defendant only when their conflicting interests can be normatively distinguished).

the plaintiff's unreasonable conduct as the sole cause of the accident (compare the first two rows). The converse holds in a case of last clear chance, which requires that the defendant either knew or should have known that the plaintiff had acted unreasonably. In these circumstances, the defendant cannot reasonably assume otherwise (eliminating the second row), so the defendant's failure to exercise reasonable care can be singled out as the cause of accident (compare the first and third rows). Unlike a case of contributory negligence, the conflicting interests of the parties can be distinguished in cases of assumption of risk and last clear chance, explaining the distinctive role played by these doctrines.

This interpretation does not depend on the writ system's requirements of direct causation and the like. It instead utilizes the causal question to determine whether the conflicting interests of the plaintiff and defendant can be normatively distinguished. By doing so, the interpretation unifies the doctrines of assumption of risk, last clear chance, and contributory negligence.

Of course, the common law did not have to evaluate the conduct of the plaintiff and defendant in causal terms. The common law did so because it refused to apportion damages among multiple tortious actors, requiring courts to identify a single proximate cause of the accident.

As one treatise explained:

> The common law refuses to apportion damages which arise from negligence. This it does upon considerations of public policy, and upon this principle, it is said, depends also the rule which makes the contributory negligence of the plaintiff a complete defense. For the same reason, when there is an action in tort, where injury results from the negligence of two or more persons, the sufferer has a full remedy against one of them [under the doctrine of joint and several liability], and no contribution can be enforced between the tort feasors. The policy of the law in this respect is founded upon the inability

of human tribunals to mete out exact justice. A perfect code would render each man responsible for the unmixed consequences of his own default; but the common law, in view of the impossibility of assigning all effects to their respective causes, refuses to [apportion damages].[17]

Having concluded that damages cannot be objectively apportioned "to mete out exact justice," courts had an important policy reason for identifying one tortious actor as *the* proximate cause of injury. Following the abolition of the writ system, courts initially conceptualized the tort duty as a general or universal obligation that each individual owed to everyone else. To limit liability in a particular case, courts had to rely on the requirement of proximate cause.* "If the question of which of several acts caused the plaintiff's injury was open to judicial discretion, how could private law stay clear of the political uses of law for purposes of redistribution?"[18] To prevent tort law from functioning as a form of social engineering that inappropriately redistributed wealth — a particular concern of that era — courts adopted rules of objective causation. "Only if it was possible to say objectively that A caused B's injury would courts be able to take money from A and give damages to B without being charged with redistribution." Objective causation provided an apparently neutral method for limiting liability that also ruled out the apportionment of damages, thereby producing the otherwise puzzling common-law defenses based on the plaintiff's conduct.

III. COMPARATIVE RESPONSIBILITY

During the twentieth century, negligence doctrine was substantially refined from the cruder version that first emerged

---

* *Compare* Chapter 9, section II.D (discussing how courts first limited liability for pure emotional and economic harms by concluding that these injuries are not proximately caused by negligence).

in the nineteenth century. The elements of duty, breach, and causation became distinctive requirements, enabling courts to address policy issues about excessive liability with duty analysis rather than proximate cause. Once duty became relational, tort liability was necessarily limited to parties standing in the requisite right-duty relationship.* The limitation obviated the need for courts to limit liability with the concept of objective causation.

As the twentieth century progressed, the very idea of objective causation also became increasingly difficult to defend. In the natural sciences, for example, the mechanistic causal reasoning of Newtonian physics was replaced by the probabilistic reasoning of quantum mechanics. Outside of the natural sciences, there was "a general decline of causal analysis in American social thought beginning around the turn of the century." The increasingly urbanized, industrialized world was "understood . . . as radically more interdependent." Social phenomena, including accidental injuries, were readily attributed to multiple probabilistic causes.[19]

Largely for these reasons, the concept of objective causation was rejected by courts in the twentieth century, allowing them to apportion damages among multiple tortious actors. Common-law tort rules were made by judges and could be revised by judges.

In considering the issue of apportionment, judges were able to draw on admiralty law — a close cousin of tort law — which had long divided damages among faulty actors.[20] Beginning in 1908, the federal statutory law governing claims of railroad workers against interstate railroads allowed for the apportionment of damages based on a comparison of the parties' negligence.[21] The majority of states adopted similar statutes for intrastate railroads. Mississippi legislatively adopted comparative negligence in 1910 for all personal injury claims, something Georgia had already

---

* *See* Chapter 8, section I.B (discussing the *Palsgraf* rule).

done. By midcentury, more states adopted statutes of this type, and by the 1970s judges in other states began to overturn the common-law rule against apportionment.[22] Except for a few southeastern states, every jurisdiction in the United States, like many other countries around the world, has adopted some form of *comparative responsibility* that apportions liability among multiple tortfeasors.

The Determination of Comparative Responsibility   The comparative responsibility of each party is determined by the jury. According to the *Restatement (Third)*:

> Factors for assigning percentages of responsibility to each person whose legal responsibility has been established include
>
> (a) the nature of the person's risk-creating conduct, including any awareness or indifference with respect to the risks created by the conduct and any intent with respect to the harm created by the conduct; and
>
> (b) the strength of the causal connection between the person's risk-creating conduct and the harm.[23]

Comparative responsibility depends on both relative culpability and the relative strength of the causal connection, a combination that is usefully illustrated by the case involving the 1993 terrorist bombing of the World Trade Center that killed six people, injured hundreds of others, and caused extensive damage to tenants. Plaintiffs proved that the defendant owner and operator of the iconic buildings knew of the substantial risk that terrorists could easily explode a car bomb in the subterranean parking garage of the complex. Despite knowledge of the risk and repeated recommendations by outside consultants to reduce the threat, the defendant failed to take reasonable precautions that would have prevented the bombing. The terrorists were able "to drive into the subgrade public parking garage, park on the access ramp, set a fuse and leave — all without a scintilla of resistance." Because the defendant's negligence made it so easy for terrorists to bomb the building, the jury determined that the defendant was 68 percent responsible for the bombing, with the more culpable terrorists being only 32 percent responsible.

The jury's finding was affirmed on appeal:

> Were the dispositive consideration in passing upon the jury's allocation of responsibility simply one of comparative reprehensibility, we would not hesitate to vacate the allocation as against the weight of the evidence; there is no question that the bombers' conduct was utterly wanton and that defendant's negligence, albeit great and facilitative of enormous harm, was not deserving of equal odium. The jury, however, in assigning fault, was required to consider more than the moral quality of the respective tortfeasors' conduct; its determination was also necessarily, and even more essentially, premised upon the extent to which each tortfeasor contributed to the harm, and the evidence, fairly considered, clearly supported the view that defendant's negligence had been extraordinarily conducive of the terrorists' conduct — so much so that the fulfilment of the terrorists' plot and the ensuing harm could with clear justification have been understood as primarily attributable to that negligence. This being the case, we see no basis to disturb the jury's apportionment. . . .[24]

The case illustrates how comparative responsibility depends on both relative culpability and the relative strength of each party's causal contribution, although it is not clear how the jury determined the exact amount of comparative responsibility. What explains why the defendant was 68 percent responsible? Typically, "juries are given very little, if any, guidance on how to proceed." The lack of guidance matters, because "there are at least two conceptually distinct ways of apportioning negligence" that can produce substantially different outcomes.[25] At best, the current practice involves the jury determining apportionment based on its notion of what is equitable or fair.

Apportionment of Liability   Once the jury has determined the comparative responsibility of the parties, the impact of that finding on the apportionment of liability depends on the form of comparative responsibility.

The majority of states have adopted *impure comparative responsibility*, which allows the plaintiff to recover only if the defendant's comparative responsibility is equal to (in some jurisdictions) or greater than the plaintiff's comparative responsibility. This method of apportionment reflects an interpersonal priority of the parties' conflicting interests. A plaintiff who was "more" responsible has a normatively distinguishable liberty interest that is legally subordinate to the defendant's conflicting ("less" responsible) liberty interest, preventing tort law from shifting the loss from the plaintiff to the defendant. The approach is impure, however, because it is not symmetrical. By the same reasoning, a defendant who was "more" responsible should be liable for the entire injury, and yet a defendant deemed to be 75 percent responsible for the injury is liable for only 75 percent of the damages. Impure comparative responsibility gives defendants a one-sided advantage.

This problem is avoided by *pure comparative responsibility*, which apportions liability in all cases. A plaintiff deemed to be 99 percent responsible for the injury could recover 1 percent of the damages from the negligent defendant, and the converse would be true if the defendant were 99 percent responsible. This approach treats the parties symmetrically and has been adopted by a dozen or so states, typically by judicial decision.

Comparative Responsibility and Last Clear Chance
Having rejected the old common-law rule that barred the contributorily negligent plaintiff from recovery, courts then had to

determine how comparative responsibility affects the other defenses. Based on a proximate cause rationale, courts initially retained last clear chance, thereby allowing a contributorily negligent plaintiff to receive full recovery from a negligent defendant who had the last opportunity for avoiding the accident. That rationale was scathingly criticized by scholars, who deemed the doctrine to be a mere palliative for the harshness of the old contributory negligence bar to recovery. Consequently, "[t]he doctrine of last clear chance has crumbled under the assault of the rash of legislative acts and judicial decisions adopting comparative negligence. It is now an *anomaly* in comparative negligence jurisdictions and exists only in the old comparative negligence jurisdictions, notably Georgia and Mississippi."[26]

The abolition of last clear chance, though, has created problems. Should a plaintiff who was initially injured by his or her own unreasonable conduct receive reduced recovery for other injuries that were subsequently caused by the medical malpractice of the doctor? The medical injuries were factually caused by the unreasonable conduct of each party, triggering the rule of comparative responsibility. The doctor had the least clear chance to avoid those injuries, but abolition of that defense would seem to absolve the doctor of full liability for the medical injuries, with the apportionment of liability instead turning on the comparative responsibility of each party. Nevertheless, courts have allowed these plaintiffs full recovery.[27] A medical patient deserves reasonable medical care regardless of the source of the medical problem, entitling the patient to full compensation for injuries caused by malpractice. The outcome, though defensible, is puzzling because it effectively reinstates the doctrine of last clear chance in these cases.

What distinguishes other cases in which the plaintiff's prior negligence placed him or her in a vulnerable situation requiring the exercise of reasonable care by a defendant who had the last clear chance to avoid the injury? Why is the recovery of these plaintiffs reduced under comparative responsibility, unlike the recovery of medical patients? Unless the cases can be distinguished in a principled manner, each of these similarly situated parties should be treated equally by tort law. Insofar as medical patients deserve full recovery, then similarly situated plaintiffs in other cases should also receive full compensation, the result attained by the common-law rule of last clear chance.*

Comparative Responsibility and Assumption of Risk

The doctrine of assumption of risk has been only partially affected by comparative responsibility. In cases of express or primary assumption of risk, the defendant owes no duty with respect to the risk in question. Without duty, there is no basis for imposing any liability on the defendant. The adoption of comparative responsibility has instead affected implied or secondary assumption of risk. By treating implied or secondary assumption of risk as a form of contributory negligence, the vast majority of states allow a plaintiff who has assumed such a risk to recover under comparative responsibility.†

As in the case of last clear chance, courts have created problems by abolishing the distinctive defense of implied or secondary assumption of risk. Courts continue to treat express assumption of risk as a complete defense, and there is no principled distinction between express and implied assumption of risk. Express assumption of risk finds justification in consent and individual autonomy or self-determination. Someone who voluntarily chooses to face a known risk becomes responsible for the ensuing consequences. That concern applies with equal

---

* The loss-of-a-chance doctrine for medical malpractice provides a possible basis for distinction insofar as it finds justification in the special nature of a physician's duty. *See* Chapter 9, section I.A. The doctrine, however, has not been widely adopted.

† *See supra* section I.C.

force to cases of implied or secondary assumption of risk. The defense, after all, only applies if the plaintiff had sufficient knowledge of the unreasonable danger and then chose to face the risk. Why doesn't this voluntary choice to face a known risk make the plaintiff responsible for the ensuing injuries, as it does in cases of express assumption of risk? To be sure, the choice is objectively unreasonable, but the fact that others would choose differently, including the reasonable person, does not matter. Otherwise, what is the point of self-determination? By eliminating any form of assumption of risk, a regime of comparative responsibility fails to respect the right holder's autonomy, creating an inconsistency with wide swaths of tort law.*

Recognizing this problem, the *Restatement (Third)* justifies abolition of the defense on the ground that "[w]hen a party clearly and consciously chooses to confront a risk because of an actual preference for the risk, [the rule] of implied-in-fact contracts and rules about the scope of a defendant's duty provide sufficient flexibility."[28] An implied-in-fact contract would eliminate the duty, just like cases in which the plaintiff expressly assumes a risk by entering into an exculpatory contractual agreement. Reformulating the rule as an implied contract could also force courts to scrutinize more carefully the nature of the plaintiff's decision, much like they do when evaluating exculpatory contracts. Treating the plaintiff's conduct as an implied-in-fact contract would produce a desirable outcome, but this approach will not work in all cases (as when the defendant had no knowledge of the plaintiff's conduct). It would be better if courts applied the doctrine properly in the first instance, eliminating the need to reformulate implied assumption of risk as an implied-in-fact contract.

---

* The element of duty does not distinguish primary and implied assumption of risk. In each case, the plaintiff assumes the risk prior to the occurrence of injury. The plaintiff's choice to face the risk eliminates it from the defendant's duty, absolving the defendant of responsibility for the ensuing injury.

None of these issues mattered for the old common-law affirmative defenses, which barred the plaintiff from recovery regardless of the doctrinal category. With the adoption of comparative responsibility, the substantive differences among the affirmative defenses are now important. Rather than simplifying the tort inquiry, comparative responsibility has made the affirmative defenses more complex.[29]

~ 12 ~

Strict Liability for Abnormally Dangerous Activities

To address the social problem of accidental harms, tort law has adopted negligence liability as the default rule. In addition to alleging negligence liability, the plaintiff in some cases can also claim that the defendant is strictly liable. The plaintiff can recover only once for the injuries, but the claim of strict liability does not require proof that the defendant breached the duty to exercise reasonable care. A rule of strict liability, therefore, determines the outcome of a case only when the plaintiff is unable to prove negligence liability, although the negligence claim can still have strategic value in these cases as well.*

---

* Even if the claim of strict liability is meritorious, a plaintiff will often try to prove negligence liability. In doing so, the plaintiff can offer evidence that impugns the defendant's conduct, unlike the claim of strict liability for which the unreasonableness of the defendant's conduct is irrelevant. Insofar as the plaintiff can show that the defendant behaved in a questionable manner, the jury is more likely to exercise any discretion in favor of the plaintiff. *Compare* Richard L. Cupp, Jr. & Danielle Polage, *The Rhetoric of Strict Products Liability versus Negligence: An Empirical Analysis*, 77 N.Y.U. L. Rev. 874 (2002) (finding higher pain and suffering awards when jury instructions are framed in terms of negligence rather than strict liability).

Due to the dominance of negligence liability, the express rules of strict liability seem to be exceptional and practically irrelevant (outside of products liability). As we have found, however, negligence liability contains substantial strains of no-fault or strict liability, giving the rules of strict liability fundamental importance that might not otherwise be apparent.[*]

The common law has always recognized express rules of strict liability. For example, the early common law applied strict liability to injuries caused by dangerous pets and wandering cattle. The most general rule originated in the famous nineteenth-century English case *Rylands v. Fletcher* that applied strict liability to a bursting reservoir.[1] The liability rule in *Rylands* was ambiguous in important respects and has been refined by courts over time to produce the *Restatement (Second)* rule of strict liability for abnormally dangerous activities, which has been adopted by the vast majority of jurisdictions in the United States.

The paradigmatic example of an abnormally dangerous activity involves blasting by dynamite or other explosives for construction activities. Even before *Rylands*, courts in the United States imposed strict liability "on parties whose blasting projected debris that caused harm to the neighboring property or to persons on that property." Courts subsequently extended this rule "to harms caused by vibrations or concussions as well as debris."[2] After *Rylands* was decided, the catastrophic bursting of reservoirs in Pennsylvania and California facilitated the adoption of that liability rule.[3] As the rule became more generalized in form, courts applied it to an increasingly wider range

---

[*] *See* Chapter 3, section I (identifying inherent connection between negligence liability and strict liability); Chapter 8, section II.A (showing how the objective standard of the reasonable person can function as a rule of no-fault or strict liability); *see also* Chapter 7, section I.B. (illustrating strains of strict liability in the intentional torts).

of activities, including oil-well explosions, fireworks displays, and the commercial use of toxic materials to kill pests or protect crops.[*]

Due to the variety of abnormally dangerous activities, the *Restatement (Second)* does not "reduce abnormally dangerous activities to any definition," but instead lists a number of factors that "are all to be considered, and are all of importance" in determining whether an activity should be subjected to strict liability. These factors are:

(a) existence of a high degree of risk of some harm to the person, land or chattels of others;

(b) likelihood that the harm that results from it will be great;

(c) inability to eliminate the risk by the exercise of reasonable care;

(d) extent to which the activity is not a matter of common usage;

(e) inappropriateness of the activity to the place where it is carried on; and

(f) extent to which its value to the community is outweighed by its dangerous attributes.[4]

This formulation gives no guidance on what the liability rule is supposed to accomplish. One can recognize that the factors "are all to be considered, and are all of importance" without having any idea of the significance or weight to be attached to each of them. The *Restatement (Second)* does

---

[*] In particular, courts generalized the ruling by Lord Chancellor Cairns for the House of Lords in *Rylands* that limits strict liability to "a non-natural use of the defendant's land." The meaning of this limitation is unclear. For example, "a 'non-natural use' might be one that departs from a state of nature; it might be one that is uncommon or unusual; or it might be one that is unreasonable or inappropriate in light of the local circumstances." *Restatement (Third): Liability for Physical Harms* § 20, cmt. d. English courts subsequently limited the rule to the occupiers of land, whereas courts in the United States have adopted a more broad-ranging rule that defines a "non-natural use" as any activity not common in the community.

not clarify the issue by explaining that no one factor is "necessarily sufficient of itself in a particular case, and ordinarily several of them will be required for strict liability. On the other hand, it is not necessary that each of them be present, especially if others weigh heavily."[5]

To determine how these factors should be applied, we need to identify the purpose of the liability rule. As we have found, rules of strict liability typically serve one of two distinctive functions—the compensation of injuries caused by reasonable, nonreciprocal risks; or the reduction of risks not adequately regulated by negligence liability. Each function can be accommodated by the rule of strict liability for abnormally dangerous activities, making it possible to apply the rule in two different manners.

I. COMPENSATION OF PHYSICAL HARMS CAUSED BY NONRECIPROCAL RISKS

According to the *Restatement (Second)*, strict liability can apply "to an activity that is carried on with all reasonable care, and that is of such utility that the risk which is involved in it cannot be regarded as so great or so unreasonable as to make it negligence merely to carry on the activity at all."[6] The strongest case for strict liability would involve such an activity satisfying the full set of factors in the *Restatement (Second)* rule, implying that strict liability is most appropriate under the following three conditions:

1. The activity is dangerous, even though it has been conducted reasonably in all relevant respects (factors a–c).
2. The activity itself is reasonable, having overall utility that outweighs its risks (factor c), although the utility is largely enjoyed by the private actor rather than the public (factor f); and
3. The activity is not common in the community (factor d) or inappropriately located (factor e).

When all of these conditions are satisfied, strict liability would not reduce risks. The actor already exercises reasonable care in conducting the activity (condition 1) and would continue to engage in the dangerous behavior because his or her private utility from the activity exceeds the injury costs for which he or she would be strictly liable (condition 2). Whether the actor is subject to negligence or strict liability, the risky behavior would remain the same.

Lacking a deterrence rationale, the purpose of strict liability must be one of compensation. The dangerous activity (condition 1), although appropriately located, is neither common in the community nor particularly beneficial for the general public (conditions 2 and 3). The abnormally dangerous activity accordingly creates a nonreciprocal risk. As we previously found, an actor responsible for a nonreciprocal risk fairly incurs a compensatory duty for the ensuing injuries, explaining why strict liability applies to abnormally dangerous activities.*

This interpretation, although compelling, does not persuasively explain all of the *Restatement (Second)* factors. Even if the actor is fairly subject to strict liability when engaged in a dangerous, uncommon activity conducted for private purposes, what does the location of the activity have to do with the fairness of requiring compensation? As one court explained:

> Considering the ultrahazardous character of the activity, we find no reason for making a distinction between the right of the owner of a dwelling house which is damaged by a blast set off in open country 2000 feet distant from his house, and the right of an owner of a skyscraper in a large city damaged by a blast set off on adjoining property. . . . [T]he ensuing loss should be considered a cost of the blaster's business.[7]

---

* *See* Chapter 3, section III.

The activity's location—factor e of the *Restatement (Second)* rule—is simply irrelevant to the question of whether the risk was nonreciprocal and fairly subject to strict liability.

Courts have also had a hard time understanding why the social value of the activity affects the appropriateness of strict liability—factor f. As one treatise observes, "[t]he justification for strict liability . . . is that useful but dangerous activities must pay their own way. There is nothing in this reasoning that would exempt *very* useful activities from the rule."[8] Unable to understand this factor, courts have rendered it "largely irrelevant" and "rarely outcome determinative."[9]

Based on these cases, the *Restatement (Third)* has eliminated the location and social value factors in its formulation of the liability rule:

(A) A defendant who carries on an abnormally dangerous activity is subject to strict liability for physical harm resulting from the activity.

(B) An activity is abnormally dangerous if:

   (1) the activity creates a foreseeable and highly significant risk of physical harm even when reasonable care is exercised by all actors; and

   (2) the activity is not a matter of common usage.[10]

The *Restatement (Third)* justifies this rule in terms of a

position [that] resonates deeply in public attitudes: if the person in the street is asked whether a party should be liable for injuries that the party causes, the person's answer is likely to be affirmative. These perceptions and attitudes can be easily explained: when a person voluntarily acts and in doing so secures the desired benefits of that action, the person should in fairness bear responsibility for the harms the actions cause.[11]

This form of responsibility is identical to the one that justifies strict liability in cases of private necessity and vicarious liability: An actor can fairly be held responsible for the foreseeable consequences of his or her affirmative, reasonable conduct.* More generally, this form of responsibility makes it possible for tort law to subject risky actors to a compensatory tort duty that protects a correlative compensatory tort right held by those who are foreseeably threatened by the risky conduct.† Due to the inadequacies of the damages remedy, a compensatory tort right ordinarily is best protected by negligence liability, with an important exception for physical harms caused by reasonable, nonreciprocal risks.‡ Consistent with this reasoning, the *Restatement (Third)* also relies on "principles of reciprocity" to justify this rule of strict liability.[12]

II. REDUCTION OF RISKS INADEQUATELY REGULATED BY NEGLIGENCE LIABILITY

Due to the difficulty a plaintiff would face in trying to prove that the defendant did not take complex precautions required by reasonable care, negligence liability does not always reduce risks to the desired extent. Without a credible threat of negligence liability, duty holders do not have a sufficient financial incentive to incur the costs of reasonable care. Strict liability restores this incentive and reduces risk by inducing duty holders to adopt safety precautions to minimize their liability costs, thereby avoiding the need for the court to make complicated safety decisions on the basis of the plaintiff's proof.**

---

    * *See* Chapter 7, section II.B (discussing rationale for private necessity); Chapter 10, section II (discussing rationale for vicarious liability).

    † *See* Chapter 5, section I.

    ‡ *See* Chapter 5, section II (explaining why a compensatory tort right is best protected by the default rule of negligence liability for accidental harms); *id.* section III (explaining why a compensatory tort right only justifies liability for nonreciprocal risks).

    ** *See* Chapter 3, section II.

This evidentiary rationale for strict liability is most prominent in the area of products liability. Having concluded that negligence liability does not adequately regulate systems of product quality, courts adopted the rule of strict liability for defective products.* The evidentiary rationale for strict liability is not limited to product cases, however, as courts have relied on that rationale to justify other important rules of strict liability.†

Nevertheless, courts have increasingly ignored the evidentiary rationale for strict liability in determining whether an activity is abnormally dangerous and subject to strict liability. When providing compensation for nonreciprocal risks, strict liability does not require a deterrence rationale. Consequently, courts have routinely assumed that factor c of the *Restatement (Second)* rule — the "inability to eliminate the risk by the exercise of reasonable care" — means that all actors actually exercise reasonable care. By setting aside any concerns about risk reduction, courts could focus on the issue of whether the defendant should be strictly liable for injuring the plaintiff with a nonreciprocal risk. Other courts then assumed that the rule of strict liability is limited to this rationale, leading them to ignore or reject a deterrence rationale for strict liability.

Based on these cases, the *Restatement (Third)* has interpreted the rule of strict liability for abnormally dangerous activities in a manner that effectively rejects the evidentiary rationale for strict liability, even though doing so is inconsistent with its express acceptance of that identical rationale for the rule of strict products liability. According to the *Restatement*

---

* *See* Chapter 1, section III.A (discussing development of strict products liability); Chapter 13 (discussing the continued vitality of the evidentiary rationale for strict products liability).

† For example, nineteenth-century, courts relied on this rationale in holding common carriers strictly liable for lost or damaged goods. *See* Chapter 1, section II. A similar rationale was invoked to justify the adoption of workers' compensation in the early twentieth century. *See* Chapter 1, section III.A.

R3T rejects justify on civil? reverse for fuel impossible

(Third), "a prerequisite for the strict liability rule [for an abnormally dangerous activity] . . . is not merely a highly significant
risk associated with the activity itself, but a highly significant
risk that remains with the activity even when all actors exercise
reasonable care."[13]

This requirement is inconsistent with the enabling torts,
which involve duties created by a special relationship like
the one between landlords and tenants.* For the enabling
torts, the absence of perfect law enforcement, coupled with
the prevalence of self-interested unlawful behavior, makes
unlawful conduct foreseeable, creating a duty for one party
to protect another from being victimized by a third-party criminal. Inadequate protection effectively enables such foreseeable criminal misconduct, giving landlords, for example, a duty
to protect their tenants from third-party criminals such as bur-
glars. In light of the enabling torts, how could courts defensibly
assume that negligence liability induces everyone to exersise
reasonable care, thereby eliminating any deterrence rationale
for strict liability?

By assuming that an activity can be abnormally dangerous
only if a substantial risk remains after all relevant actors have
exercised reasonable care, courts have created a rule that is
inconsistent with other important tort doctrines. The courts,
moreover, have not adequately defended the assumption, even
though it "has played a major role in judicial decisions determining whether particular activities qualify as abnormally dangerous."[14] These decisions provide the doctrinal foundation for
the *Restatement (Third)* rule, creating the distinct possibility
that this important form of strict liability will be unable to
serve the deterrence function.

In applying the *Restatement (Second)* rule of strict liability
for an abnormally dangerous activity, courts do not have to
assume that everyone always acts reasonably. In other contexts,

---

* *See* Chapter 8, section I.F.

the tort duty recognizes the social fact of unlawful behavior, and there is no reason why the rule of strict liability for abnormally dangerous activities cannot do the same. The issue turns on the appropriate interpretation of factor c in the *Restatement (Second)* rule involving "the inability to eliminate the risk by the exercise of reasonable care."

Any form of tortious misconduct can constitute the unavoidable risk of harm inherent in an activity. The risk might in fact be reasonable as courts commonly assume, or it might be effectively immune from negligence liability due to the plaintiff's inability to recover from the defendant or third party tortfeasors. By identifying those risks that are not actually governed by negligence liability, factor c limits the claim of strict liability to circumstances in which it is "distinguished from negligence" as required by the liability rule.

Under this interpretation, strict liability is most appropriate — that is, factors a through f are all satisfied — when:

1. The activity creates a substantial risk of physical harm that cannot be effectively regulated by negligence liability due to problems of proof (factors a–c);
2. The activity is uncommon and not likely to have high utility, increasing the likelihood that strict liability would reduce the amount of the dangerous activity (factor d);
3. The activity could be relocated to a place where the danger would be substantially reduced (factor e); and
4. The activity does not directly benefit the public and could be reduced or eliminated without social detriment (factor f).

Interpreted in this manner, all six factors in the *Restatement (Second)* rule coherently fit together, strongly supporting a deterrence rationale for this rule of strict liability.*

---

* For further discussion of this approach, *see* Mark Geistfeld, *Should Enterprise Liability Replace the Rule of Strict Liability for Abnormally Dangerous Activities?*, 45 UCLA L. Rev. 611 (1998). At least one court has adopted this type of deterrence rationale. *See Indiana Harbor Belt R.R. Co. v. American Cyanamid*

The possibility that strict liability would reduce the risky activity was widely recognized by courts in the nineteenth century following the abolition of the writ system, which enabled them to address for the first time the substantive choice between negligence and strict liability. In rejecting *Rylands*, the court in a leading case did so on the ground that strict liability "puts a clog upon natural and reasonably necessary uses of matter, and tends to embarrass and obstruct much of the work which it seems to be man's duty carefully to do."[15] Obstructing or deterring dangerous activities is not desirable when they are socially valuable, so courts during this era often rejected strict liability due to the concern that it would deter or reduce the amount of a socially valuable activity.[16] Other courts, however, recognized that the ability of strict liability to reduce risk provided a good reason for adopting that liability rule.*

Over time, the tort system has developed into a regime dominated by negligence liability formulated to control risky behavior. The reasonable person never acts negligently, and ideally there would be no unreasonable behavior and no need for further risk reduction via the imposition of strict liability.

In our world, though, unreasonable behavior occurs all the time, and plaintiffs do not have complete evidence concerning

---

Co., 916 F.2d 1174 (7th Cir. 1990) (applying Illinois law) (Posner, J.). However, "the inquiry Judge Posner prescribed and conducted would have courts determine not only the extent to which the negligence rule leaves residual risk, but also the efficacy of strict liability in reducing that risk." David R. Rosenberg, *The Judicial Posner on Negligence versus Strict Liability: Indiana Harbor Belt Railroad Co. v. American Cyanamid Co.*, 120 Harv. L. Rev. 1210, 1215 (2007). The deterrence rationale for strict liability prevents courts from determining the extent to which negligence liability would reduce risk, making Judge Posner's inquiry self-defeating. *Id.* The court instead should determine whether one of the *Restatement (Second)* factors is present in the case, not whether the presence of that factor means that risk reduction, more likely than not, would occur.

* *See* Chapter 3, section II (providing examples of courts and commentators in the nineteenth century recognizing the evidentiary rationale for strict liability).

the varied, complicated ways in which a defendant might have been able to reduce risk by the exercise of reasonable care. These undeniable social facts can be included within the *Restatement (Second)* rule of strict liability for abnormally dangerous activities, which is sufficiently flexible to account for the way in which strict liability properly applies to nonreciprocal risks, or to cases in which strict liability might reduce risks not adequately regulated by negligence liability. Both rationales have long been recognized by courts, producing a body of case law that appears to vacillate between different types of reasoning or rationales for strict liability.[17] Based on this case law, the *Restatement (Second)* could only list the relevant factors without providing guidance on how to apply them. The *Restatement (Third)* has improved matters by clearly identifying the reciprocity rationale for strict liability, but has done so at the cost of eliminating the deterrence rationale. Whether courts will follow the *Restatement (Third)* in this respect ultimately depends on whether they recognize that the adoption of negligence liability as the default rule for controlling risky behavior does not foreclose the use of strict liability to reduce risks that are not effectively regulated by negligence liability.

⌁ 13 ⌁

Strict Products Liability

In a technologically driven, consumer-based market economy, products are regularly involved in accidents. Each year, hundreds of thousands of injuries are caused by automobiles, chemicals, cigarettes, prescription drugs, guns, and numerous other products. The problem of product-caused injury is one of the most important issues addressed by tort law, and virtually all states have adopted the rule of *strict products liability* that makes the seller of a defective product strictly liable for the physical harms proximately caused by the defect. A similar liability rule has been adopted by other jurisdictions around the world, including the European Union and Japan. The practical impact of this liability rule is enormous. Almost every product sold or used within these jurisdictions must satisfy the tort safety standard, unless legislation has preempted tort law on the matter or the transaction otherwise falls outside the scope of the tort duty.

Strict products liability has a variety of doctrines tailored to the safety problems created by product markets, making the subject a field unto itself that can constitute an entire course of study.[1] The extensive litigation of product cases over the past few decades has been the impetus for many important doctrinal developments. Consequently, our prior discussions have often relied on this body of tort law, making it possible for us to quickly cover the most important doctrines of products liability.

Origins of Strict Products Liability   The development of strict products liability fully illustrates how tort law evolved over the course of the twentieth century (*see* Chapter 1, section III.A). During the nineteenth century, a seller's duty was limited to parties with which it had a contractual relationship (the requirement of *privity*). Like many other duty limitations, the courts abolished this one in the twentieth century, turning products liability into a full-blown negligence regime.

To prove negligence, the plaintiff must prove that the product defect, more likely than not, is attributable to the seller's breach of the duty to exercise reasonable care. The mere fact that the product caused injury does not render it defective, nor does the fact of defect necessarily establish negligence. Perfect quality control ordinarily is not feasible, so the seller's exercise of reasonable care usually cannot eliminate all defects.

Due to the difficulty of identifying the specific manner in which the defendant acted unreasonably, plaintiffs regularly invoked *res ipsa loquitur*. These claims were extraordinarily successful, even though they often did not, in fact, satisfy the requirements of *res ipsa loquitur*. Product sellers were incurring liability merely because they were responsible for a defective condition in a product that caused the plaintiff's injury, an implicit rule of strict liability for the physical harms caused by a product defect.*

---

* A good example is provided by the well-known case *Escola v. Coca Cola Bottling Co.*, 150 P.2d 436 (Cal. 1944), in which the California Supreme Court upheld the jury verdict of negligence based on *res ipsa loquitur*. The plaintiff was injured by an exploding bottle of soda, and the evidence showed that the defect probably involved a hairline fracture in the bottle attributable to the recycling or re-use of the bottle. The court simply asserted that bottles should not be re-used unless there is a "commercially practicable" test for eliminating all latent defects.

Once courts recognized that negligence liability was functioning in this manner, they also recognized that plaintiffs would often be unable to prove that a defect was attributable to the seller's negligence in manufacture or quality control. Rather than deny plaintiffs recovery for failing to satisfy the burden of proving that the seller was legally at fault for the defect, courts adopted the evidentiary rationale for strict liability (*see* Chapter 3, section II).

The effort was pioneered by the California Supreme Court, which "repeatedly emphasized that one of the principal purposes behind the strict products liability doctrine is to relieve an injured plaintiff of many of the onerous evidentiary burdens inherent in a negligence cause of action."[2] Courts continue to justify the rule of strict products liability with the evidentiary rationale for strict liability.[3]

Based on this case law, the *Restatement (Second)* formulated a rule of strict products liability in the early 1960s. The rule and its commentary have been widely adopted, providing the textual source of contemporary products liability law:

§ 402A. Special Liability of Seller of Product for Physical Harm to User or Consumer

(1) One who sells any product in a defective condition unreasonably dangerous to the user or consumer or to his

---

The requirements of reasonable care, however, do not ordinarily involve the complete elimination of risk, and the court's assertion was not based on any evidence comparing the cost of such testing to the risks created by the defendant's recycling program. The plaintiff's proof did not establish that the defect, more likely than not, was caused by negligence, and yet the court expressed no concern about upholding the jury verdict, the same outcome that was regularly occurring in other product cases of the era. Rather than join the majority opinion, Justice Roger Traynor argued in a concurring opinion that the plaintiff should recover under strict liability, an argument that ultimately provided the impetus for the modern rule of strict products liability. *See* Mark A. Geistfeld, Escola v. Coca Cola Bottling Co.: *Strict Products Liability Unbound*, in *Tort Stories* 229-258 (Robert L. Rabin & Stephen D. Sugarman eds., Foundation Press 2003) (discussing the evidence in the case and showing the influence of Traynor's opinion on the development of strict products liability).

property is subject to liability for physical harm thereby caused to the ultimate user or consumer, or to his property, if

(a) the seller is engaged in the business of selling such a product, and

(b) it is expected to and does reach the user or consumer without substantial change in the condition in which it is sold.

(2) The rule stated in Subsection (1) applies although

(a) the seller has exercised all possible care in the preparation and sale of his product, and

(b) the user or consumer has not bought the product from or entered into any contractual relation with the seller.

The Different Types of Defect   Having adopted the *Restatement (Second)* rule of strict products liability, courts then confronted a hard question. The rule is one of strict liability for the physical harms caused by a defective product, and yet it describes the "defective condition" as being "unreasonably dangerous," the characteristic requirement of negligence liability. Proof that the product was unreasonably dangerous would establish negligence liability, even though the rule is supposed to be one of strict liability that applies when "the seller has exercised all possible care in the preparation and sale of his product." Is the liability rule one of negligence or strict liability?

This aspect of the liability rule has caused an enormous amount of confusion over the years. The confusing mixture of negligence and strict liability concepts became more understandable once courts recognized that there are three different types of product defect, with the nature of the defect determining the roles of negligence and strict liability.

A defect can cause the product to malfunction, rendering it unable to perform its intended function (like an exploding bottle of soda). This type of defect is defined by the fact of the self-defeating product malfunction, typically attributable to some departure from the product's intended design (such as excessive carbonation of the soda). These *construction* or *manufacturing defects* were involved in the cases that first developed the rule of strict products liability, explaining why the *Restatement (Second)* rule is formulated as one of strict liability. To prove that the product was defective in this respect, the plaintiff only needs to show that it malfunctioned in a self-defeating manner, a form of proof that does not depend on whether the seller exercised reasonable care.

After the rule had been widely adopted, plaintiffs began claiming that products were defective in design or warnings. These products did not malfunction and performed according to the manufacturer's specifications, forcing courts to look for alternative definitions of defect.

To determine whether a product design or warning was defective, many courts relied on the "unreasonably dangerous" language in the *Restatement (Second)* rule. Under this approach, a product has a defect in design or warning if that attribute of the product is unreasonably dangerous. A car that was designed without airbags, for example, can be unreasonably dangerous in that respect, thereby establishing a defect of design. By relying on negligence liability, these courts were able to extend products liability to new types of defects that had not previously been regulated by tort law, illustrating how courts used negligence liability to significantly expand the scope of tort liability over the course of the twentieth century (*see* Chapter 1, section III.A).

Based on this development in the case law, the *Restatement (Third)* reformulated the liability rule:

§ 1. Liability of Commercial Seller or Distributor for Harm Caused by Defective Products

One engaged in the business of selling or otherwise distributing products who sells or distributes a defective product is subject to liability for harm to persons or property caused by the defect.

§ 2. Categories of Product Defect

A product is defective when, at the time of sale or distribution, it contains a manufacturing defect, is defective in design, or is defective because of inadequate instructions or warnings. A product:

(a) contains a manufacturing defect when the product departs from its intended design even though all possible care was exercised in the preparation and marketing of the product;

(b) is defective in design when the foreseeable risks of harm posed by the product could have been reduced or avoided by the adoption of a reasonable alternative design by the seller or other distributor, or a predecessor in the commercial chain of distribution, and the omission of the alternative design renders the product not reasonably safe;

(c) is defective because of inadequate instructions or warnings when the foreseeable risks of harm posed by the product could have been reduced or avoided by the provision of reasonable instructions or warnings by the seller or other distributor, or a predecessor in the commercial chain of distribution, and the omission of the instructions or warnings renders the product not reasonably safe.

The Risk-Utility Test   To prove that a product is defective in design or warning under the *Restatement (Third)* rule, the plaintiff ordinarily has to identify a reasonable alternative design or a reasonable alternative warning.* According to the *Restatement (Third)*, a design or warning is a reasonable alternative to the existing design or warning if it passes the *risk-utility* test, an inquiry that is equivalent to the Hand formula for reasonable care (*see* Chapter 8, section II.B).

---

* *Compare* Chapter 8, section III.A (discussing proof of negligence by identification of an untaken precaution required by the standard of reasonable care).

Consider the claim that an automobile is defectively designed for not having airbags. The *risk* of the car design without an airbag refers to the increased risk that the ordinary consumer will suffer injury due to the absence of the airbag (the term *PL*). The *utility* of the design without an airbag involves any savings the ordinary consumer experiences by not having the airbag (the burden *B* or total cost of the airbag). Under the risk-utility test, the car is defective for not having an airbag if the *utility* of the existing design is less than the increased *risk* posed by the design:

added utility of design w/o airbag < added risk of
design w/o airbag
total cost of airbag < expected injury costs w/o airbag
$$B < PL$$

Similarly, proof showing that a warning is defective for not disclosing information required by the risk-utility test is no different from proof showing that the defendant failed to take a precaution required by the Hand formulation of reasonable care. In the typical case, the plaintiff identifies a safety instruction that is not in the allegedly defective warning, and shows that an instruction to this effect would alert the ordinary consumer to the need to take the precaution while using the product, thereby reducing risk in a cost-effective manner. For example, if the ordinary consumer is not aware of the need to wear gloves while using a chemical cleaner, then adding such an instruction to the existing warning would reduce the risk of chemically induced skin burns (the term *PL*). The existing warning is defective if the cost or disutility of the additional disclosure (*B*) is less than the risks that would be eliminated by the disclosure (*PL*), the identical inquiry required by the Hand formulation of reasonable care.

The difficulty created by the risk-utility test in warning cases involves the cost of disclosure. Initially, courts concluded that the cost of adding a new disclosure to a warning only consists of the added ink and paper, a virtually nonexistent cost ordinarily requiring disclosure ($0 = B < PL$). This liability rule gave sellers an incentive to inundate consumers with warnings, something you've undoubtedly experienced. In light of the problem of "information overload," courts have increasingly recognized that a warning creates *information costs* involving the time it takes for the ordinary consumer to read and recall the warning. Information costs can cause a new disclosure to crowd out or obscure other, potentially more important safety instructions or hazard warnings. Based on these cases, the *Restatement (Third)* incorporates information costs into the risk-utility test for warning defects.[4] Unless the cost of reading and remembering the warning is less than the safety benefit ($B < PL$), the ordinary consumer will not find it worthwhile to read the warning, rendering it unable to reduce risk.*

The Consumer Expectations Test The *Restatement (Third)* defines a defect of design or warning in terms of the risk-utility test, whereas the *Restatement (Second)* apparently adopts a different definition. The *Restatement (Second)* discusses the "defective condition" as something that is "unreasonably dangerous"—a requirement yielding the risk-utility test—but the commentary to the rule explains that a product is "unreasonably dangerous" only if it is "dangerous to an extent beyond that which would be contemplated by the ordinary consumer who purchases it, with the ordinary knowledge

---

* Notice how this proof of defect also satisfies the plaintiff's initial burden of proving factual causation. If the ordinary consumer would find it worthwhile to read and follow the disclosure, then the plaintiff, who presumably is like the ordinary consumer, would have done the same. The absence of such a warning, therefore, is presumptively a factual cause of the plaintiff's harm. *Compare Coffman v. Keene Corp.*, 628 A.2d 710 (N.J. 1993) (discussing the "heeding presumption" adopted by many courts that assumes the plaintiff would have read the disclosure and avoided injury had it been in the warning).

common to the community as to its characteristics."[5] Based on this commentary, a large number of jurisdictions evaluate product defects with the *consumer expectations test*, which deems a product to be defective for frustrating ordinary consumer expectations of product safety.

The origins of the test can be traced to an ancient tort doctrine known as the *implied warranty of merchantability*, which made product sellers strictly liable for defects that rendered the product unfit for its ordinary purpose. The rule first governed the sale of contaminated food, but its rationale subsequently generalized to other products. The liability is strict in the sense that it only requires proof that the plaintiff was injured by some attribute of the product that frustrates consumer expectations of safety (such as glass in food or an exploding bottle of soda). Courts using this approach insist that the rule is one of strict products liability and not negligence.

Controversy over the Standard of Liability The risk-utility test in the *Restatement (Third)* is a pure form of negligence liability governing design and warning defects that apparently departs from the *Restatement (Second)* rule subjecting sellers to strict liability for products that frustrate consumer safety expectations. Whether defects of design or warning should be evaluated in terms of the risk-utility test or consumer expectations is now the most controversial (and fundamental) issue in products liability.

To evaluate the issue, we can rely on concepts that we have already developed and employed in prior analyses:

- The tort duty is predicated on the assumption that the ordinary consumer does not have sufficient information about product risks, causing him or her to undervalue product safety (*see* Chapter 8, section III.B). Due to the process of price competition, these misinformed consumer choices give manufacturers an incentive to supply unreasonably dangerous products. These products are more dangerous than expected by the ordinary (misinformed) consumer, resulting in the frustration of consumer safety expectations. To address this safety problem, tort law overrides these misguided contractual choices (and customary product-safety practices more generally), subjecting product sellers to a tort duty. The frustration of consumer expectations, therefore, creates the tort duty or the predicate for *any* form of products liability, including liability rules based on the risk-utility test.*

- Once the existence of the tort duty has been established, the legal inquiry must then determine whether the product is defective. The tort duty is predicated on the product attribute frustrating the actual (misinformed) safety expectations of the ordinary consumer. Unless the separate element of defect is defined in some other manner, the existence of duty would necessarily establish the existence of defect. Because the frustration of the ordinary consumer's *actual* (misinformed) safety expectations creates the tort duty, the element of defect becomes a separate requirement when defined in terms of the ordinary consumer's *reasonable* (well-informed) safety expectations. Having received a product with the amount of safety that he or she would have chosen if adequately informed of the relevant factors, the ordinary consumer could not reasonably expect some other amount of product safety. A product satisfying the well-informed, reasonable safety expectations of the ordinary consumer is not defective.[†]

---

* *Compare* Chapter 11, section I.B (explaining the doctrine of primary assumption of risk, under which the well-informed voluntary choice of the ordinary right holder to assume a risk relieves the defendant of any duty with respect to that risk).

† Under this formulation, the consumer expectations test does not absolve a product seller of liability for product risks that are "open and obvious," a conclusion reached by a number of courts. The fact that the ordinary consumer is aware of a

- What is the amount of product safety reasonably expected by the ordinary consumer? As in the case of perfectly reciprocal risks, the consumer right holder's full set of interests is best protected by safety decisions satisfying cost-benefit analysis (*see* Chapter 8, section II.B). A liability rule requiring this amount of product safety imposes burdens on consumer right holders (via increased prices and any decreased product functionality) that are less than the associated benefit consumers derive from the enhanced product safety. A liability rule requiring the cost-benefit amount of product safety promotes consumer welfare as reasonably expected by the ordinary consumer, thereby justifying the Hand formula as the rule for determining whether a product has a defect of design or warning.*

As previously discussed, the Hand formula is equivalent to the risk-utility test. The ordinary consumer's well-informed preference for product safety—the concept of reasonable expectations—yields the risk-utility test for design and warning defects, uniting the consumer expectations test in the *Restatement (Second)* and the risk-utility test in the *Restatement (Third)*.

This reasoning explains the otherwise puzzling line of cases in which courts choose between the consumer expectations test and the risk-utility test as promulgated by the *Restatement (Third)*. In the first major case, the Connecticut Supreme Court decided that it would continue adhering to consumer

---

risk does not imply that the consumer made an informed safety choice identical to the one involved in the allegation of defect, the only type of choice that should eliminate the duty. *Compare* Chapter 11, section I.C (discussing issue in the context of implied assumption of risk). For more extensive analysis, *see* Mark A. Geistfeld, *Principles of Products Liability* 34-68 (Foundation Press 2006).

* Bystander injuries require separate analysis, although courts typically have not recognized the issue. *See* Geistfeld, *Principles of Products Liability*, at 252-259 (identifying the issue and explaining why bystander injuries should be governed by ordinary tort doctrines and not those based on consumer choice).

expectations, leading it to reject the risk-utility test in the *Restatement (Third)*.[6] The court then adopted the risk-utility test as a complement to the consumer expectations test for cases in which consumers do not have sufficiently formed expectations of product safety, a puzzling outcome. Why reject the risk-utility test and then immediately adopt it?

Of the various rationales for the risk-utility test in the *Restatement (Third)*, none expressly reference consumer expectations.[7] To base strict products liability on frustrated consumer expectations of safety, the court had to reject the *Restatement (Third)*'s rationale for the risk-utility test. After confirming that frustrated consumer expectations provide the rationale for strict products liability, the court could then defensibly define (reasonable) consumer expectations in terms of the risk-utility test.

As this case and others show, the *Restatement (Third)* controversially fails to recognize the way in which the risk-utility test depends on, and is complemented by, consumer expectations. Rather than being competing conceptions of responsibility, each turns out to be necessary for fully specifying the requirements of strict products liability.

Causation   To recover, the plaintiff must prove that the defect was both a factual and legal or proximate cause of the injury in question. These two causal elements are determined by the same rules governing other tort cases. Product cases, though, can involve distinctive factual problems that have produced some of the most difficult causal issues addressed by tort law, including the issues of enhanced injury (*see* Chapter 10, section I) and market-share liability (*see* Chapter 10, section III).

Defenses Based on the Plaintiff's Conduct   Unlike other areas of tort law, courts do not enforce contractual disclaimers of products liability (*see* Chapter 11, section I.A). The defenses in product cases are otherwise equivalent to those in other tort cases, although the defenses are not always labeled in the same manner.

Most notably, in determining whether a product satisfies the safety expectations of the ordinary consumer, courts use the same inquiry that would otherwise determine whether the seller can establish primary assumption of risk. If the ordinary consumer (right holder) has enough information to make a safety decision on an informed basis and decides to face the risk, then the seller (duty holder) is relieved of responsibility to make the identical decision in a manner that would eliminate the risk—the same inquiry for establishing primary assumption of risk (*see* Chapter 11, section I.B). The plaintiff, for example, cannot buy a subcompact car, and then claim that it is defectively designed for not having the safety features characteristic of a sport utility vehicle. Rather than conclude that the plaintiff has primarily assumed the risk inherent in the activity (driving subcompact cars), courts conclude that the product design is not defective in this respect because it satisfies consumer expectations of product safety.[8]

Most jurisdictions apply comparative responsibility to cases in which the plaintiff's negligence and the defect were each a proximate cause of the injury. The plaintiff, for example, could negligently cause a crash and suffer injuries aggravated by a defect in the car. The defendant's liability for the defect can be strict, making it impossible to apportion liability by comparing fault.* These kinds of cases help to explain why the factors for apportioning damages include the relative strength of the causal connection between a party's conduct and the injury (*see* Chapter 11, section III). The relative strength of the causal connection is determined by the relative amount of tortious

---

* Manufacturers only incur strict liability for construction or manufacturing defects. Downstream distributors and retailers, by contrast, are liable for any defect, regardless of whether they could have prevented it by exercising reasonable care. The liability of these defendants is almost always strict.

risk for which each party is responsible. Tortious risk is defined by reference to the liability rule, whether it is one of negligence, strict liability, or even an intentional tort. The amount of risk created by the plaintiff's negligence, therefore, can be compared to the amount of risk created by the defect, making it possible to apportion liability on this basis.

Damages   Having proven that the defect proximately caused some compensable damage, the plaintiff must then prove the amount of damages in the same manner that he or she would prove damages in other tort cases. The extent of liability in product cases, however, can vastly exceed the amounts in other tort cases. A product having a defect of design or warning exposes the manufacturer to liability for the entire product line. These types of defects have been involved in the mass torts, like the thousands of cases involving the failure of asbestos suppliers to warn consumers of the health hazards posed by asbestos. The amount of money at stake in products liability has made it the most politically controversial component of the tort system, placing it at the center of the debate over tort reform (*see* Chapter 1, section III.B).

~ 14 ~

Damages

Tort law redresses the defendant's violation of the plaintiff's tort right with an award of monetary damages. Despite the critical role played by the damages remedy, tort scholars traditionally have marginalized this aspect of the tort claim by simply assuming that the damages award adequately redresses the wrong. In recent years, however, damages have become a hotly contested issue. Most states have adopted tort-reform measures that cap the available amount of compensatory damages for certain types of harms, typically pain and suffering. Punitive damages have also been a target of reform. In a line of relatively recent cases, the U.S. Supreme Court has determined that the long-standing procedures used by courts to determine punitive damages can yield awards that violate the Due Process Clause of the U.S. Constitution. Like the tort-reform measures that limit compensatory damages, the Supreme Court's punitive damages jurisprudence ultimately poses difficult issues about the appropriate way to measure tort damages.

I. COMPENSATORY DAMAGES

To establish the prima facie case, the plaintiff must prove by a preponderance of the evidence that the defendant tortiously caused some compensable damage, typically a physical

353

harm of some sort. Having established a right to receive compensatory damages, the plaintiff must then prove the amount of damages. As previously discussed, this proof involves a causal question: Did the defendant's tortious misconduct cause, or will it cause, the full extent of injury claimed by the plaintiff?* The plaintiff bears the burden of proof on this element, but any inherent uncertainty in the calculation does not bar recovery. The plaintiff is required to establish the amount of damages with "as much certainty as the nature of the tort and the circumstances permit."[1]

The plaintiff can receive compensatory damages for physical harm — bodily injury or damage to tangible property — and any other harms of pain and suffering or intangible economic harms proximately caused by the tortious misconduct. The damages compensate the plaintiff's monetary losses, typically lost wages, medical expenses, and repair or replacement costs, in addition to the nonmonetary injuries of pain and suffering, including anxiety, grief, indignity, and the reduced ability to enjoy life. The plaintiff receives all these damages as a lump-sum award, covering both past and future injuries.

Compensatory tort damages "are designed to place [the plaintiff] in a position substantially equivalent in a pecuniary way to that which he would have occupied had no tort been committed."[2] This compensatory principle can be straightforwardly satisfied for a plaintiff's financial losses, such as medical expenses, lost income, and damage to fungible property having a recognized market value. A damages award equal to the amount of lost wages caused by the tortious misconduct, for example, returns the plaintiff to the pecuniary position for wage income that he or she would have been in if the tort had not occurred.

Damages for pain and suffering are much more puzzling. How do these nonmonetary injuries translate into dollars?

---

* *See* Chapter 9, section II.C (distinguishing the causal issue in the prima facie case, which is resolved by the foreseeability test, from the causal issue concerning the extent of damages, which is resolved by the directness test).

Unable to resolve this question, courts only give jurors vague instructions. The following pattern jury instruction is typical:

> You may award damages for any bodily injury that the plaintiff sustained and any pain and suffering, [disability], [disfigurement], [mental anguish], [and/or] [loss of capacity for enjoyment of life] that the plaintiff experienced in the past [or will experience in the future] as a result of the bodily injury. No evidence of the value of intangible things, such as mental or physical pain and suffering, has been or need be introduced. You are not trying to determine value, but an amount that will fairly compensate the plaintiff for the damages he has suffered. There is no exact standard for fixing the compensation to be awarded for these elements of damage. Any award that you make should be fair in the light of the evidence.[3]

not value but compensatory

Without a prescribed method for quantifying pain-and-suffering damages, it is unclear how judges review these jury awards. Judges can order a *remittitur* requiring the plaintiff to accept a specified reduction of the damages award or otherwise face a new trial, with the attendant cost and risk that the next jury might find for the defendant. In some states, judges also have the power to order an *additur* (not available in federal courts) that increases the award. To overturn a jury award under either method, the reviewing court must find that the amount of the award shocks the conscience. The court evaluates the jury award by reference to the amount "a reasonable person would estimate as fair compensation."[4] The court could derive that amount by comparing the award to those in similar cases, but most jurisdictions do not use this form of judicial review. Nevertheless, judges often find the jury award to be excessive, typically ordering a remittitur of 50 percent or more.[5] How do judges make that determination? The lack of a prescribed method for translating pain and suffering into a damages award not only makes the initial jury award problematic; it also makes the judicial review of these awards equally suspect.

The absence of well-defined standards for quantifying pain-and-suffering damages largely explains why these awards have been and continue to be a focal point in the debate over tort reform. A large number of states enacted legislative reforms in the 1980s that limit pain-and-suffering awards, with many capping these awards at amounts like $250,000.*

Studies have found that jury awards for pain and suffering vary widely for injuries that appear to be equally severe, a particularly worrisome problem in light of other studies finding that these awards, on average, comprise almost half of the total damages award.[6] If there is no defensible measure of these losses (L), how can the jury in a negligence case defensibly determine whether the burden of the precaution made it a reasonable means for eliminating the risk of such injuries ($B ® PL$)? Far from being an uninteresting aspect of tort law, the rules governing compensatory damages pose complex issues, the resolution of which is integral to the sound functioning of liability rules.

II. SURVIVAL AND WRONGFUL-DEATH ACTIONS

Under the early common law, tort claims were entirely personal. If either the tortfeasor or victim died prior to judgment, the tort claim died as well. In the mid-nineteenth century, states started enacting statutes that allow tort claims to proceed despite the death of the victim. A *survival statute* enables the deceased person's estate to recover any tort damages that would have been available to the decedent up to the moment of death. The decedent's knowledge of the impending death, for example, can produce considerable awards for pain and suffering.[7] Injuries caused by the death itself require a separate claim. A *wrongful-death statute* creates

---

* *Compare* Chapter 1, section III.B (discussing how such a damage cap affects the financial viability of cases and has a disproportionate impact on the ability of different types of individuals to pursue their claims).

such a cause of action, allowing specified beneficiaries to recover certain types of losses caused by the wrongful death. Every state recognizes these statutory causes of action, representing a complete rejection of the early common-law rule.

Survival and wrongful-death actions are each based on the defendant's violation of the decedent's individual tort right, so liability in these cases requires proof of the prima facie case for that particular rights violation. Any defenses that could be asserted against the decedent, for example, apply to the survival and wrongful-death actions.

The wrongful-death statutes are of two types. One makes the decedent's estate the statutory beneficiary of the wrongful-death claim. The compensatory damages equal the amount that the decedent would have contributed to the estate over the course of *Estate* an expected lifetime (the decedent's projected lifetime earnings less the expenditures that he or she would have made for living expenses and so on). Such an award can be zero. The other type of wrongful-death statute specifies statutory beneficiaries having a defined relationship with the decedent, typically a spouse and *Benef.* dependent children. The compensatory damages include any loss of financial support and can include pain and suffering such as loss of consortium, depending on the statutory formulation. For both types of wrongful-death statutes, the compensatory damages are for harms suffered by the plaintiff (the estate or specified survivors), even though the decedent's tort right supplies the basis for the plaintiff's wrongful-death action.

In the vast majority of jurisdictions, the wrongful-death claim excludes compensatory damages for the decedent's loss of life's pleasures or *hedonic damages*. The reason is simple: Such an award cannot provide compensation to a dead person. Because this type of loss is compensable when the tortious misconduct does not kill the victim, a tort claim for the loss of life's pleasures is unavoidably personal; it dies with the victim. Consequently, the most severe form of physical harm — premature death — often produces damage awards considerably lower than those for less severe injuries. The counterintuitive result is that often it would be "cheaper for the defendant to kill the plaintiff than to injure him."*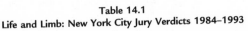

This observation is borne out by the data in Table 14.1.†

Table 14.1
Life and Limb: New York City Jury Verdicts 1984–1993

Injury	Borough	Average Verdict	Total Cases	Highest Verdict	Lowest Verdict	Average Court Verdict
Wrongful death	Manhattan	$1,900,000	84	$25,000,000	$ 2,000	$1,100,000
	Bronx	1,600,000	44	10,000,000	10,000	1,100,000
	Brooklyn	1,200,000	50	10,500,000	5,000	886,000
	Queens	1,400,000	20	7,400,000	25,000	1,400,000
Brain damage	Manhattan	5,200,000	43	67,100,000	40,000	3,300,000
	Bronx	3,600,000	34	24,500,000	41,000	2,800,000
	Brooklyn	6,200,000	25	51,300,000	30,000	3,100,000
	Queens	4,800,000	16	21,700,000	30,000	4,600,000
Herniated disc	Manhattan	652,000	77	3,300,000	4,500	560,000
	Bronx	740,000	45	3,500,000	30,000	596,000
	Brooklyn	549,000	61	6,800,000	5,000	546,000
	Queens	502,000	25	3,500,000	12,200	461,000
Knee injury	Manhattan	374,000	60	3,600,000	8,500	369,000
	Bronx	552,000	39	4,400,000	16,400	455,000
	Brooklyn	539,000	39	7,800,000	9,800	537,000
	Queens	376,000	14	1,500,000	5,000	358,000
Leg injury	Manhattan	664,000	82	4,500,000	10,000	603,000
	Bronx	827,000	37	6,200,000	36,000	615,000
	Brooklyn	776,000	45	6,500,000	5,000	587,000
	Queens	394,000	13	2,000,000	25,000	394,000
Arm injury	Manhattan	148,000	46	630,000	5,000	153,000
	Bronx	546,000	21	5,000,000	10,000	527,000
	Brooklyn	164,000	22	488,000	15,000	164,000
	Queens	145,000	9	450,000	5,500	145,000

Reprinted with permission from the April 4, 1994 edition of the New York Law Journal. © ALM Properties, Inc. All rights reserved. Further duplication without permission is prohibited.

---

* Prosser and Keeton on Torts § 127, at 945. Of course, someone who intentionally kills another is subject to criminal liability.

† Edward A. Adams, *Venue Crucial to Tort Awards: City Verdicts Depend on Counties*, N.Y. L.J., April 4, 1994, at 1, 4 (relying on data from N.Y. Jury Verdict Reporter). There is no authoritative citywide list of verdicts, but the "total represents the vast majority of personal injury awards during the decade." *Id.* at 2. The average award figures exclude cases in which the defendant won (39 percent in Manhattan; 26 percent in the Bronx; 35 percent in Brooklyn; and 45 percent in Queens) or in which the jury or trial court awarded no damages.

Contrary to the size of these damage awards, the most serious knee or leg injury is not twice as injurious as the average case of premature death. A damages award cannot compensate a dead person for the lost pleasures of living, an inherent limitation of the compensatory damages remedy that can produce surprisingly low awards for wrongful death. A case of wrongful death starkly reveals the limited degree to which compensatory damages can protect the individual interest in physical security.

III. THE MEASURE OF COMPENSATION

Tort law protects the individual interest in physical security. To do so, tort law must protect individuals from the most serious threat to their physical security — the risk of premature death. Tort law cannot adequately protect this critical component of the individual right with compensatory damages, so it protects the right by imposing a demanding duty of reasonable care on actors whose conduct foreseeably threatens the right holder's interest in physical security. The prevention of premature death is far more valuable for the right holder than a damages remedy in the event of a fatal accident, explaining why the tort system adopted negligence liability as the default rule for accidental harms.*

In some essential sense, life is infinitely valuable, suggesting that reasonable care could require duty holders to eliminate *all* risks of fatal injuries ($B < PL = $ infinity). If that were the case, no one could drive automobiles and so on, effectively eliminating a great deal of social interaction in contemporary society. Negligence liability, though, does not require the complete elimination of all fatal risks. The appropriate measure of compensation does not place an infinite value on life,

---

* *See* Chapter 5, section II.

leading to the fundamental question of how tort liability should be measured.

An individual tort right to physical security gives the right holder's interest in physical security some type of legal priority over the competing liberty interests of the duty holder. Due to this interpersonal priority of the security interest over the economic interest, life and money are *incommensurable*. The "victim's right not to be harmed" is not "commensurate with money," because the right holder's interest in physical security and the duty holder's interest in money "are not conceptually equated as fungible commodities."[8] The security interest instead has legal priority, making the tort right incommensurate with money and explaining why courts have not prescribed any method for translating pain and suffering into dollars.

This incommensurability, however, does not imply that there is no defensible way to conceptualize how the violation of the tort right can be redressed by a monetary damages award. The tort right held by an individual both creates and corresponds to an individual duty incurred by another. By breaching this duty, the defendant becomes legally responsible for the plaintiff's injuries proximately caused by the rights violation. As the source of liability, the right-duty nexus supplies an appropriate measure of tort compensation.

This compensatory measure is most easily illustrated by product cases, although it also applies, in modified form, to other tort cases. As we have found, the best protection of consumer interests involves product safety decisions formulated in terms of the risk-utility test. The ordinary consumer reasonably prefers to pay for product safety only if the benefit that he or she derives from the risk reduction exceeds the cost or disutility of the safety investment (also internalized by the consumer via the associated price increase). Consumers reasonably expect product safety decisions to be governed by a cost-benefit calculus, because that decisional rule maximizes consumer well-being or welfare. The fair protection of consumer interests — not an assumed fungibility of life and money — explains why product safety decisions are governed by the risk-utility test, the functional equivalent of the Hand formula for reasonable care.*

To focus on pain and suffering, we can decompose a product-caused injury into the constituent parts involving physical harms, emotional harms, and economic harms. So defined, the risk-utility test gives product sellers the duty to make any safety investments satisfying the following condition:

$$B < P \bullet (L_{physical} + L_{emotional} + L_{economic})$$

This duty can be effectively and fairly enforced only if the injury costs for the pain and suffering (the term $L_{emotional}$) are somehow monetized (like the associated terms $L_{physical}$ and $L_{economic}$). Without a monetary amount for the pain and suffering, the court and the product seller cannot determine the safety expenditures required by the duty of care. The liability rule would not provide the best protection of consumer interests as required by the tort right, nor would it give fair notice to the product seller as duty holder.

This attribute of the right-duty nexus can be determined by the reasonable safety preferences of the consumer as right holder. To see why, suppose there is a 1 in 10,000 chance of accident (the term P) that would cause the right holder to suffer the nonmonetary injury in question (the term $L_{emotional}$). The safety decision depends on the consumer's preference for spending money (via a price increase) to eliminate this particular risk. Suppose a well-informed consumer honestly says he or she is willing to pay no more than $10 for some product safety improvement that would eliminate the risk. Because $10 is the most the consumer would pay to eliminate the risk, the consumer must be indifferent between incurring

---

* *See* Chapter 13.

the $10 cost or otherwise facing the risk and incurring the expected injury cost of the pain and suffering:

$$\$10 = P \bullet L_{emotional}$$

$$\$10 = (1/10{,}000) \bullet L_{emotional}$$

$$\$100{,}000 = L_{emotional}$$

To determine the safety decision required by the duty of reasonable care, the consumer would prefer that this particular pain-and-suffering injury be monetized at $100,000. A different injury (or even a different probability of injury) would yield a different number. The monetization of the pain-and-suffering injury does not represent the "value" of the injury or the amount of money the consumer would accept in exchange for suffering the injury with certainty. When framed in those terms, the consumer could be willing to spend everything to avoid the most severe nonmonetary injury—the loss of life's pleasures due to premature death. The value of the injury, however, is not relevant to the safety issue in this particular case. The issue is one of determining the appropriate amount of safety expenditures for eliminating a 1 in 10,000 chance of suffering the nonmonetary injury, and for this purpose, the consumer would reasonably prefer that the pain and suffering be monetized at $100,000.

This method for monetizing a pain-and-suffering injury relies on established economic methodology commonly employed by federal administrative agencies in devising regulations for the protection of human health and safety.* The method also satisfies the relevant tort requirements.

---

* Pursuant to executive order, federal agencies must analyze proposed regulations with a cost-benefit analysis. *See, e.g.,* Exec. Order No. 12,291, 3 C.F.R. 127 (1981), *reprinted in* 5 U.S.C. § 601 (1988); Exec. Order No. 12,866, 3 C.F.R. 638 (1993), *reprinted in* 5 U.S.C. § 601 (1994). To apply cost-benefit analysis to a regulation concerning human health and safety, the impact of the regulation on physical injuries and premature death must be quantified and monetized. For example, the U.S. Environmental Protection Agency treats the

Compensatory tort damages must compensate injuries, but this fundamental requirement does not make the risk of injury irrelevant. <u>Courts do not let jurors determine pain-and-suffering damages by asking themselves how much money they or anyone else would want in exchange for actually experiencing the plaintiff's injury.</u>[9] Courts have rejected this method for determining damages because it invites sympathy or bias by the jurors, although courts have not adequately explained why the method is biased. The source of bias is made evident by the preceding analysis. An individual right holder might not be willing to accept any amount of money in exchange for the certainty of suffering a severely disabling physical injury such as quadriplegia, for example, whereas he or she would be willing to accept a finite amount of money to assume the substantially lower risk actually created by the defendant's conduct. A damages award based on the certainty of injury can vastly exceed an award based on the actual risk of injury faced by the plaintiff, creating a predictable upward bias in jury instructions that frame the damages question in terms of a certain injury. The only way to eliminate the bias is to recognize that the damages provide compensation for an *accidental* harm, thereby requiring the incorporation of contingency or risk into the damages calculation.

In the foregoing example, the award of $100,000 is based on the right holder's reasonable safety preferences with respect to the risk that caused the injury. The duty monetized the pain-and-suffering injury at $100,000, and so a breach of that duty can be redressed by obligating the defendant to pay the plaintiff $100,000 for having violated the right in this manner. The

---

prevention of each premature death as being equivalent to a savings of $6.1 million in 1999 dollars. The EPA derives this measure from the same type of inquiry that would be engaged in by a right holder trying to determine the amount of money he or she would require to assume a risk. *See generally* W. Kip Viscusi & Joseph E. Aldy, *The Value of a Statistical Life: A Critical Review of Market Estimates Throughout the World*, 27 J. Risk & Uncertainty 5, 53–56 (2003).

award compensates the plaintiff for the actual injury and not merely the risk, but does so in the manner required by the tort rule that damages cannot be based on the certainty of injury.

These damages are also fully compensatory in the appropriate respect. According to established doctrine, monetary damages for pain and suffering are not supposed to "restore the person to his previous position," but should instead "give to the injured person some pecuniary return for what he has suffered or is likely to suffer."[10] Any amount of money would provide "some pecuniary return" as literally required by this doctrine. Presumably, tort law is more demanding in this respect. Tort damages are supposed to be fully compensatory. The damages award of $100,000 is fully compensatory from the perspective of the plaintiff at the time of the risk exposure. At that time, the plaintiff would have reasonably monetized the injury at $100,000, and so the measure of full compensation can be defined in those terms as well.

This measure of damages does not apply to all cases. For cases in which the parties are not in a contractual relationship or the risks are not otherwise reciprocal, right holders do not directly incur the burdens of tort liability.* When right holders do not pay for the precautions required by the duty, they will not monetize the associated injuries in terms of their willingness to pay for the precautions. To account for this difference, the measure of compensatory damages must be modified.

Once again, suppose there is a 1 in 10,000 chance of accident (the term P) that would cause the right holder to suffer only the nonmonetary injury in question (the term $L_{emotional}$). Rather than having to pay to eliminate this risk, the right holder must be compensated to assume the risk. Suppose a well-informed right holder honestly says that he or she is willing to accept at least $12 to assume responsibility for the risk. Because $12 is the lowest amount the right holder requires

---

* *See* Chapter 8, section II.B.

to assume the risk, he or she must be indifferent between receiving the $12 or otherwise incurring the expected injury cost of the pain and suffering by assuming the risk:

$$\$12 = P \bullet L_{emotional}$$

$$\$12 = (1/10,000) \bullet L_{emotional}$$

$$\$120,000 = L_{emotional}$$

As before, this measure of the pain-and-suffering injury does not represent the "value" of the injury or the amount of money the right holder would accept in exchange for suffering the injury with certainty. Other interactions involving different magnitudes of risk or different injuries yield different compensatory measures. The damages award has this characteristic because it is based on the underlying risk of injury governed by the tort duty (the term PL), so that changes in the probability of injury (P) or the type of harm (L) will affect the amount of money the right holder requires to assume the risk. For example, in the extreme case of certain death ($P = 1$), the right holder presumably would not accept any finite amount of money, yielding a compensatory measure ($L = $ infinity) expressed by the principle that life is infinitely valuable. The substantive requirements of the tort duty, however, do not depend on the value of the injury. The issue is one of determining the appropriate amount of safety expenditures for eliminating the 1 in 10,000 tortious risk of suffering the nonmonetary injury in question, and for this particular purpose, the right holder would reasonably monetize the injury at $120,000.

This method for determining damages has some important differences with the analogous method for product cases, but the damages award still provides appropriate redress for the rights violation.* As in product cases, this award for pain

---

* When the monetization of the injury depends on the right holder's willingness to pay to reduce risk (as in product cases involving consumers), the right holder, by definition, is not entitled to receive any money prior to the risk

and suffering is defined in terms of the defendant's duty. To violate the plaintiff's tort right, the defendant must have breached the duty in a manner that caused injury to the plaintiff. The fact of breach is not sufficient, nor is the fact of injury. The rights violation necessarily requires consideration of both the breached duty and the resultant injury, justifying a damages remedy based on the manner in which the duty accounts for the injury in question.

As is true with respect to the standard of reasonable care, the most critical issue is whether this element of the tort claim can be defensibly conceptualized. The issue is not whether one can plug objectively determined numbers into an equation that will produce the correct answer in each case. The relevant factors cannot be proven in such a manner. This indeterminacy, however, does not imply that the jury has unfettered discretion. Having identified a defensible way for the jury to quantify the loss (L) for nonmonetary injuries, we then see why the jury can defensibly determine whether the defendant was obligated to eliminate that risk by taking a specific precaution as a matter of reasonable care ($B ® PL$).*

---

exposure. By contrast, when the monetization of the injury depends on the right holder's willingness to accept money in exchange for assuming the risk of injury, then the right holder is entitled to receive the risk proceeds, making his or her ability to receive the money of critical importance. Absent the receipt of money or any other benefit, why assume the risk? In noncontractual settings, the right holder could receive the risk proceeds in the form of a damages payment as per the damages method proposed in text. However, if the injury reduces the right holder's ability to enjoy the money (premature death being the extreme example), tort damages cannot be fully compensatory in this sense. As previously discussed, this compensatory problem can explain why tort law does not ordinarily define the standard of care in cost-benefit terms. By requiring more than the cost-benefit amount of safety, the standard of reasonable care can force the duty holder to spend the same amount of total resources on injury prevention as he or she would otherwise spend on damages compensation, producing a fairer distributive outcome between the parties. *See* Chapter 8, section II.B.

* Although courts have rejected expert testimony relying on this methodology, the cases are distinguishable. The expert testifies about the appropriate award by relying on studies that use this methodology. These studies involve other individuals, other types of risks, and sometimes even other types of injuries. By contrast,

Compensatory damages can be defensibly formulated by reference to the underlying duty of care only if the defendant duty holder adequately respected the plaintiff's right to be protected by reasonable care. This important requirement is satisfied in most cases. Tort liability frequently applies to behavior that was not reprehensible or even blameworthy. Lapses of attention, inadvertence, or a poor decision can cause injury and subject the actor to tort liability. In these cases, the plaintiff is entitled to compensatory damages and nothing more. The reasonable person, after all, is an unrealistic construct who is always attentive and never makes mistakes, unlike the ordinary person. As long as the defendant was engaged in ordinary or conventional safety practices, his or her negligence did not exhibit any fundamental disrespect for the right holder's interest in physical security, making it fair to measure the defendant's liability by reference to the underlying duty of reasonable care.*

This measure of compensation also reveals the inherent limitations of the compensatory damages remedy. The compensatory measure is not the monetary equivalent or value of the tort right — the plaintiff would not ordinarily accept the damages award in exchange for suffering bodily injury. The damages cannot make the plaintiff "whole" in this sense, explaining why negligence liability prohibits duty holders from choosing to be negligent in exchange for paying (inherently inadequate) compensatory damages.

---

the approach discussed in text would have the jury use this methodology, based on instructions from the judge, to derive its own measure of damages for the particular injury in question. *Compare Montalvo v. Lapez*, 884 P.2d 345, 366 (Haw. 1994) ("Testimony of an economist would not aid the jury in making such measurements because an economist is no more expert at valuing the pleasure of life than the average juror."). Indeed, at least one court has endorsed the logic of this damages measure. *See Arpin v. U.S.*, 521 F.3d 769 (7th Cir. 2008) (applying Illinois law) (Posner, J.).

* When the liability is strict, there is no proof showing that the defendant acted unreasonably. *See* Chapter 12. In these cases, the damages award can also be based on the tortious risk of injury faced by the plaintiff.

It would be absurd to exonerate the defendant with a compensatory damages award based on a duty that was flatly rejected by the defendant. A defendant, for example cannot intentionally harm someone in exchange for a payment of compensatory damages, a conclusion that is valid regardless of the compensatory measure. Such prohibited conduct merits punishment, explaining why the ordinary tort rules governing these cases are complemented by criminal liability and the extraordinary tort remedy of punitive damages.

IV. PUNITIVE DAMAGES

The plaintiff can receive punitive damages in a "great majority" of states, typically "only when the tortfeasor has committed quite serious misconduct with a bad intent or bad state of mind such as malice." Due to the reprehensible nature of the defendant's tortious misconduct, compensatory damages no longer adequately redress the violation of the plaintiff's tort right. Punishment, however, "does not adequately describe the bases for such damages, [and so] they are sometimes called extracompensatory damages."[11]

As the U.S. Supreme Court has recognized, punitive damages "serve the same purposes as criminal penalties." Both "are aimed at deterrence and retribution."[12] When punitive damages are justified solely by deterrence considerations, the award does not involve any retribution and is entirely extracompensatory.

To identify the deterrence rationale for punitive damages, consider the incentives faced by product sellers under the risk-utility test for a design or warning defect ($B < PL$). Suppose the seller expects that only one out of ten consumers with meritorious claims will actually sue and recover, perhaps because they are unable to identify the defect (like an unreasonable risk of cancer) as the cause of their injuries. To maximize profits, the seller would make the safety decision by comparing the cost of the precaution (B) with its expected liability costs ($PL \bullet 1/10$). The cost of the safety precaution could exceed the seller's expected liability costs ($B > PL \bullet 1/10$), giving the seller an incentive to sell the defective product. This deterrence problem can be addressed by punitive damages. If each plaintiff who recovers compensatory damages were to receive a total damages award ten times greater than the actual loss, the seller's expected liability costs would equal the expected injury costs ($10 \bullet PL \bullet 1/10 = PL$). When punitive damages are formulated in this manner, the seller has a sufficient financial incentive to comply with the risk-utility test ($B < 10 \bullet PL \bullet 1/10 = PL$).

Even if the duty holder fully expects to pay compensatory damages for every tortiously caused injury, <u>punitive damages can still be warranted as a matter of punishment or retribution</u>. The prior discussion unrealistically assumed that the defendant's liability or damages (D) equaled the social value of the loss (L). For a fatal risk, the duty holder is not obligated to pay any compensatory damages for the decedent's loss of life's pleasures ($D = 0$). A self-interested duty holder will predictably ignore these risks in deciding how safely to behave, reducing the incentive for taking costly precautions that would reduce the risk of a fatal accident ($B > P \bullet D = 0$). Consequently, the individual right to physical security cannot be adequately protected by compensatory damages alone. To protect the right, tort law has adopted a demanding duty of reasonable care that seeks to prevent these injuries. A defendant who flatly rejects that duty also rejects the essential protection afforded by the tort right — the requisite "bad state of mind" that merits punishment. A defendant who decides to act negligently in exchange for paying the inherently inadequate price of compensatory damages is subject to punitive damages.[13]

The retributive rationale for punitive damages has important constitutional implications. The U.S. Supreme Court has held that the Due Process Clause of the U.S. Constitution imposes procedural and substantive limitation on tort awards of punitive damages. According to the Court, the constitutionality of a punitive award depends on (1) the reprehensibility of the defendant's conduct; (2) whether the ratio between the punitive award and the amount of actual or potential harm exceeds a single digit; and (3) the disparity between the punitive award and any criminal or civil penalties for the misconduct.[14] The Court has identified the reprehensibility factor as "'[t]he most important indicium of the reasonableness of a punitive damages award.'"[15] All else being equal, greater reprehensibility merits more punishment and justifies a greater quantum of punitive damages. The constitutionality of virtually any punitive damages award depends on whether the size of the award is an excessive retributive sanction for the defendant's reprehensible misconduct.

To punish the defendant and vindicate the plaintiff's tort right, the punitive award must first disgorge any wrongful gains the defendant expected to derive by violating the right. The mere elimination of the expected wrongful gains is not enough, however, because the award would not punish the defendant for having adopted this wrongful perspective in the first instance. The punitive award must be increased further to reject altogether the wrongful perspective, thereby vindicating the right in its entirety.[16]

Consider our earlier example of a defendant manufacturer that expects to incur liability for only one out of every ten rights violations. For every tortiously caused harm (L), the defendant expects to pay damages (D) in only one out of ten cases. For the tortious risk faced by each one of these individuals, the defendant ignored the perspective required by the tort right (PL) and instead only considered its expected liability costs ($PD \bullet 1/10$). To eliminate this aspect of the expected wrongful gain, vindication of an individual tort right minimally requires the defendant to incur total damages that would equate its wrongful perspective with the perspective required by the tort right:

$$\text{Solve for } D, \text{ where } (P \bullet D) \bullet (1/10) = (P \bullet L).$$

The solution is a total damages award (D) that is ten times greater than the measure of full compensation (L). The award vindicates the individual tort right, but the amount is also equivalent to ten fully compensatory awards to ten different victims. Vindication of the individual tort right can readily account for harms to nonparties as required by the social objective of deterrence.

Vindicating the individual tort right only requires the court to consider the defendant manufacturer's misconduct toward the plaintiff, thereby satisfying the important constitutional requirement that the punitive award cannot be based on harms suffered by nonparties to the litigation.[*] That same misconduct, though, can also apply to a much larger group of similarly situated right holders (consumers). An award that vindicates the individual right will necessarily account for the duty holder's misconduct toward similarly situated right holders, increasing the award by a factor of ten in our prior example. A punitive award that vindicates the individual tort right in mass markets can involve staggering sums of money.[†]

---

[*] In a recent case, the U.S. Supreme Court held that "the Constitution's Due Process Clause forbids a State to use a punitive damages award to punish a defendant for injury that it inflicts upon nonparties or those whom they directly represent, *i.e.*, injury that inflicts on those who are, essentially, strangers to the litigation." *Phillip Morris USA v. Williams*, 127 S. Ct. 1057, 1063 (2007). For discussion of how this requirement and the others identified by the Court are satisfied by the damage award described in the text, *see* Mark A. Geistfeld, *Punitive Damages, Retribution and Due Process*, 81 S. Cal. L. Rev. 263 (2008).

[†] *E.g.*, Andrew Pollack, *$4.9 Billion Jury Verdict in GM Fuel Tank Case*, N.Y. Times A8 (July 10, 1999). As should be evident by now, jury verdicts are often substantially reduced by judicial review. *See, e.g.*, *Bullock v. Philip Morris USA, Inc.*, 138 Cal. App. 4th 1029, 174–180 (2006) (affirming remittitur that reduced punitive damages award of $28 billion to $28 million).

More than any other form of tort liability, punitive damages reflect the interdependence of individual right holders in contemporary society. When the common law first developed within the writ system, the cases involved one individual wronging another. Tort cases now frequently involve widespread wrongs and mass torts, as when a particular form of corporate misconduct harms large numbers of consumers. Tort liability continues to redress the violation of the plaintiff's own tort right, but the interdependent nature of rights violations has considerably increased punitive damage awards.

Once we recognize that individual rights violations have become increasingly interdependent, we can also see why legislatures and the U.S. Supreme Court have become increasingly concerned about tort law. Due to the interdependence of rights violations, the way in which a single court redresses an individual rights violation can have widespread implications. A jury verdict finding that a widely used prescription drug has a defective warning, for example, can spur a large number of similarly situated consumers to file suit. Aware of this dynamic, corporate actors have made safety decisions on the basis of a single jury verdict. Reaching the right result in a particular case can be a national concern. Overly vague tort rules are now more worrisome than ever, motivating tort reforms like those that limit damages for pain and suffering and place controls on the jury awards of punitive damages.

These social forces will pressure the tort system to identify more clearly the rationales for tort liability. These rationales are identified by the *Restatement (Second)* for the first time in the chapter of rules governing damages:

§ 901. General Principle
The rules for determining the measure of damages in tort are based upon the purposes for which actions of tort are maintainable. These purposes are:

(a) to give compensation, indemnity or restitution for harms;

(b) to determine rights;

(c) to punish wrongdoers and deter wrongful conduct; and

(d) to vindicate parties and deter retaliation or violent and unlawful self-help.

On one view, the multiple purposes of tort liability are not attributable to an underlying principle. Tort law does different things in different circumstances for different reasons, the type of uncertain, ad hoc approach that begs for reform. In response to these problems, tort scholars have developed sophisticated rationales for liability, with the proponents of economic efficiency contesting those who maintain the tort law is best explained by a rights-based principle of fairness. As commonly formulated, each of these rationales ignores one or more of the widely recognized purposes of tort liability. Efficiency excludes a compensatory rationale for liability, and fairness excludes a deterrence rationale for liability. On the view articulated here, these multiple purposes coherently further a collective commitment to the individual rights of life, liberty, and the pursuit of happiness. As sweeping as that commitment might sound at the outset of a revolutionary war, when rigorously applied to discrete problems, it can produce a sufficiently well-defined legal inquiry that gives requisite content to the essential doctrines of tort law.

~ 15 ~

Beyond Tort Law

I ndividuals face threats from a variety of sources outside the reach of tort law. Obvious examples include natural disasters and war. A more insidious problem involves low-level risks. A widespread polluter, for example, can cause thousands to suffer cancer and yet avoid tort liability altogether. If the pollution only slightly increases the background risk of cancer, no victim could prove that his or her cancer, more likely than not, was caused by the pollution. The background risk would instead be the likely cause. To recover in tort, the plaintiff must prove that the defendant caused the injury, a form of responsibility that necessarily limits the extent to which tort law can protect individuals from harm.

Similarly, any compensation provided by tort law is inherently limited. Individuals face numerous losses not caused by the conduct of another. Individuals regularly incur medical expenses or suffer property loss caused by natural forces. To cover these contingencies, individuals must be protected by other types of insurance, including disability insurance, health insurance, and property insurance. At best, the compensation promised by the tort system can only supplement these more comprehensive forms of insurance.

Due to these inherent limitations of tort liability, any government concerned about protecting individuals from harm will use tort law in combination with other institutions. The first such institution was the criminal justice system. With the advent of the modern administrative state, the government has employed an array of other regulatory institutions. Polluters, for example, are subject to a variety of statutory and regulatory requirements enforced by the U.S. Environmental Protection Agency. A different federal agency regulates workplace safety, another one regulates prescription drugs and medical devices, and other federal agencies regulate other matters of public health and safety. The states also have regulatory agencies. All of these institutions regulate conduct posing a threat of public harm, making it possible for health and safety regulations to address the low-level risks beyond the reach of tort law. The extent to which the government protects individuals from harmful behavior now largely depends on the combined effect of administrative regulation, criminal law, and tort law.

Similarly, the compensatory significance of tort law depends on the extent to which the government otherwise provides insurance for injured citizens. Insofar as a disabled or injured individual receives government-funded insurance for health care and lost wages, the compensatory role for tort law is reduced.

One can imagine, then, a society in which tort law is largely unnecessary. All risks could be regulated administratively and all compensable harms could be covered by insurance. These institutions would adequately protect the individual interest in physical security, eliminating this role for tort law.

The unrealism of this scenario does not detract from the significance of its implications. Unlike the United States, countries in the European Union have less tort liability supplemented by more extensive administrative regulation and government-provided insurance. The reduced role of tort liability in these liberal democracies hardly makes them less fair or just than the United States, just like the increased role of tort liability in the United States hardly implies that Americans are litigation crazy. Tort law is one institution of many that protect individuals from physical harm, making the functional importance of tort law contingent on the full range of complementary institutions.

The contingency of tort law does not reduce its importance. Behavior that is wrongful as a matter of tort law can also be wrongful in other contexts, making tort doctrine useful for related legal fields. The federal securities laws, for example, rely on tort concepts of fraud and causation.[1] The protection of individual rights is also of primary concern for other important bodies of law, including civil rights and human rights more generally. Tort law is one of the oldest legal institutions for protecting individual rights, deeply influencing how we think about protecting rights in other contexts.[*]

Is the individual right to physical security best protected by cost-benefit analysis of safety decisions? Does the right require greater protection? These issues, which have long occupied the tort system, are now critically important for determining how governments should approach the problem of global warming, illustrating how tort principles can guide momentous decisions outside of the tort system.[†] Tort law originated in a world far different from our own, but the government still needs to adequately protect each individual from harm, giving tort principles significance that extends far beyond the tort system.

---

[*] The major legal systems throughout history have recognized tort law, making widely adopted tort rules a source of international law governing human rights. The International Court of Justice, for example, is supposed to apply "the general principles of law recognized by civilized nations." Stat. of the Int'l Ct. of Just., art. 38, § 1(c).

[†] Those who want governments to adopt decisive actions for immediately reducing the threat of global warming often invoke the precautionary principle, which maintains that "[w]here there are threats of serious or irreversible damage, lack of scientific certainty shall not be used as a reason for postponing cost-effective measures to prevent environmental degradation." Rio Declaration on Environment and Development, United Nations Conference on Environment and Development, U.N. Doc. A/CONF.151/5 (1992) *reprinted in* 31 I.L.M. 874, 879 (1992). The appropriate interpretation of the precautionary principle has long been in dispute, with critics claiming that the principle cannot be justified or implemented in a defensible manner. When interpreted as a solution to the type of problem addressed by tort law involving the fair protection of the individual interest in physical security, the precautionary principle translates into a well-defined decision rule. *See* Mark Geistfeld, *Implementing the Precautionary Principle*, 31 Envt'l L. Rep. 11326 (2001).

Endnotes

CHAPTER 1

1. James Q. Whitman, *At the Origins of Law and the State: Supervision of Violence, Mutilation of Bodies, or Setting of Prices?*, 71 Chi.-Kent L. Rev. 41, 42 (1995) (both describing and criticizing conventional view).

2. *Id.* at 65 (quoting Rudolf von Jhering, *Geist des Romischen Rechts auf den verschiedenen Stufen seiner Entwicklung* 118–120 (9th ed. n.d.)).

3. James Lindgren, *Why the Ancients May Not Have Needed a System of Criminal Law*, 76 B.U. L. Rev. 29, 31 (1996).

4. David J. Seipp, *The Distinction Between Crime and Tort in the Early Common Law*, 76 B.U. L. Rev. 59, 59–60 (1996).

5. Frederick Pollack & Frederick Maitland, *The History of English Law*, vol. II 530 (2d ed., Cambridge U. Press 1968).

6. Prosser and Keeton on Torts § 2, at 8.

7. John G. Bellamy, *Crime and Public Order in England in the Later Middle Ages* 3, 1 (U. Toronto Press 1973).

8. David Ibbetson, *A Historical Introduction to the Law of Obligations* 40 (Oxford U. Press 1999).

9. *Id.* at 41.

10. *Id.* at 15.

11. *Id.* at 42.

12. *Id.* at 14.

13. *Id.* at 17.

14. *See, e.g., Scott v. Shepherd*, 96 Eng. Rep. 525 (K.B. 1773).

15. Peter Karsten, *Enabling the Poor to Have Their Day in Court: The Sanctioning of Contingency Fee Contracts, A History to 1940*, 47 DePaul L. Rev. 231, 240 (1998).

16. *Id.* at 231.

17. Randolph E. Bergstrom, *Courting Danger: Injury and Law in New York City, 1870–1910* (Cornell U. Press 1992); Robert A. Silverman, *Law and Urban Growth: Civil Litigation in the Boston Trial Courts, 1880–1900* (1981).

18. G. Edward White, *Tort Law in America: An Intellectual History* 3 (Oxford U. Press 1980) (citations omitted).

19. Ibbetson, *supra* note 8, at 11.

20. *E.g., Black's Law Dictionary* 1335 (5th ed. 1979) (defining "Tort" as "A private or civil wrong or injury, other than breach of contract, for which the court will provide a remedy in the form of an action for damages").

21. White, *supra* note 18, at 14.

22. *Id.*

23. Francis H. Bohlen, *The Rule in* Rylands v. Fletcher, 59 U. Pa. L. Rev. 298, 315 (1911).

24. Thomas C. Grey, *Accidental Torts*, 54 Vand. L. Rev. 1267 (2001).

25. Oliver Wendell Holmes, *The Theory of Torts*, 7 Am. L. Rev. 652, 653 (1873).

26. Oliver Wendell Holmes, *The Common Law* 79 (Little, Brown and Co. 1881).

27. *See* John Fabian Witt, *Toward a New History of American Accident Law: Classical Tort Law and the Cooperative First-Party Insurance Movement*, 114 Harv. L. Rev. 690, 718 (2001) (citing the "best study of deaths from accidental injury," which found that the total number of accidental fatalities was roughly equivalent to the total number of fatal accidents today, despite a threefold increase in population).

28. John Stuart Mill, *On Liberty* 22 (E.P. Dutton 1859).

29. *Vaughan v. Menlove*, 132 Eng. Rep. 490 (C.P. 1837).

30. Holmes, *supra* note 26, at 108.

31. *Id.* at 161–162.

32. *Id.* at 38, 35.

33. *Norway Plains Co. v. Boston & Main R.R. Co.*, 67 Mass. 263, 267 (1854).

34. Stephen Skowronek, *Building a New American State: The Expansion of National Administrative Capacities 1877–1920*, 28, 27 (Cambridge U. Press 1982).

35. Stephen M. Feldman, *From Premodern to Modern American Jurisprudence: The Onset of Positivism*, 50 Vand. L. Rev. 1387, 1406 (1997).

36. *E.g., Brown v. Kendall*, 60 Mass. 292 (1850) ("We think, as the result of all the authorities, the [correct] rule is . . . that the plaintiff must come prepared with evidence to show either that the *intention* was unlawful, or that the defendant was *in fault*; for if the injury was unavoidable, and the conduct of the defendant was free from blame, he will not be liable.").

37. Lawrence M. Friedman, *A History of American Law* 300 (Simon & Schuster 2d ed. 1985).

38. Morton J. Horwitz, *The Transformation of American Law, 1780–1860*, 100 (Harvard U. Press 1977); *see also* Friedman, *supra* note 37, at 469 (concluding that the common-law judges reduced tort liability by adopting negligence "to limit damages to some moderate measure" so that capital could "be spared for its necessary work").

39. Gary T. Schwartz, *Tort Law and the Economy in Nineteenth-Century America: A Reinterpretation*, 90 Yale L.J. 1717, 1718–1720 (1981); *see also* Gary T. Schwartz, *The Character of Early American Tort Law*, 36 UCLA L. Rev. 641 (1989).

40. James W. Ely, Jr., *Railroads and American Law* 212 (U. Press of Kansas 2001).

41. Robert J. Kaczorowski, *The Common-Law Background of Nineteenth Century Tort Law*, 51 Ohio St. L.J. 1127, 1145 (1990).

42. *Cole v. Goodwin & Storey*, 19 Wend. 251, 272–273 (N.Y. Sup. Ct. 1838). All of the quoted language was drawn from English opinions: *Lane v. Cotton*, 88 Eng. Rep. 1458, 1462–1463 (K.B. 1721); *Riley v. Horne*, 130 Eng. Rep. 1044, 1045 (C.P. 1828). For an extended, well-documented discussion of the policy rationales for strict liability, see generally Kaczorowski, *supra* note 41.

43. White, *supra* note 18, at 38.

44. *Fletcher v. Rylands*, 159 Eng. Rep. 737 (Ex. 1865), *rev'd*, 1 L.R.-Ex. 265 (Ex. Ch. 1866), *aff'd*, 3 L.R.-E. & I. App. 330 (H.L. 1868). The rule of strict liability for abnormally dangerous activities is the subject of Chapter 12.

45. *Losee v. Buchanan*, 51 N.Y. 476 (1873); *Brown v. Collins*, 53 N.H. 442 (1873); *Marshall v. Welwood*, 38 N.J.L. 339 (1876); *Pennsylvania Coal Co. v. Sanderson*, 6 A. 453 (Pa. 1886).

46. Jeremiah Smith, *Tort and Absolute Liability: Suggested Changes in Classification*, 30 Harv. L. Rev. 409 (1917).

47. Holmes, *supra* note 26, at 1.

48. *See* Robert L. Rabin, *The Historical Development of the Fault Principle: A Reinterpretation*, 15 Ga. L. Rev. 925, 959–961 (1981); Gary T. Schwartz, *The Beginning and the Possible End of the Rise of Modern American Tort Law*, 26 Ga. L. Rev. 601, 605–606 (1992) (concluding that judicial tort opinions until the 1960s, "for the most part, sharpened and clarified tort doctrines that had been presented somewhat more crudely in nineteenth-century cases," and that the "vitality of negligence" then caused an expansion of tort liability lasting until the 1980s); Stephen D. Sugarman, *A Century of Change in Personal Injury Law*, 88 Cal. L. Rev. 2403, 2407 (2000) ("The central change in personal injury law doctrine that has taken place since 1900 is the evolution of a robust law of negligence. . . . The fault principle itself is increasingly defended on deterrence and risk-spreading grounds, rather than simply on the basis of fairness as between the plaintiff and the defendant.").

49. Crystal Eastman, *Work-Accidents and the Law* 86 (Charities Publication Committee 1910).

50. Charles O. Gregory, *Trespass to Negligence to Absolute Liability*, 37 Va. L. Rev. 359, 382–383 (1951).

51. White, *supra* note 18, at 72.

52. Jed Handelsman Shugerman, Note, *The Floodgates of Strict Liability: Bursting Reservoirs and the Adoption of* Fletcher v. Rylands *in the Gilded Age*, 110 Yale L.J. 333, 334 (2000).

53. *See* Stephen C. Yeazell, *Re-Financing Civil Litigation*, 51 DePaul L. Rev. 183, 186–190 (2001) (also describing how the increase in home ownership substantially increased the purchase of liability insurance contained in most property insurance policies — a requirement for credit).

54. *See* Kenneth S. Abraham, *The Rise and Fall of Commercial Liability Insurance*, 87 Va. L. Rev. 85, 86–90 (2001) (describing the growth until the 1980s of liability insurance covering business activity).

55. *See* Yeazell, *supra* note 53, at 198–205 (describing changes in nature of plaintiffs' bar and the ensuing consequences for tort litigation).

56. *See generally* George L. Priest, *The Invention of Enterprise Liability: A Critical History of the Intellectual Foundations of Modern Tort Law*, 14 J. Legal Stud. 461 (1985).

57. *See* Robert L. Rabin, *Some Thoughts on the Ideology of Enterprise Liability*, 55 Md. L. Rev. 1190 (1996).

58. 152 Eng. Rep. 402 (Ex. 1842).

59. Vernon Palmer, *Why Privity Entered Tort — An Historical Reexamination of* Winterbottom v. Wright, 27 Am. J. Legal Hist. 85, 94 (1983).

60. *Thomas v. Winchester*, 6 N.Y. 397, 409 (1852).

61. *Cadillac v. Johnson*, 221 F. 801, 803 (2d Cir. 1915).

62. 111 N.E. 1050 (N.Y. 1916).

63. William L. Prosser, *The Assault Upon the Citadel (Strict Liability to the Consumer)*, 69 Yale L.J. 1099, 1100–1102 (1960).

64. 152 Eng. Rep. 402 (Ex. 1842).

65. 150 P.2d 436, 441 (Cal. 1944). The facts of *Escola* supported Traynor's claim. *See* Mark A. Geistfeld, Escola v. Coca Cola Bottling Co.: *Strict Products Liability Unbound*, in *Torts Stories* 229, 233–235 (Robert L. Rabin & Stephen D. Sugarman eds., Foundation Press 2003).

66. *See supra* notes 41–42 and accompanying text.

67. For a more detailed and illuminating exposition of this range of issues, see John Fabian Witt, *The Accidental Republic: Crippled Workingmen, Destitute Widows, and the Remaking of American Law* (Harvard U. Press 2004).

68. *Greenman v. Yuba Power Products*, 377 P.2d 897 (Cal. 1963).

69. White, *supra* note 18, at 80.

70. Patrick M. Hanlon & Anne Smetak, *Asbestos Changes*, 62 N.Y.U. Ann. Surv. Am. L. 525, 526–527 (2007) (citing Stephen J. Carroll et al., *Asbestos Litigation* (RAND Inst. for Civil Justice 2005)).

71. *See* George L. Priest, *Strict Products Liability: The Original Intent*, 10 Cardozo L. Rev. 2301 (1989).

72. *Restatement (Third): Products Liability* § 2.

73. Report of the Tort Policy Working Group on the Causes, Extent and Policy Implications of the Current Crisis in Insurance Availability and Affordability, Feb. 1986 (U.S. Govt. Printing Office, 1986-491-510:40090).

74. George L. Priest, *Modern Tort Law and Its Reform*, 22 Val. U. L. Rev. 1 (1987).

75. Schwartz, *supra* note 48, at 691.

76. Address Before a Joint Session of the Congress on the State of the Union, 1990 Pub. Papers 129, 132 (Jan. 31, 1990); Dan Quayle, *Now Is the Time for Product Liability Reform*, 18 Prod. Safety & Liab. Rep. (BNA) 306, 306 (1990).

77. For a summary of these reforms, *see* Joseph Sanders & Craig Joyce, *"Off to the Races": The 1980s Tort Crisis and the Law Reform Process*, 27 Hous. L. Rev. 207, 218–223 (1990).

78. *See* James A. Henderson, Jr. & Theodore Eisenberg, *The Quiet Revolution in Products Liability: An Empirical Study of Legal Change*, 37 UCLA L. Rev. 479 (1990); Theodore Eisenberg & James A. Henderson, Jr., *Inside the Quiet Revolution in Products Liability*, 39 UCLA L. Rev. 731 (1992); Schwartz, *supra* note 48 (discussing trends for tort law more generally).

79. Michael Orey, *How Business Trounced the Trial Lawyers*, Bus. Week 445–446 (Jan. 8, 2007).

80. *See supra* notes 15–17 and accompanying text (describing contingency-fee arrangements).

81. Stephen Daniels & Joanne Martin, *Texas Plaintiffs' Practice in the Age of Tort Reform: Survival of the Fittest—It's Even More True Now*, 51 N.Y.L. Sch. L. Rev. 285, 316–317 (2006–2007). The data in the following table are reprinted with the permission of the authors.

82. *See* Ronald J. Allen & Alexia Brunet, *The Judicial Treatment of Non-Economic Compensatory Damages in the Nineteenth Century*, 4 J. Empirical Legal Stud. 365 (2007) (study finding that "no case prior to 1900 permitted a noneconomic compensatory damages award exceeding $450,000 in current dollars," in stark contrast to many contemporary awards for such injuries totaling millions of dollars).

83. Andrew Pollack, *$4.9 Billion Jury Verdict in GM Fuel Tank Case*, N.Y. Times A8 (July 10, 1999). Verdicts like this are routinely reduced by trial judges or judges on appeal.

84. *See* Richard L. Abel, *The Real Tort Crisis—Too Few Claims*, 48 Ohio St. L.J. 443 (1987); Anita Bernstein, *The Enterprise of Liability*, 39 Val. U. L. Rev. 27, 41–43 (2004).

85. Mark A. Geistfeld, *Malpractice Insurance and the (Il)legitimate Interests of the Medical Profession in Tort Reform*, 54 DePaul L. Rev. 439, 441–444 (2005) (providing empirical support for the claim).

86. Marc Galanter, *Real World Torts: An Antidote to Anecdote*, 55 Md. L. Rev. 1093, 1116 (1994) (summarizing various empirical studies).

87. Congressional Budget Office, *The Economics of U.S. Tort Liability: A Primer* 23 (Oct. 2003) ("In short, the current state of data and economic analysis do not allow CBO to judge whether the costs of the tort system are efficient or excessive on the whole.").

88. For reviews of this literature, *see* Geistfeld, *supra* note 85, at 458 & n.55.

89. *See BMW of N. Am. v. Gore*, 517 U.S. 559 (1996).

90. *See* Mark A. Geistfeld, *Constitutional Tort Reform*, 38 Loyola L.A. Law Rev. 1093 (2005).

91. Holmes, *supra* note 26, at 127. *See also* Ibbetson, *supra* note 8, at 295 (stating that "a principal motor for legal change" in the English common law of torts "has been the need to articulate formerly ambiguous rules").

CHAPTER 2

1. *See* Tom Baker, *Blood Money, New Money and the Moral Economy of Tort Law in Action*, 35 Law & Soc'y Rev. 275 (2001); *see also* Stephen Gilles, *The Judgment Proof Society*, 63 Wash. & Lee L. Rev. 603 (2006), identifying the variety of legal obstacles faced by plaintiffs trying to recover tort judgments from the personal assets of individual defendants; Kathryn Zeiler et al., *Physicians' Insurance Limits and Malpractice Payments: Evidence from Texas Closed Claims, 1990–2003*, J. Legal Stud. (2007), presenting results of an empirical study finding that the payments received by plaintiffs in cases of medical malpractice are highly correlated to the policy limits of the defendant physicians' malpractice policies.

2. Ernest Weinrib, *The Idea of Private Law* 5 (Harvard U. Press 1995).

3. *See* John C. P. Goldberg, *Twentieth-Century Tort Theory*, 91 Geo. L.J. 513, 534–535 (2003), arguing that the functions of compensation and deterrence

only limit liability by "second-order considerations such as administrability" and do not persuasively justify negligence as the default liability rule; George L. Priest, *The Invention of Enterprise Liability: A Critical History of the Intellectual Foundations of Modern Tort Law*, 14 J. Legal Stud. 461 (1985), arguing that the objectives of compensation and deterrence logically lead to "absolute liability" for injuries caused by business enterprise.

4. *See generally* Geoffrey W. R. Palmer, *Compensation for Incapacity: A Study of Law and Social Change in New Zealand and Australia* (Oxford U. Press 1979), comprehensively describing the New Zealand plan and the failed effort to implement the plan in Australia.

5. *E.g.*, Charles O. Gregory, *Trespass to Negligence to Absolute Liability*, 37 Va. L. Rev. 359 (1951), claiming that many tort professors have "concluded that there is no such thing as the 'law of torts' but only a mass of contradictions not teachable as a body of knowledge."

6. Gerald J. Postema, *Philosophy of the Common Law*, in *Oxford Handbook of Jurisprudence and Philosophy of the Law* 588, 594 (Jules Coleman & Scott Shapiro eds., Oxford U. Press 2002).

7. *Id.* at 604.

8. Cass R. Sunstein, *On Analogical Reasoning*, 106 Harv. L. Rev. 741, 745 (1993).

9. Neal MacCormick, *Legal Reasoning and Legal Theory* 186 (Clarendon Press 1978).

CHAPTER 3

1. George P. Fletcher, *The Fault of Not Knowing*, 3 Theoretical Inquiries in Law 2 (2002), *http://www.bepress.com/til.*

2. *Compare* David R. Rosenberg, *The Hidden Holmes: His Theory of Torts in History* (Harvard U. Press 1995), depicting the importance of strict liability in the Holmesian conception of tort law; *see also* Jules L. Coleman, *Theories of Tort Law*, in *Stanford Encyclopedia of Philosophy* 4 (2003): "The central idea in tort law is that liability is based not so much on acting badly or *wrongfully*, but on committing a *wrong* [by violating the tort right of another]." Available at *http://plato.stanford.edu.*

3. *Restatement (Second)* § 283 cmt. e.

4. *United States v. Carroll Towing Co.*, 159 F.2d 169, 173 (2d Cir. 1947).

5. *See* Steven Shavell, *Strict Liability Versus Negligence*, 9 J. Legal Stud. 1 (1980), showing how strict liability can reduce risk by reducing "activity" levels, where "activity" is any aspect of risky behavior that is outside the ambit of negligence liability due to problems of proving legal fault.

6. Oliver Wendell Holmes, *The Common Law* 117 (Little, Brown and Co. 1881).

7. *Losee v. Buchanan*, 51 N.Y. 476, 485 (1873).

8. *Restatement (Third): Liability for Physical Harm* § 20 cmt. j.

9. *Fletcher v. Rylands*, 159 Eng. Rep. 737 (Ex. 1865), *rev'd*, 1 L.R.-Ex. 265 (Ex. Ch. 1866), *aff'd*, 3 L.R.-E. & I. App. 330 (H.L. 1868). The rule of strict liability for abnormally dangerous activities is discussed in Chapter 12.

CHAPTER 4

1. William E. Nelson, *From Fairness to Efficiency: The Transformation of Tort Law in New York, 1920–1980*, 47 Buff. L. Rev. 117, 117 (1999) (claiming that "no topic has captured the attention of private law theorists in America more than the law of tort").

2. Guido Calabresi, *The Costs of Accidents* (Yale U. Press 1970); Richard A. Posner, *The Economic Analysis of Law* (Little, Brown and Co. 1972); Richard A. Posner, *A Theory of Negligence*, 1 J. Legal Stud. 29 (1972). For systematic expositions of this approach, *see* William M. Landes & Richard A. Posner, *The Economic Structure of Tort Law* (Harvard U. Press 1987); Steven Shavell, *Economic Analysis of Accident Law* (Harvard U. Press 1987).

3. *See* Louis Kaplow & Steven Shavell, *Should Legal Rules Favor the Poor? Clarifying the Role of Legal Rules and the Income Tax in Redistributing Income*, 29 J. Legal Stud. 821 (2000) (arguing that the tax system is presumptively superior to allocatively inefficient legal rules for redistributing income from rich to poor). *But see* Kyle Logue & Ronen Avraham, *Redistributing Optimally: Of Tax Rules, Legal Rules, and Insurance*, 56 Tax L. Rev. 157 (2003) (providing examples of redistributions that are best attained by legal rules and not tax transfers).

4. *See* Mark Geistfeld, *Should Enterprise Liability Replace the Rule of Strict Liability for Abnormally Dangerous Activities?*, 45 UCLA L. Rev. 611, 625–633, 639–646 (1998).

5. *See* Lewis A. Kornhauser, *Wealth Maximization*, in *The New Palgrave Dictionary of Economics and the Law* vol. 3, 679 (Peter Newman ed., Stockton Press 1998).

6. *Cf.* Madeline Morris, *The Structure of Entitlements*, 78 Cornell L. Rev. 822 (1993) (discussing the various ways in which initial entitlements can be structured to produce different types of legal rules).

7. *See* Ronald M. Dworkin, *Is Wealth a Value?*, 9 J. Legal Stud. 191 (1980). For a notable effort by economists to justify cost-minimizing tort rules with normative argument, see Louis Kaplow & Steven Shavell, *Fairness Versus Welfare* (Harvard U. Press 2002).

8. For two highly influential theories of this type, *see* Richard A. Epstein, *A Theory of Strict Liability*, 2 J. Legal Stud. 151 (1973); George P. Fletcher, *Fairness and Utility in Tort Theory*, 85 Harv. L. Rev. 537 (1972).

9. Jules L. Coleman, *The Practice of Principle: In Defence of a Pragmatist Approach to Legal Theory* 15 (Oxford U. Press 2001).

10. Ernest Weinrib, *The Idea of Private Law* 132 (Harvard U. Press 1995).

11. *See* Ronald Dworkin, *Taking Rights Seriously* 194 (Harvard U. Press 1977) (explaining why the "'rights' of the majority as such" "cannot count as a justification for overruling individual rights").

12. *E.g.*, Arthur Ripstein, *Equality, Responsibility, and the Law* 11–12 (Cambridge U. Press 1999) (describing deterrence as being "derivative" or of "secondary concern" to rights-based liability); Ernest J. Weinrib, *Deterrence and Corrective Justice*, 50 UCLA L. Rev. 621, 638 (2002) ("For corrective justice, deterrence plays no role in defining the nature of the wrong.").

13. *See* Fletcher, *supra* note 8; Gregory C. Keating, *A Social Contract Conception of the Tort Law of Accidents*, in *Philosophy and the Law of Torts* 22 (Gerald J. Postema ed., Cambridge U. Press 2001); Stephen R. Perry, *Responsibility for*

Outcomes, Risk, and the Law of Torts, in *Philosophy and the Law of Torts, supra*, at 72–130.

14. *See, e.g., Palsgraf v. Long Island Railroad Co.*, 162 N.E. 99, 100 (N.Y. 1928) (holding that a plaintiff can recover only by showing that the defendant's breach of duty constitutes "'a wrong' to herself; i.e., a violation of her own right, and not merely a wrong to someone else, nor conduct 'wrongful' because unsocial"). For discussion of this highly influential case, *see* Chapter 8, section I.B.

CHAPTER 5

1. *Losee v. Buchanan*, 51 N.Y. 476, 485 (1873).

2. Thomas C. Grey, *Accidental Torts*, 54 Vand. L. Rev. 1225, 1257 (2001).

3. *Restatement (Second)* § 1 cmt. d (defining "interest" as the "object of any human desire" and explaining the relevance of these interests for tort law).

4. *Id.*, cmt. b.

5. Prosser and Keeton on Torts § 3, at 16.

6. Oliver Wendell Holmes, *The Common Law* 84 (Little, Brown, and Co. 1881).

7. *See generally* Richard W. Wright, *Justice and Reasonable Care in Negligence Law*, 47 Amer. J. Juris. 143 (2002) (describing the positions of leading legal philosophers on the issue).

8. *Lossee*, 51 N.Y. at 485.

9. *Restatement (Second)* § 901.

10. *See, e.g., Commonwealth ex rel. Attorney General v. Russell*, 33 A. 709, 711 (Pa. 1896) ("'Sic utere tuo non alienum laedas' expresses a moral obligation that grows out of the mere fact of membership in civil society. In many instances it has been applied as a measure of civil obligation, enforceable at law among those whose interests are conflicting."); *Perkins v. F.I.E. Corp.*, 762 F.2d 1250, 1275 (5th Cir. 1985) (noting that under Louisiana law, the *sic utere* maxim is the basis for the rule of strict liability governing ultrahazardous activities).

11. *See Restatement (Third): Liability for Physical Harm* §§ 4, 6 (defining "physical harm" to include physical impairment of the body caused by death, and stating general rule of negligence liability for having caused "physical harm").

12. G. Edward White, *Tort Law in America: An Intellectual History* 61–62 (Oxford U. Press 1980).

13. Gary T. Schwartz, *The Character of Early American Tort Law*, 36 UCLA L. Rev. 641, 665 (1989).

14. *Restatement (Second)* § 283 cmt. c (justifying the objective nature of negligence liability). For elaboration, *see* Arthur Ripstein, *Equality, Responsibility, and the Law* 85–91 (Cambridge U. Press 1999).

15. Holmes, *supra* note 6, at 108.

16. *See* John C. P. Goldberg, *Twentieth-Century Tort Theory*, 91 Geo. L.J. 513, 521–537 (2003) (explaining that the "most influential tort scholars in the Twentieth Century" relied on an approach, reflected in the varied *Restatements of Tort Law*, that conceptualized tort law in the functional terms of compensation and deterrence).

17. Guido Calabresi, *The Costs of Accidents* 24 n.1 (Yale U. Press 1970); *see also* Guido Calabresi, *First Party, Third Party, and Product Liability Systems: Can Economic Analysis of Law Tell Us Anything About Them?*, 69 Iowa L. Rev. 833, 847 (1984) (observing that economic analysis "certainly does not tell us what weight to give to other distributional goals that the society seems to value. . . . It does, however, give us an analytical structure that allows us to see far better what is at stake in the choice of systems [governing accidents].").

CHAPTER 6

1. Barbara Young Welke, *Recasting American Liberty: Gender, Race, Law, and the Railroad Revolution, 1865–1920* 97 (Cambridge U. Press 2001). *See also* Margo Schlanger, *Injured Women Before Common Law Courts, 1860–1930*, 21 Harv. Women's L.J. 79 (1998).

2. *Id.*, at x.

3. *See generally* Leslie Bender, *A Lawyer's Primer on Feminist Theory and Tort*, 38 J. Legal Educ. 3 (1988) (describing interest balancing as a contextualized social construct).

4. Welke, *supra* note 1, at 104–105 (paragraph structure omitted).

5. Henry M. Hart, Jr., *The Aims of the Criminal Law*, 23 Law & Contemp. Probs. 401, 409 (1958). The quotation is altered so that the "criminal law" is replaced by "tort law."

6. Oliver Wendell Holmes, *The Common Law* 35 (Little, Brown, and Co. 1881).

CHAPTER 7

1. *Restatement (Third)* § 1 cmt. e.

2. 279 P.2d 1091 (Wash. 1955).

3. 50 N.W. 403 (Wis. 1891).

4. 47 N.W. 99, 99 (Wis. 1890) (deciding initial appeal of case).

5. *See* Craig M. Lawson, *The Puzzle of Intended Harm in the Tort of Battery*, 74 Temp. L. Rev. 355, 362–365 (2001) (using this particular example and illustrating more generally the problems of the single-intent approach).

6. *See* Kenneth W. Simons, *A Restatement (Third) of Intentional Torts?*, 48 Ariz. L. Rev. 1061, 1066 (2006) ("The courts are split on the issue: a substantial group follows the so-called dual-intent approach, requiring both an intent to contact and an intent either to harm or offend; another substantial group follows the single-intent approach, requiring only an intent to contact.") (citations omitted).

7. *Restatement (Second)* § 16 cmt. a, illus. 1.

8. Simons, *supra* note 6, at 1074 (citations omitted).

9. David Ibbetson, *A Historical Introduction to the Law of Obligations* 14 (Oxford U. Press 1999).

10. *Id.* at 17.

11. *Restatement (Second)* § 18 cmt. c.

12. *Schloendorff v. Society of New York Hosp.*, 105 N.E. 92, 93 (N.Y. 1914).

13. *E.g., Lambertson v. United States*, 528 F.2d 441 (2d Cir.), *cert. denied*, 426 U.S. 921 (1976) (finding that defendant committed battery by jumping on coworker plaintiff's back as a prank, unintentionally causing him to fall forward onto some meat hooks).

14. *Restatement (Second)* § 16 cmt. a.

15. *Id.* § 19.

16. *Id.*

17. Simons, *supra* note 6, at 1074–1075 (citations omitted).

18. *Brzoska v. Olson*, 668 A.2d 1355, 1363 (Del. 1995).

19. *Id.* at 1361 (citing estimates ranging from 1:263,158 to 1:2,631,579).

20. *Restatement (Second)* § 21.

21. William Blackstone, 3 *Commentaries* 120 (1790).

22. *See* Dobbs on Torts § 36, at 67 (indicating that the third element is the minority view).

23. *See Restatement (Second)* § 36; *id.* § 36 cmt. b; *id.* § 36 cmt. a & § 40; and *id.* § 36.

24. *Paul v. Avril*, 901 F. Supp. 330, 331 (citing 28 U.S.C.A. § 1350).

25. *Restatement (Second)* § 158.

26. *Id.* § 216.

27. *Id.* § 217.

28. *Id.* § 218.

29. 1 Harper, James and Gray on Torts § 2.3, at 169.

30. *Restatement (Second)* § 218, cmt. e.

31. *Compare* 1 Harper, James and Gray on Torts § 2.13, at 203–204 ("The concept of real property includes growing crops and trees and also chattels that have become so attached to the land or buildings as to become fixtures. After severance from the land, however, all these things are treated as personal property and subject to conversion.").

32. *See Intel Corp. v. Hamidi*, 71 P.3d 296, 303 (Cal. 2003) (requiring actual harm for injunctive relief); Chapter 14, section IV (explaining that punitive damages require an award of compensatory damages and illustrating how punitive damages can protect the individual interest in exclusive possession of land).

33. *Restatement (Second)* § 222A.

34. *Id.* cmt. d Illus. 1, 4 & 2.

35. *Id.* cmt. c.

36. Calvert Magruder, *Mental and Emotional Disturbance in the Law of Torts*, 49 Harv. L. Rev. 1033 (1936).

37. *E.g., Brooker v. Silverthorne*, 99 S.E. 350 (S.C. 1918) (denying recovery for assault to a female night operator of a telephone exchange who had been verbally abused over the phone by the male defendant, including a threat that "If I were there, I would break your God damned neck").

38. *Restatement (Second)* § 46.

39. *Id.* cmt. d.

40. Prosser and Keeton on Torts § 18, at 112.

41. Heidi M. Hurd, *The Moral Magic of Consent*, 2 Legal Theory 121, 122 (1996).

42. *Id.* at 124 (paragraph structure omitted).

43. *See, e.g., O'Brien v. Cunard S.S. Co.*, 28 N.E. 266 (1891) (absolving defendant physician from battery liability based on his actual, reasonable belief that plaintiff consented to a vaccination by standing in line with other people who received the vaccination and holding out her arm like others in the line).

44. Prosser and Keeton on Torts § 18, at 113–114.

45. Francis Bohlen, *Incomplete Privilege to Inflict Intentional Invasions of Interests of Property and Personality*, 39 Harv. L. Rev. 307, 315 (1926). Bohlen was the Reporter for the First Restatement of Torts. In the deleted portion of the quote, Bohlen says "there is a difference of opinion as to the reason why the preponderating value of the interests of the actor and of society deprives the act of its liability creative quality and makes resistance to it a source of liability." Compare Chapter 5 (showing how this type of interest analysis translates into a compensatory conception of tort liability).

46. *Id.* at 322.

47. Restatement (Second) § 63 cmt. j.

48. *Id.*

49. *Id.* § 65.

50. *Id.* § 64.

51. Joseph H. Beale, Jr., *Retreat from Murderous Assault*, 16 Harv. L. Rev. 567, 577 (1903).

52. *E.g., Courvoisier v. Raymond*, 47 P. 284 (Colo. 1896) (denying recovery to a plaintiff who was not, in fact, attacking the defendant); *Morris v. Platt*, 32 Conn. 75 (1864) (denying recovery to an innocent bystander who was shot by the defendant in the course of protecting himself from attack).

53. *Restatement (Second)* § 77 cmt. j.

54. *Id.* § 77.

55. *E.g., Katko v. Briney*, 183 N.W.2d 657 (Iowa 1971) (awarding plaintiff trespasser compensatory and punitive damages for gunshot wounds caused by defendant property owner who had used a loaded spring gun to protect the contents of an abandoned, vacant house).

56. *Restatement (Second)* § 103.

57. *Id.* cmt. c.

58. 124 N.W. 221, 222 (Minn. 1910).

59. Bohlen, *supra* note 45, at 316.

60. Daniel Friedmann, *Restitution of Benefits Obtained Through the Appropriation of Property or the Commission of a Wrong*, 80 Colum. L. Rev. 504, 510 (1980).

61. Stephen D. Sugarman, *The "Necessity" Defense and the Failure of Tort Theory: The Case Against Strict Liability for Damages Caused While Exercising Self-Help During an Emergency*, in *Issues in Legal Scholarship* (Berkeley 2005), available at *http://www.bepress.com/ils/iss7/art1* (surveying extensive scholarly discussion of private necessity and identifying problems with every effort to justify *Vincent*).

62. *Vincent*, 124 N.W. at 221–222.

63. *Restatement (Second)* §§ 196 (land) & 263 (chattels).

64. Prosser and Keeton on Torts § 24, at 146 (citations omitted).

CHAPTER 8

1. *Restatement (Third)* § 7 cmt. a.

2. Dobbs on Torts § 229, at 583.

3. Prosser and Keeton on Torts § 53, at 358. The development of this approach to duty is described and criticized in John C.P. Goldberg & Benjamin C. Zipursky, *The Moral of* MacPherson, 146 U. Pa. L. Rev. 1733 (1998).

4. *Restatement (Second)* § 314 cmt. c, Illus. 1 (italics added).

5. *Buch v. Armory Mfg. Co.*, 44 A. 809, 810 (N.H. 1898).

6. *Autonomy in Moral and Political Philosophy*, in *Stanford Encyclopedia of Philosophy*, available online at *http://plato.stanford.edu*.

7. *See* Richard Epstein, *A Theory of Strict Liability*, 2 J. Legal Stud. 151, 198 (1973) (concluding that an affirmative legal obligation to rescue is an illegitimate interference with liberty).

8. *Compare* Peter Unger, *Living High and Letting Die: Our Illusion of Innocence* (Oxford U. Press 1996) (rejecting nine possible factors that might give special normative significance to rescue cases); Liam Murphy, *Beneficence, Law, and Liberty: The Case of Required Rescue*, 89 Geo. L.J. 605 (2001) (showing the difficulty of finding a defensible normative ground for distinguishing rescue and nonrescue situations).

9. Minn. Stat. § 604.01(a); R.I. Gen. Laws § 11-56-1; Vt. Stat. Ann. tit. 12, § 519.

10. *Restatement (Third)* § 7 cmt. f. For further argument in favor of criminal liability rather than tort liability, see Murphy, *supra* note 8, at 659–663.

11. *Restatement (Second)* § 289 cmt. b.

12. Oliver Wendell Holmes, *The Common Law* 95 (Little, Brown and Co. 1871).

13. Stephen R. Perry, *Responsibility for Outcomes, Risk, and the Law of Torts*, in *Philosophy and the Law of Torts*, 72, 92–93 (Gerald Postema ed., Cambridge U. Press 2001) (footnote omitted).

14. 162 N.E. 99, 100 (N.Y. 1928).

15. *See Restatement (Second)* § 281 cmt. c.

16. *See* W. Jonathan Cardi, *Purging Foreseeability*, 58 Vand. L. Rev. 739, 778–781 (2005) (concluding that the "disarray in negligence cases surrounding the so-called '*Palsgraf* question' is replete").

17. *Palsgraf*, 162 N.E. at 101.

18. *Compare* William L. Prosser, Palsgraf *Revisited*, 52 Mich. L. Rev. 1, 31 (1953) (observing that "the technical issue was whether the jury should have the case," although "it was not debated along those lines").

19. *See Restatement (Third)* § 29 cmt. f. The element of proximate cause is discussed in Chapter 9, section II.

20. *Palsgraf*, 162 N.E. at 102 (Andrews, J., dissenting) (italics added).

21. *Miller v. Wal-Mart Stores, Inc.*, 580 N.W. 2d 233, 238 (Wis. 1998).

22. *Restatement (Third)* § 3 cmt. e.

23. *Restatement (Third): Liability for Physical Harm* § 6 cmt. f.

24. Dobbs on Torts § 309, at 839–840. For a description of the evolution of tort law in this area, see Nancy Levit, *Ethereal Torts*, 61 Geo. Wash. L. Rev. 136, 140–146 (1992).

25. *Compare Dillon v. Legg*, 441 P.2d 912 (Cal. 1968) (allowing mother who observed accident from afar to recover for emotional distress) *with Thing v. La Chusa*, 771 P.2d 814 (Cal. 1989) (barring mother from recovery because she arrived on the scene shortly after the accident had occurred).

26. Prosser and Keeton on Torts § 54, at 360.

27. *Id.* at 366.

28. For arguments that tort law inappropriately devalues emotional interests for gendered reasons, see Leslie Bender, *Feminist (Re)Torts: Thoughts on the Liability Crisis, Mass Torts, Power, and Responsibilities*, 1990 Duke L.J. 848, 851–853 (1990); Martha Chamallas, *The Architecture of Bias: Deep Structures in Tort Law*, 146 U. Pa. L. Rev. 463, 499 (1998); Levit, *supra* note 24, at 139–140.

29. *See generally* Douglas G. Baird, *The Elements of Bankruptcy* (Foundation Press 4th ed., 2006) (describing the priorities within bankruptcy law and the procedural and substantive powers that bankruptcy statutes have conferred on courts).

30. *See* Mark Geistfeld, *The Analytics of Duty: Medical Monitoring and Related Forms of Economic Loss*, 88 Va. L. Rev. 1921 (2002).

31. For wide-ranging discussion of the varied issues surrounding tort recovery for pure economic loss, see 48 Ariz. L. Rev. 693 *passim* (2006) (symposium on economic loss).

32. Robert L. Rabin, *Tort Recovery for Negligently Inflicted Economic Loss: A Reassessment*, 37 Stan. L. Rev. 1513, 1526 (1985).

33. Jay M. Feinman, *Economic Negligence* § 2.1, at 28–29 (Little, Brown and Co. 1995).

34. *See* Dobbs on Torts § 452, at 1285–1287.

35. Rabin, *supra* note 32, at 1515.

36. *Friends for All Children, Inc. v. Lockheed Aircraft Corp.*, 746 F.2d 816, 826 (D.C. Cir. 1984).

37. *Henry v. Dow Chemical Co.*, 701 N.W.2d 684, 694 (Mich. 2005).

38. *Restatement (Second)* § 315.

39. *See generally* Robert L. Rabin, *Enabling Torts*, 49 DePaul L. Rev. 435 (1999).

40. *See, e.g., Tarasoff v. Regents of University of California*, 551 P.2d 334 (Cal. 1976) (imposing duty on psychotherapist to control his patient who had revealed an intention to harm the plaintiff's decedent).

41. Rabin, *supra* note 32, at 444.

42. *Restatement (Second)* § 448 cmt. b. *Compare* Erling Eide, *Economics of Criminal Behavior*, in V *Encyclopedia of Law & Economics* 345, 355–364 (Boudewijn Bouckaert & Gerrit De Geest eds., Edward Elgar Pub. 2000) (surveying numerous empirical studies finding that a reduced likelihood of sanction is associated with an increased incidence of crime).

43. Dilan A. Esper & Gregory C. Keating, *Abusing Duty*, 79 S. Cal. L. Rev. 265, 270 (2006).

44. 482 N.E.2d 34, 38 (N.Y. 1985).

45. Dobbs on Torts § 232, at 592.

46. *Id.* at 593.

47. *Compare* Jeremiah Smith, *Liability of Landowners to Children Entering Without Permission*, 11 Harv. L. Rev. 434, 436 (1898) ("It is the policy of the law

not to expose certain classes of persons, or their acts and conduct in certain situations, to the harrowing uncertainty and vexation of litigation.").

48. *Stagl v. Delta Airlines, Inc.*, 52 F.3d 463, 469 (2d Cir. 1995) (Calabresi, J.).

49. *See generally* Esper & Keating, *supra* note 43 (showing how California courts have often treated duty in this manner and explaining why it is problematic to do so).

50. *Restatement (Third): Liability for Physical Harm* § 7 cmt. i.

51. *Id.* § 3 cmt. a.

52. For discussion of some of the associated issues, see Margo Schlanger, *Gender Matters: Teaching a Reasonable Woman Standard in Personal Injury Law*, 45 St. Louis L.J. 769 (2001).

53. Fleming James, Jr., *The Qualities of the Reasonable Man in Negligence Cases*, 16 Mo. L. Rev. 1, 1–2 (1951) (paragraph structure added).

54. *Restatement (Second)* § 283 cmt. c ("The reasonable man is a fictitious person who is never negligent, and whose conduct is always up to standard.").

55. Patrick Kelley, *Infancy, Insanity, and Infirmity in the Law of Torts*, 48 Amer. J. Juris. 179, 180 (2003).

56. *Restatement (Second)* § 283 cmt. c.

57. Dobbs on Torts, § 116 at 275.

58. *See generally* Kelley, *supra* note 55; David E. Seidelson, *Reasonable Expectations and Subjective Standards in Negligence Law: The Minor, the Mentally Impaired, and the Mentally Incompetent*, 50 Geo. Wash. L. Rev. 17 (1981).

59. Harry Shulman, *The Standard of Care Required of Children*, 37 Yale L.J. 618, 618 (1928).

60. *See Restatement (Third): Liability for Physical Harm* § 10 cmt. f (describing the inquiry as whether "children choose to engage in dangerous activities characteristically engaged in by adults.").

61. *Id.* Rptrs' N. cmt. f at 145.

62. *See id.*

63. Jacobus tenBroek, *The Right to Live in the World: The Disabled in the Law of Torts*, 54 Cal. L. Rev. 841, 842 (1966).

64. Prosser and Keeton on Torts, § 32 at 176. *But see* tenBroek, *supra* note 63, at 852 (arguing that in "some areas, the pronouncement and the policy are completely rejected; in others, they are given only halting and partial credence; and in none are they fully and positively implemented by the courts").

65. *See Roberts v. Ring*, 173 N.W. 437, 438 (Minn. 1919) (justifying the objective standard on the ground that "[s]uch infirmities . . . presented only a reason why [the defendant elderly driver] should refrain from operating an automobile on a crowded street where care was required to avoid injuring other travelers").

66. Mark P. Gergen, *The Jury's Role in Deciding Normative Issues in American Common Law*, 68 Fordham L. Rev. 407, 424–425 (1999) (citations omitted).

67. *Id.* at 434 (citations omitted).

68. *Restatement (Second)* § 283 cmt. e.

69. *Restatement (Third): Liability for Physical Harms* § 6 cmt. d.

70. *United States v. Carroll Towing Co.*, 159 F.2d 169, 173 (2d Cir. 1947).

71. *See id.* (using the formula to determine whether the plaintiff was contributorily negligent for not exercising reasonable care to protect its own barge).

72. *E.g.*, Ernest Weinrib, *The Idea of Private Law* 149 (Harvard U. Press 1995) (arguing that under a Kantian conception of tort law, "[f]or a real risk that is not small . . . the cost of precautions is irrelevant").

73. *Restatement (Third): Products Liability* § 2 cmt. f, at 23.

74. 43 N.Y. 502 (1871).

75. W. Kip Viscusi, *How Do Judges Think About Risk?*, 1 Am. L. & Econ. Rev. 26, 40–46 (1999); W. Kip Viscusi, *Jurors, Judges, and the Mistreatment of Risk by the Courts*, 30 J. Legal Stud. 107 (2001); *see also* Paul Slovic, *The Perception of Risk* 199–200 (Earthscan Pubs. Ltd. 2000) ("Research on risk perception indicates that laypeople want risk decisions to be based on additional considerations besides expected damages, injuries and dollar costs.").

76. Kenneth S. Abraham, *The Trouble with Negligence*, 53 Vand. L. Rev. 1187, 1190 (2001).

77. Mark F. Grady, *Untaken Precautions*, 18 J. Legal Stud. 139, 140 (1989).

78. *Id.* at 141.

79. *McClaren v. G.S. Robins & Co.*, 162 S.W.2d 856, 858 (Mo. 1942) (emphasis added).

80. 60 F.2d 737 (2d Cir. 1932).

81. *Restatement (Third): Liability for Physical Harm* § 13(a).

82. *Id.*, § 13 cmt. b.

83. Clarence Morris, *Custom and Negligence*, 42 Colum. L. Rev. 1147, 1155 (1942).

84. *Id.* at 1163.

85. *Id.* at 1164.

86. For a more complete analysis, including other economic rationales for regulating product safety with tort law, see Mark A. Geistfeld, *Principles of Products Liability* 34–50 (Foundation Press 2006).

87. James Surowiecki, *Fuel for Thought*, The New Yorker, July 23, 2007, at 25.

88. *See generally* Shannon Brownlee, *Overtreated: Why Too Much Medicine Is Making Us Sicker and Poorer* (Bloomsbury USA 2007) (arguing that between one-fifth and one-third of health care expenditures in the United States is for unnecessary treatment).

89. *Restatement (Third): Liability for Physical Harm*, § 13(b).

90. *Id.* at 1161.

91. *Restatement (Third): Liability for Physical Harm*, § 13 cmt. c.

92. Morris, *supra* note 83, at 1155.

93. For extended analysis of the different types of safety customs and the conditions under which they can be efficient, see Steven Hetcher, *Creating Safe Social Norms in a Dangerous World*, 73 S. Cal. L. Rev. 1, 17 (1999).

94. Caroline Forell, *Statutory Torts, Statutory Duty Actions, and Negligence Per Se: What's the Difference?*, 77 Or. L. Rev. 497, 497–498 (1998) (citations omitted).

95. *Restatement (Third): Liability for Physical Harm*, § 14 cmt. b.

96. *Id.* § 14.

97. *Clinkscales v. Carver*, 136 P.2d 777, 778 (Cal. 1943) (Traynor, J.).

98. *Restatement (Third): Liability for Physical Harm*, § 14 cmt. c (paragraph structure omitted).

99. *Id.* § 15 cmt. a.

100. *Id.* cmt. c.

101. *Id.* cmt. a.

102. James B. Jacobs, *Drunk Driving: An American Dilemma* 139 (U. Chicago Press 1989).

103. *See Restatement (Third): Liability for Physical Harm*, § 14 cmt. i (explaining that the violation of a statute is relevant to duty analysis and can lead courts to recognize a duty that they would not otherwise recognize absent the statute).

104. *Bertelmann v. Taas Assoc.*, 735 P.2d 930, 934 (Haw. 1987).

105. *Id.*

106. Dobbs on Torts § 332, at 900.

107. *Id.* § 139, at 328.

108. *Restatement (Third): Liability for Physical Harm* § 8 cmt. c.

109. Holmes, *supra* note 12, at 123–124.

110. *Baltimore and Ohio R.R. v. Goodman*, 275 U.S. 66, 69–70 (1927) (Holmes, J.) (citation omitted).

111. *Pokora v. Wabash Ry.*, 292 U.S. 98, 106 (1934). *See generally* Jason Scott Johnston, *Uncertainty, Chaos, and the Torts Process: An Economic Analysis of Legal Form*, 76 Cornell L. Rev. 341 (1991) (explaining how litigation incentives bias the selection of cases decided by courts, creating a dynamic in which courts can vacillate between rules and standards applied on a case-by-case basis).

112. *Restatement (Third): Liability for Physical Harm* § 8 cmt. c.

113. Fleming James, Jr., *Proof of Breach in Negligence Cases (Including Res Ipsa Loquitur)*, 37 Va. L. Rev. 179, 180–181 (1951) (citations omitted) (italics partially supplied).

114. *Id.*, at 194–195.

115. 159 Eng. Rep. 299 (Exch. 1863).

116. *See generally* Mark F. Grady, *Res Ipsa Loquitur and Compliance Error*, 142 U. Pa. L. Rev. 887 (1994).

117. *Id.* at 922 (citation omitted).

118. *See* G. Gregg Webb, Note, *The Law of Falling Objects: Byrne v. Boadle and the Birth of Res Ipsa Loquitur*, 59 Stan. L. Rev. 1065 (2007) (describing how the development of *res ipsa loquitur* was largely influenced by cases involving common carriers).

119. *Restatement (Third): Liability for Physical Harm* § 17 cmt. a.

CHAPTER 9

1. David W. Robertson, *The Common Sense of Cause in Fact*, 75 Tex. L. Rev. 1765, 1770–1771 (citations omitted).

2. *Zuchowicz v. United States*, 140 F.3d 381, 390–391 (2d Cir. 1998) (Calbresi, J.) (citing Prosser and Keeton on Torts § 41, at 270) (citation omitted).

3. *Reyes v. Vantage S.S. Co.*, 609 F.2d 140, 144 (5th Cir. 1980).

4. Wex S. Malone, *Ruminations on Cause-In-Fact*, 9 Stan. L. Rev. 60, 77 (1956). *See also Haft v. Lone Palm Hotel*, 478 P.2d 465 (Cal. 1970).

5. *Martin v. Herzog*, 126 N.E. 814, 816 (N.Y. 1920) (Cardozo, J.).

6. *Healy v. Hoy*, 132 N.W. 208, 209 (Minn. 1911).

7. Lars Noah, *An Inventory of Mathematical Blunders in Applying the Loss-of-a-Chance Doctrine*, 24 Rev. Litig. 369, 375–378 (2005) (paragraph structure and citations omitted).

8. David A. Fischer, *Tort Recovery for Loss of a Chance*, 36 Wake Forest L. Rev. 605, 606 (2001).

9. *Id.* at 612–613.

10. *See generally* Mark Geistfeld, *Scientific Uncertainty and Causation in Tort Law*, 54 Vand. L. Rev. 1011 (2001).

11. David A. Fischer, *Successive Causes and the Enigma of Duplicated Harm*, 66 Tenn. L. Rev. 1127, 1129–1130 (1999) (citations omitted).

12. *Eagle-Picher Indus. Inc. v. Balbos*, 604 A.2d 445, 459 (Md. 1992).

13. *Restatement (Third): Liability for Physical Harm* § 27 cmt. g.

14. *Restatement (Second)* § 431.

15. *Restatement (Third): Liability for Physical Harm* § 26 cmt. b.

16. Richard W. Wright, *Once More into the Bramble Bush: Duty, Causal Contribution, and the Extent of Legal Responsibility*, 54 Vand. L. Rev. 1071, 1104 (2001). For more extensive elaboration of the NESS test, see Richard W. Wright, *Causation in Tort Law*, 73 Cal. L. Rev. 1735 (1985).

17. *Restatement (Third): Liability for Physical Harm* § 27.

18. *Id.* at § 27 cmt. f.

19. William L. Prosser, *Handbook of the Law of Torts* § 45, at 311 (West Pub. 1941).

20. *In re Polemis & Furness Withy & Co.*, [1921] 3 K.B. 560, 577.

21. 43 A. 240 (Pa. 1899).

22. *Petition of Kinsman Transit Co.*, 338 F.2d 708, 723 (2d Cir. 1964) (Friendly, J.).

23. *Id.* at 724.

24. 4 Harper, James, and Gray on Torts § 20.5, at 179–185 (citations omitted).

25. *Overseas Tankship (U.K.) Ltd. v. Morts Dock & Eng'g Co., Ltd.* [1961] A.C. 388 (P.C. Aust.).

26. *Id.*

27. Dobbs on Torts § 185, at 458.

28. *Restatement (Third): Liability for Physical Harm* § 29 cmt. p.

29. *Id.*

30. *Petition of Kinsman Transit Co.*, 338 F.2d at 724.

31. Dobbs on Torts § 185, at 458.

32. *Petition of Kinsman Transit Co.*, 338 F.2d at 723.

33. *Restatement (Third): Liability for Physical Harm* § 29.

34. *Story Parchment Co. v. Paterson Parchment Paper Co.*, 282 U.S. 555, 563 (1931).

35. *Restatement (Second)* § 912 cmt. a.

36. *Petition of Kinsman Transit Co.*, 338 F.2d at 724.

37. *See* Warren Seavey, *Mr. Justice Cardozo and the Law of Torts*, 39 Colum. L. Rev. 20, 32–33; 52 Harv. L. Rev. 372, 384–385; 48 Yale L.J. 390, 402–403 (1939) (recognizing that *Polemis* can be interpreted in this manner, making it consistent with the rule "that the negligent person takes his victims as they are").

38. *Restatement (Third): Liability for Physical Harm* § 29 cmt. i.

39. *Consolidated Rail Corp. v. Gottshall*, 512 U.S. 532, 553 (1994).

40. Pub. L. No. 107-42, 115 Stat. 230 (2001) (codified at 49 U.S.C. § 40101). For discussion by the Special Master vested with responsibility for implementing the fund, see Kenneth R. Feinberg, *What Is Life Worth?: The Unprecedented Effort to Compensate the Victims of 9/11* (Public Affairs 2005).

CHAPTER 10

1. 3 Harper, James and Gray on Torts § 10.1, at 1 (paragraph structure omitted).

2. *Larsen v. General Motors Corp.*, 391 F.2d 495, 503 (8th Cir. 1968) (applying Minn. law).

3. 5 Harper, James and Gray on Torts § 26.1, at 2 (citations and paragraph structure omitted).

4. Gary T. Schwartz, *The Hidden and Fundamental Issue of Employer Vicarious Liability*, 69 S. Cal. L. Rev. 1739, 1740 (1996).

5. *Cf.* Jennifer Arlen, *The Potentially Perverse Effects of Corporate Criminal Liability*, 23 J. Legal Stud. 833 (1994).

6. For more extensive analysis, see Schwartz, *supra* note 4, at 1755–1764.

7. 398 F.2d 167, 171 (2d Cir. 1968).

8. Schwartz, *supra* note 4, at 1750.

9. *Hartford Accident & Indemnity Co. v. Cardillo*, 112 F.2d 11, 15 (D.C. Cir. 1940), *quoted in Bushey*, 398 F.2d at 171 (other citations omitted).

10. *Restatement (Second)* § 413 cmt. b.

11. *See* Prosser and Keeton on Torts § 71, at 512.

12. 199 P.2d 1 (Cal. 1948).

13. *Restatement (Second)* § 433B(3).

14. *Id.* cmt. f.

15. *Restatement (Third): Liability for Physical Harm* § 28(b) cmt. f.

16. *Id.* cmt. g.

17. 607 P.2d 924, 937 (Cal. 1980).

18. *See, e.g.*, Glen O. Robinson, *Multiple Causation in Tort Law: Reflections on the DES Cases*, 68 Va. L. Rev. 713, 749 (1982) (concluding that *Sindell* "point[s] toward a rule that imposes liability for the creation of a risk and apportions liability according to the magnitude of that risk"); David Rosenberg, *The Causal Connection in Mass Exposure Cases: A "Public Law" Vision of the Tort System*, 97 Harv. L. Rev. 849, 866–868 (1984) (identifying market-share liability as a form of proportional liability based on the risk that the defendant caused injury). Advocates of this position also rely on the loss-of-a-chance doctrine, discussed in Chapter 9, section I.A.

19. *Restatement (Third): Liability for Physical Harm* § 28 cmt. o (collecting cases showing that no more than 20 jurisdictions have decided the issue, with nine rejecting market-share liability).

20. *Senn v. Merrell-Dow Pharmaceuticals, Inc.*, 751 P.2d 215, 223 (Or. 1988). *See also Smith v. Eli Lilly Co.*, 560 N.E.2d 324, 334–340 (Ill. 1990) (providing a survey of cases rejecting market-share liability and stressing the common theme that the liability rule is a "radical" departure from tort principles).

21. *Sindell*, 607 P.2d at 928.

22. *Senn*, 751 P.2d at 222.

23. *Summers*, 199 P.2d at 2.

24. Prosser and Keeton on Torts § 41, at 268.

25. *See generally* Mark A. Geistfeld, *The Doctrinal Unity of Alternative Liability and Market-Share Liability*, 155 U. Pa. L. Rev. 147 (2007) (developing and defending proof of causation by evidential grouping).

26. *Compare Brown v. Superior Court*, 751 P.2d 470, 487 (Cal. 1988) (justifying market-share liability with the "goal of achieving a balance between the interests of DES plaintiffs and manufacturers of the drug").

27. *Brown*, 751 P.2d at 486.

28. *See* Allen Rostron, *Beyond Market-Share Liability: A Theory of Proportional Share Liability for Nonfungible Products*, 52 UCLA L. Rev. 151 (2004).

CHAPTER 11

1. *Black's Law Dictionary* 1569 (West 7th ed. 1999).

2. *Restatement (Third): Apportionment of Liability* § 2 cmt. f.

3. *Restatement (Second)* § 496B cmt. b.

4. *Tunkl v. Regents of Univ. of Cal.*, 383 P.2d 441, 444–446 (Cal. 1963) (citations omitted and factor numbers added).

5. *Restatement (Third): Products Liability* § 18.

6. *Id.* cmt. a.

7. *Milligan v. Big Valley Corp.*, 754 P.2d 1063, 1066–1067 (Wyo. 1988).

8. *Dalury v. S-K-I, Ltd.*, 670 A.2d 795 (Vt. 1995).

9. 58 N.E. 585 (Mass. 1900).

10. *See* Kenneth W. Simons, *Assumption of Risk and Consent in the Law of Torts: A Theory of Full Preference*, 67 B.U. L. Rev. 213 (1987).

11. Fowler V. Harper & James Fleming, Jr., 2 *The Law of Torts* 1191 (Little, Brown and Co. 1956).

12. *Restatement (Third): Apportionment of Liability* § 3 cmt. c (treating implied assumption of risk as a form of plaintiff negligence).

13. 103 Eng. Rep. 926 (K.B. 1809).

14. Ernest A. Turk, *Comparative Negligence on the March*, 28 Chi.-Kent L. Rev. 189, 196 (1950) (citations omitted).

15. The doctrine was first announced in *Davies v. Mann*, 10 M & W 546, 152 Eng. Rep. 588 (1842).

16. Kenneth W. Simons, *The Puzzling Doctrine of Contributory Negligence*, 16 Cardozo L. Rev. 1693, 1747 (1995).

17. Charles F. Beach, Jr., *Contributory Negligence* 12–13 (Baker, Voorhis 2d ed. 1892).

18. Morton J. Horwitz, *The Transformation of American Law 1870–1960: The Crisis of Legal Orthodoxy* 52 (Oxford U. Press 1992).

19. *Id.* at 63. *See generally* Peter L. Bernstein, *Against the Gods: The Remarkable Story of Risk* (John Wiley and Sons 1996).

20. *See The Schooner Catharine v. Dickinson*, 58 U.S. 170 (1854).

21. 45 U.S.C. §§ 51 et seq.

22. *E.g., Li v. Yellow Cab Co. of California*, 532 P.2d 1226 (Cal. 1975).

23. *Restatement (Third): Apportionment of Liability* § 8.

24. *Nash v. Port Authority of New York and New Jersey*, 2008 WL 1869554 (N.Y. App. Div. 2008).

25. Paul H. Edelman, *What Are We Comparing in Comparative Negligence?*, 85 Wash. U. L. Rev. 73, 95 (2007).

26. Henry Woods & Beth Deere, *Comparative Fault* § 8:2, at 172 (Clark Boardman Callaghan 3d ed. 1996).

27. *E.g., Fritts v. McKinne*, 934 P.2d 371 (Okla. Ct. Civ. App. 1996).

28. *Restatement (Third): Apportionment of Liability* § 2 cmt. i, Rptrs' Note at 27.

29. *See generally* Ellen M. Bublick, *Comparative Fault to the Limits*, 56 Vand. L. Rev. 977 (2003); William K. Jones, *Tort Triad: Slumbering Sentinels, Vicious Assailants, and Victims Variously Vigilant*, 30 Hofstra L. Rev. 253 (2001) (discussing apportionment for joint and several liability).

CHAPTER 12

1. 159 Eng. Rep. 737 (Ex. 1865), *rev'd*, 1 L.R.-Ex. 265 (Ex. Ch. 1866), *aff'd*, 3 L.R.-E & I. App. 330 (H.L. 1868). For further discussion of the case, see Chapter 1, section III.

2. *Restatement (Third): Liability for Physical Harms* § 20, cmt. e.

3. *See generally* Jed Handelsman Shugerman, Note, *The Floodgates of Strict Liability: Bursting Reservoirs and the Adoption of* Fletchers v. Rylands *in the Gilded Age*, 110 Yale L.J. 333 (2000). A catastrophic dam accident in England also preceded *Rylands*. *See* A. W. B. Simpson, *Legal Liability for Bursting Reservoirs: The Historical Context of* Rylands v. Fletcher, 13 J. Legal Stud. 209 (1984).

4. *Restatement (Second)* § 520.

5. *Id.* cmt. f.

6. *Id.* cmt. b & cmt. h.

7. *Bedell v. Goulter*, 261 P.2d 842, 850 (Or. 1953).

8. 3 Harper, James, and Gray on Torts § 14.4, at 251.

9. Gerald W. Boston, *Strict Liability for Abnormally Dangerous Activity: The Negligence Barrier*, 36 San Diego L. Rev. 597, 627 (1999).

10. *Restatement (Third): Liability for Physical Harm* § 20.

11. *Id.* cmt. f.

12. *Id.* cmt. j (using reciprocity to explain why strict liability is limited to uncommon activities).

13. *Restatement (Third): Liability for Physical Harms* § 20 cmt. b. Compare *Restatement (Third): Products Liability* § 2 cmt. a (recognizing that strict liability

for defective products serves "an instrumental function of creating safety incentives" greater than those in a negligence regime "under which, as a practical matter, sellers may escape their appropriate share of responsibility").

14. *Restatement (Third): Liability for Physical Harm* § 20 Rptr's N. cmt. h, at 303.

15. *Brown v. Collins*, 53 N.H. 442 (1873).

16. *E.g., Pennsylvania Coal Co. v. Sanderson*, 6 A. 453, 459 (Pa. 1886) (rejecting claim of strict liability against a coal company for polluting a stream: "[t]o encourage the development of the great natural resources of a country trifling inconveniences to particular persons must sometimes give way to the necessities of a great community").

17. *See generally* Jed Handelsman Shugerman, *A Watershed Moment: Disasters and the Reversals of Tort Doctrine and Ideology*, J. Tort Law (forthcoming 2008), *at http://www.bepress.com/* (showing how courts vacillated between moral justifications for strict liability and instrumental justifications like risk reduction).

CHAPTER 13

1. *See generally* Mark A. Geistfeld, *Principles of Products Liability* (Foundation Press 2006).

2. *Barker v. Lull Eng'g Co.*, 573 P.2d 443, 445 (Cal. 1978).

3. *Restatement (Third): Products Liability* § 2 cmt. a (recognizing that strict liability for defective products serves "an instrumental function of creating safety incentives" greater than those in a negligence regime "under which, as a practical matter, sellers may escape their appropriate share of responsibility").

4. *Id.* cmts. i–j.

5. *Restatement (Second)* § 402A cmt. i.

6. *Potter v. Chicago Pneumatic Tool Company*, 694 A.2d 1319 (Conn. 1997).

7. *See Restatement (Third)*, § 2 cmt. a; *see also id.* cmt. g (stating that consumer expectations are relevant only insofar as they "affect how risks are perceived and relate to foreseeability and frequency of the risks of harm").

8. *See, e.g., Dreisonstok v. Volkswagenwerk*, A.G., 489 F.2d 1066 (4th Cir. 1974) (rejecting plaintiff's claim that minibus was defectively designed for not having safety features available in ordinary sedan on ground that minibus design satisfies consumer expectations); *Linegar v. Armour of America*, 909 F.2d 1150 (8th Cir. 1990) (concluding that a bulletproof vest satisfied consumer expectations and was not defectively designed because the consumer had the option of choosing safer vests).

CHAPTER 14

1. *Restatement (Second)* § 912 cmt. a. See Chapter 9, section II.C (explaining this principle and using it to justify the eggshell-skull rule).

2. *Restatement (Second)* § 903 cmt. a.

3. Committee on Pattern Jury Instructions, District Judges Association Fifth Circuit, *Pattern Jury Instructions: Fifth Circuit, Civil Cases* § 15.4 (2006).

4. *Restatement (Second)* § 912 cmt. b.

5. *E.g.*, Eric Schnapper, *Judges Against Juries — Appellate Review of Federal Civil Jury Verdicts*, 1989 Wis. L. Rev. 237, 341 (finding that typical remittitur "was at least half the size of the original verdict").

6. *See* Mark Geistfeld, *Placing a Price on Pain and Suffering: A Method for Helping Juries Determine Tort Damages for Nonmonetary Injuries*, 83 Cal. L. Rev. 773, 784–785 (1995) (describing these studies and providing more thorough analysis of the issues discussed in this section); Edward J. McCaffrey et al., *Framing the Jury: Cognitive Perspectives on Pain and Suffering Awards*, 81 Va. L. Rev. 1341 (1995) (presenting an empirical study that found the wording of jury instructions can double the award of compensatory damages for a given pain-and-suffering injury).

7. David W. Leebron, *Final Moments: Damages for Pain and Suffering Prior to Death*, 64 N.Y.U. L. Rev. 256, 266, 308 (1989).

8. Margaret Jane Radin, *Compensation and Commensurability*, 43 Duke L.J. 56, 61 (1993).

9. *See generally* L. R. James, Annotation, *Instructions in a Personal Injury Action Which, in Effect, Tell Jurors That in Assessing Damages They Should Put Themselves in Injured Person's Place*, 96 A.L.R.2d 760 (1964); *see also* 4 Harper, James and Gray on Torts § 25.10, at 697 ("All agree that [full compensation for pain and suffering] does not mean the sum that the plaintiff — or anyone else — would be willing to suffer the injury for.").

10. *Restatement (Second)* § 903 cmt. a.

11. Dobbs on Torts § 381, at 1062.

12. *State Farm Mut. Auto. Ins. Co. v. Campbell*, 538 U.S. 408, 416–417 (2003).

13. *See, e.g., Grimshaw v. Ford Motor Co.*, 174 Cal. Rptr. 348, 382 (Ct. App. 1981) (upholding a substantial punitive award based on the defendant's conclusion that it would be cheaper to pay compensatory damages than to remedy a defectively designed automobile); *Jacque v. Steenberg Homes, Inc.*, 563 N.W.2d 154, 156 (Wis. 1997) (upholding a substantial punitive award as a means of preventing the defendant trespasser from using compensatory damages to purchase an easement).

14. *BMW of N. Am., Inc. v. Gore*, 517 U.S. 559 (1996).

15. *Campbell*, 538 U.S. at 419 (quoting *Gore*, 517 U.S. at 575) (citations omitted).

16. *See, e.g.*, Arthur Ripstein, *Equality, Responsibility, and the Law* 152–153 (Cambridge U. Press 1999).

CHAPTER 15

1. *See, e.g.*, Louis Loss, *The Assault on Securities Action Section 12(2)*, 105 Harv. L. Rev. 908, 911 (1992) (explaining how courts have effectively "develop[ed] a new federal tort" under the Securities Exchange Act).

Glossary*

Affirmative defense. A set of elements that must be proven by the defendant with a preponderance of the evidence in order to defeat or diminish the plaintiff's prima facie case for liability. In tort law, the affirmative defenses involve privileged behavior (like self-defense) and do not recognize excuses (like insanity).

Allocative efficiency. In tort law, a property or objective involving the minimization of the social cost of accidents, which consists of (1) the cost of injuries; (2) the cost of safety precautions; and (3) administrative costs of the tort system and related insurance mechanisms.

Answer. A defending party's response to the complaint.

Appeal. The process of requesting a higher court to correct an error of fact or law made by a lower court. Higher courts ordinarily defer to findings of fact made by the trial court, whereas higher courts give no deference (or de novo review) to a lower court's conclusions of law.

Assault. *See also* intentional torts. A tort prohibiting one from intentionally causing another to apprehend a nonconsensual, imminent harmful or offensive contact.

Autonomy. In tort law, the value of self-determination.

Battery. *See also* intentional torts. A tort prohibiting one from intentionally causing a nonconsensual, harmful or offensive contact to the person of another.

Cause of action. *See also* claim. A set of facts sufficient to establish a claim.

Chattel. Personal or movable property, distinguished from real property (land or real estate) and intangible property (like money or financial instruments).

Claim. The formal allegation of a legal wrong. Each alleged violation of tort law constitutes a separate claim, making it possible for the same set of facts to support more than one tort claim.

Class action. A lawsuit brought by or against a representative party who represents similarly situated plaintiffs or defendants, ordinarily governed by restrictive procedural requirements concerning questions of law or fact that must be common to all class members.

---

* Selected terms of civil procedure have been included as an aid to those who are new to the study of law. These entries were provided by Suzanna Sherry and Jay Tidmarsh, *Civil Procedure: The Essentials* (Aspen Pub. 2007).

Common law. A legal regime in which judges rely on prior cases in determining the substantive content of the law.

Complaint. The plaintiff's initial pleading, containing the claims against the defendant.

Conclusions of law. The legal principles that a trial judge uses to resolve a dispute.

Contingency fee contract. A contract pursuant to which a lawyer represents a plaintiff in exchange for a percentage of the damages award in the (contingent) event that the plaintiff prevails.

Contribution. In tort law, the claim by a defendant in the underlying tort suit that is brought against a third party, alleging that this party is a tortfeasor who is legally responsible for a portion of the defendant's liability to the plaintiff.

Conversion. *See also* intentional torts. A tort prohibiting one from intentionally interfering with another's ownership interest in property.

Corrective justice. *See also* distributive justice. A form of justice involving the correction or annulment of a wrong that occurs when a duty holder violates the correlative right held by another.

Damages. The payment of money in satisfaction of a judgment the plaintiff has obtained against the defendant. Compensatory damages provide compensation for harms, and punitive damages provide an extracompensatory remedy for egregious wrongdoing.

Default rule. *See* negligence liability.

Defendant. The party who responds to the plaintiff's claims in a lawsuit, and from whom the plaintiff typically is seeking damages.

Deterrence. In tort law, the reduced risk of injury attributable to a liability rule. A rule can deter risky behavior in general (general deterrence) and/or deter the risky behavior of certain individual duty holders (specific or individual deterrence).

Directed verdict. A judgment in favor of a party issued by a judge in a jury trial that either preempts or displaces the jury's verdict, typically on the ground that no reasonable juror could have made an alternative finding. Also called "judgment as a matter of law."

Discovery. The process by which one party can obtain, on request, relevant, nonprivileged, and proportional information concerning the lawsuit from another party or third person.

Discretion. The authority of a judge to make a particular decision with few or no legal constraints.

Distributive justice. *See also* corrective justice. A form of justice involving the distribution of resources among all members of society.

Due process of law. Constitutionally sufficient procedural protections. Both the Fifth and Fourteenth Amendments to the U.S. Constitution prohibit the taking of life, liberty, or property without due process of law.

Duty. *See also* immunity; individual right. In tort law, the legal obligation owed by one party (the duty holder) to another (the right holder). Duty is not always an express element of a tort, but there can be no tort liability without such an antecedent legal obligation between the parties.

Economic loss. In tort law, damage to intangible property (like the loss of money) as distinguished from bodily injury or damage to tangible property (real property or chattels). In products liability, economic loss includes damage to the defective product itself.

Efficiency. *See* allocative efficiency.

Element. In tort law, a particular requirement that must be satisfied for either the plaintiff to prove a prima facie case for liability or the defendant to prove an affirmative defense. Each individual tort or affirmative defense is conventionally defined in terms of its distinctive set of elements.

Fact finder. The person or persons who determine which disputed facts are true in adjudication. The jury typically is the fact finder in tort cases.

False imprisonment. *See also* intentional torts. A tort prohibiting one from intentionally causing another to be completely confined against his or her will.

Immunity. *See also* duty. A doctrine that prevents the defendant from being subject to liability, often expressed in rules that exempt specific types of actors (like government officials) from certain types of tort liability, regardless of whether the conduct otherwise satisfies the elements of these torts. An immunity eliminates any antecedent legal obligation for the conduct in question, making it equivalent to a rule of no duty.

Indemnification. In tort law, by a defendant in the underlying tort suit that is brought against a third party, alleging that this party is a tortfeasor who is legally responsible to cover all of the defendant's liability to the plaintiff.

Individual right. In tort law, the protection of an individual interest from being harmed by the conflicting, distinguishable interests of others (duty holders).

Injunction. A court order requiring a party to act or refrain from acting, rarely available in tort cases.

Intent. *See also* intentional torts. In tort law, conduct with the purpose or desire to bring about a consequence or done with knowledge that such a consequence was substantially certain to occur.

Intentional infliction of emotional distress. *See also* intentional torts. A tort prohibiting one from engaging in extreme and outrageous conduct with the intent of causing emotional distress to another.

Intentional torts. *See also* intent. The group of torts sharing the common element that the defendant intended to produce a consequence or outcome that is prohibited by tort law. Each of the intentional torts, such as assault, battery, and trespass on land, specify a particular type of prohibited consequence or outcome.

Interest analysis. In tort law, the characterization of a liability rule by the way in which it mediates the conflicting interests of the right holder and duty holder. For this purpose, an interest is the object of any human desire.

Joinder. The joining of multiple claims or parties in a single lawsuit.

Joint and several liability. *See also* several liability. In tort law, a substantive doctrine that makes a defendant liable for the entirety of the plaintiff's harm for cases in which more than one tortfeasor is legally responsible for the harm.

Judgment. The final decision of a court on the merits of a claim or case.

Jurisdiction. The authority of a court to decide a case, requiring both jurisdiction over the person (personal jurisdiction) and the particular type of dispute (subject matter jurisdiction).

Jury instructions. The judge's directions to the jury about the findings it must make in order to reach a verdict on a disputed claim.

Liberty interest. The interest one has in freedom of action, including access to money and other economic resources.

Mixed questions of law and fact. An issue determined by a judge or jury that involves fact finding and the interpretation of a legal principle as applied to those facts, such as the jury's determination of whether the defendant failed to exercise "reasonable care" as alleged by the plaintiff's claim for negligence liability.

Motion. A request directed to a judge and seeking an order or other relief from the judge.

Necessity. *See also* affirmative defenses. An affirmative defense that privileges the defendant's conduct, which would otherwise be tortious, in order to prevent substantially greater damage to person or property.

Negligence. Often used by courts and commentators to refer to the type of unreasonable conduct that can result in negligence liability.

Negligence liability. A tort consisting of the elements of a duty to exercise reasonable care; breach of that duty; causation (both factual and legal or proximate); and damages. Negligence liability provides the most general conditions under which a defendant may be liable to the plaintiff, making it the default rule for accidental harms.

Negligence per se. Proof of negligence liability based on the violation of a safety statute or administrative regulation.

New trial. A trial ordered after a court determines that a legal error impermissibly affected the result in an earlier trial concerning the same dispute.

Physical harm. In tort law, bodily injury or damage to tangible property, corresponding to the individual interest in physical security that traditionally has been the core concern of tort law.

Plaintiff. The complaining party in a lawsuit.

Pleadings. The formal papers in a case that set out the allegations of a party.

Precedent. Prior decisions on an issue by the same court or a court that is superior in the judicial hierarchy. Under the doctrine of stare decisis, it is presumed that a court will adhere to precedent.

Preemption. In tort law, the displacement of a liability rule by a statute enacted by a governmental body exercising higher law-making authority.

Prima facie case. In tort law, production of sufficient evidence to establish a claim.

Proximate cause. *See also* superseding cause. An element of a tort requiring a specified causal connection between the tortious conduct and the injury for which the plaintiff seeks compensation. The term traditionally refers to both factual and legal causation, but recent usage is limited to legal causation alone.

Punitive damages. *See* damages.

Reciprocity. A concept based on the bilateral nature of risky interactions. Under conditions of perfect reciprocity, the interacting parties are equivalent in all relevant respects, making each a right holder and duty holder vis-à-vis one another to the same extent. The concept of reciprocity, therefore, also refers to the way in which a tort rule can simultaneously affect an individual in his or her capacity as both right holder and duty holder.

Relevance. The ability of a piece of evidence to help prove or disprove a disputed matter of consequence to a claim.

Remittitur. A judicially ordered decrease in the amount of damages awarded by a jury, which a plaintiff can accept as a means of avoiding a new trial.

Reply. The complaining party's response to the defendant's answer, if ordered by a judge.

Res ipsa loquitur. Proof of negligence liability entirely by circumstantial evidence. "The thing (accident) speaks for itself (on the issue of negligence)."

Right. *See* individual right.

Security interest. *See* physical harm.

Settlement. An agreement reached among the parties to a dispute, obviating the need for judicial resolution.

Several liability. *See also* joint and several liability. In tort law, a substantive doctrine governing the liability of a defendant for harms that are also the legal responsibility of other tortfeasors. A severally liable defendant can be liable for only a portion of these harms (under some forms of comparative responsibility or market share liability, for example).

Special relationship. In tort law, the type of relationship that creates a duty to protect the right holder from being harmed by a third party.

Strict liability. A type of tort consisting of a duty owed to the right holder to compensate harms proximately caused by conduct subject to the duty. Such a tort does not have any element requiring that the defendant acted unreasonably or was legally at fault for the injury, so it often is called "no-fault" liability. A rule of strict liability can otherwise be limited in various respects, including the form of conduct subject to the tort, distinguishing it from a rule of absolute liability that only requires some causal connection between the defendant's conduct and the plaintiff's injury.

Strict products liability. A tort that makes a product seller of a defective product liable to a right holder for physical harms proximately caused by the defect. The liability rule is limited by the requirement of defect, distinguishing it from a rule that would make a product seller absolutely liable for all injuries caused by the product.

Summary judgment. A judicial order terminating the lawsuit in favor of one party, prior to trial, after consideration of the evidence, typically when construed as favorably as possible for the nonmoving party.

Superseding cause. *See also* proximate cause. A cause that prevents other factual causes from being a proximate cause of the injury.

Trespass on land. *See also* intentional torts. A tort prohibiting one from intentionally interfering with another's interest in the exclusive possession of land.

Trespass to chattels. *See also* intentional torts. A tort prohibiting one from intentionally interfering with another's interest in the exclusive possession of chattels.

Unitary civil action. Pleading rules that allow a party to bring more than one claim in the same lawsuit.

Verdict. The determination by the jury. A general verdict only specifies the winning party and the amount of damages, if any, whereas a special verdict only involves the determination of specific facts and leaves to the judge the task of applying the verdict to the legal principles in order to determine the winning party.

Vicarious liability. In tort law, a doctrine that makes one party (the principal) legally responsible for the torts committed by another (the agent). The responsibility is based on a pre-existing relationship that enables the principal to exercise control over the agent, like the relationship between an employer and employee.

Workers' compensation. An administrative regulatory system that gives injured workers a right to receive compensation for injuries that arise in and out of the course of employment. The compensation ordinarily is limited to medical expenses and a portion of lost wages, often determined by schedule. The employee does not have to prove any fault on the employer's part, but loses any right to sue the employer in tort to recover for accidental harms. The employee typically retains the right to recover for an intentional tort.

Writ. In common-law pleading, the formal document that stated the type of claim a plaintiff was asserting against a defendant, such as the writ of trespass or the writ of trespass on the case.

Index